PERCEPTION,
EMPATHY,
AND
JUDGMENT

Arne Johan Vetlesen

PERCEPTION, EMPATHY, AND JUDGMENT

An Inquiry into the Preconditions of Moral Performance

The Pennsylvania State University Press
University Park, Pennsylvania

Library of Congress Cataloging-in-Publication Data

Vetlesen, Arne Johan, 1960–
    Perception, empathy, and judgment / an inquiry into the
    preconditions of moral performance / Arne Johan Vetlesen.
            p.   cm.
    Includes bibliographical references and index.
    ISBN 0-271-01056-8 (cloth)—ISBN 0-271-01012-6 (paper)
    1. Judgment (Ethics)   2. Empathy.   I. Title.
BJ1408.5V48   1994
170—dc20   92-43991
                                                            CIP

Published by The Pennsylvania State University Press,
Barbara Building, Suite C, University Park, PA 16802-1003

To my mother and father

Contents

List of Abbreviations

Chapter 1
AV	MacIntyre, *After Virtue*
NE	Aristotle, *Nicomachean Ethics*
OT	Arendt, *The Origins of Totalitarianism*
WJ	MacIntyre, *Whose Justice? Which Rationality?*

Chapter 2
BPF	Arendt, *Between Past and Future*
CJ	Kant, *Critique of Judgment*
EJ	Arendt, *Eichmann in Jerusalem*
HC	Arendt, *The Human Condition*
LK	Arendt, *Lectures on Kant's Political Philosophy*
LM	Arendt, *The Life of the Mind*
OR	Arendt, *On Revolution*
OT	Arendt, *The Origins of Totalitarianism*
NA	Arendt, *Nach Auschwitz*
TMC	Arendt, "Thinking and Moral Considerations"
UP	Arendt, "Understanding and Politics"

Chapter 3
Fo	Scheler, *Formalism in Ethics*
OA	Scheler, *Ordo Amoris*
Sym	Scheler, *The Nature of Sympathy*

Chapter 4
FAM	Blum, *Friendship, Altruism, and Morality*
GM	Schopenhauer, "Über die Grundlage der Moral"
NG	Lang, *Act and Idea in the Nazi Genocide*
PP	Charles Taylor, *Philosophical Papers*
ROE	de Sousa, "The Rationality of Emotions"

Chapter 5
AHD	Fromm, *The Anatomy of Human Destructiveness*
AuF	Horkheimer, "Autorität und Familie in der Gegenwart"
AP	Adorno et al., *The Authoritarian Personality*
CD	Freud, *Civilization and Its Discontents*
DE	Horkheimer and Adorno, *Dialectic of Enlightenment*
EF	Fromm, *Escape from Freedom*
FT	Adorno, "Freudian Theory and the Pattern of Fascist Propaganda"
I	Milo, *Immorality*
OG	Miller, *For Your Own Good*
RS	Kohut, *The Restoration of the Self*
UK	Miller, *The Untouched Key*

Chapter 6
E	Habermas, "Entgegnung"
ED	Habermas, *Erläuterungen zur Diskursethik*
FS	Honneth et al., *Zwischenbetrachtungen: Im Prozeß der Aufklärung, Festschrift für Jürgen Habermas*
JS	Habermas, "Justice and Solidarity"
KHI	Habermas, *Knowledge and Human Interests*
KN	Habermas, "Kohlberg and Neo-Aristotelianism"
L	Habermas, "Law and Morality"
MC	Habermas, *Moral Consciousness and Communicative Action*
ND	Habermas, *Nachmetaphysisches Denken*
NR	Habermas, *Die Nachholende Revolution*
TCA	Habermas, *The Theory of Communicative Action*
TK	Habermas, *Texte und Kontexte*
TW	Habermas, *Technik und Wissenschaft als "Ideologie"*
VE	Habermas, *Vorstudien und Ergänzungen zur Theorie des kommunikativen Handelns*

Chapter 7
DV	Gilligan, *In A Different Voice*

Preface

This book is a study in moral theory. Its subject is the relation between morality and emotions. The thesis I wish to establish is that our emotional abilities provide us with our principal mode of access to the domain of the moral. In the course of building my argument I use a number of examples—some of them fictitious and construed, others strictly empirical. Looming large among the latter is the Holocaust, the near-total destruction of the European Jews.

Thus, the present study is more interdisciplinary in scope and method than most philosophical treatises in the field of moral theory. This range is well reflected in the variety of disciplines represented in the group of persons from whom I have received stimulating criticism and advice: persons who all share an interest in moral theory and to whom the Holocaust is a historical event, indeed a warning, of never-ending concern, yet persons whose views on the ideas advanced in my study differ widely. More often than not, therefore, what some of my critics will find convincing, others will find wanting.

The work was conceived and drafted in Frankfurt between 1988 and 1990. Those in Frankfurt to whom my thanks are due include Jürgen Habermas, Martin Löw-Beer, Richard J. Bernstein, Seyla Benhabib, Axel Honneth, Chris Latiolais, Joel Anderson, Rainer Forst, William Rehg, and, last but not least, my most critical critic, Joachim Renn. In Oslo I have benefited from discussions, and disagreements, with Alastair Hannay, Audun Øfsti, and Jon Wetlesen.

As to the sociological aspects of my study, I am greatly indebted to Zygmunt Bauman, whose thought-provoking response to my ideas has been a major inspiration. As to the psychological aspects, in particular those touching on psychoanalysis and object-relations theory, I have learned much from discussions with Bjørn Killingmo and Siri Gullestad.

Finally I thank Roger Maier for our never-ending conversation about the matters that matter most.

Introduction

A much-discussed topic in moral philosophy is the relation between reason and emotion. The distinction between the two is often framed as a hierarchy, an order of priority possessing a normative content and not merely a descriptive one. In this hierarchy, reason is presented as the universal and objective foundation of morality and, furthermore, as the power that guides moral conduct and enables respect for the dignity of others. Emotions, by contrast, are said to be of secondary importance in regard to morality; moreover, some theorists even question whether they possess any real moral significance at all. Because of this hierarchy, the input of reason is solicited in any moral context, whereas the influence of emotion is repressed.

The distinction between reason and emotion is reflected, somewhat roughly, in the distinction between respect for and concern for others. Again, the distinction commonly appears in the form of a hierarchy. Hence, in speaking of *Achtung*, Kant, probably with the overwhelming majority of contemporary moral philosophers, holds that having respect, not showing concern, captures the essence of morality. The respect for another person "not merely as a means but as an end in him- or herself" is a respect commanded by the moral law laid down in us qua rational beings, or *Vernunftwesen*, and it is precisely in our capacity as beings endowed with the gift of reason that we observe the moral law. Concern, according to this view, turns not on our capacity for reason but on our capacity for feeling; and Kant strictly reserves the attribution "truly moral" for the former, that is, for actions done out of duty, as distinct from inclination, to use his own terms.

The order of priority claimed to obtain between respect and concern makes us suspect them of being opposites. To challenge such an impression, we should consider whether respect and concern do not in fact include rather than preclude each other. We could argue that it makes no sense to say that one person has concern for another person without having any respect for that person. The notion of concern intended here is a strong one; it is not to be confused with a fleeting and quickly fading impulse of a particular emotion such as sympathy, pity, or compassion. Rather, one person's concern for another is a concern *with* the other, a concern in which the other's status as an autonomous being is addressed. As such, the concern for the other person that deserves calling itself a *moral* concern ipso facto contains a respect for the *integrity* of that person, for that person's inviolable right to decide for him- or herself what best serves his or her goals and interests. If one does not observe this, one risks conflating concern with paternalism.[1]

The normative distinction between respect and concern could also be called into question using respect as the frame of reference. For difficult as it is to conceive of concern without respect, it is just as difficult to conceive of respect without concern. Would we find credible those who assured us that they had respect for others, "respect" in the moral sense, although they failed to show any concern for the weal and woe of those others? Hardly. In this case, as in the first case, when the one principle is considered exclusive of the other, its claim to moral importance is found wanting.

What I propose, then, and what this study takes pains to articulate, is the following view: that morality per se, or the domain of the moral, includes both respect and concern for others. Hence, I am committed neither to the position that although both principles belong to "morality," one of them possesses greater importance than the other, nor to the more radical position that only one of the two principles possesses genuine moral relevance. Instead, I recognize respect and concern as being moral principles of equal significance.

In the present study, however, although I acknowledge the irreducible moral importance of respect, I am systematically interested in concern only. This helps locate my study in terms of a philosophical division of labor. Consequently, the notion of *moral performance* that is developed in the course of this inquiry does not aspire to the status of an exhaustive or full-fledged moral theory.

I focus mainly on concern, instead of respect, because my starting point is the relation between emotions and morality. But one cannot engage in a philosophical discussion of the role of emotion in moral performance without paying attention to the ways in which emotion has been barred from "ethics proper" because of the primacy traditionally accorded to reason; the Kantian hierarchy is only a case in point, though a tremendously influential one at that. Thus, a central aim is to question the assumption of inferior status assigned to human emotional capacities in this hierarchy. We need to investigate whether the mutual inclusion seen to obtain in the relation between respect and concern does so in the case of reason and emotion as well. Specifically, we need to ascertain whether a balance between our cognitive powers and our emotional powers is required for moral performance to be successful. I speak, therefore, of the *interplay* I see between the faculties of reason and of emotion in moral performance.

In addition, there is a crucial sense in which my interest in moral theory from the viewpoint of emotions favors an examination of the prerequisites of developing concern for others, as distinct from respect for others. The path from emotions to concern seems to be shorter and more direct than that from emotions to respect—at least with regard to the intuition from which I depart. Part of the subsequent argument, however, is that the distinction between the two is not at all that clear-cut. I have already indicated how this argument may be advanced by questioning the contraposition of reason and emotion so pervasive in the Western tradition of moral thought. Once this distinction has been subjected to critique, the very idea of giving a "full" treatment of the one principle without regard to the other will appear mistaken, indeed a gross distortion of the subject matter.

This study's focus on concern is throughout on *concern as between humans*, concern as an interpersonal process and phenomenon. Hence, nonhuman objects of concern are not considered. And this pertains to morality as well: since I restrict discussion of "morality" to what obtains—or fails to obtain— between human subjects, the type of moral theory to which this work hopes to make a contribution is a *human-centered* one. But note that this does not imply that I hold only humans to have a moral standing. Far from it. What carries chief importance for the purposes of the present work is that the acting *subjects* in moral performance are humans and humans only.

The choice of emotion, rather than reason, as the point of departure renders the bulk of current as well as traditional philosophical discourse on morality vulnerable to the charge of cognitivistic one-sidedness. Certainly Kant is far from alone in highlighting the cognitive at the expense of the emotional—this applies to moral psychology no less than to moral philosophy. To note this is to identify a major selectivity characteristic of Anglo-American theorizing about morality. However, to identify a selectivity is to take a first, tentative step toward redress. But this step calls for great caution. For in compensating for this particular type of imbalance, one can easily overcompensate, committing exactly the same mistake as before, only this time weighting the other side. Thus, the danger for the present study is to replace the rejected overemphasis on the cognitive with a no less selective emphasis on the emotional.

Having given this warning, I turn now to my conception of moral performance. My study sets out to examine the preconditions of moral performance in the individual subject. What essential cognitive and emotional *resources in the subject* are required for the subject to recognize the other as a moral addressee? As I define it, moral performance runs through a sequence made up of three distinct levels: perception, judgment, and action. The logical connection between the three levels is such that the first necessarily precedes the last—that is, an act of moral judgment rests on an act of moral perception preceding it. The sequence, however, is also dialectical; it allows for movement back and forth between perception and judgment before a decision to act. My analysis of moral performance takes the form of a descriptive reconstruction of its basic preconditions. The main emphasis is on (1) the relation between moral perception and judgment and in particular on (2) the interplay between cognitive and emotional faculties in moral perception.

We experience the objects of moral judgments through emotion. Judgments do not constitute *what* is judged, nor do they supply our first access to the objects judged. Judgment presupposes perception in the sense that perception "gives" judgment its object; we pass moral judgment on things that are already given, or disclosed, to us through acts of perception. It is on this level, which logically precedes that of judgment, lest judgment be empty, that we locate the emotions. Emotions anchor us to the *particular* moral circumstance, to the aspect of a situation that addresses us immediately, to the *here and now*. To "see" the circumstance and to see oneself as addressed by it, and thus to be susceptible to the way a situation affects the weal and woe of others, in short, to identify a situation as carrying *moral significance* in the first place—all of this is required in order to enter the domain of the moral, and none of it would come about without the basic emotional faculty of empathy.

Moral perception provides and shapes the setting for moral judgment and moral action. Moral judgment is concerned with the cognitive grasp, assessment, and weighing of the weal and woe, of the well-being, interests, and rights of all the parties affected by a situation, in this very wide sense of being affected. In passing judgment on how best to act considering the viewpoints of all concerned (I consider this the yardstick of moral judgment; see Chapter 6), I will need norms and principles to guide me in my deliberations. But my cognitive-intellectual knowledge in this field—about principles and norms and how "best" to weigh and apply them in a particular situation—comes to naught and remains impotent if I am not sensitive to, if I do not "see" (as defined above), the situation at hand as a *morally* relevant one, calling upon me to *make use*, here and now, of my judgmental powers.

The sequence of moral performance is set in motion by an act of moral perception. Moral perception takes place prior to moral judgment and provides the basis for its exercise. To inquire into the function of moral perception is to explore the *Vorfeld* (periphery) of much of contemporary moral theory: inasmuch as the latter is predominantly preoccupied with the criteria for morally right judgment and with the justification of norms, principles, and rights, the question of how the object of moral judgment is arrived at in the first place tends to be underemphasized, as is the question of what is required of the subject—in terms of cognitive and emotional abilities—for the subject to recognize the other as a *moral* addressee and hence as an object of respect and concern and as a carrier of rights and human dignity.

In asking these questions I have become interested in the role played by emotions in moral performance. Emotions are a crucial part of the picture if we want to know what we are up to as moral agents. But to say that emotions are morally important is one thing; to explain what their importance consists of is quite another. Justin Oakley, who deals with this topic in *Morality and the Emotions*, holds "that emotions are morally significant, not that they are always morally wrong or right" (56). But significant in what sense? Oakley's position is that "emotions are morally significant because they constitute in various ways human relationships of love and friendship, and such relationships are among the most valuable things we can have" (57–58). Accordingly, "emotions are among the things which contribute to a good life, and therefore have deep moral significance" (186).

My own case for the moral significance of emotions is very different from Oakley's. The question I pursue is not whether and to what extent emotions contribute to a good life. Rather, it is what the role of emotions is in providing us with an entry into the moral domain. My thesis is that emotions—or more accurately, the faculty of empathy—are indispensable in providing us with an access to the domain of the moral. I conceive the domain of the moral in a wide sense; I take it to include every "other" whom we look on as a moral addressee, that is, as an object of respect and concern. The morally relevant features in a situation are the features that carry importance for the weal and woe of human beings involved in it. Suffering is doubtless a feature of this kind, and indeed the one that springs most immediately to mind. But I am against any reduction of morality, of what is morally crucial, to suffering—that is to say, to the task of mitigating and preventing the suffering of others. In my view, the features of a situation that bear on justice, honesty, dignity, and trust affect the people involved in a morally significant way. Whereas the woe of others has to do with their suffering, their weal has to do with the degree to which they are treated with a sense of justice and with trust and the degree to which their dignity and autonomy as persons is respected. My promotion of these positive values is no poorer in moral significance than my attention to the negative value of others' suffering. In acknowledging a balance between positive and negative values in the context of their moral relevance in a given situation, I oppose the many moral theories that hold—though starting from emotions, as I do—that suffering, and thus the "woe" side, is what renders the other's situation morally important.

When we want to examine how we identify some features in a particular situation as carrying moral significance, the accomplishments we focus on are those of moral perception. The features bearing on the weal and woe of others are the subject matter of moral perception. If for some reason we are inattentive or indifferent to the existence of such features, we will be incapable of initiating the sequence of moral performance. To put it differently, if our moral perception fails, we will be incapable of recognizing that the situation at hand is a morally relevant one. And since the level of perception is logically the first one in the sequence of moral performance, to fail here is to fail to reach, and thus to exercise, the powers required for the ensuing levels of moral judgment and moral action. Not least because of its logical primacy in this sequence have I chosen to spend so much effort examining moral perception and its prerequisites in the moral subject.

I am tempted to call my task one of retrieval. The term captures the sense of reintroduction, rather than introduction, that I set out to offer. My key concepts, notably moral perception and the faculty of empathy, are not so much novel as largely neglected. To be sure, this state of affairs might have led me to appropriate the "moral sense" theories of Adam Smith, Shaftesbury,

Hutcheson, and Hume, yet I devote no chapter to the proponents of moral sentiment. To be frank, I have learned more about the phenomenology of the moral in general and of moral emotion in particular from Continental philosophers, primarily Scheler, than from the celebrated British school. One reason for this is that Scheler—irrespective of how one assesses his philosophy—has the merit of being a successor to Kant; and it is precisely Scheler's attempted repudiation of the "cognitivistic" moral theory of his great predecessor that attracts my interest. The fact—or so my critique has it—that Scheler *inverts* and so perpetuates (rather than refutes) the Kantian framework renders Scheler's program for an ethics in which emotion is stressed on a par with intellect no less instructive, even though it fails in the respects where I would most like to succeed. A second point worth making is that the doctrines of Hutcheson and Hume have received considerable attention in recent books by Alasdair MacIntyre and Charles Taylor,[2] yet it is not their interest in the British school that motivates my interest in MacIntyre and Taylor.

Moral perception tends to be a blind spot in moral theories where the object or phenomenon of judgment is so often taken for granted—as if the act of identifying and recognizing a situation as morally significant merited no theoretical inquiry and met with no practical obstacles. In this work, however, moral perception is not conceived as something to be naïvely taken for granted, to be presupposed as a mere given, but is conceived as an accomplishment, a complex feat, and an utterly precarious one at that. The vulnerability of moral perception is in large part due to the frailty of the faculty of empathy on which it rests.

A main thesis of this work is that moral perception rests on the faculty of empathy and that the latter is a precondition for the former. Empathy is a concept more familiar to psychologists than to philosophers; it has recently enjoyed a revival in psychoanalysis thanks to the work of Heinz Kohut;[3] and some contemporary moral philosophers, notably the Americans Lawrence Blum, Amelie Rorty, and Robert Solomon, have drawn on it in their treatment of moral emotions.[4] What is lacking, however, is a systematic elucidation of the concept of empathy within a comprehensive moral theory. By this I mean an elucidation that details the full importance of empathy at work between a moral subject and his or her addressee, indeed that shows empathy as being instrumental in *disclosing* the addressee to the subject, even—I shall argue in Chapter 4—in providing the subject a first *access* to the domain of the moral as such. I am thinking, therefore, of a conception of empathy different from that worked out by Kohut, where its context remains that set up by the interaction between analyst and analysand. By contrast, a conception suited for moral theory would have to free empathy from the specific limits of "analytic" interaction and apply it to interpersonal relations in general and, further, would have to show that empathy is not just any "feeling"—such as, say, an impulse of pity or anger—but is instead anchored in a deep-seated human faculty, one disposing a subject to develop concern for others. Hence, empathy as defined in this study is irreducibly *other*-regarding or -directed; whereas there is such a thing as self-pity or self-love, there is no self-empathy.[5] In empathy there is always a thou, never only a me. Empathy sets up, indeed helps produce and sustain, a relation, a *between* or (to use Hans-Georg Gadamer's term) *Zwischen*,[6] involving one subject's relating to another; its locus is the interpersonal as distinct from the intrapersonal. To call empathy humankind's basic emotional faculty means that it lies at the bottom of all the particular and manifest feelings for others. It is by virtue of this faculty that I can put myself in the place of the other by way of a feeling-into and feeling-with. Empathy allows me to develop an appreciation of how the other experiences his or her situation; empathy facilitates the first reaching out toward and gaining access to the other's experience, but empathy does not imply that I become "contaminated" by the other's emotional state; it does not mean that I myself come to feel what the other feels. I do not have to feel the other's feeling in order to grasp, and thereupon be able to judge in light of, how the other experiences the situation he or she is in. The feeling-with made possible by the faculty of empathy is no mere projection; it neither presupposes nor demands that the other be identical to myself. I argue for this view in my critique of Schopenhauer's ethics in Chapter 4. Empathy, in short, involves the recognition of the otherness of the other, yet it does not seek the *enhancement* of this otherness as an end in itself, as does love; this I discuss in Chapter 3 on Max Scheler.

The empathy at work in moral perception not only turns on the ability to see; it also requires an ability to listen. Both seeing and listening mean paying attention to. They are characteristics of what might generally be called attentiveness. Perception always requires attentiveness; attentiveness is made possible by receptivity, by the capacity to view oneself as "addressed" by some situation or incident. If it is appropriate to talk about a flow of movement in moral life, the flow is not, properly speaking, from thought to action but from receptivity-attentiveness-perception to action; and the subject is not foremost an epistemic self highly skilled at reasoning clearly and without contradiction but a full-blooded person with a body as well as a brain, with emotional faculties as well as intellectual ones, with a particular gender, and with all his or her senses intact. Stressing that may border on belaboring the obvious, yet I want it to serve as a reminder that the arena of moral life, as well as the locus for acquiring the morally essential human faculties, is that of everyday social interactions, not that of sophisticated puzzle solving in the rarefied air of practical discourses, to allude to Karl-Otto Apel and Jürgen Habermas. The inquiry into the moral that starts from a notion of concern for others must focus on, to quote from Tom Kitwood's *Concern for Others*, "our countless small and unreflective actions towards each other, and the patterns of living and relating which each human being gradually creates. It is here that we are systematically respected or discounted, accepted or rejected, enhanced or diminished in our personal being" (149). This point adds weight to my previous one about the appeal to experience.

Attentiveness, however, does not arise in a vacuum; it needs to be learned, cultivated, maintained. In short, attentiveness is linked with what Kitwood calls "moral space." Moral space, he writes, is "the source of those good feelings which give a sense of inner freedom and of agency, on the basis of which a person can face the many and exacting demands of everyday life."[7] Attentiveness, perhaps the nucleus of everyday moral life, can be promoted or prevented; therefore, as Kitwood asserts, the most crucial agenda item is to "bring about the creation and extension of moral space, and to change those situations where it is diminished or extinguished" (100). At heart the fostering of attentiveness and the creation of moral space is a social, indeed a political, issue. And politics means power: the power relations at work *between* people, and often invisible to them, and the forces of repression at work *within* the individual. As I demonstrate in Chapters 2 and 4, it is no mere accident that the Nazi ideology encouraged precisely the closing not only of the public sphere but also of the moral space, in which the humanity of one's fellow subjects—regardless of race, gender, nationality, conviction—can come to be fully recognized. It is especially noteworthy that the closing of moral space between subjects first and foremost assumed the form of a suppression of the emotional capacities in each of them. There is a road from hardening to numbing, from the stereotypes of propaganda to the reality of mass murder.

My use of illustrations and historical examples, such as the one just alluded to, is intended to lend empirical support to my thesis that we perceive the moral dimension of a situation by virtue of perceiving the human reality it involves. This is—mutatis mutandis—to argue that processes of *dehumanization* are likely to lead to *moral neutralization* and thus to pave the way for immoral acts. I postulate a link between the human and the moral, one bearing on the connection between our being and our doing. The link is such that the perceived human reality of a situation involving the weal and woe of others *addresses* me, calls upon me, lays a moral obligation on me because I am, see myself as, and wish to be able to continue to see myself as a human being. But it must be emphasized that this link is recognized by the subject only if he or she adopts a participatory, rather than an objectifying and detached, attitude toward others. Given a detached attitude, there is a danger that I shall remain blind to the human reality of the situation in front of me, that it will awaken no engagement on my part but will instead leave me indifferent. And indifference is a prime threat to morality, even more destructive to it than hatred or resentment, because the intrinsic logic of indifference sets no limits to its spread. What is threatened, often effectively suspended, in indifference is what I term the "emotional bond" between humans. To miss the human dimension of a situation is also to miss its moral dimension. Chapters 4 and 5 draw on psychology (Mitscherlich and Mitscherlich, Lifton, Fromm), object-relations theory (Bowlby, Kohut), and sociology (Adorno, Horkheimer, Bauman) in exploring these issues. So, to sum up, in failing to perceive a situation for the human reality it involves, I also fail to see myself as addressed by it.

Some observations need to be made concerning this work's method. First, the discussion of emotions that follows frequently involves an appeal to experience. For just as I have drawn on, or rather have had to draw on, parts of my own body of experience in the course of the argument, so my reflections, insofar as they are sometimes recollections, take the form of appeals to the experience of the reader. To the objection that such appeals unavoidably jeopardize the work's scientific character, my response is that the objection is ill-founded: experiences need not be *private*; they need not be inaccessible to the public or to the reader. By appealing to experiences, I offer to *share* them with others, be they similar to or divergent from the experiences of those others. In any case, I seek to promote the entry of experience into an area that is common, intersubjective, shared; an open space, not a closed one; a familiar territory, not a foreign one.

There is a crucial sense in which my subject matter is substantively, and therefore also analytically and methodologically, inseparable from the human capacity for making experiences in general. To put it succinctly: what we know about emotions we know from experience. To be sure, a particular emotion not (yet) personally experienced can nonetheless be related to, be imagined, be the subject of desires, longings, or fears, or be talked about with someone who has experienced it firsthand. However, emotions cannot be divorced from experience, whether that experience has already been had or is yet to be had. It is this—at bottom existential—link between human emotion and human experience I want to do justice to in building my argument about the role of emotion in morality. So, in writing of empathy, the appeal is to a subject capable of experiencing empathy and of showing the concern for others made possible—so I shall argue—by the faculty of empathy. The capacity for emotion involved here has in fact two aspects: in experiencing an emotion, we can be either at the giving or at the receiving end of it. Accordingly, what we "know" about, say, concern or love or compassion we know either as the emotion's author or as its recipient, or both. To discuss emotions, then, is to move within the domain of human—and therefore intersubjectively shareable—experience.

Second, a general feature of our understanding (*Verstehen*) is that it moves within a horizon of preconceived categories. That it does so, and that understanding therefore is never starting from scratch, *ex nihilo*, makes it noncontingent; *what* categories we bring with us as we approach a given topic, however, vary depending on the more specific nature of the topic at hand. The present topic—the role of emotions in morality—is no exception. This inquiry proceeds in a manner indebted to the philosophical hermeneutics of Gadamer, from which these points concerning understanding in general stem. Gadamer (in *Wahrheit und Methode*) teaches that the structure of understanding is dialogic. This entails that when we approach a text, we must be attentive to it in a twofold sense: we must allow it to question us no less than we intend to question it. In other words, not only do we turn to a text with certain preoccupations and questions, we also must allow the text to be a speaker in a dialogue, that is, to challenge and call into question—and so enhance our awareness about—the "prejudices" we invariably bring along as our cognitive ballast whenever we turn to a text and expect "answers" from it.

In more specific terms, what is inspired by Gadamer's hermeneutics in this study is the ideal of letting the other voice speak and present its case in the strongest possible manner before subjecting it to critique. Each chapter dealing with a particular philosopher's position—namely, Chapter 1 on MacIntyre, Chapter 2 on Arendt, Chapter 3 on Scheler, and Chapter 6 on Habermas—seeks to live up to this ideal. Accordingly, each of these chapters begins with an extensive exposition of the works of the philosopher considered; the critical assessment that then follows seeks to proceed immanently and so grow out of the respective author's own concerns.

Third, some words of explanation concerning the structure of the study. The first three chapters make up Part One of the study. Each examines the work of a specific philosopher, whose position is subsequently contrasted with my own notions of moral performance in general and of empathy and moral perception in particular. This latter, then, is the acid test to which each considered position is exposed. How do the philosophers in question conceive of emotions? Do they analyze emotions only on the manifest level of particular feelings for others, such as sympathy, love, or compassion, or do they also endeavor to locate a constitutive level of emotion, one where we may identify a basic emotional faculty in humankind that lies at the bottom of and so facilitates the whole series of manifest feelings for others? What is the account given of the preconditions of moral perception and moral judgment, especially in terms of the contributions made by cognitive and emotional capacities? Is the overall picture given of emotions in ethics a positive one or, rather, one seeking to limit or even exclude, the impact of emotional capacities on moral performance? If the latter, what are the arguments put forward in defending such a negative (albeit widespread) view of emotions in moral conduct? These are the main questions put to Mac-Intyre, Arendt, and Scheler in the three chapters that form Part One of the inquiry. I conclude that MacIntyre is dismissive of the role of emotions in morality, that Arendt in the final instance rather neglects it, and that Scheler overemphasizes it. The case of Scheler carries systematic importance for the development of my own general position, since it exemplifies what I call emotivistic one-sidedness in moral theory, as opposed to (the much more frequently found) cognitivistic one-sidedness. The fact that I oppose both versions of one-sidedness testifies to my aim of working out a philosophical position that does justice to the irreducible function possessed by both the cognitive and the emotional faculties without granting primacy to either.

Chapters 4 and 5 form Part Two of the study. These chapters are devoted to two large and complex themes: the perception of the "moral" and the relation between emotions and immorality, respectively. Chapter 4 develops the thesis that emotion, or more accurately, the faculty of empathy, is indispensable in the disclosure of moral phenomena. My thesis holds that emotion enters morality from the very beginning, that is to say, as soon as that peculiar entity naïvely referred to as a moral "object," or "phenomenon," or "situation," is given to us in the first place. It is precisely this naïve and, as it were, inconspicuous "givenness" of the so-called moral that demands closer scrutiny; namely, the act of perceiving something *as* morally significant. I argue that our ability to feel, which rests on the faculty of empathy, provides us with our principal mode of access to the domain of human experience and that without an access to this domain, we would remain blind to the specifically moral character of situations where the weal and woe of others is somehow at stake. This being so, the wish to exclude emotional abilities from morality would have the effect of excluding humanity from it.

Chapter 4 also returns to the topic introduced at the outset, the relation between reason and emotion. The position advanced discards the influential dichotomy according to which cognition is active, something we do and for which we assume responsibility, and emotion passive, something we suffer and for which we can take no, or only minor, responsibility. Contrary to what is assumed in the pervasive dichotomy, or rather hierarchy, I argue that emotions do reflect morally on the person having them. To feel a particular way about something or someone means to be committed to seeing the object, or target, of the feeling in a particular way, to ascribe to it a certain "import," to use Charles Taylor's term. Such ascription of import entails a commitment to rationality, to intersubjectivity and justification. When I try to make you see on what grounds I feel the way I do about someone or something, all of this is involved.

This connects with my discussion of MacIntyre. When I explore what might be called the intentionality of emotion—the relation between emotion on the one hand and belief, evaluation, and judgment, in a word, rational discourse, on the other—I in effect challenge MacIntyre's critique of "emotivism" in *After Virtue*. In that book, MacIntyre is content to have demonstrated that the Enlightenment and its present-day politico-philosophical heir, liberalism, have paved the way for emotivism's current reduction of morality to personal preference beyond the reach of argumentation. The case of MacIntyre's shallow critique of emotivism is illuminating for two reasons. First, MacIntyre lets stand the impression that emotions (always unspecified) interfere with and undermine intersubjectivity and rationality in moral discourse and moral conduct. Hence, MacIntyre leaves unquestioned the view that emotions are "nothing but" a means of interpersonal manipulation, disclosing our fellow subject as someone to be acted upon rather than with. Second, it is truly remarkable, considering the large volume of critical commentary devoted to MacIntyre's book, that so far as I can see no one has singled out for discussion its negative portrait of emotions in morality. So, not only MacIntyre has let emotivism get away with its distorted picture of emotions in general and of their moral importance in particular; numerous commentators as well have allowed MacIntyre to get away with letting this feature of emotivism stand unchallenged. The explanation for this cannot avoid being speculative, yet that explanation must include Western moral philosophy's traditional suspicion of human emotion as something dark and dangerous, opposed to the objectivity-sustaining power of human reason.

However, there is more to the (from my perspective, conspicuous) passing over of the possible *constructive*, perhaps even *constitutive*, role of emotions in moral performance than the characteristic bias and blindness just noted with regard to MacIntyre. What needs to be taken seriously is the deep-seated distrust of human emotion as a dark and dangerous power, in a word, as threatening, instead of preserving, what we understand by morality. Therefore, the claim that there is a connection between human emotional capacities on the one hand and morality on the other gives rise to a fundamental objection. This connection cannot be the whole story about emotions and morality: we all know only too well that there is also a story to be told about emotions and *immorality*, that emotions can lead us not to concern for others but to its opposite. It is an empirical fact that a large number of immoral acts spring from the feelings that people have against one another—hate being the supreme example.

This objection poses the challenge I try to meet in Chapter 5. My study would be incomplete and severely deficient if it were to ignore the dark sides of emotion and with them emotion's undeniable potential for immorality. I hope to demonstrate that the existence of all-too-human aggressive feelings such as hate represents no repudiation of my position. To establish why, I clarify where I do see a link and where I see none. I see a link between the faculty of empathy on the one hand and morality, especially moral perception, on the other; the former I hold to be a precondition of the latter. But I see no link between emotions *as such*—emotions in general, emotions in their phenomenological manifoldness—and morality. Hence, I do not hold that a subject's mere "having" of some particular feeling would *eo ipso* constitute a guarantee that this person's ensuing performance would be a "moral" one. Far from that, my position allows that the performance may just as well be immoral. Consider the crucial distinction between "emotion," or some one particular "feeling," on the one hand and the faculty of empathy on the other. It is thanks to the latter, and not by virtue of the former (as Charles Taylor seems to imply), that a person gains first access to the domain of the moral. Much conceptual work is required to elaborate this vital distinction. To fail to observe it easily leads one to throw the baby out with the bathwater—as in the view that hate (i.e., a particular feeling) represents a compelling argument against any constitutive link between human emotionality and morality.

Whereas in Part Two I develop the central claims and elaborate the overall conceptual framework of my thesis, I turn in Part Three to an assessment of Habermas's discourse ethics. In so doing I am able to draw on the theoretical position established in the course of the thematic chapters that make up Part Two.

Even though Habermas locates his discourse ethics within the Kantian tradition of moral philosophy, one of his programmatic aims is to do more justice to the positive moral significance of emotions than did Kant himself. Habermas's moral theory explicitly voices (yet until very recently seldom thematizes) an ambition to portray moral judgment as involving an "integration" of a cognitive and an emotional component. In his account of solidarity—recognized as the twin principle to justice—Habermas acknowledges that emotional capacities play a vital role in morality. This being so, his account provides me with an opportunity to advance an immanent critique of the way discourse ethics à la Habermas treats emotions in morality. Suffice it to say here that the cognitivism inherited from Kant's ethics prevails in the end, despite Habermas's occasional claims to the contrary.

Feminist theorists, in particular, have contended that any discourse on emotion is also—if not explicitly, then at least implicitly—a discourse on gender. Chapter 7 is devoted to this gender-oriented perspective on morality. At the center of my discussion stands Carol Gilligan's influential book *In a Different Voice*. Gilligan proposes to delineate a distinct "ethic of care and responsibility" on the basis of her many in-depth interviews with young American women facing moral dilemmas such as abortion. One of Gilligan's key findings is that women seem to give emotions priority over the cognitivistic, detached, and rule-oriented approach to moral issues known from academic literature and, Gilligan suggests, representative of male thinking about morality. However, Gilligan's theoretical approach differs from mine in vital respects. Gilligan seems to believe there are two kinds of ethics, one typically male, the other typically female; because my own approach to moral performance is to investigate the necessary cognitive and emotional preconditions for a subject's successful constitution and recognition of *moral phenomena*, the preconditions I examine are taken to apply equally to all moral agents, irrespective of their gender identity. My position is that gender identity makes no difference on the level of constitution (my primary focus); rather, gender identity makes a difference, or *is made to make a difference*, with respect to power, social organization, division of labor, and so on; but to discuss such eminently *culture-dependent* implications, or meanings, of gender is to engage in an inquiry of a very different type from that here.

I asserted above that unless the subject adopts a participatory, not an objectifying and detached, attitude toward others, there is a danger that he or she will remain blind to the human reality and thus also to the moral significance of the situation at hand. My thesis is that to miss the human dimension of a situation is also to miss its moral dimension. I make the case for this thesis (primarily) in Chapter 4; therefore, here I will abstain from going further into the implied link between the human and the moral. What does require some attention at this stage, however, is the fact that the thesis referred to is not first and foremost about (moral) motivation (e.g., that which moves us to show concern and respect for others). Rather, at its deeper level, the thesis is an epistemological one.

It may be possible to do moral philosophy without engaging in epistemology. Not in the present case, however. The notion of moral performance proposed here clearly involves epistemological assumptions.

I undertake to build a case for the indispensable role of emotion, of empathy, in moral performance; in so doing, I theorize that the latter consists of perception and judgment (and action), that is to say, of largely *cognitive* categories. Considering that the argument is about *emotion* in morality, this may seem a rather contradictory strategy, but only to one who subscribes to a cognitivistic understanding of moral perception and moral judgment. Such an understanding depicts both (moral) perception and judgment as faculties that passively register the way things, or situations, or people, present themselves to pure cognition, where "pure" means "disinterested" and "detached." In the history of Western epistemology from Plato to Descartes to present-day cognitivism, the pervasive assumption is that one can always know something best by gaining a reflective and detached comprehension of it; to achieve this, it is required that the knower step out of and take a stand at some distance from what he seeks knowledge about. [8]

This model of how knowledge is attained has been subjected to powerful critique from a host of modern philosophical positions, counting pragmatism, phenomenology, and existentialism. There is neither need nor space to deal with this critique here. What matters for the purposes of the present study is the following: Since, in my view, moral perception and moral judgment alike contain an emotional component (resting on the faculty of empathy) as well as a cognitive one, and since the joint accomplishment or, better still, the *interplay* of these two components is what facilitates the exercise of moral perception and judgment (all of which will be argued in the chapters to follow), clearly the notions of "perception" and "judgment" defended here are *not* of the cognitivist kind just referred to.

According to the view advanced in this study, moral perception is what sets the sequence of moral performance in motion. Yet, significantly, moral perception does not "awaken" and get going by itself, as it were. Far from that, perception needs to be given a direction. But how does this happen? What is it that precedes perception in order that it can direct itself at something in the first place? The answer has to be sought in human *receptivity*, by which I mean "to be attentive to," "to be alert to," "to become aware of." The important point here is that such receptivity, such attentiveness, is something *active*, not passive; yet it is not something the subject self-consciously "does," "produces," or "brings about."

In elucidating the implications of this, I am indebted to Heidegger for his account of understanding, affectedness, and attunement in *Sein und Zeit*. A central idea in Heidegger, relevant to the point just made, is that something we encounter in the world is never encountered as an "isolated occurrent entity"; rather, it is encountered in terms of an "involvement-whole." Whether this general epistemological claim holds true for all the sciences need not be considered here. What is vital for my case is that it is immediately relevant to what I have to say about moral performance. My notions of moral perception and moral judgment have in common with Heidegger's critique of cognitivist epistemology the strong emphasis on being receptive (or attentive or attuned) to the human and moral phenomena we encounter in order that we can gain access to them, focus on them as distinct objects of perception, and subsequently be able to pass (moral) judgment on them. In other words, insofar as a "knowledge" is involved in our deciding that the weal and woe of others is at stake in a particular situation (i.e., a case of moral perception) and furthermore that a particular course of action is the appropriate response to that situation (i.e., a case of moral judgment), this knowledge is not gained by way of detachment and disinterestedness. To the contrary, it is by way of having the ability to be involved in the situation in front of us, that is, of having it matter to us, make a difference to us, that a situation we encounter in the world is constituted as a distinct "object" for perception and thereupon for judgment.

This may be pure Heidegger. However, my account differs from the Heideggerian one in a crucial respect. Whereas Heidegger develops his anticognitivist epistemology out of his more "profound" concern with laying out a "fundamental ontology" about *Dasein's* being-in-the-world, I take no such recourse to ontology. More important for my inquiry is the difference between Heidegger's point of departure and my own. Heidegger's argument about how understanding, according to its very structure, is active and nondetached—in the sense of being "attuned to" and "involved in"—is an argument from *Dasein*'s existential-ontological care structure. By contrast, my argument about how (moral) perception and judgment are constituted by virtue of being receptive to and susceptible to is an argument from human emotion; more precisely, what I hold to be man's basic emotional faculty: empathy. Thus, the respective points of departure are distinctly dissimilar. Although my ideas about how detachment bars, rather than secures, understanding demonstrate indebtedness to Heidegger, the way I start *Mitsein* from empathy is very un-Heideggerian.[9]

In summary, the account of moral performance advanced here has epistemological implications because in speaking of moral perception and judgment we need to know *how* the moral agent gains access to that over which perception and judgment are exercised. The thesis that receptivity is logically prior to perception, and perception logically prior to judgment, is basically an epistemological thesis. The critique of Western philosophy's traditional privileging of a detached attitude in the agent is likewise basically an epistemological critique.

Fundamentally and most generally, human receptivity means an openness to the world and all that we encounter in it. Receptivity as I conceive of it signifies a "readiness to"—to attend to, to perceive, to judge, to act toward— whereby the *what*, the specificity, of that at which all of this is to be directed is not yet given but is rather what the subject, in his or her *active* readiness, is awaiting and what will set in motion the entire sequence of human response.

For the purposes of this inquiry, however, it is not this very broad sense of human receptivity that demands attention. The perspective is more limited; it is confined to receptivity as it bears on moral performance. This imposes a limit on the scope of receptivity and understanding as analyzed by Heidegger (and Gadamer). What is of interest to this inquiry is not receptivity per se, receptivity to "intraworldly entities" in general, but receptivity to moral phenomena and thus *others*.

What, then, is the specific role of receptivity in morality? I turn to my concept of empathy to give an answer: in the domain of morality, human receptivity takes the form of empathy with others. Receptivity in its derivative and restricted sense as receptivity to phenomena belonging within the moral domain is viewed here as a crucial characteristic of a subject's being-in-the-world-*with-others*. In putting the emphasis on the latter, I leave the larger Heideggerian framework behind and seek a separate road to the study of morality as being with others.

Part One

1

From Aristotle to Emotivism—and Back Again

Alasdair MacIntyre's work offers a broad and provocative assessment of contemporary moral philosophy. MacIntyre sets the stage for my concern with emotions in ethics by way of his critique of emotivism.

MacIntyre's position is that of the self-conscious neo-Aristotelian. His case for a return to key precepts of Aristotle's ethics rests on a phenomenology of the moral that shows "emotivism" to pervade current thought and practices. Emotivism is a doctrine reducing morality to nonrational personal preference. Its historical emergence, argues MacIntyre, was prepared by the failure of the Enlightenment philosophers to furnish morality with a rational justification; it is sustained today, he continues, by a liberal philosophy that pays lip service to fighting it though wholly incapable of doing so.

Morality in Contemporary Emotivist Culture

After Virtue begins with a "disquieting suggestion": a "catastrophe" has oc-
curred, turning our present world into one in which the language of morality
is in a state of "grave disorder." What we possess are "the fragments of a
conceptual scheme, parts which now lack those contexts from which their
significance derived" (AV, 2). Accordingly we have lost our comprehension
of morality. This, however, we fail to acknowledge; the catastrophe in
question "will have to have been of such a kind that it was not and has not
been—except perhaps by a very few—recognized as a catastrophe" (AV, 3).
This means that people act and talk *as if* what they refer to as morality still
made sense, still was coherent and rational. At the same time, so-called
moral philosophers do their best to confirm our naïve belief in the coherence
and rationality of our language and practice of morality. A point is reached
where everybody possesses simulacra of morality and where there exists little
hope that anyone will be able to unmask the fictitious character of what we
take to be "morality" and to inform us of the actual gap between the latter
and the "genuine" morality we have lost without our knowing it.

Although MacIntyre singles out the Enlightenment project of justifying
morality as the primary focus of his criticism, he does set out to play the
role of the *Aufklärer*: he wants us to become aware of the nature and causes of
the "grave disorder" in which morality has come to be in contemporary
society and culture. To trace the causes of the present malaise means to go
all the way back to the Aristotelian conception of morality and of man. The
great Aristotelian tradition, argues MacIntyre, is the one with which we have
lost contact; showing the mistakenness of liberal modernity's endeavor to
distance itself from its Aristotelian heritage, MacIntyre hopes to restore the
practical and the theoretical supremacy of the latter. Consequently, *After
Virtue* reads like a narrative. Being a conflation of philosophical and historical
argument, the book offers a diagnosis of present-day Western society and
culture as well as a systematic argument *against* the kind of morality embodied
in this culture and *in defense* of the lost Aristotelian tradition.

MacIntyre names *emotivism* as the conception of morality most characteristic
of the current mentality. When MacIntyre contends that people act and talk
as if what they refer to as morality still made sense, his claim is that people
act and talk as if "morality" equaled that which the emotivist doctrine takes
it to be, namely, the expression of personal preferences. "Emotivism is the
doctrine that all evaluative judgments and more specifically all moral judgments are *nothing but* expressions of preference, expressions of attitude or

feeling, insofar as they are moral or evaluative in character" (AV, 12). Emotivism makes a sharp distinction between factual and moral judgments. Whereas factual judgments can be true or false, because in the realm of fact there are rational criteria allowing us to secure agreement concerning what is true and what is false, moral judgments, being expressions of attitude or feeling, are neither true nor false; hence, agreement in moral judgment is not to be secured by any rational method, for there is none. Thus, two purposes are served by our use of moral judgments: we express our personal feelings and attitudes, and we seek to produce certain nonrational effects on the emotions or attitudes of those with whom we interact. Rationality having been reserved for the realm of factual judgments, moral judgments are barred from any appeal to nonpersonal rational criteria. Therefore, all attempts to reach agreement in matters involving conflicting preferences are in vain; having no independent impersonal criteria to appeal to, argument is unable to settle conflicts; what remains is the expression of feelings to others in a more or less manipulative way. Taken as a theory of meaning, emotivism asserts that the sentence "This is good" means roughly the same as "I approve of this; do so as well" (AV, 12). Again, this example brings out the view that the purpose of moral or evaluative judgment is to influence a hearer's attitudes.

MacIntyre rejects the emotivist doctrine considered as a philosophical theory of meaning. However, his reasons for doing so are technical and do not concern me here. What merits attention is his strong conviction that emotivism, in reducing morality to personal preference, reflects a correct sociological hypothesis about the way in which people now act, talk, and think. Thus, what matters is that emotivism, its theoretical weaknesses notwithstanding, has today come to be the dominant way of understanding what "morality" is and what we are up to when we pass evaluative judgments. The crucial issue for MacIntyre, then, is not whether emotivism is true as a theory (he believes himself able to show it is not) but rather what difference it would make to morality if emotivism were more and more widely *believed* to be true, thereby pervading the domain of social practices. This, to repeat, is indeed what he holds to be the case. Given this assumption, the crucial question becomes the following: Can a particular theory of morality, however sound or unsound from a theoretical point of view, become "real" and hence "true" when (almost) universally believed to be true, that is, when systematically *acted* on?

The possibility of this being so chills MacIntyre. He sees emotivism as the third and final stage in modernity's long history of moral decline. At the first stage, moral theory and practice embodied genuine objective and impersonal standards that provided rational justification for particular policies, actions, and judgments. These standards were themselves susceptible to rational justification. At the second stage, the many attempts to maintain the objectivity and impersonality of moral judgments proved unsuccessful; in the course of this period—later to be identified by MacIntyre as the era of the Enlightenment—the project of furnishing the standards with rational justification broke down. Finally, at the third stage, theories of an emotivist kind have achieved wide implicit acceptance because of a general implicit recognition that, in practice, though to a somewhat lesser extent in philosophical theory, claims to objectivity and impersonality cannot be made good. MacIntyre contends that although emotivism reflects a correct sociological hypothesis about morality's conception and practice in our society, it is wrong in its assertion that objective and impersonal moral standards can *never* be rationally vindicated. What emotivism holds to be universally and thus principally the case—namely, that the sought-for justifications do and must fail—MacIntyre holds to be true only with regard to the second and third stages in his scheme: although both the Enlightenment and its modern "heir," liberalism, have in fact failed to deliver such a justification, this does not mean that all such attempts have always and will always come to naught. Indeed, what MacIntyre endeavors to show is that the Aristotelian tradition offers a coherent account of what a rational justification for an objective morality must look like; in their rejection of this tradition, emotivism and the Enlightenment and modern liberalism have all gone wrong. Thus, the moment of "truth" in emotivism is merely the restricted sociological "truism" about the culture in which we live—that "in moral argument the apparent assertion of principles functions as a mask for expressions of personal preference" (AV, 19). But MacIntyre, albeit often tacitly and implicitly, assents as well to a number of *philosophical* claims entailed in the moral outlook of emotivism.

The integral connection between morality and sociology is in no way limited to the case of emotivism. When MacIntyre states that "emotivism has become embodied in our culture," the point he wants to make is a general one. For him, every moral philosophy characteristically presupposes a sociology; to understand the claims of any moral philosophy, we should be able to spell out what its specific social embodiment would be. Whereas emotivist doctrine is "mirrored" in the social practices in which we are engaged today, emotivist theory is affirmed and sustained in and through those practices. MacIntyre describes the social content of emotivism as "the obliteration of any genuine distinction between manipulative and nonmanipulative social relations" (AV, 23). Emotivism takes human interaction universally to be a relation in which each person treats another primarily as a means to his or her ends. Far from being an end in the sense of Kantian ethics, the other emerges as an instrument of my purposes, as someone to be acted upon rather than with. Barred from the possibility of appealing to impersonal criteria—allegedly there are none—what remains for the agent is his or her nonrational attempt to align the attitudes, feelings, preferences, and choices of the other with his or her own. Emotivism therefore sees in the social world nothing but "a meeting place for individual wills, each with its own set of attitudes and preferences and who understand that world solely as an arena for the achievement of their own achievement of their own satisfaction" (AV, 25).

Hence, the individual as conceived by emotivism does not view herself or himself as belonging to a community, let alone as having any obligations whatsoever to a larger social world. Belongingness and obligations are viewed as wholly negative, as artificial constraints that would only restrict the agent's zone of operation and so more fundamentally what has come to be understood as the agent's "freedom." In this conception, to be a moral agent is to be able to *stand back* from each and every situation in which one may happen to be involved. The moral agent believes himself or herself capable of passing judgment on every situation from a "purely universal and abstract point of view that is totally detached from all social particularity" (AV, 32). Accordingly, moral agency is located not in socially defined roles or practices but in the *self*—a self, that is, having no necessary or inescapable social content and no necessary or inescapable social identity. And because this self is in and for itself nothing, it can "be" anything, assume any role or take any point of view. Fundamentally unsituated and uncommitted, this "democratized" self can slip into, drop out of, and move between an endless series of unconnected situations, roles, and identities; belonging nowhere, this self sees itself as realizing its "freedom" precisely to the degree that it is entirely set over and against the social world, the latter being not something to which it belongs but an arena spanning the plurality of selves, as it were, and on which they all pursue their more or less conflicting projects. It is no accident that I speak here in the language of Sartre's existentialism, the scenario being familiar to all readers of *Being and Nothingness*.[1] Indeed, MacIntyre perceives in the early works of Sartre a picture of the human self and of moral (or not so moral) agency wholly in line with emotivism. Sartre's self is defined negatively precisely by its being devoid of any substance—be it of a social, cultural, or historical nature—and hence positively by its inescapable openness (occasionally repressed through "bad faith") to the projects through which it relates itself to a social world from which, significantly, it is always able to withdraw. People's freedom lies in their capacity to negate and transcend the facticity of the world and what "is," to keep the world of human affairs at such a distance that all commitments in and to it appear as entirely contingent and never as substantial.

In this model, the self carries nothing with it in its perpetual transitions from one situation and set of moral commitments to another; it is a self with no history, with no social past, with no cultural heritage. This of course is the reason it is thought of as radically "free." But this freedom, argues MacIntyre, is only to be had at the price of abandoning rationality. The emotivist self, lacking any ultimate criteria, offers no *reasons* in its transitions from one set of moral commitments to another. This self thus possesses a *negative freedom* in the double sense of being utterly distinct from its social embodiments on the one hand and bound by no rational criteria or standards on the other. The latter point entails that "whatever criteria or principles or evaluative allegiances the emotivist self may profess, they are to be construed as expressions of attitudes, preferences and choices which are themselves not governed by criterion, principle or value, since they underlie and are prior to all allegiance to criterion, principle or value" (AV, 33). Insofar as the self in the course of its transitions from one set of moral commitments to another has a history, this history is not governed by the individual's membership in a variety of social groups furnishing the self with a noncontingent and therefore inexchangeable identity; nor is this history directed toward a given end, or telos; nor finally is this history guided by any rational criteria according to which the choices made en route by the individual can expect to be justified by the self and judged by his or her peers. In short, the content of negative freedom is wholly negative.

MacIntyre rejects the picture of the self and moral agent conveyed by a culture in which the emotivist reduction of morality to personal preference has become embodied—our own. His claim is that this self is a nobody, a ghost; lacking everything the Aristotelian tradition understood by an individual, the pseudoself pictured here mirrors the self-image of a culture suffering from grave moral disorder and decline. What MacIntyre sets out to argue in *After Virtue* is that the decline is the outcome of a philosophical desire to reject and discredit the Aristotelian conceptions of human life and of moral agency. MacIntyre's attack on the emotivism entailed in much of modern moral philosophy and political theory—which he sees sustained in present-day social practices—therefore takes the form of a strong defense of the Aristotelian tradition from which emotivism wishes to distance itself.

The Aristotelian Tradition

MacIntyre's diagnosis of contemporary emotivist morality rests on the assumption that emotivism owes its dominant position to the fact that the Aristotelian tradition has not been entirely lost but only partially so. Today we possess only the fragments of a larger conceptual scheme and historical context of morality, and the interminable character MacIntyre attributes to moral disagreement today is to a large degree due to the problem or, better, impossibility of putting these fragments together in some coherent set of beliefs about what morality is. Proceeding genealogically, MacIntyre hopes to show that what now appears as an arbitrary multitude of more or less implicit beliefs in fact once formed part of a coherent and systematically worked-out moral theory. That theory's classical expression is Aristotle's *Nicomachean Ethics*, and its historical context is the Greek city-state, or polis.

Aristotle's individual—being a man as opposed to a woman, an owner of property as opposed to a slave—understands himself as *belonging* to this community, not as set antagonistically over and against it. Indeed, only through its acknowledged membership in the polis is the individual able to identify himself and to be identified by others. The individual is defined by his social embodiment. But in addition to his recognition that he belongs to a particular society and inhabits certain well-defined roles within it, the individual also recognizes that his life has an end, or a telos. Man's telos lies in the perfection of what it means to be a man. This view makes sense as soon as we look upon human life from a teleological perspective. Central to the latter are Aristotle's concepts of actuality and potentiality; there is a fundamental contrast between "man as he happens to be" and "man as he could be if he realized his essential nature." Ethics, then, is "the science which is to enable men to understand how they make the transition from the former state to the latter" (AV, 52). It follows that Aristotle's ethics puts its main emphasis on features for which there is no place in the emotivist doctrine: there is an account of potentiality and act, of the essence of man as a rational animal, and of the human telos. And what is more, this scheme allows a place for *reason* in ethics, a place denied it in emotivist theory and practice.

Aristotle teaches that reason tells us both what our true end is and how to reach it. Practical reason tells us how to govern our lives according to the *virtues*. Instructing us how to move from potentiality to act, how to realize our true nature, and how to reach our true end are the precepts enjoining the various virtues and prohibiting the vices that are their counterparts. Whereas emotivism asserts that human conduct in general is determined by the nonrational and strictly private feelings and mental states of each individual, Aristotle holds that the task of ethics is to teach man how to *direct* and *cultivate* his "given" feelings and mental states. Through instruction and habituation, that is, we have to learn how to *master* our feelings and inclinations in order to avoid being mastered by them. Feelings, admitted in emotivism to have the first and final word in all human interaction, are to be shaped and then *thereafter* acted on. It is only through such an ongoing process of education and habituation that we acquire the virtues; far from arising in us by nature, the virtues are developed in us by our consciously activating and practicing them. This is what Aristotle has in mind when he says that "we become just by doing just actions, temperate by doing temperate actions, brave by doing brave actions" (NE, 1103a26). We should act, Aristotle goes on to say, in such a manner that our actions "express correct reason." What he means by this formulation is threefold: first, the agent must know that he is doing virtuous actions; second, he must decide on them, and decide on them for themselves; and third, he must also do them from a firm and unchanging state. Thus, for actions to express correct reason and hence virtue, "the agent must be in the right state when he does them," in the threefold sense just given (NE, 1105a30). As a condition for having a virtue, however, the knowing counts for little as compared to the doing; or, to be more precise, the frequent *doing* of virtuous actions, though of course expressing correct reason only when informed by the correct knowing, is what makes a man truly virtuous. A just man is just only as long as he continues to perform just actions for the sake of being just; he does what is virtuous because it is virtuous.

In Aristotle's account of the virtues a crucial distinction is made between what any particular individual at any particular time takes to be good or right for him and what is really good and right for him qua man. For it is not for the sake of my good but for the sake of achieving the good for man in general that I practice the virtues. Aristotle's all-important thesis is that the good for me qua man *equals* the good for me qua individual; what I strive toward as an individual is the perfection of what it means to be a man. To the good for man that he aims at in all his knowing and doing, Aristotle gives the name *eudaimonia*—it is, writes MacIntyre, "the state of being well and doing well in being well" (AV, 148). However, a capacity to judge is required if we are to make the right choices about means to achieve that superior end. Insofar as the exercise of the virtues involves such choices, to act virtuously presupposes a capacity to judge in the sense of knowing "how to do the right thing in the right place at the right time in the right way" (AV, 150). The "knowledge" implied here, Aristotle tells us, is not of a universal kind. Being concerned with action, with "what is open to deliberation," the practical intelligence, or *phronēsis*, required to judge is about particulars; hence, its exercise, stresses MacIntyre, has nothing to do with "a routinizable application of rules" (AV, 150). It follows that the capacity to judge cannot be learned in the way, say, a craft, involving *technē*, can be learned. *Phronēsis* is not a skill; it is not to be learned and had once and for all. The situations in which it is to be exercised differ, and although Aristotle says that *phronēsis* involves experience because "particulars become known from experience" (NE, 1142a15), it is clear that present and future situations will call upon different deliberations than past ones, however successfully we may have judged and acted in the past. Practical intelligence nevertheless serves something that is general; it is concerned with "what is just, fine and good for a human being" (NE, 1143b25). The task of judgment, then, is one of mediation: while practical intelligence gives us an idea of what it means for man as such to "be well and do well in being well," that is, to seek the highest good known as *eudaimonia*, the task reserved for judgment is to consider how this idea of what is good is to be realized in the context of a particular situation.

The virtues are practiced not for the sake of pursuing what is good for me qua individual but for the sake of achieving what is good for man qua man. Admittedly, this is an awkward rendition of Aristotle's thesis. In his account of the virtues, there is no contradiction between what is good for the individual and what is good for man in general, that is, for the community. Indeed, only as a member of a community can the individual acquire and perform the virtues; being a *zōon politikon*, the individual can only flourish as a human being when acting in concert with his fellow men in a common pursuit of what is the highest good for man per se. Belonging to a community is a good in itself without which no single man would be happy; to be excluded from recognition by and in the community he belongs to would mean to be alienated not only from the others but also from himself: he simply would not know who he was. However, in attributing the realization of the human good to the community at large, Aristotle of course presupposes the existence of a wide range of agreement in that community on goods and virtues; and it is this agreement, observes MacIntyre, "which makes possible the kind of bond between citizens which constitutes a *polis*" (AV, 155). Appearing here is the central importance ascribed to friendship in Aristotle's ethics. The bond between citizens of a community in which there is basic agreement on goods and virtues is the bond of friendship, and friendship is itself a virtue. Far from being founded merely on mutual advantage or on taking pleasure in one another's company, friendship as intended by Aristotle embodies a shared recognition and pursuit of a human good. To act virtuously and thereby to achieve that good thus means to act not against others but with them, acknowledging that they pursue goals similar to mine. Consequently, there is no place for deeper conflicts within the polis; should conflicts nevertheless occur, they can only be the result either of character flaws in individuals or of unintelligent political arrangements. Hence, conflicts are contingent rather than basic.

The self that is the bearer of the Aristotelian virtues differs in several important respects from the self as conceived in emotivism. I have already referred to the latter's separation between the roles that the individual (in a revealing term) "plays." Therefore, the life of the individual appears as nothing but a series of unconnected episodes. But a self thus separated from its roles "loses that arena of social relationships in which the Aristotelian virtues function if they function at all" (AV, 205). In Sartre, a representative proponent of the modern outlook, the self lives an "authentic" life precisely to the degree that it refuses to commit itself to social relations; indeed, this very refusal to make any substantial commitment to a social world discredited as conventionalized and inauthentic is what makes for the integrity of the self as depicted in Sartre. But when the self is fragmented into a contingent set of demarcated areas of role-playing, no scope is permitted for the exercise of cultivated dispositions that could genuinely be accounted virtues in the Aristotelian sense. To possess a virtue is to be able to manifest it in very different types of situations; it requires a knowledge of what is good and right for man, a knowledge attained through intellectual learning, and an ability to mediate prudently between this general knowledge and the particular situations in which it is to be realized in particular ways, an ability, that is, fostered not by theoretical learning but by practical experience. Today, however, dispositions refer not to virtues but to professionalized skills. What the emotivist self seeks to do is to acquire certain skills that make for success in a given situation. To be "good" is not to be a good person but to be *good at*—good at doing certain things and acting in certain ways in order that a certain pregiven aim be fulfilled. In this view it is simply taken for granted that others appear solely as means to my ends and never as ends in themselves.

Even though according to Aristotle some virtues are available only to certain types of people—an idea with which the proponent of emotivism would not hesitate to agree—his claim is that virtues nonetheless attach not to men as inhabiting social roles but to man as such. Aristotle's account of the virtues is part of his overall teleological scheme; the telos of man as a species determines what human qualities count as virtues. And although Aristotle treats the acquisition and exercise of the virtues as means to an end, the relation of means to end is internal and not external or arbitrary, as is the case in the emotivist, instrumentalist understanding of skills as techniques to achieve individual goals. Aristotle teaches that a means is internal to a given end when forming a constitutive part of it, in the sense that the end cannot be adequately characterized independent of a characterization of the means. Thus, the virtues are a means in the sense of being internal to the telos that is the good life for man qua man. The exercise of the virtues is therefore itself a crucial component of the good life for man. Far from being a means that succeeds in a particular situation, a virtue as defined in Aristotelian ethics is a quality that enables an individual to move toward the achievement of the specifically human telos.

The emotivist self characteristically fails to perceive such a telos; it asserts that there can be no such thing, either for itself or for man per se. Walking "freely" in and out of a series of unrelated social contexts, this self pursues goods that Aristotle would count as external, insofar as they are always in some single individual's possession. Consequently, the more someone has of external goods, the fewer there are for other people; external goods are objects of a competition where there must be winners and losers. However, in exercising the virtues—be they those of character, such as generosity and temperance, or those of thought, such as wisdom and intelligence—the Aristotelian self pursues internal goods the achievement of which is a good for the whole community. To share in the pursuit of certain socially recognized internal goods, being what friends (in the sense intended by Aristotle) in fact do, is to share in what MacIntyre calls a practice. "The virtues are those goods by reference to which we define our relationships to those other people with whom we share the kind of purposes and standards which inform practices" (AV, 191). To enter into a practice means to accept the authority of a set of standards of excellence; it is to subject my own attitudes, choices, preferences, and tastes to the standards that currently define the practice. MacIntyre echoes the Aristotelian contention that "in the realm of practices the authority of both goods and standards operates in such a way as to rule out all subjectivist and emotivist analyses of judgment" (AV, 190). The argument against the atomism and instrumentalism of emotivist morality, then, is that it is not for the individual agent to decide what is to count as appropriate conduct and sound judgment in a particular situation; conduct and judgment are not geared toward success and utility. Situations, as viewed here, are part of practices; and a practice—be it playing a game of baseball or taking part in a public meeting—demands that each participant act in a manner laid down by standards that are intersubjectively recognized as defining the practice in question. This recalls Aristotle's contention that an ability to pass sound moral judgment necessarily presupposes the acquisition of the virtues. Wholly in line with this view, MacIntyre defines a virtue as "an acquired human quality the possession and exercise of which tends to enable us to achieve those goods which are internal to practices and the lack of which effectively prevents us from achieving any such goods" (AV, 191). A practice, moreover, may flourish or it may disintegrate; its sustenance and integrity depend on the exercise of the appropriate virtues by the individual's taking part in it.

The self as conceived in the Aristotelian tradition is not only an actor but an author. MacIntyre introduces a narrative concept of selfhood in order to elucidate the teleological character Aristotle ascribes to human life. My life is an enacted narrative in the sense that "I am what I may justifiably be taken by others to be in the course of living out a story that runs from my birth to my death; I am the *subject* of a history that is my own and no one else's, that has its own peculiar meaning" (AV, 217). To be the author of a narrative running from birth to death is to understand one's life as directed toward a telos and hence as having a purpose and an overall unity; at the same time, it is to be ready to be held accountable for the actions and experiences that compose the narrative I enact. My life is meaningful to myself and intelligible to others only as long as it is a movement toward a telos of which I never stop being aware. So the unity of an individual life is the unity of a narrative embodied in a single life. When I ask myself, What is the good for me? I ask how best I might live out such a unity and bring it to completion; when I ask, What is the good for man? I ask what all answers to the former question must have in common. The story of my life, however, is not exclusively mine; others will be part of my story, as I will be part of theirs. The point here is that I am never in a position to seek for the good or to exercise the virtues only qua individual. I am born into a certain community and at a certain time, into a particular social setting having a particular history. The picture of selfhood elaborated here, as opposed to that of the emotivist self, is of a self not in any way detachable from its social and historical context. Selfhood is inseparable from situatedness. The self as presented by Sartre, however, believes itself to be what it chooses itself to be. That is to say, the self is entirely free to question, negate, or "transcend" what it typically takes to be the merely contingent features of its social existence. Dismissing the Sartrean self as an emotivist fiction, MacIntyre argues the case for perceiving the self as socially and historically situated: my identity is not something I am free to develop but something I *derive*.

The practices in which I take part all have a history; they belong to a *tradition*, and it is from this tradition that my identity in a broad sense derives. In asking the seemingly personal question, What is the good for me? I in fact pose the universal question, What is the good for man? The answer to the former question is presupposed by the latter, there being in Aristotle's view no antagonism between the good for me and the good for man. However—and this is where social and historical particularity enters—there is no universal or timeless answer to the question addressing the good for man. The answer will change from time to time because always asked by a particular individual belonging to a particular tradition, and it is the tradition of which he is a bearer, rather than the individual himself, that defines what may count as a cogent answer. A living tradition then is "an historically extended, socially embodied argument" continually defining and redefining the standards to which questions concerning the good for man must appeal in order to receive an answer for which rationality may be claimed. In other words, MacIntyre advances the historicist thesis that *to every particular tradition there corresponds a particular standard of rationality and justification*. This, then, is what I take to be the deeper philosophical thrust of his claim that different traditions have different answers to the same question concerning the good for man. (I return to this thesis in the last two sections of this chapter.)

The concept of a tradition involved here is a complex one. On the one hand, a tradition is said to have a *sociological* aspect; it consists of a multitude of practices sustained on the microlevel by individuals and on the macrolevel by a set of social institutions. On the other hand, a tradition is said to have an *epistemological* aspect (the terms are mine); it defines the standards all evaluative questions about the good for man and all normative questions about the good for man and all normative questions about right human action must appeal to in order to receive answers admitting of *rational* agreement. Moreover, both aspects are historical in nature. Practices, transmitted and handed down by and through generations of social actors, change in the course of time, as do the cognitive standards peculiar to a specific tradition. Hence, to say of the individual that he searches for his good entails, first, that he does this qua member of a particular community and qua participant in a variety of social practices and, second, that he searches for his good as defined by the tradition to which he belongs. In other words, what is to count as the good for the individual is not a matter of individual choice, this being of course what emotivist theory and practice assure us; rather, it is a matter of the individual's recognizing the authority of certain intersubjective and tradition-constituted standards.

If MacIntyre is right in his claim that the virtues are always defined in a way peculiar to a particular tradition, then each and every tradition may be expected to make its own truth claim about the nature of the virtues. Therefore, different traditions will tend to make different, if not squarely incompatible, claims to truth about what we really are, what is our telos, and what is to count as actions expressing the appropriate virtues. To use the example given by MacIntyre, "in the Homeric account the concept of a virtue is secondary to that of *a social role*, in Aristotle's account it is secondary to that of *the good life for man* conceived as the *telos* of human action and in Benjamin Franklin's much later account it is secondary to that of *utility*" (AV, 186). Confronted with such rival claims about the virtues, what we want to know is, Who is right? What are the standards, or criteria, for passing a rational judgment about such rival and competing claims to truth? How are we to decide in favor of one of them?

MacIntyre's initial response is to assure us that "a unitary core concept of the virtues" can in fact be disentangled from the rival claims just referred to, that the rival claims are not rivals after all but instead just different *Erscheinungen* of a common core concept. Such a core concept can indeed be discovered, and "it turns out to provide the [Aristotelian] tradition with its conceptual unity" (AV, 186). MacIntyre goes on to identify three stages in "the logical development of the core concept of virtue." The first is an account of what MacIntyre defines as a practice, the second is an account of the narrative order of a single human life, and the third is an account of what constitutes a moral tradition. MacIntyre, intending to demonstrate what rival claims about the virtues have as their common core, argues that the virtues are acquired and exercised in the course of practices, that their exercise is required if the individual is to live his life as a narrative order directed toward a given telos, and, finally, that the individual as well as the practices he participates in belong to a tradition in which "man" and man's ends are defined in a particular way. But in so arguing, MacIntyre unwittingly stresses the importance of *particularity* at all three stages, whereas what he had set out to demonstrate in offering this model was the *universality* of his core concept of the virtues. How can we encounter something truly universal in the midst of all this particularity?

A practice as defined by MacIntyre involves standards of excellence and obedience to rules as well as the achievement of internal goods. Entering into a practice, I accept the authority of those standards, and I recognize that the goods internal to the practice can only be secured by my subordinating myself within the practice to my relation to other practitioners. Subjecting my attitudes, choices, and preferences to the standards currently defining the practice, I learn to recognize "what is due to whom"; furthermore, I have to be prepared to "take whatever self-endangering risks are demanded along the way"; and finally, I have to "listen carefully to what I am told about my own inadequacies and to reply with the same carefulness for the facts." From these very general remarks, MacIntyre immediately goes on to make the strong claim that "we have to accept as necessary components of any practice with internal goods and standards of excellence the virtues of justice, courage and honesty." These, then, are the *virtues required for every practice;* they are what MacIntyre holds to be the "core," common to the different accounts of the virtues offered by the Homeric, the Aristotelian, and the utilitarian (the reference is to Franklin) traditions. Not to accept the virtues of justice, courage, and honesty, says MacIntyre, "so far bars us from achieving the standards of excellence or the goods internal to the practice that it renders the practice pointless except as a device for achieving external goods" (AV, 191).

I believe, however, that MacIntyre has not really shown that these three virtues are required for every practice, and that he has not argued convincingly that there is such a thing as a core concept of the virtues to be disentangled from its long philosophical and etymological history. What he has done is to construct a definition of "practice" such that it would seem to be universally dependent on the exercise of at least the three virtues pointed to—else the practice would turn "pointless." Prima facie, however, it remains to be argued why, for instance, justice is as much an all-important virtue in architecture as it is in chess, or why courage, say, is as much a sine qua non to the practice of farming as it is to that of fighting a (prenuclear) war—all of these being examples of practices drawn on by MacIntyre himself. Indeed, it remains unclear in what sense the virtues mentioned are "required" for every practice. One interpretation, as proposed by Richard J. Bernstein,[2] is that they are required in order to *sustain* practices. But to grant this leads to new problems. For if it really be the case that such practices as chess and farming require justice, courage, and honesty in order to be sustained, then it follows that the very existence of these practices today provides evidence that the virtues in question have lost none of their social force and significance. This, however, is a conclusion effectively ruled out in MacIntyre's diagnosis of contemporary emotivist society, according to which, what we witness in today's society is the *decline* in the virtues—in their acquisition, cultivation, and exercise, and in their centrality in the life of the individual as well as in the community at large.

The Enlightenment Project of Justifying Morality

Emotivism is for MacIntyre the third and final stage in the history of moral decline; Aristotelianism is the first. The Aristotelian tradition succeeds in demonstrating what emotivism occasionally pays lip service to but nonetheless fundamentally denies: that moral theory and practice can in fact embody genuine objective and impersonal standards that provide rational justification for particular actions and judgments. What has happened in the course of this history? Why has such a decline come about? In short, why has the project of justifying morality been a failure, giving way to the emotivist reduction of morality to nonrational personal preference?

MacIntyre's answer is that the Enlightenment, identified as the second stage in the scheme, failed to maintain the objectivity and impersonality of moral reasoning that had been its object. It failed because it dismissed certain features of the Aristotelian ethics without which the ambition to give morality a rational foundation cannot be fulfilled. "What then the conjunction of philosophical and historical argument reveals is that *either* one must follow through the aspirations and the collapse of the different versions of the Enlightenment project until there remains only the Nietzschean diagnosis and the Nietzschean problematic *or* one must hold that the Enlightenment project was not only mistaken, but should never have been commenced in the first place. There is no third alternative" (AV, 118). Thus, the moral philosophers of the Enlightenment were wrong from the start; they were mistaken in their belief that key parts of Aristotle's ethics had to be rejected if one were to secure the rationality of morality. MacIntyre holds the opposite to be the truth: that morality is *deprived* of its rational foundation as soon as and to the extent that the key features of the Aristotelian ethics are discredited.

What, then, are these features so crucial to morality? Referring to philosophers as different as Hume and Kant, Pascal and Diderot, Adam Smith and Kierkegaard, MacIntyre contends that "all reject any teleological view of human nature, any view of man as having an essence which defines his true end. But to understand this is to understand why their project of finding a basis for morality had to fail." Now, the moral scheme that forms the historical background to these thinkers had, being of Aristotelian origin, a teleological structure that required three elements: untutored human nature, "man as he could be if he realized his telos," and the moral precepts that enable him to pass from one state to the other or to actualize his potentiality. However, the scientific and philosophical dismissal of Aristotelianism was to have the effect of eliminating any such notion of "man as he could be if he realized his telos"; no place remained for the notions of actuality and potentiality entailed in the Aristotelian model. "Since the whole point of ethics . . . is to enable man to pass from his present state to his true end, the elimination of any notion of essential human nature and with it the abandonment of any notion of a *telos* leaves behind a moral scheme composed of two remaining elements whose relationship becomes quite unclear" (AV, 54). On the one hand, a certain content for morality, inherited from the Aristotelian tradition, gradually comes to be lost: a set of injunctions coming to be deprived of their original teleological context. On the other hand, a certain view of "untutored human nature as it is," handed down by a tradition from which the Enlightenment wishes to distance itself, permits a series of disagreements on human nature to emerge: In what does it consist? Or there is perhaps no such thing as a human nature at all? The moral philosophers of the Enlightenment thus inherited incoherent fragments of what MacIntyre holds to be a once coherent scheme of thought and action; failing to understand "their own peculiar historical and cultural situation, they could not recognize the impossible and quixotic character of their self-appointed task" (AV, 55)—the task, that is, of rationally justifying a morality devoid of any specific notion of man and of human nature, of the "essence to be actualized in man" and of his telos. MacIntyre's thesis is that if you detach morality from "the teleological scheme of God, freedom and happiness as the final crown of virtue," you will "no longer have morality; or, at the very least, you will have radically transformed its character" (AV, 56). In what ways then does this transformation manifest itself?

Taking ethics to be the science teaching man how to pass from his present state to his true end, Aristotle maintains an internal connection between the facts of human nature and the precepts of morality. However, the philosophical plausibility of such a connection suffered a serious blow, from which it has yet to recover, when Hume in his *Treatise* made the claim that one is never allowed to pass from an "is" to an "ought": no transition can be made from statements about human nature to moral judgments, that is, from factual premises to a moral or evaluative conclusion.[3] At stake here is the status of *functional concepts*. For moral arguments within the Aristotelian tradition involve at least one central functional concept, that of *man* understood as having an essential nature and an essential purpose or function. This means that the concept of "man" cannot be defined independent of the concept of a "good man"; and the criterion of someone's being a man and someone's being a good man are not independent of each other, notwithstanding Hume's celebrated argument to the contrary. Aristotle therefore starts his ethics with the statement that the relation of "man" to "living well" is analogous to that of "harpist" to "playing the harp well" (NE, 1095a16). To understand what a "man" is thus requires an understanding of what it means to be a "good man," the two elements being inseparable. Man has a function or a purpose: to actualize his essential nature and to attain the telos giving meaning and unity to his life. The use made of "good" here presupposes that every type of item that can appropriately be called good or bad—including persons and actions—has some given specific purpose or function. To call something good, therefore, is also to make a factual statement; to call a particular action just is to make a factual statement about what a just man would do in such a situation. The argument advanced here leads MacIntyre to the contention that within the Aristotelian tradition "moral and evaluative statements can be called true or false in precisely the way in which all other factual statements can be so called." However, "once the notion of essential human purposes or functions disappears from morality, it begins to appear implausible to treat moral judgments as factual statements" (AV, 59).

But it is not only that no human nature is agreed on or that "man" has ceased to be a functional concept; it is also that man is no longer seen as filling a set of roles each of which has its own purpose: member of a family, soldier, philosopher. What MacIntyre describes in terms of a loss of traditional context was seen by the Enlightenment thinkers as the achievement by the self of its proper autonomy. However, this much-celebrated liberation of the modern self is had at the price of detaching it from the traditional morality without which the would-be moral utterances of the newly autonomous agent are devoid of any authoritative content. "Each moral agent now spoke unconstrained by the externalities of divine law, natural teleology or hierarchical authority," writes MacIntyre, and immediately proceeds to pose the polemical question, "But why should anyone else now be expected to listen to him?" (AV, 68). What the Enlightenment, the utilitarianism of the nineteenth century, and the analytical moral philosophy of the twentieth have in common is that they have all failed to give this question a cogent answer. The result is that contemporary moral experience has taken on a "paradoxical character": although taught to see ourselves as autonomous moral agents, we cannot help becoming engaged in modes of practice involving us in downright manipulative relations with others; seeking to protect the autonomy we think we, being "enlightened" selves, have achieved, we find "no way open to us to do so except by directing towards others those very manipulative modes of relationship which each of us aspires to resist in our own case" (AV, 68). Again, the incoherence of the moral scheme transmitted to us today prepares the way for emotivism; morality, once rationally justified in theory and in practice, is reduced to the rationality-evading domain of personal preference and social manipulation.

MacIntyre, an adherent of a moral tradition largely lost to us, therefore writes his history of the moral decline into emotivism in such a way as to say that, Aristotelianism having been disavowed, emotivism was not to be avoided. But certainly a philosopher like Kant, albeit for good reasons unfamiliar with the word, wished to avoid "emotivism" and the like at all costs. This being so, MacIntyre's diagnosis presupposes that Kant, the seminal Enlightenment thinker, can be shown to have failed in *his* attempt to furnish morality with a rational foundation.

Kant sees ethics as having its foundation in reason. Practical reason appeals to no content derived from experience, such as our conception of human happiness. Reason lays down principles that are universal, categorical, and internally consistent. A rational morality as intended by Kant will lay down principles that can and ought to be held by *all* human beings, independent of circumstances and conditions, and that could therefore consistently be obeyed by every rational agent on every occasion. MacIntyre interprets Kant to mean that "the project of discovering a rational justification of morality simply is the project of discovering a rational test which will discriminate those maxims which are a genuine expression of the moral law when they determine the will from those maxims which are not such an expression" (AV, 44). The moral law takes the form of a categorical imperative to "always act so as to treat humanity, whether in your own person or in that of the other, as an end, and not merely as a means." This is a moral law that demands that we offer to the other *reasons* for acting in a certain proposed manner rather than try to influence and manipulate the other in nonrational ways, hence treating that other as a means and not as an end. In other words, Kant's seems to be an ethics showing us how emotivism and the like can be avoided. MacIntyre, however, although sympathetic with Kant's ambition, argues that Kant failed to do what he set out to do. Kant, says MacIntyre, gives us "no good reason" for holding the position that I should always treat the other as an end and never merely as a means. "I can," writes he, "without any inconsistency whatsoever flout this position; 'Let everyone except me be treated as a means' may be immoral, but it is not inconsistent and there is not even any inconsistency in willing a universe of egotists all of whom live by this maxim" (AV, 46). Believing himself to have demonstrated that Kantian ethics is unsuccessful in its attempt to rule out a universe of egotists, MacIntyre draws the conclusion that "the attempt to found what Kant takes to be the maxims of morality on what Kant takes to be reason therefore fails just as surely as Kierkegaard's attempt to discover a foundation for them in an act of choice failed." So "Kant's failure provided Kierkegaard with his starting-point: the act of choice had to be called in to do the work that reason could not do" (AV, 47).

MacIntyre has perhaps gotten a little ahead of himself. Consider the claims he wishes to justify: First, in emotivism the difference—all-important in ethics—between manipulative and nonmanipulative human relations is obliterated. Second, the philosophers of the Enlightenment, the most prominent among whom is Kant, set out to furnish morality with a rational vindication that, if successful, would maintain the crucial difference between manipulative and nonmanipulative human relations. Third, what we witness today is the hegemony of emotivism. Fourth, and in conclusion, this being so, something must have gone terribly wrong with the Enlightenment project that was to have secured the ethical difference in question and hence to have ruled out the possibility that emotivism would reign. The opposite being the case in our society, this project must have failed to accomplish what it set out to do.

This, then, is what I take to be the structure of MacIntyre's argument. But it is not convincing. The whole point of Kant's ethics was precisely to underscore the difference between a relationship in which each person treats the other primarily as a means to that other's (overt or covert) ends and one in which each treats the other as an end. But Kant, according to MacIntyre, fails; Kant does not succeed in showing why a universe of egotists would be inconsistent with the moral law as embodied in the categorical imperative.

MacIntyre argues that "it might be inconvenient for each if everyone lived by this maxim ['Let everyone except me be treated as a means'], but it would not be impossible and to invoke considerations of convenience would in any case be to introduce just that prudential reference to happiness which Kant aspires to eliminate from all considerations of morality" (AV, 47). This in fact is the only clear-cut philosophical argument that MacIntyre offers in his criticism of Kant; he is content to leave the substantial part of his case against Kant to the historical and sociological "evidence" provided by the "fact" of the current hegemony of emotivism. In other words, twentieth-century emotivism is used as an "argument," or demonstration, that Kant's attempt to justify morality has failed. This strategy seems highly problematic.

MacIntyre's philosophical argument against Kant maintains that his ethics allows for a universe of egotists. According to MacIntyre's conception of Kant's ethics, the test for any proposed maxim is whether we can consistently will that everyone should always act on it. Proposing the maxim "Let everyone except me be treated as a means," MacIntyre asserts that this maxim, despite its obvious immoral nature, in fact passes the test. That is to say, there is no inconsistency in my willing to act on this maxim and hence in my willing a universe of egotists. Permitting what is prima facie a downright immoral maxim successfully to pass the test of consistency, Kantian ethics is scandalized. Or so MacIntyre claims to have shown. But he has not. Morality as argued for by Kant does *not* allow a universe of egotists; it allows only a "kingdom of ends" where each person treats all others not as means but as ends. Why should we treat the other thus? MacIntyre holds that Kant's failure consists in his failure to answer this question. Furthermore, he holds that the only way to give the question a cogent answer is by recourse to Aristotelian ethics, according to which "a prudential reference to happiness" delivers what is needed. Kant, however, opposing this tradition, does not trust the ability of conceptions of happiness or of the human telos to provide a foundation for morality; such conceptions being vague and shifting, reason itself, relying on no content derived from experience, will have to provide the sought-for foundation. MacIntyre, in his attempted repudiation of Kant, observes that reason lays down formal principles such as that concerning internal consistency, but he ignores the fact that Kant's ethics entails a certain definition of man or, more precisely, of what is meant by the noumenal self. John Rawls observes that "though acting on any consistent set of principles could be the outcome of a decision on the part of the noumenal self, not all such action by the phenomenal self expresses this decision as that of a free and equal rational being." The implication is that "if a person realizes his true self by expressing it in his actions, and if he desires above all else to realize this self, then he will choose to act from principles that manifest his nature as a free and equal rational being."[4] So the reason it is morally wrong to treat others as means and not as ends is that it would be plainly inconsistent with the definition of the noumenal self as a free and equal rational being; it is only when treated as an end that we recognize—in ourselves as well as in others—what it means to be what we are: free and equal rational beings.

I conclude that MacIntyre's philosophical argument against Kant is unconvincing. Further, I contend that the central argument in *After Virtue* depends on this rejection of Kant and that it, too, is therefore essentially unsound. In contriving this argument, MacIntyre next takes up Nietzsche. Nietzsche, we are told, is *"the* moral philosopher of the present age"; it was his "historic achievement to understand more clearly than any other philosopher . . . not only that what purported to be appeals to objectivity were in fact expressions of subjective will, but also the nature of the problems that this posed for moral philosophy" (AV, 113). The inherited notions of natural rights, of utility, of the greatest happiness of the greatest number are all unmasked as fictions; likewise, the autonomous moral subject as envisaged in Kant is said to be but an illusion. What these fictions and illusions try to hide is the scandalous and disturbing "truth" that there is nothing to morality but expressions of my thoroughly nonrational will, and that morality can only mean *my* morality in the sense of being dictated by what my subjective will creates. Will replaces reason, be it Aristotelian or Kantian. But there is no need to spell out Nietzsche's philosophy here. What matters is the role it plays in MacIntyre's argument. His main contention is that "the power of Nietzsche's position depends upon the truth of one central thesis: that all rational vindications of morality manifestly fail and that *therefore* belief in the tenets of morality needs to be explained in terms of a set of rationalizations which conceal the fundamentally non-rational phenomena of the will. My own argument obliges me to agree with Nietzsche that the philosophers of the Enlightenment never succeeded in providing grounds for [Nietzsche's] central thesis. But . . . that failure itself was nothing other than an historical sequel to the rejection of the Aristotelian tradition" (AV, 117–18). And toward the end of his book, MacIntyre writes that "against the Aristotelian tradition the Nietzschean polemic is completely unsuccessful"; moreover, "it is from the perspective of that tradition that we can best understand the mistakes at the heart of the Nietzschean position" (AV, 257, 258).

So MacIntyre ascribes to Nietzsche the role of a philosopher who was partly right, partly wrong. He was right in rejecting the morality of the Enlightenment, because hidden behind the appeals to objectivity and impersonality were "in fact" the much more "profound" phenomena of the will. Rationality, then, is but a facade designed to conceal the primacy of the nonrational powers whose embodiment humanity is. Witnessing "nihilism" as the unavoidable outcome of the philosophical failure of the Enlightenment, Nietzsche was able to anticipate the emotivism that was to emerge as the reality of twentieth-century Western society.[5] But he was wrong in generalizing from the condition of moral judgment in his own day to the nature of morality as such. Had Nietzsche understood that the deeper reason for the failure of the Enlightenment thinkers lay in their initial rejection of the Aristotelian tradition rather than in the "nonrational" nature of what he took to be morality per se, he would have seen something that he, as an heir of the Enlightenment, never even considered: namely, that the only way out of the impasse of nineteenth- and twentieth-century morality is made possible by a rejection of the rejection of Aristotle, and, hence, by some sort of *return* to the latter. Nietzsche was wrong because he failed to question whether it was right to abandon Aristotle. On the other hand, if Aristotle's position in ethics and politics had been sustained—this of course is what MacIntyre holds—then the whole Nietzschean enterprise would have been pointless from the start.

The history of moral philosophy from Hume onward, in MacIntyre's reading, is the history of a series of failures preparing for present-day emotivism. The sheer *plurality* of post-Aristotelian philosophical attempts to provide morality with a rational vindication and so with a fixed set of objective standards is used by MacIntyre as an argument against the philosophical validity of each of these attempts. In other words, MacIntyre holds the view that if, say, Hume were right, then we would have had no Kant; and if Kant were right, then we would have had no Hegel; and if Hegel were right, then we would have had no Kierkegaard, and so on, all the way up to the various positions in modern analytic philosophy. What MacIntyre does is infer from the fact that there has been and still is a plurality of attempts to justify morality, each making its own truth claim, the conclusion that every one of these attempts has "therefore" failed. Since Hume, at least, disagreement about morality is said to have taken on an "interminable" character because every position has rivals as well as successors. So when we ask the question posed earlier—What are the criteria for making a rational judgment about these rival and clashing claims to truth?—we get no answer; each and every position in contemporary debate about morality fails when it comes to the crucial task of convincing its rivals that *its* claim to truth is the only legitimate and redeemable one. What we have then is a situation where the rival positions relate to one another the way Hume did to Kant and vice versa: just as Hume seeks to found morality on the passions because his arguments have excluded the possibility of founding it on reason, so Kant founds it on reason because *his* arguments have excluded the possibility of founding it on the passions. In short, the failure of the one provides the other with his starting point; since no single one of the attempted justifications of morality appears philosophically compelling from the standpoint of its many rivals, the debate goes on and on and on and ultimately assumes interminability.

Is MacIntyre's inference sound? Is it legitimate to infer from *historical* plurality to *philosophical* invalidity? Does the historical circumstance of plurality and thus of theoretical rivalry carry the kind of *falsifying* power MacIntyre wishes to attribute to it? Can philosophical theories be said to "fail" other than as philosophical argumentation—proceeding as it does immanently, as opposed to historically or sociologically—shows them to fail? In short, is the argumentative use MacIntyre wishes to make of the sheer historical fact of a plurality of positions really philosophically sound? I think not. Again, my impression is that MacIntyre illegitimately turns an alleged historical and sociological "fact" into a philosophical argument, whereas he, on closer scrutiny, can be seen to have none.

The Rationality of Tradition-Constituted Inquiry

Whose Justice? Which Rationality?—the title chosen for the sequel to *After Virtue*—signals a core thesis of the book: that to each determinate form of practical rationality there corresponds a determinate conception of justice and, moreover, that there is no neutral set of criteria by which rival claims to what rationality and justice is can be adjudicated. Whereas in his earlier book MacIntyre hoped to show that the Enlightenment thinkers were unable to agree on what precisely those principles were that would be found undeniable by all so-called rational persons, in his latest book he develops this failure as the misconceived attempt to construct a morality for "tradition-free individuals," an attempt thwarted during several centuries of unresolved disputes because there has emerged as yet no uncontested account of what tradition-independent morality consists.

One might wonder where these notions of "tradition-free individuals" and "tradition-independent morality" come from. MacIntyre's answer is that they are part of the Enlightenment legacy and that they have been embraced by that Enlightenment heir known as liberalism. Being essentially a critique of modern liberalism, MacIntyre's new book devotes much space to showing that "the [liberal] project of founding a form of social order in which individuals could emancipate themselves from the contingency and particularity of tradition by appealing to genuinely universal, tradition-independent norms" has been and is doomed to remain a failure and, furthermore, that the liberal hope of a "tradition-independent rational universality" is an illusion (WJ, 335). Thus, there is no rationality as such, no justice as such, no morality as such; there is only that peculiar to a tradition. It follows that all appeals to tradition-independent criteria are misconceived.

What MacIntyre understands by a tradition "is an argument extended through time in which certain fundamental agreements are defined and redefined in terms of two kinds of conflict: those with critics and enemies external to the tradition who reject all or at least key parts of those fundamental agreements, and those internal, interpretative debates through which the meaning and rationale of the fundamental agreements come to be expressed and by whose progress a tradition is constituted" (WJ, 12). Given this definition of a tradition, there is no way to engage in the practices of advancing, evaluating, accepting, and rejecting accounts of practical rationality and justice except from within some one particular tradition. Those who inhabit the same tradition engage in conversation, cooperation, and conflict with regard to the core beliefs of that tradition. Each tradition, however, can at each stage of its development provide rational justification for its central theses in its own terms, employing the concepts and standards peculiar to it and by which it defines itself. But, argues MacIntyre, "there is no set of independent standards of rational justification by appeal to which the issues between contending traditions can be decided." Granting this, how are we to judge rationally between rival claims to truth about rationality, justice, and morality? Again, practical rationality is always what a particular tradition understands by it; justice likewise is always justice as defined by, say, the Aristotelian or the Augustinian or the utilitarian tradition. So to give an example, Hume and Rawls agree in "excluding application for any Aristotelian concept of desert, in the framing of rules of justice, while they disagree with each other on whether a certain type of equality is required by justice." Different traditions make rival and competing claims to our allegiance with respect to our understanding of practical rationality and justice, and "we can have no good reason to decide in favor of any one rather than of the others. (WJ, 351).

What are we to conclude from such an argument? If it really be the case that the only standards of rationality are those made available by and within different traditions, then the conclusion that no issue between contending traditions is rationally decidable seems unavoidable. This is indeed the conclusion drawn by two related philosophical positions. The first MacIntyre identifies as the *relativist* position. It denies the possibility of rational debate between rival traditions; it holds that every set of standards, that is to say, every tradition incorporating a particular set of standards, has as much and as little claim to our allegiance as any other; therefore, no one tradition is rightfully entitled to arrogate to itself an exclusive title. Accordingly, no one tradition can deny legitimacy to its rivals; hence, rational choice among rival traditions is impossible. The second position relevant here is that of *perspectivism*. Although it shares the kind of argument just made, it withdraws the ascription of "truth" and "falsity" altogether. In the perspectivist view, rival traditions are not mutually exclusive and incompatible claims to understand one and the same world. Rather, they provide radically different but nonetheless complementary perspectives for envisaging the realities about which they speak to us.

Now, it may seem that MacIntyre, given his own argument as just sketched, has no choice but to endorse the conclusions drawn by relativism and perspectivism. But no. His thesis is that they are both "fundamentally misconceived and misdirected." Relativism and perspectivism, he goes on to assert, are in fact "the negative counterpart of the Enlightenment, its inverted mirror image" (WJ, 353). What they claim is that if the Enlightenment conceptions of truth and rationality cannot be sustained, then theirs is the only possible alternative. MacIntyre agrees with this claim only insofar as he agrees that the Enlightenment thinkers all failed in their attempts to establish a particular view of truth and rationality, one in which truth is guaranteed by rational method and where rational method appeals to principles undeniable by any fully reflective rational person. No agreement has as yet been reached as to what precisely the principles in question are. Correctly acknowledging this "fact," relativism and perspectivism, however, draw conclusions unacceptable to MacIntyre. In short, theirs is not the only possible alternative; a third way can in fact be found, one recognizing "the rationality possessed by traditions," a rationality overlooked by the Enlightenment as well as by its more recent philosophical heirs.

The rationality possessed by traditions, writes MacIntyre, has not been explicitly articulated in the form of a *theory* of rationality within one or more of the traditions with which he is concerned in his new book: the traditions, that is, of Aristotelianism, of Augustinianism, of the Scottish Enlightenment, and of liberalism. Rather, the sought-for theory of rationality is one "embodied in and presupposed by" the *practices* of inquiry *common* to the four full-fledged traditions referred to. "The rationality of a tradition-constituted and tradition-constitutive enquiry is in key and essential part a matter of the kind of progress which it makes through a number of well-defined types of stage. Every such form of enquiry begins in and from some condition of pure historical contingency, from the beliefs, institutions, and practices of some particular community which constitute a given" (WJ, 354). Thus does MacIntyre introduce the first stage in the development of a tradition in which the beliefs, utterances, texts, and persons taken to be authoritative are referred to uncritically, there being as yet no systematic endeavor to call them into question. In a second stage, however, the inevitable confrontation by new situations, generating new questions, may reveal within established practices and beliefs "a lack of resources for offering or for justifying answers" to these new questions. Inadequacies of various types are identified but not yet remedied. Finally, in a third stage, the systematic attempts to respond to those inadequacies result in a set of reformulations and reevaluations of beliefs formerly taken for granted, reformulations intended to overcome the identified limitations. Notice that the inquiry is undertaken by the adherents of the tradition, by individuals remaining at all three stages loyal to the tradition and working exclusively from within the tradition they belong to. Notice also that some core of shared belief, constituting allegiance to the tradition, has to survive every rupture. Having taken part in the third stage of development, the individuals belonging to a tradition are in a position to contrast their new beliefs with the old, the former being but reformulations of the latter.

At this point MacIntyre introduces the concept of *falsity* as defined by his theory of the rationality entailed in the practices of inquiry. In this definition, those earlier judgments and beliefs are called false insofar as the individuals come to perceive a radical discrepancy or a lack of correspondence between what they once believed and the world as they have now come to see it, their tradition having gone through all three stages of development. Falsity, then, is recognized retrospectively as a past inadequacy now successfully overcome. It follows that the decisive reason for inquiring further is the identification of incoherence within established belief and that established belief will not be rejected until something perceived as more adequate, because less incoherent, has been discovered. Thus, the third stage is never reached once and for all; sooner or later it is likely to assume the kind of taken-for-grantedness characteristic of the first stage, thus in turn preparing the way for a second stage concerned with critical questioning. At every stage, beliefs and judgments are criticized and justified by reference to those of the previous stage. Therefore, tradition-constituted inquiry is "anti-Cartesian" in what it moves *from*, and it is "anti-Hegelian" in what it moves *toward*. Always taking the sheer contingency and facticity of some set of established beliefs as the starting point for inquiry, the adherents of a tradition may well assign a certain primacy to certain "truths" and treat them as first metaphysical or practical principles. Such principles, however, are anti-Cartesian insofar as they have to vindicate themselves in the historical process of dialectical justification described above. This means that they must succeed in vindicating themselves as superior to their historical predecessors, as more coherent and adequate in the face of novel situations and problems. Conceived in this manner, first principles are not self-sufficient, self-justifying epistemological first principles in the sense intended by Descartes; their primacy is purely provisional in that they are subject to falsification in the course of future dialectical questioning. Furthermore, it follows from this latter point that anything like the Absolute Knowledge of the Hegelian system is a chimera; the possibility that present beliefs will in the future be revealed as inadequate is one that can never be precluded.

But it also happens that a tradition-constituted inquiry is subjected to a much more serious questioning than the one referred to as the second stage in the above model. To the kind of occurrence MacIntyre has in mind here he gives the name *epistemological crisis*. Such a crisis begins to emerge when the inquiry ceases to make progress by its own standards of progress. Conflicts and disagreements over rival answers to key questions can no longer be settled rationally and hence come to assume an interminable character. In this situation, sticking to the established methods of inquiry no longer has the intended effect of solving the problems encountered but has the opposite effect of increasingly disclosing new inadequacies and hitherto unrecognized incoherences within the established fabric of beliefs. Hence, the mark of an epistemological crisis is a "dissolution of historically founded certitudes" (WJ, 362). Here the inquiry falls into a state of impasse. It proves unable to solve the new problems by its old standards of problem solving; it lacks the methodological and theoretical resources needed to make further progress. What this means is that the tradition cannot *by itself* overcome the radical crisis and the increasing self-doubt it has run into. At this particular point, says MacIntyre, the adherents of a tradition may be expected to "encounter in a new way the claims of some particular rival tradition."

> When the adherents of a tradition have understood the beliefs of the alien tradition, they may find themselves compelled to recognize that within this other tradition it is possible to construct from the concepts and theories peculiar to it what they were unable to provide from their own conceptual and theoretical resources, a cogent and illuminating explanation—cogent and illuminating, that is, by their own standards—of why their own intellectual tradition had been unable to solve its problems or restore its coherence. . . . What the explanation afforded from within the alien tradition will have disclosed is a lack of correspondence between the dominant beliefs of their own tradition and the reality disclosed by the most successful explanation, and it may well be the only successful explanation which they have been able to discover. Hence the claim to truth for what have hitherto been their own beliefs has been defeated. (WJ, 364–65)

This, then, is the argument MacIntyre makes in trying, on the one hand, to defend his thesis of the rationality of tradition-constituted inquiry and, on the other, to meet the double challenge posed by relativism and perspectivism.

The relativist maintains that if each tradition carries within it its own standards of rational justification, the possibility of one tradition entering into rational debate with any other is precluded; therefore, no tradition can vindicate its rational superiority over its rivals, and allegiance to any one tradition is and must remain nonrational and arbitrary. But MacIntyre takes it that he has shown this argument to be unsound. "It is untrue," he contends, "that traditions, understood as each possessing its own account of and practices of rational justification, therefore cannot defeat or be defeated by other traditions." It is untrue because "it is in respect of their adequacy or inadequacy in their responses to epistemological crises that traditions are vindicated or fail to be vindicated" (WJ, 366).

The perspectivist calls into question the possibility or, better, legitimacy of making truth claims from any one particular tradition. Perspectivism assumes a multiplicity of perspectives, mutually enriching one another, and thereby supposes that one could temporarily adopt the standpoint of one tradition and then, at will, as it were, exchange it for another. Insofar as perspectivism is a doctrine presupposing the possibility of moving freely between contending traditions, it rests on an illusion. This is so because the person outside all traditions "lacks sufficient rational resources for enquiry and a fortiori for enquiry into what tradition is to be rationally preferred"; "to be outside all traditions is to be a stranger to enquiry" (WJ, 367).

In stressing every person's ineradicable belongingness to a particular tradition, MacIntyre's response to the challenge coming from relativism and perspectivism seems to run along lines similar to Gadamer's in *Wahrheit und Methode* (esp. 205ff.), a work nowhere mentioned by MacIntyre. But I believe that Gadamer would hesitate to accept the conclusions drawn in *Whose Justice? Which Rationality?* MacIntyre's theory of the rationality possessed by tradition-constituted inquiry requires that a tradition enter a serious internal epistemological crisis for it to "open up" and to enter into conversation with other, rival traditions. The idea here is that the beliefs and judgments held by that alien tradition may prove helpful in solving the problems run into in one's own. In other words, it is in attempting to secure and restore the jeopardized truth claim embodied in a tradition that the adherents of that tradition—for the first time, as it were—come to take interest in the ways in which rival traditions go about solving their problems, which are viewed as having an adequate degree of similarity, and thus relevance, to one's own problems. MacIntyre's point, then, is not only the familiar Gadamerian one that inquiry always begins from *within* some one tradition; it is also, and more interestingly, that the move *outward* from within one's own tradition is always caused, motivated, and *necessitated* by the tradition's running into a series of internal problems that it reveals itself incapable of solving. The tradition's own standards and methods of inquiry proving utterly inadequate in the face of crisis, its only way out is that made possible by invoking the standards and methods of a rival tradition. It follows that a tradition remains fully self-occupied and self-sufficient as long as it develops through the three stages depicted in MacIntyre's model and as long as it continues to make "progress" as defined by the standards of inquiry peculiar to it. From such a perspective, alien traditions must appear alien in the strong sense of precluding any possibility that they might in fact *contribute in some way or another—methodologically or conceptually*—to the course of development taken by one's own tradition. However, this possibility is not precluded by an act of consideration; it is precluded because not entertained. The assumption is that rival traditions simply are given no chance to make any contribution whatsoever. This is so because it takes a breakdown or crisis within one's own tradition for the alien ones to be viewed not simply as "alien" but as "interesting" or "relevant"—interesting or relevant, that is, on the condition that they demonstrate some efficacy in overcoming problems that one's own tradition has been unsuccessful in resolving by itself. In short, a conversation between two or more traditions comes about when, and only when, one of them suffers an epistemological crisis, implying by "suffers" that the crisis is actually *perceived* as being one. Conversation therefore presupposes a situation of acknowledged emergency.

However, I suspect that there is a logical inconsistency in this account of the rationality possessed by tradition-constituted inquiry. MacIntyre states that "the standards by which the adherents of a tradition judge the explanation [offered by an alien tradition] to be cogent and illuminating will be the very same standards by which they have found their tradition wanting in the face of epistemological crisis" (WJ, 364). Viewed in its broader context, this statement involves two inconsistent claims. First, MacIntyre claims an epistemological crisis renders the standards thus far adhered to rationally untenable; this being the case, they need to be substituted by more coherent and adequate standards. This explains the interest taken in the rival standards of inquiry maintained by alien and hitherto "uninteresting" traditions. Second, these very same "untenable" standards are not questioned, let alone rejected, but are still held on to; indeed, they are what allows the explanation offered by the alien tradition to appear as "cogent and illuminating." In other words, MacIntyre makes the incompatible claims that the standards in question are both rejected and held on to.

But MacIntyre can't have it both ways. Surely there is no easy way out here. Indeed, it sounds very plausible that in times of crisis the adherents of one tradition develop, out of sheer necessity, a new interest in the alternative standards of inquiry embodied in a rival tradition. Given that this happens precisely at the moment when their own standards are perceived to collapse, the hard question becomes, By recourse to what standards is the explanation to one's own problems as offered by the alien tradition allowed to be vindicated as rationally "superior"? With the old standards collapsing and about to be substituted, and with no new ones having as yet been developed or adopted, there seem to be *no* standards available for determining whether the truth claim made by the rival tradition is in fact rationally superior to the one made by one's own. My assumption is that MacIntyre has failed to give a consistent argument for the kind of rationality he attributes to the conversation between rival traditions. At stake here is nothing less than the persuasiveness of MacIntyre's response to relativism and perspectivism. That is to say, if the argument to establish the rationality allowing one to decide between contending truth claims should fail, then the thesis that such a rationality is not to be had is not repudiated after all, which would mean that relativism and perspectivism win—if only by default.

To be sure, the argument required must be of a more sophisticated nature than that needed to explain the rationality working within one single tradition. In the case of the latter argument, MacIntyre's three-stage model offers what in my view is a convincing argument, showing as it does how earlier beliefs and judgments are rendered inadequate by later ones, these later ones successfully overcoming problems left unresolved by the former. In this vertical, or diachronic, dimension, the rational superiority claimed for the problem solving of the present, as opposed to that of the past, is determined by invoking one and the same standard of inquiry—the standard, that is, by which a tradition defines itself and is recognized by others as this or that particular tradition, in short, the standard furnishing a tradition with its specific identity through the course of time. But this ceases to be the case when we move from conversation within one tradition to conversation between two or more coexisting traditions. In this case, not one and the same but two or more rival standards of rationality and justification are involved, each making a distinct truth claim. Moreover, to repeat a central point, the possibility of there being a neutral, "third" standard, or standing ground, external to all tradition is an option squarely ruled out by MacIntyre.

The question remains, How are we to decide rationally between a plurality of truth claims? This question will remain with us as long as a number of traditions continue to coexist, confronting us with a number of more or less incompatible truth claims. "The initial answer," says MacIntyre, "is: that will depend upon who you are and how you understand yourself" (WJ, 393). Prima facie, this suggestion seems merely to echo Fichte's dictum that the kind of philosophy one chooses is decided by the kind of person one is. But this hardly suffices as a cogent answer. The point of MacIntyre's provisional answer is to remind us once again that there are no standards of rationality equally available to all persons, regardless of what tradition they may happen to find themselves in. This being his major contention, MacIntyre asserts that "what rationality then requires of such a person is that he or she . . . engage, to whatever degree is appropriate, both in the ongoing arguments within [his or her] tradition and in the argumentative debates and conflicts of that tradition of enquiry with one or more of its rivals." The two tasks involved are not at all the same. The latter task of engaging in conversation between one's own tradition and one of its rivals "requires a work of imagination whereby the individual is able to place him or herself imaginatively within the scheme of belief inhabited by those whose allegiance is to the rival tradition, so as to perceive and conceive the natural and social worlds as they perceive and conceive them." To acquire such alien concepts, we have to learn to speak in a voice that is not our own, as it were; we are not really able to employ such concepts in the first person, except as dramatic impersonators. Hence, "acts of emphatic conceptual imagination" allow us to come to understand "what it is to be and to believe within another tradition" (WJ, 394). Notwithstanding the plausibility or lack of such of this account (I find it uncomfortably close to the almost unanimously discarded "empathy model" going back at least to the hermeneutics of Dilthey), it can scarcely be said to deliver a satisfactory answer to the question of how the individual is rationally to decide between contending truth claims. Understanding the outlook of the alien tradition "from within" certainly may be one requisite among others for reaching the sought-for decisions, but it just as surely does not suffice to tell us exactly *how* we are to go about actually deciding. That is to say, having learned the language of the alien tradition and having thereby "understood" the beliefs and standards of justification peculiar to it, the problem of how to decide between the alien truth claims and one's own—or between any other truth claims, for that matter—remains unresolved.

However, the criticism I have voiced needs to be substantiated by other arguments in order to uncover the more basic weaknesses of the neo-Aristotelian position defended in MacIntyre's work. The crucial point in this regard doubtless is MacIntyre's negative assessment of modern liberalism, that is, of liberal modernity as well as of liberal political theory.

MacIntyre's Neo-Aristotelian Critique of Modern Liberalism

MacIntyre contrasts his own position with that of modern liberalism as follows:

> Where the standpoint of a tradition involves an acknowledgment that fundamental debate is between competing and conflicting under-

standings of rationality, the standpoint of the forums of modern
liberal culture presupposes the fiction of shared, even if unformulable,
universal standards of rationality. Where the standpoint of a tradition
cannot be presented except in a way which takes account of the
history and the historical situatedness, both of traditions themselves
and of those individuals who engage in dialogue with them, the
standpoint of the forums of modern liberal culture presupposes the
irrelevance of one's history to one's status in debate. We confront one
another in such forums abstracted from and deprived of the particularities of our histories. (WJ, 400)

The standpoint of liberalism is said to involve a double abstraction: the
particular theses of practical rationality and justice that are to be debated
and evaluated are abstracted from their context within traditions of inquiry;
correspondingly, the attempt is made to debate and evaluate such theses in
terms of their rational justifiability *to any rational person*, to individuals
abstracted from their particularities of character, history, and circumstance.
So liberalism perceives conceptions of rationality and justice as detached
from their respective traditions, and likewise it perceives the individual as
detached from his or her particular background and history. What remains,
then, are conceptions without contexts, individuals without histories, that is
to say, two fictions, the one as devoid of content as the other. What
liberalism thus essentially comes down to is the attempt to formulate a
morality for tradition-free individuals who, when taking part in moral
debates, appeal to genuinely universal, tradition-independent norms and
principles. "Initially," writes MacIntyre,"the liberal claim was to provide a
political, legal, and economic framework in which assent to one and the
same set of rationally justifiable principles would enable those who espouse
widely different and incompatible conceptions of the good life for human
beings to live together peacefully within the same society, enjoying the same
political status and engaging in the same economic relationships" (WJ, 335–
36). The self as envisaged in liberalism is one that moves from sphere to
sphere, compartmentalizing its attitudes and possessing its own ordered
schedule of "preferences." The preferences are beyond reasoning; what they
in fact do is provide all practical reasoning with its all-important initial
premise. Moreover, in being treated as simply given rather than as sociohis-
torically constituted, preferences guide actions in such a way that the latter
are understood as designed to implement the former, making the success of
the course of action chosen dependent on whether it is a pragmatically

effective implementation. What this self seeks to do, then, is to act so as to maximize the satisfaction of its peculiar preferences in accordance with their internal ordering. Whereas in the public realms of liberal politics (the market being the most prominent one) the ultimate data are preferences, weighed against each other regardless of how they have been arrived at, the basic unit and nucleus of social life is the individual, being held to possess his or her essential human capacities apart from and prior to membership in any particular social and political order.

The liberal picture of the self obviously has enormous consequences for its conceptions of rationality and justice. MacIntyre's argument in this regard rests on the premise that freedom as defined by liberalism means "negative freedom" and, furthermore, that in liberalism the concept of right is prior to that of the good. As opposed to the Aristotelian, the liberal is committed to there being no one overriding good. The recognition of a range of human goods dovetails with the liberal definition of freedom insofar as every individual is to be equally free to propose and to live by whatever conception of the good he or she pleases, on the condition that the conception in no serious way interfere with the life and freedom of the rest of the community. From this it follows that no systematic attempt to embody a particular conception of the human good in public life—by individuals or groups of individuals—is proscribed. Given the multiplicity of preferences and the plurality of human goods, it is inevitable that conflicts between rival conceptions occur. Thus, there arises a need for some set of regulating principles, recognized by everyone concerned, by which cooperation in the implementation of preferences may be achieved. This is where MacIntyre sees liberalism put to the test. He argues that "the only *rational* way in which these disagreements could be resolved would be by means of a philosophical enquiry aimed at deciding which out of the conflicting sets of premises, if any, is true. But a liberal order . . . is one in which each standpoint may make its claims but can do no more within the framework of the public order, since no overall theory of the human good is to be regarded as justified" (WJ, 343). MacIntyre's thesis is that debate at the so-called first level, debate about the human good in general, is necessarily barren of substantive consensual conclusions in a liberal social order. Rival appeals to accounts of the human good or of justice therefore assume a rhetorical form; nonrational persuasion displaces rational agreement because "standpoints are construed as the expressions of attitude and feeling and often enough come to be no more than that." From this, in turn, it follows that "the philosophical theorists who had claimed that all evaluative and normative judgments *can be* no more than expressions of attitude and feeling, that all such judgments are emotive, turn out to have told us the truth not about evaluative and normative judgments as such, but about what such judgments become in this kind of increasingly emotivist culture" (WJ, 343).

We have come full circle and reached the point where MacIntyre's attack on modern liberalism links up with his diagnosis of contemporary emotivist culture in *After Virtue*. The two books discussed in this chapter in fact advance *one single major thesis:* that modern liberalism in theory and in practice *sustains* the present-day emotivist culture whose historical emergence was prepared for by the failure of the Enlightenment project to work out a universal morality compelling to all persons qua rational human beings. This means that liberal theory has nothing to offer as a way out of the ethical impasse that is the real content of the sociocultural hegemony achieved by emotivism. "Liberally" allowing for a multiplicity of preferences and goods, seeing the latter as the possession of sovereign individuals and hence as being beyond the force of argument, liberalism bars these rival conceptions from rational dispute at the so-called first level and therefore cannot but implicitly accept the conclusion celebrated in emotivism that normative judgments are and can be no more than subjective expressions of attitude and feeling. But MacIntyre is not content to leave it at that. He goes on to claim—and this I take to be the second part of his major thesis—that liberalism also fails with regard to the second level of moral debate. This is the level where preferences are tallied and weighed, thereby presupposing that "the procedures and rules which govern such tallying and weighing are themselves the outcome of rational debate of quite another kind, that at which the principles of shared rationality have been identified by philosophical enquiry" (WJ, 343). As is familiar from the argument in *After Virtue*, such debate about the principles of justice to which universal assent can be found has proved "perpetually inconclusive." That is to say, of whatever kind the universality sought for might be, it is doomed to be a false one; it can be nothing but a *specific particularity for which universality is falsely claimed*.

The reason this is so, according to MacIntyre, is that there can be no "morality as such," just as there can be no morality for "tradition-free individuals." MacIntyre puts forward, somewhat surprisingly, a clear-cut Marxian argument at home in the critique of ideology. Hence, in the postscript to the second edition of *After Virtue*, he writes that "what Kant took to be the principles and presuppositions of morality as such turned out to be the principles and presuppositions of one highly specific morality, a secularized version of Protestantism which furnished modern liberal individualism with one of its founding charters." Consequently, "there are *no* grounds for belief in universal necessary principles—outside purely formal enquiries—except relative to some set of assumptions" (AV, 266). The argument applies a fortiori to liberalism. So the principles that inform practical reasoning in a liberal polity and the theory and practice of justice within it are "not neutral with respect to rival and conflicting theories of the human good. Where they are in force they impose a particular conception of the good life, of practical reasoning, and of justice upon those who willingly or unwillingly accept the liberal procedures and the liberal terms of debate. The overriding good of liberalism is no more and no less than the continued sustenance of the liberal social and political order." What this amounts to is that "liberalism can provide no compelling arguments in favor of its conception of the human good except by appeal to premises which collectively already presuppose just such an overriding theory of the good. The starting points of liberal theorizing are never neutral as between conceptions of the human good; they are always liberal starting points." In the end, there is no escaping the conclusion that liberal theory is itself the articulation of a particular tradition, having, just "like other traditions, internal to it its own standards of rational justification" (WJ, 345).

   This being the structure of the argument MacIntyre develops against liberalism, I cannot help remarking that he has put forward much effort to come up with a critique remarkable perhaps only for its predictability. To start with, surely the proponents of liberal theory need not be reminded that theirs is a starting point within and not outside of history and hence of tradition. I hold the opposite to be the case, meaning by this that the thinkers of the Enlightenment, some of whom count among the founders of liberalism, were extremely aware of the historical situatedness of their philosophical enterprise. Indeed, they saw themselves as coming to grips with the peculiar character of what they self-consciously viewed as a radically novel and unprecedented era in world history, coined in the late eighteenth century as *die Neuzeit.*[6] It belongs to the self-image of this era that humanity is not tradition-free or in any way liberated from history (whatever that might mean) but is its bearer, maker, and subject. History, that is, not only "happens" but can also be shaped by humanity itself, being—following Vico's famous dictum—*its* domain, the arena of its making, as opposed to the principally alien reality of nature. Implied in this development is a change in the view of humanity, for to picture humanity as the doer and maker of the history in which it is situated entails, as far as ethics is concerned, a *universal attribution of moral personality,* meaning moral autonomy and moral responsibility, to the effect that, in fundamental ethical matters, everyone ought to count, no one ought to be excluded (recall here Aristotle's banning slaves and women from the polis); in short, all ought to count in the same way.[7] It is this kind of universalism that is the seminal historical achievement of the Enlightenment; and insofar as liberalism is an heir to the latter, this obliges it to defend—in theory and in practice—the universal or unrestricted right to take part in the ethical discourse.

However, to remind liberal theory that it took and continues to take its departure from within a context that is not universal but particular is not what MacIntyre set out to do. MacIntyre set out to demonstrate not only that liberalism is a *particular* kind of theory embodied in a *particular* set of practices and institutions but also that it is, more significantly, a *false* theory. But he makes a serious mistake when he takes it that the (allegedly unadmitted) particularity of this theory—being one tradition among others—in any way shows it to be false. In my view, MacIntyre makes an inference from particularity to falsity that is philosophically unsound.

What precisely has gone wrong with MacIntyre's argument? In answering this question, I turn briefly to the discussion of rights—a key term in liberal theory—in *After Virtue*. "Human rights" as we understand them are to be truly universal; they are supposed to "attach equally to all individuals, whatever their sex, race, religion, talents or desert." However, the concept as such has a relatively short history; "there is no expression in any ancient or medieval language correctly translated by our expression 'a right' until near the close of the middle ages." But "from this it does not of course follow that there are no natural or human rights; it only follows that no one could have known that there were. And this at least raises certain questions." To which MacIntyre significantly adds, "But we do not need to be distracted into answering them, for the truth is plain: there are no such rights, and belief in them is one with belief in witches and in unicorns." We may wonder why exactly that is so. MacIntyre's response is that "the best reason for asserting so bluntly that there are no such rights [is that] every attempt to give good reasons for believing that there *are* such rights has failed." And from this the scarcely unexpected conclusion is drawn that "natural or human rights . . . are fictions" (AV, 69–70).

My thesis is this: MacIntyre repeatedly makes a philosophically unsound inference from a de facto plurality of rival conceptions to the conclusion that no single one of them can be true or, put differently, that all of them are in fact false. He deduces falsity from multiplicity. I say "repeatedly" because I have detected this move in MacIntyre's argument on three separate occasions.

First, there is the central thesis in *After Virtue* that each attempt made by the Enlightenment thinkers to provide morality with a rational vindication has failed "because" there can be seen to be a plurality of such attempts, all of them setting out to achieve the same goal, all of them disagreeing among themselves about how that goal can be reached. So if Hume had been right, then we would have had no Kant, and so on. Second, there is the thesis in *Whose Justice? Which Rationality?* that liberalism is not a neutral and tradition-free moral and political theory but a theory having a particular history and articulating the beliefs and practices peculiar to a particular tradition; there being a multiplicity of coexisting traditions, liberalism is in effect but one of them. Having established that liberalism is a tradition in this sense, MacIntyre takes it that he has relativized liberalism's (alleged) claim to historical independence and so also its purported theoretical "primacy"; from this relativization the conclusion is drawn that liberal theory is false. Third, there is the thesis, explicit in the first book and implicit in the second, that the concept of universal human rights in fact has a very particular history and that a number of attempts to give good reasons for making us believe in such rights have been undertaken, although no overall reason has as yet been globally assented to; "therefore," each and every one of these different attempts has been a failure.

I asked in an earlier section whether it is legitimate to infer from *historical* plurality to *philosophical* validity. As has become clear from my discussion, the answer is no. MacIntyre's critique of liberalism is a case in point, in that it commits precisely this unsound inference. For to show that liberalism is in fact a particular tradition having a particular history is to show nothing whatsoever regarding its *validity* as a philosophical theory. What is wrong with MacIntyre's critique is that it fails to recognize the distinction between the origin of the theory and its validity, that is, between its *Genese* and its *Geltung*. To infer from the former to the latter is to violate the crucial logical distinction between them; it is to commit a category mistake. Therefore, the indisputable fact that liberalism is a particular theory developing out of a particular historical context in no way *falsifies* its claim to validity, that is, its truth claim as a philosophical theory. In fact, according to MacIntyre's own account of the rationality possessed by tradition-constituted inquiry, all truth claims put forward in philosophical debate are truth claims emerging within and arising out of a context that is always particular and never universal. But there is no need to "remind" the liberal theorists that theirs is a theory as context-specific as any other; quite to the contrary, the thinkers of the Enlightenment all had a very strong historical awareness. Hence, any claim to the effect that the liberal tradition is historically naïve is mistaken. What really matters from a philosophical point of view is that any validity claim *transcends* the particularity of its specific origin; it aims at universal validity, at universal recognition and assent. And it is on this level, that of validity, or *Geltung*, that a critique of the soundness of liberalism qua theory must take place.

Thus, the short answer to the question of what has gone wrong with MacIntyre's critique is that it fails to offer philosophical arguments, that is, arguments at the level of validity just identified. True, he did give such an argument against Kant; on closer scrutiny, however, it proved to be faulty. I find it noteworthy in itself that a distinguished philosopher offers so few philosophical arguments in setting out to substantiate nothing less than his major theses. The arguments in his books are basically empirical. Or to be more precise, what are held by MacIntyre to be empirical facts are invoked to make what he holds to be a philosophical case against certain philosophical theories, especially moral ones.

MacIntyre claims that our culture is one pervaded by emotivist beliefs and practices; in order to show that this is so, he has recourse to certain conceptions allegedly characteristic of our culture: the conception of the modern self, or individual; the conceptions of the therapist, the expert, and the manager; the conception of what constitutes human relations; the conceptions of what justice, rationality, and rights are; and so forth. The close relation among historical development, social life, and moral theory that emerges from the very structure of MacIntyre's line of argument is chosen very deliberately. Thus, MacIntyre frequently says that "a moral philosophy characteristically presupposes a sociology." And he presents the all-important thesis—empirical in form but philosophical in its much-discussed implications—that "to a large degree people now think, talk and act *as if* emotivism were true" (AV, 22). But what if this thesis is empirically false? Granting this for the sake of the argument, what becomes—or rather remains—of the *philosophical* arguments MacIntyre wishes to advance? Not very much, I am afraid.

This is not the appropriate place to put MacIntyre's claim that we live in an emotivist culture to the comprehensive empirical test it demands; indeed, that is a task for historians and sociologists. What I can do, however, is examine the contention that every moral theory takes as its point of departure some particular conceptions of, for instance, "freedom," "right," and "justice." To that end, I invoke the theory of John Rawls.

Rawls writes, in *A Theory of Justice*, that "it has seemed to many philosophers, and it appears to be supported by convictions of common sense, that we distinguish as a matter of principle between the claims of liberty and right on the one hand and the desirability of increasing aggregate social welfare on the other; and that we give a certain priority, if not absolute weight, to the former. Each member of society is thought to have an inviolability founded on justice or, as some say, on natural right, which even the welfare of everyone else cannot override" (27). This being so, "the conditions embodied in the description of the original position are ones that we do in fact [i. e., empirically] accept" (21). Rawls goes on to argue that in justice as fairness "the concept of right is prior to that of the good" (31). Apparently, Rawls does just what MacIntyre does: he begins his philosophical argument by invoking what he takes to be certain pregiven "convictions of common sense," that is to say, beliefs of empirical nature and import. However, Rawls and MacIntyre part company at the actual *content* of their empirical assumptions. MacIntyre, to put it succinctly, holds that common sense amounts to emotivism, a doctrine according to which normative and evaluative judgments are, more or less, but manipulatively directed expressions of nonrational private feelings and attitudes. Rawls, on the other hand, holds that common sense amounts to justice as fairness, a doctrine according to which each member of society has an inviolability founded on justice or natural right, justice in effect denying that the loss of freedom for some is made right by a greater good shared by others. What differs here is the role rationality is to be accorded in morality. Whereas in emotivism morality is reduced to personal preferences beyond the reach of rational criticism, justice as fairness allows rational deliberation to work out the basic principles of justice. So the similarity between the two authors' moves from theory to empirical fact and back again conceals a substantial dissimilarity in the content the commonsense convictions alluded to are held to have. These are two profoundly different assumptions about common sense that are linked up with two just as profoundly different theories of morality. And what is more, MacIntyre and Rawls cannot both be right.

Leaving aside that issue, however, the train of thought just developed leads to a more general point about morality and ethos, or about *Moralität* as opposed to *Sittlichkeit*. This pair of concepts can be traced back to Hegel's critique of the abstract formalism of Kant's ethics, but for my present purposes, I need not recite that long and fascinating history.[8] The point I have in mind is made by Charles Taylor when, referring to Aristotelian ethics, he writes that "our conception of the good is . . . intimately linked with a particular praxis, to which it immanently belongs."[9] In a similar vein,

Herbert Schnädelbach believes that "the essential indebtedness of Aristotle's practical philosophy to practical life experience indicates that the ethics in every Aristotelian or neo-Aristotelian position is at any given time systematically *rooted in a preexisting ethos.*" In this model, what the moral philosopher seeks to accomplish is "a reconstruction of the ethos through ethics," being convinced that "the good already exists in the world." What this amounts to on the part of Aristotelian ethics is "the rejection of a normative foundation of action that is independent of existing reality,"[10] the implication being, to quote Karl-Otto Apel, that "no further critical standard of evaluation can then be imposed on the substantial *Sittlichkeit,* too powerful in any case, of the lifeworld [*Lebenswelt*]."[11] In Apel's view, neo-Aristotelian moral theory is "conventional" in that it treats the application of ethical principles as "a problem concerning the prudent application of conventional norms." This raises a question about the place allowed for ethos-transcending critique in theories inspired by Aristotle. MacIntyre again and again stresses that morality is socially and culturally "embodied," and that standards of rational vindication as well as notions of justice and rights are wholly "defined" by and "internal" to a particular tradition. He thereby confirms Schnädelbach's description of neo-Aristotelianism as entailing the systematic rooting of ethics in a preexisting ethos or, to cite Apel, a linking of ethics with "the natural substantial *Sittlichkeit.*" Apel points out that "on the level of post-Kantian discourse ethics, this means that the interests that normally underlie the conventional norms . . . are explicitly made the subject matter of practical discourses."[12]

Apel's point contains a rather serious accusation: that in neo-Aristotelian morality the culturally defined interests underlying the established conventional norms escape thematization and, hence, criticism. So it appears that morality, depicted as entirely embedded within and part of a given tradition, or ethos, cannot critically question but only affirm and sustain the latter. Let us call the level of ethical debate involved here the first level, that at which the factual *social* validity of conventional and ethos-embodied norms are counterfactually questioned with regard to their *rational* validity. Do these norms deserve the prima facie social validity granted them? If universalized, can they be expected to attain assent by all parties concerned?[13] I see no denying the critical force of these questions; indeed, it seems to me that MacIntyre's apparently sympathetic emphasis on the social embodiedness of morality pays the all too high price of precluding the possibility of ethos-transcending critique.

On the other hand, was it not MacIntyre himself who accused liberal theory of the very same thing—of barring ethical debate at the so-called first level? Sure it was. In his attack on liberalism, however, first-level debate was defined as "debate about the human good in general." That, of course, is a typically Aristotelian way of defining such debate. MacIntyre's quarrel with liberalism is that it allows no place for an overall theory of the human good or for a specific conception of human telos—these being the key tenets in all Aristotelian ethics. In this definition, the Aristotelian position seems to allow first-level ethical debate, whereas the liberal position must be content to tally and weigh a multitude of given individual "preferences" at the so-called second level, thereby being forced to invoke principles the nature of which has yet to be agreed on. According to MacIntyre's critique, then, liberalism fails at both levels.

In *A Theory of Justice*, Rawls argues to the contrary. Following him, the first level of ethical debate deals with the principles of justice and of right generally, these principles being those that would be chosen in the original position. The concept of right being prior to that of the good, questions concerning the latter are secondary ones not belonging to the first level. "In general," contends Rawls, "it is a good thing that individuals' conceptions of their good should differ in significant ways, whereas this is not so for conceptions of right. In a well-ordered society citizens hold the same principles of right and they try to reach the same judgment in particular cases" (447–48). The moral priority of the right over the good consists in the deontological thesis that the principles of justice limit the conceptions of the good the individuals may choose to pursue; and where a person's values clash with justice, it is justice that prevails. Only the basic principles of justice, not the human good or humanity's ends, are determined by reason. As Rawls assures us, "That we have one conception of the good rather than another is not relevant from a moral standpoint. In acquiring it we are influenced by the same sort of contingencies that lead us to rule out knowledge of our sex and class." As observed by Michael Sandel, the conclusion to be drawn from this statement is the vigorously anti-Aristotelian one that "deliberation about ends can only be an exercise in arbitrariness."[14] Behind this is a deontological conception of the self asserting that "the self is prior to the ends which are affirmed by it." The self as conceived in justice as fairness is not a unity in the Aristotelian sense of being *one* self devoted to the enactment of *one* coherent life plan guided by *one* overriding goal or telos. "Human good," says Rawls, "is heterogenous because the aims of the self are heterogenous"; accordingly, "to subordinate all our aims to one end . . . strikes us as irrational, or more likely as mad. The self is disfigured." In contradistinction to what is held by teleological doctrines, "it is not our aims that primarily reveal our nature but rather the principles that we would acknowledge to govern the background conditions under which these aims are to be founded and the manner in which they are to be pursued."[15]

MacIntyre's rejoinder is to say that Rawls's account is wrongheaded. Hence, by implication, each philosopher holds that the other reverses the correct order of priorities. Not only are the contending priorities of right and good incompatible; the *self* perceived as "having" those rights and "pursuing" those goods is radically different in the two moral theories. In MacIntyre's reading of Rawls, individuals are primary and society secondary, and the identification of individual interests is prior to and independent of the construction of any moral or social bonds between them. Consequently, Rawls takes it for granted and even makes it a presupposition of his theory that we must always expect to disagree with others about what the good life for the human individual is; indeed, that individuals be free to choose what is the good for them and to go about doing so in total independence is (1) what the priority of right is to secure and (2) what basically constitutes freedom. Hence, Rawls—turning again to MacIntyre's reading—views it as a historical "truth" that the good for me as an individual and the good for humanity as such differ and conflict; in a certain sense, this is not just the way things are but also how they should be. Hence, disagreements about rival notions of the good assume an interminable character; they fall beyond the scope of argument.

But MacIntyre, following Aristotle, acknowledges no such inevitable or ahistorical difference and conflict. In his view, the self is not prior to community. Contrary to the deontological notion defended by Rawls, the identity of the self is not independent of its interests and ends and relations with others. MacIntyre's community is one in which the "primary bond is a shared understanding both of the good for man and of the good of that community and where individuals identify their primary interests with reference to those goods" (AV, 250). Thus conceived, community penetrates and constitutes the self; allowing the good of community to have a hand in the constitution of the self entails that the self have no priority over its (noncontingent) ends, which means that the deontological notion of its antecedent individuation is denied. In Rawls's view, however, the constitution of the self is untouched by any—individual or social—conception of the good; it is reserved instead to the concept of right. But to assert, as Rawls does, that "the essential unity of the self is already given by the concept of right" is to narrow the scope of self-reflection.[16] For if the self is "given" by the purely formal and, hence, impersonal principles of right, it is admitted that the self *itself* is excluded from any possibility of participating in the constitution of its identity and unity, the sheer abstract givenness of the latter implying that it is never mundanely arrived at, as it were. Self-reflection in Rawls's scheme, then, can only take as its objects the allegedly contingent wants and desires and preferences of the self, but not the self itself. Reflection here, as Sandel has argued in his book *Liberalism and the Limits of Justice,* "does not extend its lights to the self standing behind the wants and desires it surveys; it cannot reach the self qua subject of desires" (159). So whereas for Aristotle and for MacIntyre all moral deliberation must take as its starting point the question Who am I? Rawlsian justice as fairness bars this question and asks instead, What ends shall I choose? thereby restricting the role of deliberation to assessing the desires and preferences of a subject whose identity is not *constituted* by community and *developed* by the subject itself; far from that, the deontological subject is given in advance by a set of formal principles of right.

The so-called individualistic outlook MacIntyre ascribes to Rawls has a "distinguished ancestry" going back to Hobbes, Locke, and Machiavelli, and "it contains within itself," concedes MacIntyre, "a certain note of realism about modern society; modern society is indeed often, at least in surface appearance, nothing but a collection of strangers, each pursuing his or her own interests under minimal constraints" (AV, 250). What this amounts to comes as no surprise: Rawls, a proponent of modern liberalism, takes the particular *Gestalt* of the modern self or individual to express a "universal truth" about the human condition and about humanity as such; in doing so, he contributes—however unwittingly—to sustaining contemporary emotivist culture. Merely confirming the current self-understanding of humanity, Rawls is of course unable to call it into question and to uncover its historicity; as to the latter task, recourse has to be taken to the very different conception of humanity, of the individual, and of community to be founded in Aristotle.

Above, I made the point that MacIntyre's strong emphasis on the social embodiedness of morality is purchased at the high price of precluding the possibility of tradition or ethos-transcending critique. My claim was that MacIntyre fails to distinguish between the *social* and the *rational* validity of tradition-embodied norms; he fails to demonstrate how the former can be criticized by virtue of the latter. Furthermore, in his account of the rationality possessed by tradition-constituted inquiry, MacIntyre stresses that standards of rational justification as well as notions of rights and justice are entirely defined by and internal to a particular tradition. In this account, a critique directed *against* these standards and notions can only arise by way of a so-called epistemological crisis. This means that critique in the sense intended by MacIntyre is always preceded by, and so made possible by, a breakdown within a particular tradition's ongoing collectively undertaken process of inquiry, the breakdown having the effect that progress—as defined by the tradition's own standards—no longer appears possible.

Given this account of what critique amounts to, my question is, Where does this leave the individual? What is the possibility of the individual's undertaking a critique of the standards and notions of his or her tradition, of his or her doing so even when the standards and notions are still cognitively successful as defined by the tradition's own definitions of inquiry and progress? In other words, what room is allowed for the individual to criticize the tradition of which he or she is a member, in times when that tradition *does not* experience an epistemological crisis? How is the individual, to take an example, to respond to a situation in which certain rights accorded to Aryans come to be denied to Jews? What is the individual to think of such an officially orchestrated transformation? How, that is, is the individual to resist attempts at systematic revision of central moral notions within "his" or "her" tradition, when such attempts are undertaken from *within* that tradition itself? By recourse to what standards is he or she to call such revisions into question?[17]

These questions are never addressed by MacIntyre because they presuppose that a critique within and of a tradition is undertaken as a collective project of inquiry not only *by* the tradition itself but also by individuals who might *oppose* and *disagree* with the standards and notions peculiar to "their" tradition and who therefore call the tradition into question irrespective of an epistemological crisis. This being so, I find it deeply unsatisfactory to make—as does MacIntyre—epistemological crisis the sole and all-important presupposition and criterion for the possibility of advancing a critique.

What is at stake here is nothing less than the *autonomy* of the individual or, even more fundamentally, his or her *freedom*. Put bluntly, my claim is that autonomy and freedom simply are not an issue in the moral theory of MacIntyre. Of course, he might reply that to expect or even to demand them to be is to take it for granted—as do all kinds of liberal theory—that autonomy and freedom are, and indeed ought to be, the key tenets of all moral philosophies. So rather than naïvely presuppose these tenets or, better, values, one would have to argue for their presumed primacy. To make such an argument, one would normally—as does Rawls, as does Apel, as does Habermas—go back to Kant and start from his conception of autonomy. I shall abstain from recapitulating how this Kantian or post-Kantian argument goes. What matters here is that MacIntyre's account, for all its disquieting silence on the issue of autonomy and freedom, at least shows that humanity is not morally self-sufficient, as liberal theorists from Hobbes and Locke onward have maintained, taking the atomistically pictured individual and his or her desires as their point of departure. MacIntyre, that is, shows that *belonging* to a society is *the* essential condition of people's developing their basic human capacities, implying by this that a person must be part of society to be human in the full sense and to realize the human good. Regrettably, the philosophical *argument* for this ultra-Aristotelian view— humanity being *zōon politikon*—is not systematically carried out by MacIntyre in his rather polemical attack on liberalism. The argument required would have to show that the liberal thesis of the priority of right over the good, which MacIntyre criticizes in Rawls, is untenable because it is impossible to make good the notion of right without invoking the notion of *belonging to a society* in which the *good* is defined, that is to say, without invoking the very notion of the good that primacy-of-right theories set out to deny, or at least to do without at this "first level." Charles Taylor has argued that "if we cannot ascribe natural rights without affirming the worth of certain human capacities, and if this affirmation has other normative consequences (e.g., that we should foster and nurture these capacities in ourselves and others), then any proof that *these capacities can only develop in society* or in a society of a certain kind is a proof that we ought to belong to or sustain society or this kind of society."[18] If a "social thesis" of this kind is true, "an assertion of the primary of rights is impossible; for to assert the rights in question is to affirm the capacities, and granted the social thesis is true concerning these capacities, this commits us to an obligation to belong. This will be as fundamental as the assertion of rights, because it will be inseparable from it."[19] To argue that the rights and the freedom of the individual are ensured only if linked up with living in a society where there is a *common* pursuit of the good life, as defined by that society, is of course to concede a Hegelian legacy as much as a distinctly Aristotelian one. In his *Philosophy of Right* Hegel writes, "Das Recht der Individuen für ihre subjektive Bestimmung zur Freiheit hat darin, daß sie der sittlichen Wirklichkeit angehören, seine Erfüllung, indem die Gewißheit ihrer Freiheit in solcher Objektivität ihre Wahrheit hat und sie im Sittlichen ihr eigenes Wesen, ihre innere Allgemeinheit wirklich besitzen."[20] The basic idea is that the concrete ethos, or *Sittlichkeit*, is the fundamental precondition of *Moralität*; to recognize the constitutive role of the former is not—as has so often been objected—to sacrifice the Kantian autonomy entailed in the latter but to make possible its realization. Given this conception, the claim made by Taylor concerning primacy-of-right theories is twofold: first, all such theories (justice as fairness included) presuppose—however implicitly or unwittingly—a specific notion of the good; and second, they *cannot avoid* making such a presupposition. Were it not for its intrinsic and irreducible relation to the notion of the good, the notion of right would remain merely formal and abstract; to assert rights is to affirm the worth of certain capacities inherent in humanity, which in turn is to affirm belonging to a society, which in turn is to affirm the common pursuit of the good as made possible by belonging to that society. So it is not only that we, in theory, cannot assert rights without having recourse to the good; it is that we—in real life—recognize our belonging to society as a *good in itself* without which all other goods would be unattainable, to echo Aristotle's *Politics*. (I return to this argument in the section "Why Be Moral?" in Chapter 6.)

But this is not all. For although it is true that belonging to a society is a good that makes possible the pursuit of a host of goods, recent history has shown a more specific condition must obtain, indeed is of pivotal importance, in order that rights—including the very basic ones, the so-called Rights of Man, that is, the rights pertaining to a human simply qua human—achieve genuine political recognition. This condition requires that a subject be able to prove his or her belongingness—not, as we would expect from the general discussion above, to a community or society—but only to a nation. Although this point is empirical, because dependent on the policies adhered to by different regimes, it is not devoid of philosophical significance. To see this, consider Hannah Arendt's analysis of the utter precariousness, or ultimate valuelessness, of human rights in the section "The Decline of the Nation-State and the End of the Rights of Man" in her book *The Origins of Totalitarianism*. Regardless of the specific reasons for their enforced status as refugees—be they of political, religious, or ethnic origin—the stateless people searching, mostly in vain, for a safe place to settle down in the Europe of the twenties and thirties were forced to realize that loss of national rights was identical with loss of human rights: "The Rights of Man, supposedly inalienable, proved to be unenforceable . . . whenever people appeared who were no longer citizens of any sovereign state" (OT, 293). Thus, "the calamity of the rightless is not that they are deprived of life, liberty, and the pursuit of happiness [viz., goods of the kind intended by Taylor in the preceding paragraph] but that they no longer belong to any community whatsoever" (OT, 295). What is so dramatically brought out in Arendt's historical examples is the fateful—in the end, lethal—lack of a sufficiently secured *right to have rights,* which for Arendt is the right "to live in a framework where one is judged by one's actions and opinions" and, further, the right to "belong to some kind of organized community" (OT, 296–97). The all-important point is that the second right proved to be a condition, a sine qua non, of the first—and this in flagrant contradiction to the idea behind the universal Rights of Man. From this dark historical lesson, Arendt draws the sinister conclusion that "the conception of human rights, based upon the assumed existence of a human being as such, broke down at the very moment when those who professed to believe in it were for the first time confronted with people who had indeed lost all other qualities and specific relationships—except that they were still human" (OT, 299). In Arendt's (unmistakably Aristotelian) reading, this demonstrates that "only the loss of a polity itself expels [Man] from humanity" (OT, 297). If, however, the right to have rights is devoid of any force, save an impotent rhetorical one, unless a person is a recognized full member of a community willing and able to guarantee any rights whatsoever, then I take it to follow, since the right to have rights is to apply to *all* people, that the community guaranteeing *this* right must be as universal and all-encompassing as the notion of "humanity" as such; it must, in the final analysis, be a "world-community" coextensive with humankind. Nothing less will do, because "less" is bound to imply some sort of restriction, to invoke some kind of particularity, and thus to put the sought-for inclusiveness in jeopardy. In this regard, MacIntyre seems to me unable to establish the most fundamental of rights, namely the right to rights; indeed, all theories claiming the primacy of "belongingness to some *particular* community" have to face the challenge highlighted in Arendt's historical examples.

Philosophers asserting the primacy of *Sittlichkeit* refuse to see it as "opposed" to *Moralität;* they view the latter as truly realized in the former and hence the opposition as artificial. Yet it is clear that not just any political order will do. For belonging to a political community is a good in itself by virtue of which all other goods can be attained only on the condition that the given community *foster* and *sustain* the sense of such belonging as being *primary* to all other goods, that is, those goods people might wish to pursue for themselves. In short, only communities actively affirming the primacy of belongingness deserve our allegiance and hence our continued belonging to them. And it is precisely in this respect that MacIntyre holds liberalism to "fail" as a political order and so to be unworthy of allegiance and belonging. Encouraging antagonistic individualism and acquisitiveness rather than communality, elevating the values of the market to an unchallenged importance in social relations, the present-day liberal order is one MacIntyre rejects in practice as much as in philosophical theory: "The modern political order, whether liberal, conservative, radical or socialist, simply has to be rejected from a standpoint that owes genuine allegiance to the tradition of the virtues; for modern politics itself expresses in its institutional forms a systematic rejection of that tradition" (AV, 255). Not content to leave it at that, MacIntyre concludes his book with a grim "we are at war" passage asserting that the present powers that be are but "barbarians," to be fought only through participation in a certain kind of ethos: "What matters at this stage is the construction of local forms of community within which civility and the intellectual and moral life can be sustained through the new dark ages which are already upon us. And if the tradition of the virtues was able to survive the horrors of the last dark ages, we are not entirely without grounds for hope. This time however the barbarians are not waiting beyond the frontiers; they have already been governing us for some time" (AV, 263).

Concluding Remarks

MacIntyre's attempt to rehabilitate key tenets of Aristotelian ethics takes the form of a comprehensive critique of liberal modernity and liberal moral and political theory. His two books discussed in this chapter advance one major thesis: that modern liberalism in theory and in practice sustains the present-day emotivist culture whose historical emergence was prepared for by the failure of the Enlightenment project to work out a universal morality compelling to all persons alike qua rational human beings. The structure of this formulation highlights the fact that MacIntyre's approach is a conjunction of philosophical and historical argument; his diagnosis of the present state of moral philosophy is inseparably linked with his diagnosis of the present state of modern society. But is this approach convincing? Is it philosophically sound?

According to Rawls, liberal society seeks not to impose a single way of life but to leave its citizens as free as possible to choose their own values and ends. People individually, not the society they belong to, must define what the "good" is. Therefore, a liberal society must govern by principles of justice that do not presuppose any particular vision of the good life. The question is, Can any such principles be found? MacIntyre answers in the negative. But in doing so he draws from the plurality of the proposed principles the conclusion that the candidates so far have all failed, because no one set of principles has received the universal assent theoretically claimed for it. My view is that this inference is false; it is not a philosophical argument at all but a category mistake, inducing philosophical validity from historical plurality, that is, the domain of *Geltung* from that of *Genese*. Having committed this mistake, MacIntyre is at a loss to do justice to the philosophically all-important distinction between the social and the rational validity of tradition- or ethos-embodied norms. From these criticisms, I conclude that the conjunction of philosophical and historical argument characteristic of MacIntyre's approach is philosophically unsound; alleged historical "facts" cannot do the work of immanent philosophical arguments.

Furthermore, MacIntyre's theory of the rationality possessed by tradition-constituted inquiry provides a persuasive account of how rationality works internally or within one particular tradition, in the diachronic dimension of inquiry. However, a serious weakness in MacIntyre's theory is his attempt to repudiate the double challenge of relativism and perspectivism. His argument that "conversation" between coexisting rival traditions is indeed possible and that it is conducted according to a rationality recognized by all parties is unconvincing, because it fails to clarify the standards of rational justification by virtue of which such conversation can take place. In MacIntyre's theory, conversation between contending traditions arises only in situations of "epistemological crisis." Granted this assumption, if the old cognitive standards of a tradition are affected by crisis and hence about to break down, and if no new ones have as yet been adopted, *which* standards make rational conversation and questioning still possible? MacIntyre provides no satisfactory answer, and this is to say that he has not succeeded in refuting relativism and perspectivism after all.

Following the assertion that critique comes about only as the result of an epistemological crisis, MacIntyre's silence on the topic of the autonomy and the freedom of the individual seems odd, especially considering that by these qualities is implied the individual's ability as well as right to criticize "his" or "her" tradition or society, to oppose it even in times of normalcy, rather than breakdown. But MacIntyre, having polemically rather than argumentatively dismissed en bloc the notion of (natural or universal) rights in *After Virtue*, fails to thematize the issue of individual autonomy and freedom altogether. (My suspicion is that he holds the issue to be a proof of liberal bias.) Yet MacIntyre's is an intellectualist and inquiry-oriented conception of critique in the vein of Gadamerian hermeneutics, whereas the critique I have in mind is of a straightforward political kind prone to raise the notion of (democrati-cally founded) rights MacIntyre so vehemently rejects.

For all his preoccupation with the widely recognized crisis of contempo-rary emotivist society, MacIntyre is surprisingly little interested in addressing the crisis of moral and political judgment so central to philosophers with a similar outlook, such as Hannah Arendt. Judgment having become something utterly fragile and precarious, in what way and to what extent can *phronēsis* be cultivated and exercised in present-day society? Our crisis is one high-lighted by, say, the Holocaust, but MacIntyre remains silent on how the individual can be capable of judging and ethically coming to terms with such an unprecedented historical event. This silence is a pity; the Holocaust would have provided MacIntyre with an opportunity to be more concrete in his diagnosis of what the current malaise in moral theory and practice consists in.

In the end there is the question whether the unsoundness of some core philosophical arguments, not to speak of the sheer lack of such, in the moral theory of MacIntyre can be taken to have demonstrated that the neo-Aristotelian position in moral theory is untenable. Put otherwise, to have revealed systematic weaknesses in the books of MacIntyre, recognizing his reputation as a prominent neo-Aristotelian philosopher, is not a fortiori to have shown that neo-Aristotelianism per se is invalid. In order to see more clearly why it is that such an inference is unwarranted, one has only to bear in mind the references I made above to the work of Charles Taylor and Michael Sandel. In these authors, to mention but two, an unmistakably Aristotelian outlook interestingly mingles with a considerable influence from Hegel, in particular from the latter's critique of Kant's ethics. Indeed, it is getting hard to distinguish between neo-Aristotelians and neo-Hegelians; perhaps tomorrow we will no longer see any sense in doing so. Given this state of affairs, the case made by Taylor against the liberal priority of the right over the good is more convincing than the one made by MacIntyre in *After Virtue;* similarly, the case made by Sandel against the liberal priority of the self over its ends is more penetrating than the one made by MacIntyre in *Whose Justice? Which Rationality?*

So it may appear that the argumentation carried out by a number of other theorists "makes good" the damage done to the neo-Aristotelian position by my critique of MacIntyre. Besides, there will always be some disagreement about whether this or that theorist "really" is representative of this or that tradition. Yet the neo-Aristotelian position, like any other, is only as strong as its proponents' defense of it. Thus, on the one hand, it is obviously true that a critique proceeding immanently—as intends my assessment of Mac-Intyre—can only warrant conclusions themselves of an immanent nature, which means that only the persuasiveness of MacIntyre's case is affected by the criticisms made in this chapter. But on the other hand, the flaws I have detected in the very structure of MacIntyre's argument cannot be completely without relevance for the specific tradition of moral thinking he sets out to defend. MacIntyre has devoted two books to demonstrating that liberal theory fails—as did the Enlightenment philosophy to which liberalism is the intellectual heir—to give compelling answers to the following central questions: What are the criteria for making a rational judgment about the rival truth claims put forward by the plurality of traditions coexisting today? How are we to decide, by the use of argument, which truth claim to accept and which to reject? What makes the notion of, say, justice embodied in the Aristotelian tradition more convincing than its liberal rival?

But although MacIntyre claims that Enlightenment and liberal moral philosophers fail to answer these questions, my claim is that *he* fails. What we are ultimately left with is an "answer" invoking Fichte's dictum that the philosophy one chooses depends on what kind of person one is. *Behind* this answer, which of course in a sense is none, lies the more substantial thesis that "our education in and about philosophy has by and large presupposed what is in fact not true, that there are standards of rationality . . . equality available, at least in principle, to all persons, whatever tradition they may happen to find themselves in and whether or not they inhabit any tradition." All of this is directed against the Enlightenment and its heir liberalism; arguing against the latter, MacIntyre's point is that "genuine intellectual encounter does not and cannot take place in some generalized, abstract way" (WJ, 393).

Hence, in the end we are *not* left with the particularity of the *person*, as apparently suggested by the initial answer echoing Fichte; rather, we are left—in theory and in practice, and as always in vehement opposition to the Enlightenment and to liberalism—with the particularity of *tradition*, of the constitutive and irreducible moment of any person's belonging-to. This is the way MacIntyre, taking himself to be an Aristotelian as true as they come, dismisses all talk of universality as abstract talk, as talk devoid of substance, as liberal bias, if not downright indoctrination. However, if the intended recognition of particularity is to be purchased at the price of restricting the force of argument and of critique, to speak philosophically, or of the autonomy and freedom of the individual, to speak politically, then one begins to wonder whether this price is not too high and, finally, whether such restrictions are at all in line with the work of that great tradition-founding father, the philosopher par excellence, Aristotle.

After MacIntyre: The Philosophical Urgency of Overcoming Emotivism

Recall the definition of "emotivism" that serves as the basis for MacIntyre's case against it: "Emotivism is the doctrine that all evaluative judgments and more specifically all moral judgments are *nothing but* expressions of preference, expressions of attitude or feeling, insofar as they are moral or evaluative in character" (AV, 12).

According to MacIntyre's account of emotivism, two purposes are served by our use of moral judgments: we express our personal feelings and attitudes, and we seek to produce certain nonrational effects on the feelings and attitudes of those with whom we interact. Argument is unable to settle conflicts; what remains and what prevails is the expression of feelings to others in a more or less manipulative way. Indeed, in emotivism the very distinction between manipulative and nonmanipulative social relations is obliterated. Taken as a theory of meaning, emotivism asserts that the sentence "This is good" means roughly the same as "I approve of this; do so as well." Hence, the evaluative and normative, masquerading as objective and rational, turn out to be nothing of the sort but rather the reverse: namely, the facade of subjectivity, ultimately of sheer self-interest.

A double reductionism is involved in emotivism as portrayed by MacIntyre: (1) emotivism reduces morality to personal preference, and (2) emotivism reduces the role of emotions in ethics to that of an instrument the subject uses in seeking to influence the feelings and critiques of another in a manner presumably advancing his or her nonrational personal preferences.

What matters from my viewpoint is that MacIntyre is systematically preoccupied with a critique of the *first* reductionism only; and I have devoted my discussion of MacIntyre's case to this critique of his, in the framework of which he works out his notions of the moral self, moral agency, virtues, practices, tradition, and rationality. The introduction and elaboration of all these core issues falls within the framework of analysis that is set up by what I call the first reductionism committed by the emotivist doctrine. Although MacIntyre initially calls attention to the *second* reductionism, he subsequently neglects it. In other words, MacIntyre, invoking Aristotelianism, seeks to show that emotivism is wrong in reducing morality to personal preference; but he nowhere attempts to show, by way of systematic argument, that emotivism is *just as wrong* in depicting emotions as "nothing but" a means of interpersonal manipulation, as "nothing but" more or less clever and covert strategic devices at the mercy of competing personal preferences, in short, as disclosing our cosubject as someone to be acted upon rather than with.

The uncovered deficit in MacIntyre's otherwise impressively far-reaching account means that he lets emotivism get away with its not merely prejudiced and one-sided but downright false picture of emotions in ethics. The falsity of the emotivist picture of emotions as but a means of social manipulation is to be seen and treated as a philosophical challenge. It challenges us to do what MacIntyre neglects to—namely, to subject to scrutiny the popular claim that ethics can and should do without and hence can and should relinquish emotions, that emotions represent "nothing but" bias in relation to ethics, especially in relation to the exercise of moral judgment. If this claim is false—and I hold it to be fundamentally false—the challenge it poses is the rehabilitation of the role of emotions in ethics in general and in moral judgment in particular. In support of that rehabilitation, I argue that emotions, rather than being "instrumental" in the pejorative sense of (mutual) manipulation, are partly *constitutive* of both perception and judgment, playing in addition a role in our (moral or not so moral) action for which we in fact, however reluctantly, must assume responsibility.

In letting emotivism's portrait of emotions stand, MacIntyre joins the company of many prominent philosophers, including Kant, the main target in *After Virtue*. When emotivism—taken more often as a current practice than as a philosophical theory by MacIntyre—presents emotions as nonrational devices of interpersonal manipulation, it just echoes the grim view of human emotions in general that moved Kant to regard them with such deep suspicion. There is nothing in what MacIntyre has to say about emotivism that will lead followers of Kant on this topic to reconsider their position. For all the differences among them, there is one vital point of agreement in Kant, MacIntyre, and emotivism: this is the claim that emotions, or feelings, owing to their very nature, are capricious, changeable, transitory, and weak. Observing as much, Kant drew the conclusion that emotions are unreliable as moral motives.

But this leaves us with a very undifferentiated idea of human emotions. First of all, a distinction needs to be made between feelings and emotions. In Chapter 3 I elaborate such a distinction in discussing Scheler's typology of feelings, and in Chapter 4 I pursue the distinction further in examining the emotional prerequisites of moral perception. Here I wish only to observe some main characteristics.

A feeling is something "rawer" than an emotion or a mood or a state. A feeling is situational in the sense that it signifies a specific way of approaching, taking in, and responding to the situation in which we find ourselves. Hence, we may point out the specific features in a situation that elicit or trigger the corollary feeling that we experience in it. When Sartre says of shame that it is "an immediate shudder which runs through me from head to foot without any discursive preparation,"[21] he captures the instantaneous, urgent, sometimes downright eruptive force with which we live our affective experience *here* and *now*. In feeling thus conceived, there is an original element of absorption, of being *in*, as distinct from standing apart from, a quality of being at one with what catches our attention in the situation, of being so "close" to it as to be virtually engrossed in it. Together with this goes a lack of distance, of detachment, of the kind of consciousness of ourselves and *of our feeling* that is gained only when we become aware— perhaps by way of the look of the other (Sartre's focus), but not necessarily— of ourselves as blushing, turning red, perspiring, and so on.

An emotion, by contrast, develops out of the instantaneous affective intake of the situation just described. An emotion does not possess the same eminent concreteness and here-and-now directedness as a feeling. There is in emotion a step back, a quality of being aware of the more immediate feeling; the emotion adds an element of reflection absent in the feeling. Hence, an emotion signifies a more mature grasp of and stance toward the object or person at which it directs itself; it involves a stronger component of interpretation, evaluation, and reflection than does feeling. In a distinct emotion there is a blend of affectivity and cognition. In an emotion such as love, the love we feel, we feel not blindly, unknowingly; rather, we are aware of ourselves as experiencing this love for reasons that we may—more or less successfully, and (as Scheler maintains) never quite exhaustively—point to when challenged to justify why we feel this love.

The possibility of *justifying* a particular emotion raises a lot of questions. We need to know how an emotion is connected with responsibility, with rationality, with intersubjectivity and discourse. If you challenge me to offer the reasons why I love, you make a number of presuppositions: for example, that I identify myself as having the emotion, as being its subject; that I am prepared to assume responsibility for having it and will not dismiss it as something that "has nothing to do with me" or that is completely external to me; that communication and, presumedly, justification are something to which emotions lend themselves as proper objects; that my offered reasons for having the emotion may be either appropriate or inappropriate with regard to its target; hence, that the emotion is capable of being "backed up" by reasons you may find convincing or unconvincing.

On the *moral* significance of emotion, Lawrence Blum contrasts what is naïvely conflated in the "emotivism" MacIntyre leaves conceptually unchallenged. Blum distinguishes between personal feelings and altruistic emotions. Altruistic emotions, he tells us, "are not like changeable moods, such as good-spirits and exuberance." Accordingly "acting from altruistic emotion is not characteristically acting "on impulse" or "impulsively"; nor is it acting "on inclination" or doing what one is "in the mood" to do.[22] Altruistic emotions such as sympathy and compassion are grounded in a concern for the weal and woe of others; personal feelings such as liking and affection are grounded in personal (but not necessarily moral, Blum is quick to add) characteristics of the other person. The implication, as Blum sees it, is that altruistic emotions have the capacity to overcome the subjectivism and partiality pertaining to personal feelings, and hence the capacity to provide a reliable motivational basis for moral action.

In his depiction of emotivism, MacIntyre reduces "emotions" and "feelings" alike to what Blum terms "personal feelings." Lacking the distinction proposed by Blum, emotivism as portrayed by MacIntyre all too easily encourages the conclusion that "emotions" per se are completely unsuited to fulfill any morally significant task. We are led to believe that emotions, owing to their "nature," undermine moral performance; hence, they must be barred from taking part in it.

Unlike personal feelings, which are bound up with the person's strictly subjective preferences, altruistic emotions such as concern, sympathy, and compassion meet the requirement of reliability, consistency, and rationality. Stronger still, they are necessary prerequisites for developing a regard for the well-being of another person. Sympathy and compassion deserve to be called *moral* emotions, since they are not reducible to, or at the mercy of, the agent's private desires and affections. Blum's claim is that compassion, for example, can in fact counterweight moods and inclinations that are self-interested. So "the regard for the other's good which compassion implies means that one's compassionate acts often involve acting very much contrary to one's moods and inclinations."[23]

To be sure, these claims need extended argument. However, at this point it is enough to indicate the questionable assumptions implicit in emotivism understood as a doctrine reducing morality to personal preferences beyond the reach of argumentation. My first step in calling this position into question has been to emphasize that emotions are not noncognitive phenomena over which we have no control. Mature moral emotions can be cultivated; they are something for which we as moral agents are prepared to assume responsibility. But even if this is granted, it may still be asked whether emotions, as opposed to Kantian duty, are reliable as a source of moral motivation. My reply is that they are fallible: we may fail to develop, say, compassion; or, when acted on, compassion may lead to immoral rather than moral results. But so may acting from duty, as Justin Oakley shows;[24] indeed, so may acting from any category of motivation; no motive is such that it can *never* be involved in immorality. But I find the level of *constitution*—that is, the degree to which emotion may be *indispensable* in moral performance—to be of greater philosophical interest than the (ultimately empirical) issue of motivation.

Stated briefly, the antiemotivist thesis I subsequently develop, and that MacIntyre nowhere considers, holds that emotion—or, more specifically, the faculty of empathy—is indispensable in the disclosure of moral phenomena. To say this is to assert that *emotion enters morality from the very start*, that is to say, as soon as that peculiar entity naïvely referred to as a moral "object" or "phenomenon" or "situation" is given to us in the first place. It is precisely this naïve and "inconspicuous givenness" of the so-called moral that demands closer scrutiny: namely, the act of *perceiving* something *as* morally significant, *as* belonging to the domain of the moral. Emotion provides us with our principal mode of access to the entire domain of human experience; without an access to this domain we would remain blind to the specifically moral reality of situations where the weal and woe of a cosubject is somehow at stake. My thesis entails that emotion be partly constitutive of acts of perception and, furthermore, that judgment, being in my view logically preceded by perception, is no less based on the joint performance of our emotional and cognitive faculties than is perception, so that a manifest failure to exercise moral judgment is just as likely to have as its cause an emotional impairment as a cognitive one.

So MacIntyre permits emotivism its grossly mistaken picture of the role taken by emotion in perception, judgment, and action. What I have programmatically stated here is my *philosophical* case against the doctrine of emotivism. But in addition, there is the *sociological* part of that doctrine to pay attention to. For it might still be true, as MacIntyre maintains, that people in contemporary society to an increasing extent "act, talk, and think" in the manner affirmed by emotivism, so that our emotional capacities are—or, in any case, are about to become—but a means in the endless pursuit of personal preferences. Now, I think it is very hard to determine whether this is actually the case; perhaps we had better be more modest than both MacIntyre and the emotivists and speak instead only, and less loudly, of a prevailing "tendency." What is warranted is caution rather than sweeping generalizations. However, sociological descriptions or predictions are not the main issue here. Rather, what is important and remains so throughout is my thesis that we dispose of no other principal access to the domain of the human—and a fortiori, I argue, to the domain of the moral—than that gained through emotion. Although this thesis is a philosophical one, it nonetheless contains a sociological dimension in the sense of MacIntyre's view that every morality contains, even presupposes, a sociology. Thus, even though I would defend a somewhat weaker version of this link, it remains the case, to take an example, that the degree to which the human faculty of empathy is intact and not impaired or even fatally damaged must be settled empirically rather than by philosophical argument. The *performance* of our emotional capacities is not indifferent to the social setting in which it takes place; rather, a faculty such as empathy—giving rise to care, compassion, sympathy—is highly susceptible to changes in the moral subject's social environment, which means that the social environment may help encourage or impede the faculty's actual exercise. In this sense one social setting may cultivate empathy, whereas another may undermine it. I therefore include a number of psychological, sociological, and historical studies in my later account of the moral significance of man's emotional capacities.

One might wonder whether MacIntyre's neglect of emotion reflects an omission of the topic by Aristotle himself. The question is quickly settled by turning to Aristotle's writings on politics, ethics, and rhetoric. Far from bypassing the importance of human emotion in these various areas, Aristotle in fact devotes considerable attention to it. W. W. Fortenbaugh, in his book *Aristotle on Emotion*, shows that Aristotle endeavored to offer a view of emotion where "emotional appeal would no longer be viewed as extra-rational enchantment." I take this to signify that the missing "second half" of MacIntyre's attempted refutation of the emotivist doctrine can indeed be found in Aristotle. According to the interpretation given by Fortenbaugh, "Once Aristotle focused on the cognitive side of emotional response and made clear that an emotion can be altered by argument because beliefs can be altered in this way, it was possible to adopt a positive attitude towards emotional appeal."[25] Brought to bear on ethical theory, an investigation into the nature of emotional response comes to the fore in Aristotle's conviction that moral virtue must be seen as tied to emotional response. Fortenbaugh shows Aristotle to work with a distinction between two fundamental modes of human behavior—namely, emotional response and reasoned reflection—and to correlate this distinction with an ethical distinction between moral virtue and practical wisdom. Moral virtue makes the end correct, and practical wisdom provides the means to the end (see NE, 1144a7–9), so that "as a perfection of man's emotional side, moral virtue makes correct the judgments and goals involved in emotional response."[26]

Nancy Sherman has given a particularly instructive interpretation of Aristotle's assessment of the role of emotions in moral life. Sherman emphasizes that Aristotle "intends us to understand virtue as both a way of acting and a way of feeling"; hence, in Aristotle's view, ways of feeling are included with the specific virtues and vices.[27] To hit the mean is not only to act in a way that is appropriate to the case, it is also to respond with the right sort of emotional sensitivity (NE, 1109a23). Sherman also draws attention to the *Rhetoric*, where Aristotle develops an intentional theory in which "passions are viewed not as blind promptings and urgings that merely happen to us, but rather as selective responses to articulated features of our environment."[28] These few observations allow us to see that Aristotle would be strongly opposed to Kant's dismissive depiction of emotions as partial and unreliable and therefore as devoid of moral worth. Far from sharing such a negative view, Aristotle helps us realize that, to cite Sherman, "without emotions, we do not fully register the facts or record them with the sort of resonance and importance that only emotional involvement can sustain."[29] To be sure, Aristotle is mainly interested in the role assumed by emotions in motivating action and in adding depth to interpersonal attachment in general and friendship (*philia*) in particular, and thus as indispensable for living a good life. In this respect, Aristotle differs from my own perspective: he is less concerned with the part played by emotion as a necessary precondition for moral perception and judgment than with the indispensability of emotion in the "good life."

I shall not pursue what Aristotle has said on emotions and how his view of them helps shape his ethics. What I want to note is simply that MacIntyre is silent on this aspect of Aristotle's teaching, and this holds in particular for the topic one would expect MacIntyre to draw explicitly on, namely, moral virtue.

MacIntyre holds Kantian ethics in general and the categorical imperative in particular to be defenseless in the face of the attack leveled against them by emotivism. In this I believe MacIntyre is wrong. In my view, MacIntyre—

on this occasion aligning himself with emotivism—attacks Kant in an area where Kant is at his strongest, namely, in his attempt to establish the universality of moral principles, whereas MacIntyre ignores the problematic on which Kant is at his weakest, namely, in his dismissive account of human emotion. As I see it, MacIntyre's case against Kant would have been much stronger if he had chosen to address Kant on the issue of emotion in ethics rather than on universalization in practical reasoning. But, again, what MacIntyre neglects to do should be converted into and taken up as a challenging philosophical task.

2

Hannah Arendt and
the Crisis of Judgment

Whereas Alasdair MacIntyre's diagnosis of contemporary moral life is of the most general kind, Hannah Arendt's reflections always start from—and retain—a moment of particularity. Time and again Arendt emphasizes the particularity of the persons, events, and actions we judge as well as of the circumstances in which we do so. Her view of moral judgment as an exceedingly precarious business informs all her basic themes—the nature of unprecedented or "radical" evil, the connection between deeds and motives, and the interrelation between thinking and judgment. The case of Adolf Eichmann serves to illuminate all these themes. It also, I argue, illustrates the shortcomings of Arendt's conviction that Eichmann's was a cognitive failure, to be located on the level of judgment. I propose a different view. In doing so I start to develop a notion of moral performance that accords crucial importance to the category of perception and to the emotional faculty of empathy.

Coming to Terms with Moral Judgment:
The Challenge of Eichmann

Husserl's late *Krisis* book developed the insight that it is only through a crisis, in the sense of a breakdown of the *Lebenswelt*, that we become aware of such a world: stripped of its innocence, of its quality as something profoundly taken for granted, the lifeworld becomes an object of consciousness.[1] Due to the impact of unprecedented historical change, what had up till then been unproblematic becomes eminently problematic. This pertains not only to the structures of our lifeworld but to such vital mental capacities as thinking and judgment as well. Hannah Arendt makes the observation that through the breakdown of judgment we come to question its nature. Recent history teaches us that the capacity for judgment seems to disappear exactly when most urgently needed, namely, in the event of a crisis. This, Arendt's point of departure, rests on a paradox: although a crisis is said to have led us to examine the capacity of judgment, it is hard to see how an examination thus provoked can succeed in shedding any light on this capacity, given that it is considered to have suffered a breakdown.

That the ability to judge seems to vanish when most needed is the conclusion Arendt came to at the trial of Adolf Eichmann in Jerusalem in 1961. It was beyond doubt that Eichmann had caused "radical evil" and that his deeds were monstrous, but it turned out the doer was not. Eichmann left Arendt with a puzzle: his actions clearly did not spring from base personal motives or firm ideological convictions; far from that, he just appeared shallow and mediocre. This being so, the actual consequences of the measures to which the SS officer Eichmann had contributed seemed to stand in flagrant contradiction to the apparent harmlessness of his personality.

What are we to make of this gap between the deeds and the doer? This question gave rise to Arendt's much-discussed thesis of the "banality of evil." Today, thirty years after it was coined, it is fair to say that the thesis has been nearly as much misunderstood as discussed. For this she must herself be blamed: in choosing to speak about "banality" with regard to the evil Eichmann had caused, Arendt—however unwittingly—encouraged the accusation of being engaged in a kind of apologia. Nothing could have been further from her intentions. The unfortunate term "banality" having been chosen, we have to live with it and make the best possible sense of it. What is "banal" about the evil to which Eichmann made his by no means minor contribution is not the evil itself, that is, *die Endlösung*, but the fact—or what

Arendt took to be the fact—that "banal" motives were behind the radical evil eventually produced, such noncriminal and apparently innocent motives as seeking to do one's job, to obey all orders from above in order to avoid criticism, and to be loyal to superiors and always do what they think right. Reflecting on Eichmann's mediocre personality, she wrote, "That such remoteness from reality and such thoughtlessness can wreak more havoc than all the evil instincts taken together which, perhaps, are inherent in man— that was, in fact, the lesson one could learn in Jerusalem. But it was a lesson, neither an explanation of the phenomenon nor a theory about it" (EJ, 288). In The Origins of Totalitarianism, Arendt connects the unprecedentedness of the Holocaust with what she views as the "aim" of totalitarian ideologies: "the transformation of human nature itself" (OT, 458). The implication is that natality, by which Arendt understands the human capacity to act spontaneously, must be liquidated; "spontaneity as such, with its incalculability, is the greatest of all obstacles to total domination over man" (OT, 456). Witnessing Eichmann in the setting of the Israeli court, Arendt was struck by his cliché-ridden language, by his "adherence to conventional standardized codes of expression and conduct" (LM, 1:4). Eichmann personified the dull nonspontaneity that totalitarianism aims at producing. The ambition to transform human nature reflects the totalitarian belief that everything is possible; and when the impossible was made possible—as in the case of the industrialized extermination of millions of innocent men, women, and children—it became "the unpunishable, unforgivable absolute evil which could no longer be understood by the evil motives of self-interest, greed, covetousness, resentment, lust for power, and cowardice." Arendt draws the conclusion that the radical evil produced not by wickedness but by a diffuse mixture of unconditional obedience, lack of spontaneity, and sheer thoughtlessness "breaks down all standards we know" (OT, 459). Consequently, this phenomenon cannot be understood or punished or forgiven. Faced with the unprecedented horror of totalitarianism, we suddenly discover that our standards of comprehension are utterly inadequate; radical evil "has clearly exploded our categories of political thought and our standards for moral judgment" (UP, 379). In this, then, Arendt sees a profound challenge to any future ethics worthy of its name.

Arendt noticed a lack of spontaneity in Eichmann's conduct in the courtroom: far from demonstrating the all too familiar traits of overt wickedness and hatred, Eichmann turned out to be a remote and unconcerned figure. Face to face with survivors who gave testimony to the atrocities in which he had taken part and who in doing so would show great distress or even break down in despair, Eichmann kept his cool. He is reported to have remained emotionally unaffected throughout the proceedings. Clearly the survivors as well as the victims for whose death he was responsible were not fellow human beings to him. Far from being persons whom he could hate—or, for that matter, with whom he could have sympathy—the Jews were turned into an abstract category, a category consisting not of persons but of cases (*Sachen*). Jews meant but figures, statistics, administrative tasks. Thus, Eichmann's lack of spontaneity and humanity is reflected in the way he, the perpetrator, views his victims, the Jews: on both sides a *dehumanization* takes place. In other words, Eichmann not only fails to see a group of human beings *as* human beings, because he has dehumanized this particular group, he also, in the course of dehumanizing this group, dehumanizes himself.

Arendt is right in pointing out that "the essence of totalitarian government . . . is to make functionaries and mere cogs in the machinery out of men" (EJ, 289). The dehumanization of the Jews is the real content of the Nuremberg Laws; from the mid-thirties onward, the physical extermination that eventually followed was prepared for step by step. In Nazi Germany, the canons of legislation were systematically changed so as to render all measures taken against the Jews strictly "legal." Because the whole jurisdiction was turned into an instrument of mass murder, an officer like Eichmann acted fully within the framework of the judgments expected of him. That is to say, he acted in accordance with the rule; he examined the order issued to him for its "manifest" legality and regularity. It is the claim of totalitarian lawfulness to have bridged the discrepancy between legality and justice, a discrepancy that the legality of positive law has always acknowledged and never sought to abolish. Hence, totalitarian lawfulness, "defying legality and pretending to establish the direct reign of justice on earth, executes the law of History or of Nature without translating it into standards of right or wrong for individual behaviour. It applies the law directly to mankind without bothering with the behaviour of men." The totalitarian ambition to transform man himself here takes the form of transforming the human species into "an active unfailing carrier of a law to which human beings otherwise would only passively and reluctantly be subjected" (OT, 462). As transformed by totalitarian policy, all laws become laws of movement; nature and history are no longer the stabilizing sources of authority for the actions of mortal men, but rather movements in themselves. Terror, according to Arendt, is the realization of the law of movement; "its chief aim is to make it possible for the force of nature or of history to race freely through mankind, unhindered by any spontaneous human action" (OT, 465). A situation is created in which

> no free action of either opposition or sympathy can be permitted to interfere with the elimination of the "objective enemy" of History or Nature, of the class or the race. Guilt and innocence become senseless notions; "guilty" is he who stands in the way of the natural or historical process which has passed judgment over "inferior races," over individuals "unfit to live." Terror executes these judgments, and before its court, all concerned are subjectively innocent: the murdered because they did nothing against the system, and the murderers because they do not really murder but execute a death sentence pronounced by some higher tribunal. (OT, 465)

What totalitarian rule thus ultimately strives toward is not despotic rule over men but a system in which "all men are made equally superfluous" (OT, 453). In this system, each man does not receive his right place and his due fate according to sources of authority stemming from man and subject to his approval or disapproval; instead, the suprahuman forces of nature and history in a direct manner *von oben herab* (from on high) and unmediated by the world of human affairs dictate to him his course of action. Stripped of his individuality, of his uniqueness in the sense of being a new beginning in the world, man is not only utterly superfluous, he is totally exchangeable as well. Anyone can take his place; he may fill the place of anybody else; whether tomorrow he will be an instrument or a victim of the suprahuman forces is not for him but exclusively for the suprahuman forces to decide. This abstraction from the individuality of all involved makes for what Adorno calls the "total depersonalization of murder": "With the murder of millions through administration . . . the individual is robbed of the very last and poorest that had been left to him."[2] The indifference toward death reflects the "indifference of subjects toward others," which, according to Detlev Claussen, "derives from an immanent tendency in bourgeois society." Consequently, anti-Semitism was stripped of its emotional fanaticism, of every moment of spontaneity on the part of the mobilized masses that might make them less controllable and thus potentially dangerous. In the words of Claussen, the anti-Semitism of the National Socialists "was transposed into an objectified, purely instrumental praxis that becomes indifferent toward the specific character of the objects in the camp."[3]

The indifference toward death that is prepared for ideologically by subjecting men to the "laws" of suprahuman forces and psychologically by a process of dehumanization affecting the perpetrator himself as well as his so-called objective enemies is complemented by the indifference to the actual killing itself. The Nazis industrialized the act of murder; by turning killing into an administrative task and by defining it in purely bureaucratic terms, they made sure that the sheer abstractness of large-scale planning and modern technology helped maintain the indifference that was widespread among the personnel involved due to the ideological and psychological features just mentioned. Franz Suchomel, SS *Unterscharführer* in Treblinka, practices the resulting jargon when he (in Lanzmann's film *Shoah*) says that "Belzec was the studio. Treblinka was an admittedly primitive, yet well-functioning assembly line of death [*Fließband des Todes*]. Auschwitz was a factory."[4] As Raul Hilberg observes:

> Killing is not as difficult as it used to be. The modern administrative apparatus has facilities for rapid, concerted movements and for efficient massive killings. These devices not only trap a larger number of victims; they also require a greater degree of specialization, and with that division of labor, the moral burden too is fragmented among the participants. The perpetrator can now kill his victims without touching them, without hearing them, without seeing them. He may feel sure of his success and safe from its repercussions. The ever-growing capacity for destruction cannot be arrested anywhere.[5]

The advanced technical division of labor yields a fragmentation of the total human act: no one man decides to carry out the evil act and is confronted with its consequences. The person who assumes full responsibility for the act has evaporated. The individual agent does not see himself as a moral subject but as an exchangeable part of a larger unit. His self-understanding perceives him not as wicked but as loyal, not as someone doing something wrong but as someone doing his job. Indeed, as Stanley Milgram observes when summing up the findings in his famous psychological experiments, "men do become angry; they do act hatefully and explode in rage against others. But not here. Something far more dangerous is revealed: the capacity for man to abandon his humanity, indeed, the inevitability that he does so, as he merges his unique personality into larger institutional structures."[6]

To the surprise of everybody, Eichmann at one point during his trial invoked Kant, claiming that he had lived his whole life according to a Kantian definition of duty. Though able to come up with an approximately correct definition of the categorical imperative, Eichmann went on to admit that he had ceased to live according to Kantian principles from the moment he was charged with carrying out the Final Solution. He also admitted having been aware of this, but explained that he had consoled himself with the thought that he no longer "was master of his own deeds," that he was "unable to change anything" (EJ, 136). In Kant's ethics, the principle according to which we ought to act is that of practical reason; in the distorted reading of Eichmann, the principle was the will of the Führer, making the categorical imperative read, "Act in such a way that the Führer, if he knew your action, would approve it" (this, in fact, is an authentic formulation of Hans Frank; see EJ, 136). This implies that conscience, the tribunal of the mind, which witnesses all one's acts and thoughts and before which they are put to the test, in the mind of Eichmann spoke with the voice of neither God nor practical reason but of Hitler; and what the Führer had sanctioned, no man could question. In Freudian terms, the Führer is the externalization of the superego.[7]

As Arendt observes, Eichmann's violation of Kantian ethics consists in his treating others, that is, the Jews, merely as means and not as ends in themselves. This is to say that Eichmann was guilty of the dehumanization of his victims. But this is not the whole story. The point I made above must be made once again, namely, that there is a *double* dehumanization involved here: not only does the perpetrator dehumanize his victims, he dehumanizes himself as well. By this I mean that Eichmann treats himself as well as his victims as a mere means and not as an end in itself. And I maintain that to treat oneself in this way—as nothing but a tool in the service of some external or suprahuman force—is just as immoral as treating others this way. At work in the Final Solution, then, is a leveling on both sides, affecting the killer as well as those to be killed. In viewing himself as a mere instrument in the carrying out of the unconditional commands of the pseudo-Darwinist "laws of nature," the individual agent has already killed himself as such, which is to say that the "murder of the moral person in man" of which Arendt speaks with regard to the *Nacht und Nebel* prisoners comprises the moral person in the SS officer as well. I would even go so far as to venture the hypothesis that the murder of the moral person—in the victim and in the perpetrator—is a sine qua non for the physical murder subsequently following. If this is granted, then moral responsibility takes the form of the individual agent having to assume responsibility for having killed the moral person in himself, which in its turn makes it possible for him to take part in the business of murder without being at odds with his own self-understanding. Thus, the issue of moral responsibility must address the fact that a person like Eichmann sees himself as a mere means and "therefore" as not responsible for the total consequences of his highly specialized and fragmented contribution. That is, he must be held morally responsible for the immoral act of *letting* himself become a mere means or tool within some larger administrative unit. I of course acknowledge that the responsibility for the actual murder, the "final" outcome of the whole process, still remains; but the point I want to make is that this responsibility for the consequences is *preceded* by a responsibility for adjusting oneself to the status of a mere tool, a dehumanization on the part of the acting ego without which that concerning his fellow men would not come about.

Reflecting on the problems raised by the trials against the Nazis who had committed "crimes against humanity," Arendt writes, "what we have demanded in these trials, where the defendants had committed 'legal crimes,' is that human beings be capable of telling right from wrong even when all they have to guide them is their own judgment, which, moreover, happens to be completely at odds with what they must regard as the unanimous opinion of all those around them" (EJ, 295). The traditional discrepancy between legality and justice (of which I spoke earlier) having been repealed (if not de facto, then at least allegedly), an officer like Eichmann would have to break the rules and challenge the canons of the legal system were he to act "morally" in my sense of the term. But because "the law of Hitler's land demanded that the voice of conscience tell everybody: 'Thou shalt kill' . . . , evil in the Third Reich had lost the quality by which most people recognize it—the quality of temptation" (EJ, 150). By doing what was expected of him, by conscientiously [sic] following the rules, by loyally obeying all orders, Eichmann in his own eyes as well as in the eyes of those around him was a "law-abiding citizen." Were he deliberately to have broken these rules, he would have had to do so only for the sake of some *other* rules or principles, ones he would have considered not more legal but more legitimate. In short, he would have had to adhere to a set of norms and principles that at the time was being systematically, that is, de jure, violated. In this, he would have had nothing but his own judgment to guide him. Eichmann, however, was content to let Hitler's words and the principles subscribed to by the Nazis serve as judge—as the only judge to be recognized. For those few who were still able to tell right from wrong, Arendt says that "they went really only by their own judgments, and they did so freely; there were no rules to be abided by, under which the particular cases with which they were confronted could be subsumed. They had to decide each instance as it arose, because no rules existed for the unprecedented" (EJ, 295).

This recalls the problem I addressed at the very beginning: How is judging possible in times of breakdown and crisis? How can we pass sound moral judgments in a world in which the standards for doing so seem to break down before our eyes? The involved dialectic between historical change and human cognition may be described as follows: only with the help of knowledge stemming from (collective as well as personal) experience can man pass judgment. But what if the particular to be judged is so novel as to lack any similarity with the past to which we owe our knowledge? What, in the terms of Reinhart Koselleck, if the *Erwartungshorizont* (horizon of expectation) has radically dissociated itself from our *Erfahrungsraum* (realm of experience), leaving us with the task of bridging an abyss?[8]

Arendt turns to Kant's *Critique of Judgment* in order to come to grips with the puzzle that Eichmann left her. In his third *Critique*, Kant makes a distinction between determinate and reflective judgments. Determinate judgments subsume the particular under a general rule existing prior to it; reflective judgments "derive" the rule from the particular. The distinction equals that between "subsuming under a concept" and "bringing to a concept." Arendt seeks to show the relevance of Kant's analysis of aesthetic judgment for political and moral theory; indeed, she holds that his aesthetics contains Kant's real, albeit "secret," political philosophy. Arendt's assumption is that the kind of judgment we are engaged in when we deliberate in political and moral affairs is captured in what Kant called reflective judgment. As was just brought out in the case of those few who were able to tell right from wrong under the Nazi dictatorship, judgment here refers to the mode of thinking that does not subsume particulars under general rules but instead ascends from the particular to the universal. In this respect, Arendt seems close to Aristotle's concept of *phronēsis*, even though she does not refer to it. Aristotle in his *Nicomachean Ethics* (1141b10) says of *phronēsis* that "it is concerned with action, and hence with particulars; it is about what is open to deliberation." But reflective judgment, which seeks to appreciate the particular in its irreducible particularity, cannot fulfill this task without some concept or rule transcending the particular that we want to judge. This is the point where the *Krisis* motif turns up in Arendt's assessment of what it is to judge: the alarming fact is that we no longer possess the reliable universal categories required for our cognitive and evaluative appreciation of something particular. As Arendt observes, in a passage reminiscent of MacIntyre's thesis in *After Virtue*, "The very framework within which understanding and judging could arise is gone" (LK, 95–96). Responding to this challenge, Arendt writes, "Even though we have lost yardsticks by which to measure, and rules under which to subsume the particular, a being whose essence is beginning may have enough of origin within himself to understand without preconceived categories and to judge without the set of customary rules which is morality" (UP, 391). For all the attractiveness of Arendt's conception of man as a "new beginning," I find it hard to accept her assumption. I do not believe that understanding "without preconceived categories" is possible. As is shown by the philosophical hermeneutics of Gadamer (which Arendt nowhere mentions), every act of understanding presupposes some larger horizon that transcends and thereby cognitively situates the particular to be understood. Far from working from scratch, understanding is a process in which we go beyond, as it were, what we seek to understand in order to understand it. Moreover, would not Arendt concede that "those few who were still able to tell right from wrong" in Nazi Germany and who deliberately broke the rules and principles officially valid at that time did so—as I argued above—only on the condition that they adhered to some *other* rules and principles? Clearly, the people who protested did so in strong opposition to the powers that be and the legal canons of the day, but from this it does not follow that they acted and judged in a conceptual vacuum, for wherever there is deliberate action and judgment, preconceived categories—however counterfactual, however at odds with the prevalent *Zeitgeist*—are always called upon and at work in the minds of the actors.

At stake here is nothing less than the question of how to envision the interconnectedness of thinking and judging. In her unfinished work *The Life of the Mind*, Arendt offers the following definition of the two mental activities: "Thinking deals with invisibles, with representations of things that are absent; judging always concerns particulars and things that are close at hand" (LM, 1:193). Still, the two are interrelated, as are consciousness and conscience. She goes on to explain:

> If thinking—the two-in-one of the soundless dialogue—actualizes the difference within our identity as given in consciousness and thereby results in conscience as its by-product, then judging, the by-product of the liberating effect of thinking, realizes thinking, makes it manifest in the world of appearances, where I am never alone and always too busy to be able to think. The manifestation of the wind of thought is not knowledge; it is the ability to tell right from wrong, beautiful from ugly. (LM, 1:193)

A number of points are worth dwelling on in this dense passage. First of all, recall the nature of Arendt's interest in the problematic: taken aback by the discovery that Eichmann was not wicked but thoughtless—"he *merely* . . .

never realized what he was doing" (EJ, 287)—Arendt sets out to examine "the strange interdependence of thoughtlessness and evil" (EJ, 288). The question that imposed itself was, "Could the activity of thinking as such . . . be among the conditions that make men abstain from evil-doing and even actually 'condition' them against it?" And she goes on to speculate, "Is wickedness . . . *not* a necessary condition for evil-doing?" (LM, 1:5). This is indeed what Arendt maintained when she coined the phrase "banality of evil." But what are we to make of her claim in the passage just cited that judgment, being the worldly manifestation of thought, is not knowledge? In fact, Arendt states quite categorically that judgment is not a cognitive faculty. In this she believes herself to follow Kant, whose position she reads as follows: "Judgment is not practical reason; practical reason 'reasons' and tells me what to do and what not to do; it lays down the law and is identical with the will, and the will utters commands; it speaks in imperatives. Judgment, on the contrary, arises from a merely contemplative pleasure or inactive delight [*untätiges Wohlgefallen*]" (LK, 15). However, it is difficult to see how this Kantian concept of judgment, intended as it was for the domain of aesthetics, can fit into the sphere of *praxis*, of politics and morals.

Arendt herself was well aware of the implied tension between judgment as contemplative and judgment as engaged in ongoing social action. As a number of commentators have pointed out (among them Beiner and Bernstein), Arendt oscillated between at least two profoundly different views of judgment. According to what might be called the early version, judging was conceived in terms of the deliberations of political actors with regard to possible courses of future action. Judging belonged to the world of action, or praxis; the judging subjects were men of action, having to develop and pass their judgments *in medias res*, as it were. A shift in Arendt's conception came about when she took up Kant's third *Critique*, believing there to have found a concept—namely, reflective judgment—that provided her with a way out of the philosophical impasse in which the Eichmann controversy had left her. Following Kant in stressing the disinterested quality of judging, Arendt situated its exercise within the world of contemplation. The shift implied is equal to that from the actor to the spectator. Hence, the temporal modality of judging changes; it comes to mean reflection on the past as opposed to deliberation about how to act in the future. Given this conceptualization, judgment is free from all practical interest. According to this late version, judgment no longer participates in the *vita activa*; it is confined to the *vita contemplativa* as an autonomous faculty to be separated from the other faculties of the mind and claiming its own modus operandi (see LM, 1:216).

This development in Arendt's thought justifies Beiner's claim that judging, for Arendt, ultimately comes to serve an *ontological* function: "Judgment has the function of anchoring man in a world that would otherwise be without meaning and existential reality: a world unjudged would have no human import for us" (LK, 152). Judging furnishes that which has happened with meaning; it makes possible man's reconciliation with what was but no longer is. Viewed as the saving power of remembrance, judging "lets endure what is essentially perishable"; its ultimate function is to "reconcile time and world-liness" (LK, 155).

Notwithstanding the philosophical merit of Arendt's late attempt to work out the ontological function of judgment, this turn in her reflections seems to betray her initial intention of coming to terms with the moral-political significance of judgment. In order to find out whether such a betrayal does take place, we have to go somewhat deeper into the use Arendt makes of Kant in her *Lectures on Kant's Political Philosophy*. Central to Arendt's discussion is Kant's section "Taste as a kind of sensus communis" in his *Critique of Judgment*, where he says:

> Under the *sensus communis* we must include the idea of a sense *common to all*, i.e. of a faculty of judgment which, in its reflection, takes account (*a priori*) of the mode of representation of all other men in thought, in order, as it were, to compare its judgment with the collective reason of humanity. . . . This is done by comparing our judgment with the possible rather than the actual judgments of others, and by putting ourselves in the place of any other man, by abstracting from the limitations which contingently attach to our own judgment. (CJ, §40, p. 136)

Accordingly, Kant's "maxim of enlarged thought" reads, "to put ourselves in thought in the place of everyone else" (CJ, §40, p. 136); the faculty making this possible Kant calls imagination, or *Einbildungskraft*. Though still a solitary business in the sense of taking place in the isolation of my own mind, the critical, or *representative*, thinking for which imagination is a necessary presupposition is public, in that it renders the others—who are actually absent—present. To think with an enlarged mentality is to move in a space that is essentially public, open to all sides; it demands that one "trains one's imagination to go visiting" (LK, 43). As Arendt describes the process of representation, "I form an opinion by considering a given issue from different viewpoints, by making present to my mind the standpoints of those who are absent; that is, I represent them." Through representation, the opinion I form ceases to be purely private or subjective, it achieves intersubjective quality: "The more people's standpoints I have present in my mind while I am pondering a given issue, and the better I can imagine how I would think and feel if I were in their place, the stronger will be my capacity for representative thinking and the more valid my final conclusions, my opinion" (BPF, 241). In other words, the basic condition for this exertion of the imagination is what Kant called disinterestedness, the liberation from one's own private interests.

Arendt now has to face the question of the *validity* of the opinions I form and the judgments I pass. "The power of judgment," she tells us, "rests on a potential agreement with others"; and the thinking process that is active in judging "finds itself always and primarily . . . in an anticipated communication with others with whom I must come to some agreement." Arendt's claim is that "from this potential agreement judgment derives its specific validity" (BPF, 220). Hence, to be valid, my judgment depends on my ability to "represent" the standpoints of the absent others in my own mind. Unexpectedly, Arendt goes on to assert that judging "is not valid for those who do not judge or for those who are not members of the public realm where the objects of judgment appear" (BPF, 221). So, whereas such thinkers as Apel and Habermas would recognize one of their own leitmotivs in Arendt's Kantian idea of representative thinking, they would certainly oppose her limitation of valid judgment to the actual members of the public realm. For Arendt, that is, the person passing judgment has only to take into consideration the members of the *reale Kommunikationsgemeinschaft*, whereas discourse ethics demands that we transcend the boundaries of the local community to which we belong and judge on behalf of the members of a *ideale Kommunikationsgemeinschaft*. To advance a more immanent critique, I find problematic Arendt's sudden insistence that judging be restricted to the actually existing public realm, insofar as it contradicts the Kantian demand, always approvingly cited by Arendt, to take into account "not so much actual as merely possible judgments." Indeed, the fact that Eichmann was accused of "crimes against humanity" implies that he had failed to go beyond the positivity of the Nazi jurisdiction and the facticity of the Nazi society to which he belonged—and from which, significantly, the Jews had been systematically excluded since the enactment of the Nuremberg Laws of 1935. Eichmann's crime was not only against the Jews excluded from the public realm of contemporary German society; it was a crime against future generations of Jews as well, against people not yet born and whose birth he in effect denied them, killing their would-be mothers and fathers. Hence, my claim is that the demand to take account of those absent must be viewed temporally as well as spatially; that is, the concept of absence points to the not-yet of the future as well as to the somewhere else of geography.[9] This being so, the notion of a crime against humanity, if it is to make sense, presupposes that "humanity as a whole is the community which we have to anticipate in our judgment and whose possible agreement renders our judgment valid" (Rainer Forst).[10]

By conceiving of the thinking process involved in judging as "an anticipated communication with others with whom I have to come to some agreement" (BPF, 220), Arendt at the stage of her Kant lectures and in the essays published in *Between Past and Future* still sees judging as participating in the *vita activa*. Judging is not yet, as it came to be toward the end of *The Life of the Mind*, purely contemplative and retrospective; while certainly resting on a disinterested withdrawal (à la Kant) from the ongoing decision making in which the actors are engaged, the spectator seeking to judge these worldly affairs has not dissociated himself from them to the extent of no longer being prepared to let the actors take a future stand on the judgment he passes— indeed, he is expected to *anticipate* their stand. Far from simply seeking to lend meaning to events already having taken place, saving their particular dignity by an act of remembrance, the person who judges sees himself as directly affected by the actions of his contemporaries. Hence, Arendt, in her essay "The Crisis in Culture," tells us that "judging is one, if not the most, important activity in which this sharing-the-world-with-others comes to pass" (BPF, 221).

The Kantian insight Arendt wants to make fruitful for the domains of politics and ethics, then, is that to judge particulars—and judging is always of particulars—we have to be able to represent in our thinking the standpoints of all concerned. Only by way of this moment of mental *universalization* can we judge as members of a larger community. Having learned this from Kant's notion of *erweiterte Denkungsart* (enlarged thought), Arendt puts forward the claim that Eichmann failed to judge, because he was incapable of representing others in his own mind. Now, the condition of the autonomy of judging qua mental faculty is the ability to think—this, I believe, is what Arendt had in mind when she stressed that thoughtlessness rather than wickedness led Eichmann into doing evil. It is in the *refusal to judge* that Arendt locates the greatest evils in the political realm; the evil of totalitarianism epitomized in Eichmann was manifest in his lack of imagination, "of having present before your eyes and taking into consideration the others whom you must represent." It is worth emphasizing that the representation demanded here must be understood as a stretching out *from* something particular and context-bound *toward* something universal and ideal. Viewing moral responsibility in this strong sense is what the early Sartre did when he said that "our responsibility is . . . much greater than we had supposed, for it concerns mankind as a whole." In choosing what the right kind of action would be, "my action is, in consequence, a commitment on behalf of all mankind."[11]

The Interrelation Between Thinking and Judgment

> Never is he more active than when he does
> nothing, never is he less alone than when
> he is by himself.
>   —Cato

I take the crucial question concerning Arendt's views about thinking and judgment to be, How are we to make sense of the claim that the condition of the exercise of the faculty of judgment is the ability to think? In her lecture "Thinking and Moral Considerations," Arendt sets out to examine whether our ability to judge, to tell right from wrong, is indeed dependent on our faculty of thought. Can it be, she asks, that the activity of thinking *as such* might be such that it "conditions" men against evildoing? Thinking, Arendt says, deals with objects that are absent, removed from direct sense perception. To think means to move outside the world of appearances. Hence, an object of thought is always a re-presentation, "something actually absent and present only to the mind which, by virtue of imagination, can make it present in the form of an image" (TMC, 423; the "imagination" referred to is the *Einbildungskraft* of which Kant speaks in his *Critique of Judgment*). Insofar as thinking is a dwelling on invisibles, a preoccupation with what is absent, thinking is not of this world, entailing that it—by itself—bring about nothing at all, no "results" of which it can boast that these are the worldly manifestations of its activity. Indeed, thinking's chief characteristic is precisely that it interrupts all doing. Thinking and doing, that is, are mutually exclusive of each other. As Heidegger observed, thinking as such is "out of order." Thus conceived, thinking is subversive; it inevitably has "a destructive, undermining effect on all established criteria, values, measurements for good and evil" (TMC, 434). Due to its very nature, therefore, thinking will never furnish morality with a foundation or grounding; far from that, thinking will always lead us to question the belief in any such foundation. In other words, no moral propositions or commandments, no final code of conduct, and no allegedly final definition of what is good and what is evil may be expected to issue from the activity of thinking.

But does the subversive nature of thinking render it completely negative? Or is there still a possibility that something positive and affirmative might emanate from the sheer thinking experience? Brought to bear on the hypothesis from which Arendt starts her inquiry, to ask these questions assumes that if there is anything in thinking that can prevent men from doing evil, and in this sense be of a positive nature, then it must be some property inherent in the activity itself, regardless of its objects. Socrates, to whom Arendt now turns, is notorious for engaging in dialogues whose outcomes are largely, if not entirely, negative or aporetic. Arendt points out that Socrates nevertheless formulated two positive propositions, both occurring in the *Gorgias*: first, "It is better to be wronged than to do wrong" (474), and second, "It would be better for me that . . . multitudes of men should disagree with me rather than that I, *being one*, should be out of harmony with myself and contradict me" (482). Hardly surprising, Arendt sees as mistaken the view that the propositions are the results of some cogitation about morality. "They are insights," she tells us, "but insights of experience," by which she means the thinking experience as such (TMC, 439). Her proposal is that we view the second proposition as the prerequisite for the first one. The key to the interpretation she advocates lies in the "being one" so heavily stressed by Socrates. What he has in mind is this: When I appear and am seen by others, and as long as I enjoy the company of others, I am as I am seen by others; that is, I am one, and hence recognizable. However, I am not only for others but also for myself, and in the latter case, I am not just one. Rather, I am my own company, I am with myself, and with this a difference is inserted into my oneness. Thinking is this very difference; thinking is the activity in which I engage with myself, it is my relating to myself, my taking part in a soundless dialogue between me and myself. When thinking, I am not one but two-in-one. In solitude (to be strictly distinguished from loneliness), in my keeping myself company, my merely being conscious of myself comes to be actualized in a duality during the thinking activity; and "it is this *duality* of myself with myself that makes thinking a true activity, in which I am both the one who asks and the one who answers" (LM, 1:185).

This is the searched-for positive moment in Socrates' propositions. The only (positive) criterion of thinking as understood or, better, experienced by

Socrates, Arendt asserts, is agreement, "to be consistent with oneself . . . ; the opposite, to be in contradiction with oneself, actually means becoming one's own adversary" (LM, 1:186). This is exactly what is at stake in both of Socrates' propositions; moreover, it contains the justification for Arendt's urge that we view the second proposition as the prerequisite for the first one. The "being one" referred to by Socrates reminds us that "it would be worse for me to be at odds with myself than in disagreement with multitudes of men" (TMC, 439); therefore, "it is better to be wronged than to do wrong." Having suffered wrong, that is, I can still remain the friend of the sufferer; but who would want to be the friend of and have to live the rest of his life with a murderer? The issue here—that of either being in harmony or in conflict with oneself—is one of eminent moral impact. Yet it is, to repeat, not a moral cogitation but an insight arising out of the experience of thinking as such. The latter teaches us that it does not take a plurality of egos in order to establish difference; rather, the ego carries the difference within itself when it says, "I am I." Being conscious of myself, I am inevitably two-in-one, the embodiment of difference and hence a self faced with the Socratic issue of the success or failure of being in harmony and at peace with itself.

The meaning of "thoughtlessness" follows directly from the above. It means to "shun the intercourse with oneself" (TMC, 445). In Arendt's view, Eichmann did just that. Drawing on the only positive statements of Socrates and using Eichmann as her negative example, Arendt reaches the conclusion that the question whether the thinking activity as such may condition men against evildoing is to be answered in the affirmative.

What does this conclusion really mean? How literally are we to interpret the thesis that thinking "as such" may condition men against evildoing? Are we to understand that thinking in itself is a *sufficient* condition for preventing us from doing evil; or is it rather one among a number of *necessary* conditions? What is the force to be attributed to thinking with regard to motivation? Put otherwise, how sure can we be that a person practicing the "silent inner dialogue" will be a person who, *on that very account*, as it were, is likely to resist participation in evil deeds? To what extent is the likelihood of such participation to be seen as determined by the presence or absence of thinking in a person? In a passage that is not to be misinterpreted as arguing ad hominem, Richard Bernstein writes, "The most generous claim that one can make about Heidegger—the *thinker* par excellence—is that 'when the stakes were on the table,' he exercised such poor *judgment*."[12]

In my view, for Arendt's thesis to carry the *moral* significance that is her central concern, the thesis must imply that thinking upholds its own criterion for action. If this is Arendt's meaning, then how can thinking be "connected" to action? How are we to conceive of this assumed link between thinking, depicted as a withdrawal from the world of appearances, and action, depicted as our willful intervention into that world? The link, I take Arendt to answer, is provided by our faculty of judgment. Judgment mediates between thought and action, between thinking and doing. Thinking, we recall, deals with generalities; judgment, with particulars. The point of importance in the present context is that thinking turns into judgment insofar as it emerges from its withdrawal and returns to the world of appearances in order to deal with the particular as it appears there. The criterion for action inherent in thinking as such is not the usual rules of conduct, recognized by the many and agreed on by society, but whether I shall be able to live in peace with myself when the time has come to think about my deeds. To put it thus is, of course, to invoke conscience. To Arendt, the inability to think coincides with a failure of conscience, the absence of the former entailing the absence of the latter, whereby conscience is described as "the anticipation of the fellow who awaits you if and when you come home" (LM, 1:191). Brought to bear on the case of Eichmann—whose fame stems primarily from his *actions*—this train of thought suggests that Eichmann's failure to judge was not his original failure but rather one following from a logically prior and truly original failure to think and a fortiori to contemplate the prospect of having to live in disharmony with himself. Not thinking, Eichmann has no such thing as conscience. Devoid of conscience in the sense of an inner tribunal before which he has to justify himself, Eichmann could not "of himself" prevent himself from committing evil deeds.

Eichmann was far from alone in renouncing judgment in Nazi Germany. According to Arendt, his failure is symptomatic rather than unique. The unwillingness to abstain from passing judgment became rare, the exception rather than the rule; it increasingly became the prerogative of a small minority of people, namely, those few who were never prepared to bypass the summons from themselves, from that other I contained in the two-in-one. The lesson to be learned here highlights one of my criticisms of MacIntyre. That lesson, in the final instance, is that judgment requires of individuals that they be prepared to set themselves apart from and actively oppose the ethos of their society. Judgment entails—and will principally always entail—a preparedness to defy the rule of the many and to contradict current practices and the powers that be in order not to risk having to contradict oneself. The latter contradiction is primary to the former because my being able to forgive myself is primary to my not being forgiven by others. This primacy is not logical but existential; it touches on what kind of forgiving carries the largest weight *for me*. Ultimately at stake, therefore, is the question whether a deed would allow or disallow me to retain my self-respect.

Presupposing as it does a withdrawal from the world of appearances and thus from the realm of action, thinking as such is deeply apolitical. However, in political emergencies, those who go on thinking and who, for that very reason, refrain from action, are "drawn out of hiding because their refusal to join in is conspicuous and thereby becomes a kind of action" (LM, 1:192). In such emergencies, says Arendt, thinking is political by implication because it not only brings about the destruction of unexamined opinions, values, doctrines, and theories but also has a downright *liberating* effect on another faculty, that of judgment; and judgment was held by Arendt to be the "most political" of man's mental capacities. Thus, thinking always carries a political potential within itself, a potential actualized, however, only in cases of crises, breakdowns, and emergencies—only in times, that is to say, when thinking seems to become even *more* "out of order," even *more* at odds with the worldly affairs of the day, than it used to be. So, a crisis not only calls urgently for the capability for judgment, it also renders visible the peculiar connectedness of thinking and judgment, making us painfully aware of the utmost *precariousness* of the link thereby uncovered.

The conclusion arrived at by Arendt in her reflections on Eichmann over so many years can be briefly summarized as follows. Eichmann's overt failure to act morally stems from his failure to exercise judgment, and the latter in its turn stems from his original and, as it stands, irreducible failure to think. In philosophizing over Eichmann, Arendt, in my interpretation, makes use of the following explanatory scheme:

Level: THINKING $\longrightarrow$ JUDGMENT $\longrightarrow$ ACTION
Faculties involved: intellectual   intellectual   —

In this scheme, Arendt's reflections assume the form of a two-stage deduction: first, she examines Eichmann's actions by drawing attention to his incapacity for judgment; then she analyzes his alleged failure to judge by resorting to an examination of his inability to think, ending her inquiry by emphasizing the moral significance of the inner tribunal of conscience said to be a product of the two-in-one actualized in thinking, and in thinking only.

Leaving aside the commonplace complaint that Arendt, in endorsing the so-called positive legacy of Socrates, commits the philosopher's classic "idealistic" fallacy of assuming that action is at all preceded by thinking, the suggestion I make here—and pursue in a systematic manner in later chapters—is that the philosophical "challenge" posed by Eichmann is in fact more fully appreciated and met when the following scheme is adopted:

Level: PERCEPTION —→   JUDGMENT—→   ACTION

Faculties involved: cognitive-emotional   cogn.-emot.   —

Again, a two-stage deduction is being encouraged: first, the familiar move from action back to judgment; then a second move from judgment back to *perception*, as distinguished from Arendt's "thinking." "Perception," aptly captured in the German *Wahrnehmung*, is intended to mean the capability of recognizing and identifying the object or phenomenon about which judgment is subsequently to be passed. It is necessary that recognition and identification be adequate and appropriate; that is, they must satisfy the condition of *doing justice* to the phenomenon to be judged as belonging to a specific class of phenomena, for example, as being a moral phenomenon as opposed to a physical one. To exchange Arendt's "thinking" for "perception" carries the advantage of introducing into the explanatory scheme a category that is not purely and exclusively intellectual. (My choosing the term "intellectual" instead of, say, "cognitive" here is very deliberate; it follows partly from Arendt's view of judgment as "opinion" and *not* cognition.) It is a central thesis of mine that not only "perception" but also "judgment" is to be conceived of as not purely and exclusively presupposing intellectual capacities. To the contrary, what I argue is that both categories—perception as well as judgment—must be split into two components, one of which is cognitive, the other of which is emotional. Furthermore, I urge that the components be considered equally important and *necessary*, so that a failure on the part of one of the two components will prove a sufficient condition for the failure of perception per se as well as judgment per se. In other words, each component is *indispensable*.

The explanatory scheme that I have proposed holds out the promise of representing a considerable gain in conceptual richness. To assess this gain, consider once more Arendt's response to the challenge presented by the Eichmann trial. What is the eventual outcome of Arendt's applying her scheme to the challenge? It is the claim that Eichmann was "merely thoughtless." But, it must be asked, what other possibilities did she explore, apart from rejecting as false the popular assumption that Eichmann was some kind of a "monster"? More to the point, what other hypotheses does Arendt's scheme *allow for*? Because her category of "judgment" as well as that of "thinking" is wholly, one-sidedly *intellectualistic*, no path of inquiry is open to her except to question Eichmann's intellectual capacities (*in casu*: the path of "representative thinking"). To say that her scheme permitted no other path is to contend that her conclusion was in fact largely predetermined. Having for conceptual reasons ruled out the possibility that the failure of Eichmann might be strictly cognitive (in Arendt's sense of cognition as securing knowledge in the form of *epistēmē*), Arendt could only assert that it was intellectual, and this in the strong sense of touching on the very nature of the thinking activity per se.

Because my scheme acknowledges the existence of an emotional as well as a cognitive component, not only to "judgment" but also to "perception," two distinct paths of inquiry can be embarked upon: the path of cognition and the path of emotion. However, this is not to say that one should pursue one path to the analytic exclusion of the other. Quite to the contrary, to ask what has gone wrong on the level of judgment or on the prior level of perception is to try to locate the source of the failure; and this source can be purely cognitive or purely emotional or, finally, in the more complex cases, *jointly* cognitive and emotional.

In light of the analytic and conceptual distinctions I have introduced, I am prepared to claim that what Eichmann epitomizes is not so much thought-lessness as *insensitivity*. The capacity he failed to exercise is emotional rather than intellectual or cognitive; it is the capacity to develop *empathy* with other human beings, to take an emotional interest in the human "import" of the situation in which the persons affected by his actions found themselves. To be more accurate, the empathy Eichmann failed to develop is not just one "emotional capacity" among others; rather, what I intend by "empathy" is people's basic *emotional faculty*. Corresponding to this is my conception of "representative thinking," that is, the mental process of making present to the mind the standpoints of those who are absent, as the basic *cognitive faculty* required for the exercise of moral judgment.

It follows from what I have said above about Arendt's explanatory scheme that in her reflections the possible "insensitivity" of Eichmann could never be thematized, let alone explored in any systematic manner. Arendt, that is, had at her disposal no category with which she could pin down the "failure" of Eichmann as emotional; she lacked the specifically emotional analytic category that is required if the question of Eichmann's insensitivity, as opposed to his thoughtlessness, is to be raised at all.

Admittedly, I cannot prove that Eichmann was insensitive. Nor, for that matter, could Arendt prove that he was "merely thoughtless." To observe this, however, is not to make an argument either pro my thesis or contra Arendt's. Eichmann is often reported (even by Arendt) to have been "unimpressed" by the testimony given by victims of the Holocaust during his trial. He is said to have remained largely unaffected by the proceedings, even at the moments of great psychological distress and occasional breakdown on the part of the witnesses. In short, he seemed *disinterested*. This unaffected-ness, this disinterestedness in the face of evident distress and pain in people physically present with Eichmann in the courtroom, I find worthy of reflection. More than that, I find it downright conspicuous; and I find it equally conspicuous that Arendt (herself present to cover the trial for the *New Yorker*) throughout fails to dwell on it. In my view, this shows two things: first, that there exists a considerable amount of empirical evidence (including the television coverage of the proceedings) to support my claim about Eichmann's being insensitive; second, that what I call Arendt's *intellectualist bias* effectively prevents her from reflecting on the point just made.

However, this is not the place to go into a comprehensive account of the explanatory scheme I have put forward. But before returning to my discussion of Arendt, I wish to make a general and a specific observation concerning the status of the scheme.

The general observation is that the scheme, though introduced in the context of attempting to come to grips with Eichmann, is in no way tailor-made to "fit" with that one particular case. The scheme is not confined to but survives the empirical illustration provided by Eichmann, so that instead of being launched ad hoc, the scheme is the other way around—that is, Eichmann is invoked to lend some human flesh, as it were, to the proposed analytic categories. Indeed, these categories have come to remain, and a great number of examples—some empirical, some hypothetical—are offered in order to account for them. Moreover, no one example can suffice to prove the overall theoretical and analytic value of an explanatory scheme. Signifi-cantly, and in all fairness, this applies to Arendt's scheme no less than to mine: just as the case of Eichmann hardly provides me with a cogent falsification of Arendt's scheme, so does it bestow on my own scheme hardly anything like an adequate verification.

The specific observation is that my scheme has the advantage of permitting more hypotheses to be explored than Arendt's. *In concreto*, it allows me to contend that Eichmann's was an *emotional* failure. That is my first claim. The second claim, which remained implicit in the above discussion, is that Eichmann's *original* failure is to be located on the level of *perception*. Eichmann failed to *perceive* the Jews as human beings, and he did so because he failed to develop empathy toward them, to take an emotional interest in the human import of the situation in which they found themselves. According to my scheme, this failure on the level of perception serves to explain the (perhaps more evident) failure of judgment; it can do so because I take the former level to be logically prior to the latter.

Ronald Beiner has made a point of immediate relevance here: "When we say 'Eichmann lacks judgment' we want to say: 'He does not lack the power to judge in any sense whatever, but he does lack the power of *humane* judgment, he fails to identify correctly particulars that would be evident to any normal, civilized, morally sighted judging subject.'" And further: "[Eichmann] seems to be missing the *human* significance of these events, his very faculty of moral *perception* (not just political evaluation and foresight) seems to be essentially deficient."[13] So political judgment as conceived of by Beiner incorporates or, rather, presupposes "humane" judgment. I think that Beiner is right and that his emphasis on "moral perception" takes him an important step beyond Arendt's reflections on the subject. Yet for all the merit of this, the gain achieved as compared to Arendt's account is rather meager. As I see it, Beiner should have gone one step further. He should have asked what, in its turn, is presupposed in the humane judgment of which he so rightly speaks. But because Beiner fails to take this step, his insight into the nature of humane judgment and of moral perception remains but the beginning of a major insight. His perspective appears too intellectualist, too influenced by Arendt, to allow him to fully appreciate the emotional capacities of persons as distinct from their intellectual ones.

Seeking to substantiate her claim that evil is implicit in the refusal to judge, which in its turn is implicit in the inability to practice representative thinking, Arendt says, "In the last analysis . . . our decisions about right and wrong will depend upon our choice of company, with whom we wish to spend our lives." Today, however, "the likelihood that someone would come and tell us that he does not mind and that any company will be good for him is, I think, very great. Morally and even politically speaking, this indifference . . . is the greatest danger" (LK, 113). Arendt holds that this indifference lies at the heart of the widespread tendency to refuse to judge at all. In the final lecture of her Chicago course "Basic Moral Propositions," she ends on a pessimistic note:

> Out of the unwillingness or inability to choose one's examples and one's company, and out of the unwillingness or inability to relate to others through judgment, arise the real *skandala*, the real stumbling-blocks which human powers cannot remove because they were not

caused by human and humanly understandable motives. Therein lies
the horror and, at the same time, the banality of evil. (LK, 113)

In my view, the roots of this prevailing indifference must be sought not in
the psychology of the individual but in the bureaucratic institutions that
structure modern life, make killing abstract, and undermine the actor's sense
of responsibility by fragmenting his or her acts as well as comprehension of
the acts' final consequences. Failing to achieve an overview of the administrative body to which he or she belongs, always one among many and as such
perfectly exchangeable, the individual is less inclined to assume responsibility; failing to see the people affected by his or her actions as humans rather
than as dull objects, or *Sachen*: the individual is less capable of representative
thinking; hence, the individual will not refuse to but will be unable to judge.
My claim here is that the question of individual responsibility must take the
form of *not allowing oneself to become incapable of judging*. Demanding this means
demanding that the individual always questions the legitimacy—as opposed
to the factual legality—of the institutional framework he or she is about to
enter, *before* being trapped by it, *before* becoming its helpless victim. To judge
soundly in such a setting means to be able to anticipate, that is, foresee, the
total consequences of a number of highly specialized activities and measures.
This, from a moral point of view, we *have* to demand of the individual; but
in doing so we should know that we probably ask for too much. Indeed, our
demand is empirically undermined from three sides, each of them jeopardiz-
ing the individual's sense of moral responsibility. First, and as acknowledged
by Arendt, the standards of judgment handed down by and through tradition
are no longer authoritative but have been *exploded* by radical historical change,
and ultimate values and norms have ceased to be valid. Second, the probability that we will be successful in anticipating the outcome of a complex web
of activities seems very small in view of the *unprecedented* nature of the activities
(as is clearly the case with the Holocaust). Third, the situatedness of the
individuals within modern administrative bodies allows for a *fragmentation* of
their consciousness that robs them of their ability to comprehend the
significance of their own actions. To sum up, we demand of actors—always
in medias res—that they judge soundly in the face of unprecedented events
while being affected by cognitive fragmentation and while having but
exploded categories at their disposal.

I have wanted to radicalize our understanding of the crisis of judgment in
order that Arendt's Kantian response to the challenge it posed for her could
be put to the test. The Eichmann trial provoked Arendt to address the issue

of judgment from two different perspectives: there is the question whether and how Eichmann judged, and there is the question whether and how we are to judge Eichmann. Arendt reached the conclusion that Eichmann did not judge, that he failed to do so because he was unable to think in Kant's sense of representing others in his own mind. Regarding our own judgment of Eichmann, the controversy triggered off by Arendt's thesis of the banality of evil raised the question *whether* we—who have never been faced with the situation he was in—have any right to judge Eichmann at all. To this a number of contributors, Gershom Scholem among them, answered in the negative; he took the view that the nonparticipants do better to abstain from judgment altogether. To this Arendt replies, "The argument that we cannot judge if we were not present and involved ourselves seems to convince everybody everywhere, although it seems obvious that if it were true, neither the administration of justice nor the writing of history would ever be possible" (EJ, 295–96). Arendt sees "a reluctance evident everywhere to make judgments in terms of individual moral responsibility" (EJ, 297). While granting that Arendt could and should have been more careful and less crude in her criticism of the role played by the Jewish councils during the deportation to the concentration camps, I think that the force of her stand must be recognized: Arendt demands that we judge what happened because Eichmann taught us the dark lesson of what may happen if we choose not to judge. For her, abstaining from judgment is not the same as showing some kind of Socratic wisdom but equals an unwillingness to assume responsibility; the spectator as well as the actor is obliged to judge. In short, the inability of Eichmann himself to judge teaches us the importance of our doing so—even though from a vantage point temporally and spatially removed from the events in question.

But what about the three factors mentioned that undermine the prospect of judging? Is the spectator unaffected by the explosion of our moral categories, by the unprecedentedness of the events, and by the fragmentation of consciousness? Indeed, it was in setting out to judge Eichmann, in the spectator's attempt to come to grips with the actor, that Arendt *discovered* that our traditional standards of judgment are radically inadequate. And with regard to the Final Solution, it still remains something genuinely novel, or *einzigartig*, as was brought out recently in the German *Historikerstreit*. This does not imply, however, that our view of the Final Solution should be on an equal footing with Eichmann's, insofar as he was—but failed—to judge what was happening, whereas we are to pass judgment on what did happen. Again, the difference between the actor and the spectator comes to the fore as one of temporal modality, as one of anticipating as opposed to contemplating in retrospect. Nevertheless, both parties are confronted with the quality of unprecedentedness, making the particular to be judged a particular such as never has been, neither before nor after. Here, then, judging concerns particularity in the strongest possible sense; that is, even if the moral categories were still intact—which they, however, are not—they would not be able to offer us any guidance. In this extreme case, the sought-for universal would have to be derived from an as yet fully unknown particular, invoking here Kant's "reflective judgment." As Arendt remarks, we are forced to a "thinking without banisters [*Denken ohne Geländer*]." As to my point about the fragmentation of consciousness, finally, we have no reason to believe that this process does not haunt the spectator as well as the actor. In fact, I would argue, with Habermas, though for different reasons, that the fragmented consciousness today is the new *Gestalt* of the false one and that the fragmentation on the level of the individual's cognitive faculties is part of a larger societal process from which no one, including the theoretician, is exempted.[14]

For all the force of Arendt's view, I suggest that a different understanding of what it is to judge be acknowledged, one permitting us to say—contrary to Arendt—that Eichmann did in fact judge. By this I mean that there is a sense in which Eichmann *knew* that the business he was involved in was one of plain murder. This being the case, a need existed to justify murder, to make it not only legally but also morally acceptable to the personnel professionally engaged in it. In short, I claim that the Final Solution was in need of a moral justification, making sure that the people carrying it out felt that what they were doing was "right" rather than "wrong." Heinrich Himmler recognized this need; in his speeches, he addressed it explicitly on a number of occasions. Thus, in a speech given in front of an SS *Gruppenführer* audience at Poznan in October 1943, Himmler said, "We had the moral right vis-à-vis *our* people to annihilate *this* people which wanted to annihilate us. But we had no right to take a single fur, a single watch, a single mark, a single cigarette, or anything whatsoever. . . . On the whole we can say that we have fulfilled this heavy task with love for our people, and we have not been damaged in the innermost of our being, our soul, our character."[15] What we have here then is the peculiar SS morality according to which the individual theft of a cigarette is wrong, but the collective murder of millions is right, the former being done for personal gain, the latter for the sake of the German people and the Aryan race. Hence, Martin Broszat remarks about Auschwitz *Lagerkommandant* Rudolf Höss that "he is one of those people who are willing to accept the most brutal measures of extermination as correct and reasonable, indeed as unavoidable and as a command of duty, yet who are shocked and full of indignation when they hear about 'criminal offenders' and who self-righteously turn their noses up at sexual anomalies."[16]

The point Arendt made in the Eichmann controversy was that the responsibility for making judgments cannot be shirked; judgment cannot be suspended, because the supreme danger is abstention from judgment; therefore, we have to judge Eichmann for not judging. But should we not be ready to admit that a kind of judgment *is* involved in Himmler's apologia for the implementation of the Final Solution, invoking as he does the traditional language of morals, including such virtues as duty, loyalty, and unselfishness? Of course, the kind of morality at work here is perverted and indeed immoral, violating everything that was and is meant by the virtues referred to. But in saying so, do I not, exactly at the moment when I make this critical observation, engage in a debate, regarding what morality is, with the proponents of the "Nazi morality"? In a sense I do. Still, however much I might treat the Nazis as participants in such a debate, they would not be prepared to treat me the same way. That is, I would have a discussion without reciprocity, without a mutual recognition among those taking part.

In my earlier account of the suprahuman forces Nazi ideology ultimately has recourse to, I pointed out that the annihilation of the Jews is "necessitated" by the objective law of nature. What this implies is twofold: first, the law guiding human action—thus, deciding on what is right and what is wrong—is not the work of humankind but a product of nature, that is, of the principle of selection; second, individuals do not consider themselves responsible in the sense of being autonomous but rather see themselves as mere instruments obeying forces superior to humankind. Now, the autonomy of agents is a premise for any discussion addressing moral questions; denying their autonomy, Nazis place themselves outside the domain in which argumentation makes a difference; hence, the discussion breaks down. Still, the fact remains that the Nazi ideologues perceived a need to borrow parasitically and arbitrarily from the canons of conventional morality in order to make of atrocities a "heavy task," as it were, demanding the supreme virtues of humanity (see Chapters 4 and 5).

In view of this train of thought, one might say that Eichmann failed to exercise judgment, because he robbed himself of the requisite for doing so, namely, his autonomy. Whereas I stated above that individuals must assume responsibility by "not allowing themselves to become incapable of judging," I now refine that statement to the effect that individuals must *not allow themselves to be robbed of their autonomy. In concreto,* and as emphasized by Stanley Milgram, this demand requires of individuals that they refuse to let their unique personalities merge into larger institutional structures. Arendt remarked that Eichmann seemed to hold no firm ideological convictions; and even though this might have been the case, at least to some extent, it must be recognized that he did share the Nazi *Weltanschauung* voiced by Himmler and accordingly enjoyed the kind of "good conscience" this worldview promised its adherents. Hence, there remains a specific ideology of which Eichmann is both follower and victim: the ideology of the end of the individual and thus of human autonomy. Indeed, this is the very ideology preparing for anti-Semitism, preparing ultimately for anti-Semitism's transformation into a practice of industrialized murder. For who is the Jew but the other, the embodiment of the transcending moment of freedom? I think Sartre is right in defining anti-Semitism as "fear of the human condition."[17] Held, to a large degree falsely, to refuse assimilation, the Jew came to symbolize an otherness—with Adorno, "pure nonidentity"—that was felt as unbearable and that therefore in the end had to be physically done away with. Doing away with otherness means *Gleichmachen* (equalizing), as noted by Adorno and Horkheimer in their "Elements of Anti-Semitism."[18] The Jews, the anti-Semite assures us, are all the same; the equality for which the anti-Semite craves, however, can only be secured by death: only through death itself are all humans made equal, only through death is the unbearable moment of otherness negated. But according to Sartre's analysis of hate, the memory of the other, the inescapable fact that the other once existed, perpetually haunts the killer; having wiped out the other, the killer still cannot get rid of the other. Hence the project of the anti-Semite is bound to fail.[19] (I take this up in greater detail in Chapter 5.)

The exchangeability of one person for another results from the liquidation of their uniqueness as individuals and prepares for the indifference between people that made the Holocaust possible. Eichmann's indifference to his victims forced Arendt to reject the notion of "radical evil" as she had initially conceived it in her book on totalitarianism. Radical evil, she had maintained, is unpunishable in the sense that no punishment can be adequate or commensurate; it is unforgivable; and it is rooted in motives so base as to be beyond human comprehension. The Nazi atrocities had revealed that people are unable to forgive what they cannot punish and that they are unable to punish what has turned out to be unforgivable. Our difficulties in judging Eichmann—philosophically as well as juridically—stem from the discovery that his crime has exploded the standards we rely on when we are to punish and to forgive. As to the third characteristic of radical evil, its escaping human comprehension because rooted in motives so bad as to be simply incomprehensible, the encounter with Eichmann left Arendt with the demand for a reconsideration: finding that Eichmann did not act from base motives, she attributed superfluity to his motives; and *when motives become superfluous, evil is banal rather than radical.* In short, evil deeds do not necessarily imply evil motives. If evil is banal in this sense, no faulty nature or original sinfulness is required to become ensnarled in it. We must be prepared to recognize that the presence of an evil will or of base personal motives was not required of the persons involved in order that they carry out the extermination of the Jews. Confronted with evil deeds, we go searching for evil natures in which to ground them, moral philosophy having taught us that people *do* evil because they *are* evil and, moreover, that to know the good is to do the good. These, then, are the commonplaces of conventional morality that Arendt saw challenged or even crushed by the nondemonic personality of Eichmann, that is to say, by the superfluity of his motives. In this lies the core of Arendt's thesis that evil does not necessarily stem from evil but that it is just as likely to stem from thoughtlessness, especially in the age of "administrative massacres organized by the state apparatus." In this modern setting, the (in psychological terms) aggressively "evil" personality would pose a threat to the sought-for effectiveness of the administrative measures; that personality would only interfere with the smoothness of the apparatus. When motives turn personal as distinguished from professional, they merge with the individuality of the person having them; and because individuality, at least potentially, equals incalculability, the all-important totalitarian aim of controlling people's actions would here be jeopardized. People are not allowed to act but only to execute, insofar as the human ability to act means the ability to "start new unprecedented processes whose outcome remains uncertain and unpredictable." The burden of action, Arendt tells us in *The Human Condition,* is that of "irreversibility and unpredictability" (HC, 233). So, insofar as Eichmann is guilty of allowing himself to be robbed of his autonomy—the autonomy involved being that of the actor whose self-confirmation as a unique individual is evident in every act undertaken—he has allowed himself to be made into a mere executor in the apparatus of the SS, assuming no personal responsibility for the actions he was involved in; and it is exactly for letting this happen that I hold him morally responsible.

Concerning the problem of judgment, Arendt's thesis is that Eichmann failed to judge because he was incapable of representing others in his own mind; he failed to exercise what Kant called the *erweiterte Denkungsart*. The gap separating the particularity of our own position from the universality of that of all others or of society at large is thus bridged by representative thinking; and to foster our faculty of this mode of thinking is what ethics is all about, if my interpretation of Arendt is correct. Prima facie this sounds like a very persuasive conception of the nature of judgment. Nevertheless, I am disturbed by the way in which this conception advocates what I call a mental jump from the particular to the universal. Does not the individual's transcending his or her particularity in order to reach an all-embracing universal point of view actually *endanger* the appreciation of particularity it was supposed to secure? Is there not a paradox involved in the Kantian idea of leaving my own particularity behind in order to reach an ideal universality from which the particularity that judging is concerned with can come to be genuinely appreciated? Arendt, to repeat, claims that Eichmann failed to judge, implying by this that he failed to practice the mental universalization of representative thinking. But my claim is that Eichmann failed to judge because he *failed to identify with his victims as individual human beings*. That is to say, he epitomizes what Adorno called "the inability to identify with the suffering of others."[20] In his case, to judge would have required him qua particularity to identify with other qua particularity; judging, he would see himself as one unique individual approaching another just as unique individual. When we accuse Eichmann of having failed to understand that the murder of millions of innocent people is morally wrong, then we are in reality demanding of him that he should—*e contrario*—have understood what it means to kill *one* out of these millions of people. I would indeed hold that there is no way in which any one of us can comprehend the murder of millions—it simply would mean to ask too much. What we can hope for and strive toward is comprehension of the murder of one human individual. This comprehension may be brought about by identification—by one individual's identifying with another. I claim that moral judgment as exemplified by Eichmann has to do with the meeting of particulars; judgment in the sense here intended comes about when the person who judges frankly *confronts his or her own particularity with the particularity of that which is to be judged*. As in Kant, judgment concerns particulars; but according to the conception here advanced, and thus against Kant, judgment does not approach the particular by way of a preceding mental reaching out toward universality. In denying his victims their right to emerge as individuals, Eichmann abstracted from the feature he was to judge; this abstraction I earlier referred to as dehumanization, making mere numbers, or statistics, out of humans. To be sure, the crime of which I, in agreement with Arendt, hold Eichmann to be guilty, is one against humanity and thus against something universal; this I established above and still subscribe to. My claim, however, is that Eichmann, the actor, and we, judging retrospectively, have to concentrate on the *particular* human being rather than on some collective unit in order to grasp, and thereafter to judge, the concrete reality of the Holocaust.

Given the argument just advanced, the plea I want to repeat is that we differentiate between a cognitive and an emotional aspect of moral judgment. To acknowledge the existence of an emotional moment is of course to go against the view held by Arendt, according to which judgment arises from a merely contemplative pleasure or inactive delight, that is, from what Kant called *untätiges Wohlgefallen*. Applied to the way we judge aesthetically, in saying, This is beautiful, this going against may be correct; applied to the way we judge morally, in saying, This is right, or This is wrong, I hold it to be false. Why? Because we utter moral judgments as participants, as engaged members of a community, not as disinterested spectators emotionally unaffected by the phenomena awaiting our judgment. The point is echoed by Habermas when he asserts that "the objectivating attitude of the nonparticipant observer annuls the communicative roles of I and thou, the first and second persons, and neutralizes the realm of moral phenomena as such." Recognizing that "the world of moral phenomena can be grasped only in the performative attitude of participants in interaction," Habermas notes that "feelings seem to have a similar function for the moral justification of action as sense perceptions have for the theoretical justification of facts."[21]

Arendt on Emotions and Empathy

The systematic function admitted to feelings in the passage cited from Habermas finds no support in the writings of Arendt. Rather than endorse the entry of feelings into ethics or, for that matter, politics, Arendt sees it as crucial that feelings be precluded from the exercise of moral as well as political judgment. Her principal position is brought out in an unequivocal manner in the section on the role of compassion in Rousseau and Robespierre in her book *On Revolution*. The leading ideologues of the French Revolution, she writes, saw reason and the passions as set against each other; identifying thought with reason, they drew the conclusion that reason interfered with passion and compassion alike. Reason, that is, makes a person selfish; it allegedly "prevents nature from identifying itself with the unfortunate sufferer." Arendt continues, "It is as though Rousseau, in his rebellion against reason, had put a soul, torn into two, into the place of the two-in-one that manifests itself in the silent dialogue of the mind with itself which we call thinking. And since the two-in-one of the soul is a conflict and not a dialogue, it engenders passion in its twofold sense of intense suffering and of intense passionateness" (OR, 80). What counted to Rousseau, then, was "selflessness, the capacity to lose oneself in the sufferings of others"; and selflessness in its turn gave rise to compassion, whose magic was that it "opened the heart of the sufferer to the sufferings of others" (OR, 81). In Arendt's account, compassion is cosuffering and concerns only the particular; it "cannot reach out farther than what is suffered by one person" and is therefore not generalizable. Compassion is intrinsically antipolitical and in this respect, Arendt tells us, not unlike love: in both, the distance, the in-between that always exists in human intercourse, is abolished. Arendt accordingly depicts love as "unworldly"; because antipolitical, "love is killed the moment it is displayed in public" (HC, 243, 51). However, in the French Revolution and especially in the course of its aftermath, compassion, unlike love, broke into the worldly domain of political affairs and thus came to claim a political role for which Arendt holds it to be entirely unsuited. Compassion, she asserts, "lends its voice to the suffering itself, which must claim for swift and direct action, that is, for action with the means of violence" (OR, 87). So it is not only that compassion "illegitimately" interfered into politics; more disastrous, compassion, as let loose in the public realm of politics, immediately—and, Arendt holds, inevitably—took on the form of sheer terror, of the "absolute terror" of which Hegel spoke. [22] By contrast, pity, taken here as the sentiment that corresponds to the passion of compassion, does not share compassion's inescapable antipolitical features. Unlike compassion, pity can "reach out to the multitude and therefore, like solidarity, enter the market-place." However, pity owes its very existence to the presence of misfortune; due to its "vested interest in the existence of the weak . . . pity can be enjoyed for its own sake, and this will almost automatically lead to a glorification of its cause, which is the suffering of others" (OR, 89). Thus it was that Robespierre's pity-inspired virtue "played havoc with justice and made light of laws" (OR, 90). Being a sentiment and *eo ipso* boundless, pity does not admit of any limitations; it can only amplify the violence and terror initially springing from the passion of compassion.

Gershom Scholem, in a letter to Arendt addressing the controversy over her Eichmann book, charges her with a lack of "Ahabeth Israel," that is to say, with a failure "to love the Jewish people." In view of the immediately preceding, Arendt's response is no surprise. "I have never in my life," she writes back, " 'loved' any people or collective. I indeed love only my friends and the only kind of love I know of and believe in is the love of persons" (NA, 73). The advocacy of a love displayed in public and taking, as it were, a whole people as its object, amounts to a category mistake. Convinced that history is on her side, Arendt reminds Scholem of the section in *On Revolution* just dealt with, pointing to the "disastrous results" that accrue "when emotions are displayed in public and become a factor in political affairs" (NA, 74).

In all of this, Arendt's closeness to Kant is unmistakable. Kant excludes love from the moral, and sympathy is denied a moral status exactly on account of its being lovable and rooted in love. Kant's point is that we do not love the moral law, we respect it. In his *Critique of Judgment* (see esp. §§ 29, 67), love corresponds to the beautiful; respect, to the sublime (*das Erhabene*). Respect is a formal principle, whereas love is a substantive one. We respect people on account of their (formal) humanity, whereas we love them on account of their particular (substantive) qualities that endear them to us. In Kant, formal equality is rooted in formal respect, and both converge in the exercise of the formal right of autonomous judgment. All subjects are accorded this right as a matter of respect, and in this consists their formal equality.[23]

As Ronald Beiner has observed, the principal lesson to be drawn from Arendt on this issue is identical to that found in Kant: love belongs outside politics and ethics because it *impairs* judgment, and, according to this reasoning, what holds for love in this respect *holds for all other emotions too.* Hence, it is of the utmost importance that emotions en bloc be kept out of the exercise of judgment, inasmuch as their partaking in judgment inevitably and necessarily helps undermine it. In an often-quoted passage describing the "representative thinking" at work in political judgment, Arendt tells us that the process of making present to my mind the standpoints of those who are absent is "a question neither of empathy, as though I tried to be or to feel like somebody else, nor of counting noses and joining a majority, but of being and thinking in my own identity where actually I am not" (BPF, 241). Now, what Arendt says about the (possible) role of empathy in political judgment here is entirely representative of what she *in general* holds about the role of emotions in judgment—be it aesthetic, political, or moral judgment. Common to all these kinds of judgment is that judgment is and must remain *disinterested* and *impartial*, and it is precisely these features of disinterestedness and impartiality that would be seriously endangered were emotions to enter into its exercise. That, in broad terms, is Arendt's position.

What this position implies, to begin with, is that Arendt grants the dualism of "reason" and "passions" of which Rousseau spoke. Arendt's quarrel with Rousseau does not concern the dualism as such; this remains unchallenged in her argument. Rather, Rousseau favors one side of the dualism, that is, passions, whereas Arendt favors the other, that is, reason. Moreover, Arendt not only fails to call into question the tacitly presumed validity of the dualism; she also fails to subject to scrutiny the alleged "selflessness" of feelings and sentiments alike. Empathy is defined as the individual's attempt "to be or feel like somebody else." As in the critique of Rousseau, the essence of the feeling or sentiment in question is an assumed "giving oneself up," that is, *abandoning oneself* in the sense of turning self-less. But is not such a conception of empathy inadmissibly narrow? Stronger still, is it not downright erroneous? In my view, Arendt heaps empathy together with the notoriously opaque notion of *Sichhineinversetzen* (placing oneself inside) encountered in the hermeneutics of the early Dilthey.[24] There, to be sure, the feeling-with-the-other is attained only at the price of abandoning oneself and one's specific identity. In this model, then, what is demanded is that I give up my own standpoint in order to gain access to that of the other. Indeed, Dilthey's entire theory of *Fremdverstehen* rests on the idea that the one who seeks to understand others has to renounce his or her own standpoint if he or she is to succeed, so that the more I suspend my own identity the more likely it is that my recognition of the identity of the other will be a genuine and unbiased one.

Against this conventional understanding of empathy—which is largely implicit in Arendt but which I nevertheless, on the face of her dismissive definition in the passage quoted, suspect her of subscribing to—I argue in later sections that emotions do occupy a systematic place in the exercise of judgment. In particular, empathy is to be acknowledged as an emotional faculty in its own right. The very essence of empathy lies in one subject's retaining instead of abandoning his or her own standpoint and identity in the course of his or her endeavour to recognize the other *as* other—as different, not the same—by virtue of a feeling-with. Empathy entails a *Sichmitbringen*, not a *Sichaufgeben*; that is, empathy entails that I maintain my identity, not that I abandon it. The emotional "projection" (I hesitate to use the term) of myself into the place of the other leaves intact the space between myself as one and the other as other.

The conception of empathy suggested here connects with what I said above about moral judgment, namely, that moral judgment has to do with the meeting of particulars. Judgment, I wrote, comes about when the person who judges frankly confronts his or her own particularity with the particularity of that which is to be judged. Empathy I define as humanity's basic emotional faculty, and as one indispensably at work in an unimpaired exercise of moral judgment. Being essentially a *Sichmitbringen* as opposed to a *Sichaufgeben*, empathy preserves the "meeting of particulars" I earlier spoke of as the very kernel of moral judgment. In preserving this kernel, empathy leaves intact the distinctness and unique identity of the person who empathizes as well as that of his or her addressee. Having stated this, I hasten to add that empathy *maintains* distinctness; it does not *absolutize* it, nor does it *suspend* it. The phenomenon of empathy arises because your pain is yours and not mine, because we are different individual human beings; the call for empathy can be met because we are all human beings, principally sharing the same access to the experience of pain. Max Scheler wanted to make the same point when he wrote that "sympathy does not proclaim the essential identity of persons . . . but actually presupposes a pure essential *difference* between them."[25] Eichmann's principal failure was the failure to recognize the Jews as distinct human beings, as unique individuals. Because he perceived the Jews as *Sachen*, and thus not as bearers of distinctness and particularity, the very starting point for empathy was undermined. But this is not all. The case of Eichmann transcends the issue of empathy; it forces us to consider the paramount question of the connection between *dehumanization* and *moral neutralization*.

But Arendt remains a Kantian not only in denying emotions in general and empathy in particular a systematic place in ethics. She takes herself to have "discovered" the "secret" political philosophy of Kant in his third *Critique*. Her thesis is that the specific type of judgment we exercise about political affairs is in fact captured in Kant's notion of "reflective judgment." What precisely is it that justifies this assimilation of the political to the aesthetic? Prima facie, it seems that Arendt is led to her thesis on purely conceptual grounds. Arendt, that is, conceives of politics as "worldly," as a phenomenon of the "common world" and the public sphere. It follows that in politics we are concerned with judgment of appearances (*Erscheinungen*), of what appears and is displayed for all to see and comment on in the public world (*Öffentlichkeit*). And this very feature—appearing in a public world—is what Arendt holds politics and aesthetics to have in common. Publicity is constitutive of art and politics per se, and thus not simply a condition for their being intersubjectively shared and assessed. Therefore, by pressing people against one another and destroying the space between them, totalitarian ideologies undermine the most crucial prerequisite of art and politics alike: their appearing *in* a public space and *to* a public, a plurality of people (see OT, 466). Yet what is it that is said to "appear" here? Arendt answers, particulars. So in judging aesthetics and politics alike, the judgment is of appearances and hence of particulars. Indeed, it is so in the strong sense of appreciating the particular *qua* particular, that is, without subsuming it under a pregiven universal or concept or law. For this reason, aesthetic and political phenomena alike call for the exercise of "reflective" as distinguished from "determinate" judgment, and Arendt's turning to Kant here is largely prompted by his development of the former type of judgment (see esp. CJ, B XXV).

In order now to test the cogency of Arendt's thesis, let me recall how the issue arose. Toward the end of her postscript to *Eichmann in Jerusalem*, Arendt observes that "there remains, however, one fundamental problem . . . touching upon the central moral questions of all time, namely upon the nature and function of human judgment. What we have demanded in these trials . . . is that human beings be capable of telling right from wrong." She goes on to describe these individuals as having to "decide each instance as it arose, because no rules existed for the unprecedented" (EJ, 294, 295). There existing, in other words, no general rules to be abided by, what is demanded here is reflective judgment. Now, consider how "human judgment" is described in the passage: it is the ability to "tell right from wrong." This ability, as I see it, is not what human judgment or judgment in general amounts to; rather, telling right from wrong is what *moral* judgment is concerned with. However, in her *Lectures*, Arendt says of Kant that "he withdrew moral propositions from the new faculty [i.e., judgment]; . . . the moral question of right and wrong is to be decided neither by taste nor judgment but by reason alone" (LM, 2:255). In confirmation of this view, Arendt repeatedly insists that "judgment is not practical reason" and that "judgments . . . are not cognitions" (LK, 15, 77).

What seems evident from the quotations given is that Arendt's position on judgment is ambiguous. At this juncture, the uneasiness left by her various statements cannot be overcome by invoking temporality; here, it is of no avail to try to distinguish between the past-oriented judgment of the spectator and the future-oriented judgment of the actor. Rather, this time the problem concerns the relation between judgment and knowledge. Reflecting on Eichmann, Arendt depicts judgment as the ability to "tell right from wrong." Writing on Kant, she contends that "the moral question of right and wrong" is to be decided *not* by judgment but "by reason alone." But

Arendt cannot have it both ways. She cannot argue that judgment is about telling right from wrong *and* that the moral question of right and wrong is decided not by judgment but by reason alone.

If there were any way of resolving this contradiction, it might look as follows. Whereas Arendt's reflections on Eichmann helped her *pose* the question of judgment, her reflections on Kant, put to paper a good decade later, provided her with a philosophical framework in which to pursue the question in a more systematic manner, so that the latter reflections are the ones offering an "answer"—or rather the closest she ever came to one. If this reading is granted, then Arendt came to answer the question of judgment in terms different from those in which she first framed it. Hence, once she turned to Kant, his position became her own—namely, that the moral question of right and wrong is settled by reason and not by judgment, because judgments are not cognitions and therefore give us no knowledge of right and wrong.

The upshot is that Arendt's (characteristically unsystematic) refusal to bring moral judgment within the ambit of rational discourse proper entails her denying moral judgment a cognitive status. Drawing her very own lesson from the late appropriation of Kant's third *Critique*, she ends up barring knowledge from practical or moral judgment. The latter, inasmuch as it deals with praxis, deals with publicly voiced and debated opinions, beliefs, and convictions for which, Arendt holds, no truth claim can be made. Through its link to praxis, moral judgment is passed with respect to matters of *doxa*, whereas knowledge, by contrast, is linked to *theōria* and thus allows for the validity claim of *epistēmē* proper. To Arendt, "truth" equals *alētheia;* it has to do with what is universal and necessary as opposed to what is particular and contingent. Its philosophical source is not Kant after all but classical Greek epistemology. As Habermas has written, "With [an] outmoded concept of theoretical knowledge that builds upon ultimate evidence, Arendt abstains from conceiving the coming to agreement about political questions as a rational formation of consensus."[26] Consequently, Arendt's position leaves her with the problem of why we should be expected to take seriously opinions and judgments that are devoid of claims to truth. I can see no convincing answer to this problem in Arendt's work.

Since I have pursued rather diverse lines of argument in this chapter, it is useful to end by sorting out the issues that carry systematic importance. My primary concern has been with Arendt's reflections on Eichmann. Eichmann was a loyal and conscientious officer; he always saw to it that his conduct conformed to what his superiors expected from him. However, since in Nazi Germany the canons of legislation were systematically altered so as to render all measures taken against the Jews strictly "legal," the triviality of always examining an order for its manifest legality and hence of ordinary professional loyalty soon became anything but trivial: for all the inconspicuousness of his character, Eichmann made a seminal contribution to mass murder. Struck by Eichmann's dullness, cliché-ridden language, and lack of anything that might resemble spontaneity, Arendt came to assess his failure as a deficient capacity for judgment, ultimately as a manifestation of "thoughtlessness."

I have questioned Arendt's assessment. Why did she assume that Eichmann's failure was on the level of judgment and thinking? Why did she not consider the possibility that the capacity in which Eichmann was lacking was emotional, as opposed to purely cognitive? I have pointed out some immanent reasons for this selectivity in Arendt's work. These reasons mostly pertain to Arendt's attempt to straddle the Kantian and Socratic traditions. By persisting in a "thinking without banisters," Arendt aspired to an independence in her thought, yet her characteristic vacillations and many flagrant contradictions, some of which I find unresolvable, are the high price she paid.

The selectivity of Arendt's cognitivist approach to the challenge Eichmann poses to moral theory in general and to moral judgment in particular has inspired me to launch my own alternative account. I raise the hypothesis Arendt neglected: that Eichmann's original failure was of an emotional kind. Investigating this hypothesis has led me to propose a distinction between three levels of moral performance: perception, judgment, and action. In this sequence, the serial order of priority is fixed: lest action be indistinguishable from behavior devoid of intentionality, it rests on judgment; lest judgment be blind or uninformed, it rests on perception. Perception "gives" judgment its object. This implies that the initial access to the domain of moral phenomena, of entities requiring *moral* judgment, is located not on the level of judgment but on that of perception. In short, perception precedes and facilitates judgment. When we inquire into the prerequisites of perception—Arendt never did—we must distinguish between the contribution made by the cognitive and that made by the emotional faculty. A consequence of this conception is that an impairment, or a more or less selective or limited blocking, of one faculty constitutes a sufficient condition for the failure to accomplish an act of moral perception; and failing on this level, which in my scheme is logically the first one in a three-part sequence, is a fortiori a sufficient condition for a (subsequent) failure on the level of judgment. Also, a failure on the level of perception tends to be less conspicuous, less notable and discernible, than a failure on the level of judgment. Acts of judgment are more overt, more manifest and visible, than the acts of perception that precede them and constitute their sine qua non. Moreover, acts of judgment are what we encounter, what we discuss, what we defend or reject in our (verbalized) goings-on with other moral agents. By contrast, acts of perception do not from the outset possess eminent articulability; they are only indirectly open to intersubjective illumination and discussion. This is so because it is only when we dwell on a manifest act of judgment and ask, How did it come about? What made the person judge in this particular way? that we can embark on a separate analysis of perception viewed as the level logically prior to judgment. I assume that this lack of direct manifestness and, in this sense, of visibility may account for Arendt's preoccupation with judgment at the expense of perception. Later chapters show just how typical this is.

The task in the chapters that follow is to substantiate my notion of moral performance. Arendt has given me the chance to put forward a most tentative and preliminary formulation of my position; herein lies the constructive upshot of my disagreement with Arendt over Eichmann.

There is a sense, unnoted above, in which Arendt's reply to Scholem's charge that she failed to "love the Jewish people" carries systematic importance too. Arendt holds that to fail here is to make no mistake at all—at least not philosophically. Her argument is that (to her) love is and must remain restricted to the love of single persons, of individuals known within an intimate setting. It therefore amounts to a category mistake to advocate public display of love for a collective, for example, the Jewish people. I agree with Arendt's argument—with the qualification, however, that it is taken to apply to love, to the specific feeling for particular others we experience as love. Hence, I agree with Arendt that, lest love be misconstrued, love can be neither public nor directed to a collective; love thus understood is therefore correctly seen as excluded from the realm of political affairs and political discourse.

Yet Arendt must be careful not to commit her own sort of category mistake. There are two distinct levels involved here; they must be kept apart, or else the one may be conflated with the other. The category mistake I have in mind consists in inferring from the specificity and exclusivity of, for example, love qua feeling that humanity's emotional capacities per se must be barred from entering the business of moral performance in general and moral judgment in particular. This would be to infer from the level of manifest, particular feelings to the level of humanity's underlying constitutive capacity for developing the entire series of possible emotional relations with others. In other words, the inference would entail that since a particular feeling such as love—or compassion or pity, to say nothing about hate or wickedness—can be convincingly shown sometimes to mislead one's moral judgment, it has a fortiori been proved that the emotional faculty in humanity that gives rise to this host of particular feelings must be kept at arm's length from moral performance.

Arendt proves nothing of the sort. To validate the inference just sketched would take an argument of a type she nowhere offers. The main reason she gives no elaborate argument to this effect is that to do so would presuppose drawing a systematic distinction between the levels involved—but typically not acknowledged—in the inference: the level of manifest, particular feelings and the level of humanity's capacity for relating to others through emotion, through having the ability to feel. It is precisely this type of distinction Arendt fails to make, hence also to observe, in her quarrel with Scholem over love. She therefore, erroneously, held the (correctly judged) exclusiveness of love—that is, of this particular feeling—to prove that the qualities of people that make them into emotional beings must be excluded from the moral domain lest sheer terror or irrationality ensue and the moral domain be fundamentally jeopardized. In Arendt's case, the more immanent reason for her neglect to distinguish between the two levels has to do with the admittedly arguable fact that the Socratic and the Kantian traditions of moral thought from which she drew inspiration both share a priority of humanity's cognitive faculty over its emotional one—not in all matters, of course, but surely as far as the view of moral performance is concerned; and this suffices for my present point.

So it is that Arendt fails to separate the phenomenology of overt feelings such as love and compassion from the constitutive faculty in humanity from which they arise and by virtue of which their development and manifestation are made possible. It may be recalled that a similar failure to distinguish levels undermines MacIntyre's philosophically shallow "refutation" of emotivism. The difference between a level of manifestation and a level of constitution is elaborated below. Thus, in Chapter 3 I turn to a critique of Max Scheler that seeks to clarify the systematic relations among love, sympathy, and empathy; in Chapter 4 I examine the category of perception; and in Chapter 5 I discuss how the "dark side" of emotion, that is, a feeling such as hate, may endanger moral performance and even lead to downright immoral conduct—at least if allowed to have the last word. Only if we make sure to observe the difference between the levels involved here will we avoid throwing the baby out with the bathwater. If the host of possible particular feelings or emotional attitudes toward others is not kept conceptually apart from humanity's basic emotional faculty, that of empathy, the point about the genuinely moral significance of "our being emotional beings too" will be missed. In particular, I seek to demonstrate the error in all attempts to pick some particular manifest feeling—be it (positively) love, be it (negatively) hate—in order to conclude from its apparent contingency/subjectivity/irrationality that humanity's emotional abilities per se are "thus" proved to be alien to the business of moral perception and judgment. Though invariably unable to acknowledge it, such attempts jump from one level to the other, from manifestation to constitution. In a word, what I set out to show is that the inference to which they are committed is a non sequitur.

To sum up, Arendt is preoccupied with—and often offers brilliant insights into—humanity's cognitive and intellectual capacities; nowhere does she subject humanity's specific emotional faculty to proper philosophical inquiry; more to the point, she has no concept of such a faculty at her disposal. This makes it all the more important that we liberate our thinking about morality from the cognitivist framework Arendt, from beginning to end, remained a captive of—despite her sought-for independence and break with tradition.

3

Scheler's Grounding of Ethics in Love

The demonstrated absence of an affirmative assessment of humanity's emotional abilities in the work of Hannah Arendt has laid upon me the task of stating in more constructive terms what it is that she failed to offer. A philosopher who strived to put humanity's emotional being at the very center of his theory was Max Scheler, to whose program for a material ethics I now turn.

Scheler sets out to do justice to the richness and complexity of humanity's emotional life and to establish that life's central importance in ethics. Against the background of a typology of feelings, Scheler postulates a correspondence between types of feeling on the one hand and modalities of value on the other. In his scheme, sensuous feelings correspond to the values of pleasure and pain; vital feelings, to honorability and baseness; and spiritual feelings, to values of the mind.

Scheler considers Kant his great philosophical adversary. My critique of

Scheler reveals the irony of this. For, despite major criticisms, Scheler remains so impressed by Kant's analysis of pure reason that his own "critique" of the emotional life is conducted within a conceptual framework unmistakably Kantian; in fact, I call it an inverted Kantianism. My thesis is that Scheler, far from discarding Kant, mirrors the architectonics of his *Critique of Pure Reason*: Scheler treats emotions the way Kant treated theoretical cognition—as admitting of an analysis maintaining their strict apriority, objectivity, and lawlikeness.

Scheler's Program for a Material Ethics

Max Scheler's work on ethics attempts a full-scale repudiation of Kant's practical philosophy. Deeply dissatisfied with Kantian ethics' overwhelmingly negative assessment of the emotions, Scheler sets out in his moral theory to construct a comprehensive typology of feelings. The task as Scheler sees it is not only to substitute a positive account of feelings for the dismissive Kantian one but also, more important, to explode the dichotomies of formal and material, a priori and a posteriori, and to do so by virtue of a theory about humanity's emotional life.

In the introduction to his book *Der Formalismus in der Ethik und die materiale Wertethik*, Scheler declares that his aim is to scrutinize the very idea of a formal ethics rather than to provide a strictly immanent critique of Kant's philosophy. Indeed, to seek the latter would mean to remain loyal or, better, blind to the more or less tacit presuppositions of formal ethics à la Kant with which Scheler's critique is concerned. A first way of spelling out these presuppositions is to ask what Kant would hold against the idea of a *material* ethics. To Kant, contends Scheler, a material ethics must "necessarily" equal an ethics of goods and purposes: of hedonism, because having to resort to states of sensual pleasure; of heteronomy, because failing to establish the autonomy of the moral agent; of the mere legality of action, because unable to maintain the morality (*Moralität*) of the will; of inclination-based egoism, because at a loss to justify a moral law independent of man qua natural-sensuous being. Perhaps most important of all is the claim, attributed to Kant, that "every non-formal [*materiale*] ethics is necessarily of only empirical-inductive and a posteriori validity; only a formal ethics gains certainty a priori and independently of inductive experience" (Fo, 7).

It is beyond the scope of this chapter to deal with every single one of the listed charges against a material ethics. Instead, I concentrate mainly on the last one, where it is asserted that a material ethics must renounce the idea of an a priori foundation, implying that the content and the validity claim of its analyses can only be empirical.

For Kant, says Scheler, what makes people moral is their capacity for reason. People's reason stands opposed to their having feelings, inclinations, and needs, that is to say, to their sensuousness. The dichotomy of autonomy and heteronomy is but a reflection of humans being both rational and sensuous. As a result of Kant's attempt to found ethics on reason and autonomous will, all that fails to conform to the form of reason as embodied in the moral law—that is, its purity, objectivity, and universality—comes to be equated with sensuousness. Thus, the entire emotional life of man is reduced to *Sinnlichkeit* insofar as it fails to meet the Kantian definition of practical reason. Feelings are portrayed as alogical, contingent, capricious; to act from them would be to forgo reason and hence autonomy and to yield to the sheer sensory pleasures. In Kant's conception, emotional capacities such as love and empathy are but feelings; and with respect to feelings, no separate, cognitively significant *faculty* can be claimed (I shall return to this point in the last section). Rather, feelings are ultimately sensuous (*sinnliche Gefühle*); and being sensuous, feelings not only seek but also originate in pleasure (*sinnliche Lust*; see Kant's *Critique of Practical Reason*, A133ff.). Humanity is not so much the subject of feelings as subjected to them; to give in to one's feelings means to act not only heteronomously but also egoistically, to seek pleasure for its own sake and ultimately to live the life of a downright hedonist.

Scheler sets out to reject the reason-sensuousness dichotomy and thereby the entire series of assumptions deriving from it. In correcting the Kantian caricature of humanity's emotional life, Scheler wants to show that the link between feelings and sensory pleasure, and between feelings and egoism or hedonism, is but rationalist prejudice, and that a material ethics does not have to be eudaimonistic. Insofar as Kant sees "formal" and "material," "a priori" and "a posteriori," as corresponding to the division between reason and sensuousness, a critique of the latter opens the way for a novel understanding of the former. Only the stubborn hegemony of the Kantian tradition can explain why it has taken so long finally to raise the question

> whether there are original as well as essential differentiations in rank among the essences of acts and functions at the base of the alogical of our spiritual life, that is, whether these acts and foundations have

an "originality" comparable to that of the acts in which we comprehend objects in pure logic—in other words, whether there is also a *pure* intuiting and feeling, a *pure* loving and hating, a *pure* striving and willing, which are *as* independent of the psychological organization of man as pure thought, and which at the same time possess their own original laws that cannot be reduced to laws of empirical psychic life—this question is not even asked by those who share this prejudice. (Fo, 254)

In putting the question in these terms, Scheler leaves no doubt as to what kind of material ethics he seeks to work out—"an absolute, a priori, *and* emotional ethics." Scheler again and again cites Blaise Pascal's expressions "ordre du coeur," "logique du coeur," and "le coeur a ses raisons," which he takes to anticipate his idea of an "eternal and absolute lawfulness of feeling, loving, and hating which is as absolute as that of pure logic, but which is not reducible to intellectual lawfulness" (Fo, 254). Scheler offers the following outline of his program:

There is a type of experiencing whose "objects" are completely inaccessible to reason; reason is as blind to them as ears and hearing are blind to colours. It is a kind of experience that leads us to *genuinely* objective objects and the eternal order among them, i.e., to *values* and the order of ranks among them. And the order and laws contained in this experience are as exact and evident as those of logic and mathematics; that is, there are evident interconnections and oppositions among values and value-attitudes and among the acts of preferring, etc., which are built on them, and on the basis of these a genuine grounding of moral decisions and laws for such decisions is both possible and necessary. (Fo, 255)

As brought out in this passage, Scheler's program for a material ethics is part of a larger philosophy, that is, of a *Wertmetaphysik* (a metaphysics of value). In the exposition that follows, I confine myself to those aspects of Scheler's metaphysical theory that bear directly on his ethics.

According to Scheler, the existence of values is purely ideal, whereas the existence of goods (*Güter*) is real. Values are independent of emotional states and desires, as well as of the objects and carriers of goods. Values are "ideal objects" in the same sense as the qualities of color and sound; existing only ideally, values constitute an absolute, invariable sphere of being. Scheler depicts values as "facts that belong to a specific mode of experience" (Fo, 187). The organ corresponding to the values on the side of the human subject is the *emotionale Aktzentrum* (emotional center of action), which receives the given value in a spontaneous fashion, without having, as it were, to pass through a theoretical-cognitive sphere of mediation. In a word, Scheler asserts the *Unmittelbarkeit des Werterlebens* (immediacy of the perception of value) secured by a class of emotional acts in which the absolute and ideal sphere of value is grasped without any sort of recourse to human inclinations. The manner in which we come to grasp the values is as pure as these ideal values themselves, meaning that there is such a thing as "pure" feeling, "pure" loving, at work in the emotional acts Scheler sees as the peculiar cognitive organ facilitating the reception of ideal values.

Scheler postulates a strict division between emotional acts and states of feeling. To highlight the former, Scheler declares the existence of an original intentional feeling, as is found in "pure" loving or "pure" hatred. So whereas the link between states of feeling and objects is a mediated one set up through theoretical acts, the intentional feeling, preferring (*Vorziehen*), loving, is an original act directing itself at something objective, that is, at values. Admittedly, Scheler's account of intentional feeling is somewhat vague. It is clear that he wants to distinguish it from emotions (*Gefühle*), affects, and so-called *emotionale Antwortsreaktionen* (emotional response reactions). Among his numerous examples, the most helpful is perhaps that concerning anger. "Certain evils," he writes, "must be 'comprehended' beforehand in *feeling* if anger is to be aroused" (Fo, 258). I take this to mean that what I actually "feel" or experience—as "arising in me" or as "declining," as being "brought about" by this or that person or incident—is but the phenomenal response to a feeling-that preceding it and generating it; a feeling, moreover, that is not "a dead state or a factual state of affairs that can enter into associative connections or be related to them; nor is such a feeling a 'token'; [rather] it is a goal-determined movement . . . a punctual movement, whether objec-tively directed from the ego or coming toward the ego as a movement in which something *is* given to me and in which it comes to 'appearance.' " Notwithstanding the vagueness of his line of argument, Scheler's thesis is clear: "This feeling therefore has the same relation to its value-correlate as 'representing' has to its 'object,' namely, an intentional relation" (Fo, 257–58). Scheler seeks to establish the same original a priori content, the same *Beziehungsgesetzlichkeit* (lawfulness of relation), for the emotional acts of feeling and loving that he claims for their objective correlates, the values. Just as the principle of logical contradiction teaches us that we cannot consistently and in the same respect assert both p and $-p$ to be true, so we cannot consistently and in the same respect feel both F and $-F$ about a specific object. Hence, the principle of logical contradiction is no more basic or universal than the principle of so-called emotional contradiction. The category of emotional acts and the concept of original intentional feeling are assumed by Scheler to demonstrate that apriority, universality, and logicality are to be accorded to humanity's emotional life and not exclusively to its intellectual one. Asserting the irreducibility of the emotional life, Scheler purports to explode the Kantian distinction between reason and sensuousness and, with that, all the aforementioned assumptions usually derived from it. The entire schema is challenged once Scheler starts analyzing the different components of the emotional life, which is not something capricious, contingent, or subjective, to be handed over to psychology and the empirical sciences. Rather, humanity's emotional life possesses its own peculiar objectivity, and it conforms to laws and hierarchies no less a priori, no less scientifically strict than the ones studied by Kant in his *Critique of Pure Reason*.

To appreciate the full significance of Scheler's core thesis, a distinction must be made *within* the domain crudely referred to as "humanity's emotional life." This is the purpose of Scheler's endeavor to single out the emotional acts and the original intentional feeling: the *Aktzentrum* of feeling, preferring, and loving/hating constitutes a separate and autonomous sphere of the human mind (i.e., *ein geistiger Bereich*) no less distinct and "pure" than the cognitive apparatus uncovered by Kant in his first *Critique*. To repeat, there is such a thing as "pure" feeling. From this sphere of the emotional acts, Scheler divorces the sphere of the sensuous, vital-organic, and corporeal, for which no purity and thus no universality are to be claimed. The implication of the distinction drawn within our emotional life (typically neglected in Kant and in the many varieties of formal ethics) is that the dichotomies of a priori and a posteriori, having been shown to be untenable in their Kantian application to the reason-versus-sensuousness schema, come to be "imported," as it were, to grant pure emotional acts the status of apriority, and sensuousness the far less dignified status of aposteriority.

In Scheler's typology of feelings, he distinguishes among (1) sensuous feelings (*sinnliche Gefühle*), (2) bodily feelings (as states) or life feelings (as functions), (3) purely spiritual feelings (*rein seelische Gefühle*), and (4) feelings of the mind (*geistige Gefühle*). Scheler states that common to all sorts of feelings is their experienced relatedness to an I or a person; in every case of my feeling "something," the object of the feeling is more closely tied to me, the one who feels, than it is in the case of my knowing or imagining something. As opposed to the objects of intellectual cognition, feelings are *"originaliter* on the ego. They can be kept *away*, but only by way of activity. That is, they always return quasi-automatically to the ego." It follows that "feelings cannot be controlled or managed arbitrarily. They can be controlled and managed only indirectly, by controlling their causes and effects (expression, actions)" (Fo, 332–33).

Within the typology itself, Scheler defines *sensuous feeling* as eminently concrete and tangible; coming from a particular part of the body, the origin of the sensation it produces is always easily localized. A sensuous feeling essentially exists as a state, the intensity of which varies. Nowhere, however, does it arise as a function or as an act, being too primitive to attain by itself any form of intentionality whatsoever. Its relatedness to an I is a severely restricted one; qua state, it is rather the state of a limited part of my body than of myself as a person. It is, moreover, of short duration, its existence characteristically having the actuality of a here (this part of my body) and a now (at this very moment). Finally—and this is a point of crucial ethical importance—the "feeling" I have in the case of a sensuous feeling is the one that is most subject to my own will or lack of such. A sensuous feeling, that is, can be put under the control of my will, for example, intensified or even produced in the first place (I decide to cut my thumb); in short, it is to a very great extent susceptible to manipulation.

Not so—and this is the ethical significance—with a *spiritual feeling*. If I am sad, the sadness I feel is more intimately a part of me, of the very essence of the person I am, than a cut in my thumb would be. It is not for me simply to decide to produce or annul my sadness. Even when I contemplate my sadness, hoping that it will soon go away, I do not contemplate a part of me from which I am detached; I contemplate *myself* and the state in which I *am*. The feeling of my sadness is more original, spontaneous, and encompassing than the feeling or, better, sensation of my injured thumb; and the more spontaneous (as opposed to reactive) my feelings—that is, the more they are part of me and affect me qua person—the less the feelings in question will be subject to my will and hence arbitrarily changeable. Otherwise put, the more a feeling is an integral part of my whole person, the less "reactive" it is, and the less possible it is for me to influence its presence or absence. A further ethical implication of this difference is that a sensuous, reactive feeling such as (physical) pain cannot give rise to sympathy or compassion in the sense of a genuine feeling-with-another-person. "Sensuous feelings," maintains Scheler, "can be the stimuli of emotional contagion, but they can never be the foundation of fellow feeling [*Mitfühlen*]" (Fo, 335). I can even, says Scheler, "*feelingly* bring to mind a spiritual feeling [*seelisches Gefühl*] that I have never experienced, though this given content does not become an actual feeling-state" (Fo, 334). By contrast, a sensuous feeling remains tied to the here-and-now actuality of the sensation accompanying it, a sensation that is mine insofar as my thumb is mine, and from which you, my alter, are psychically distanced, in a way that you are not (I can always hope) from my—"current" rather than "actual"—sadness. So sadness (or happiness) furnishes the ethical phenomena of sympathy and compassion with a foundation denied them in the event of a feeling of (physical-sensory) pain or pleasure.

The upshot of this discussion is that the "lower," the more primitive and reactive, a feeling, the more it is to be conceived as a possible direct outcome of an action or a decision of ours. Conversely—and again, this is what counts from an ethical perspective—the "higher," the more spiritual and spontaneous, a feeling, the less it lies in our power to "decide" its presence and endurance. Spiritual feelings are characterized by the continuity of their existence as well as of their meaning or import. They are part of the person having them to the extent of coming to define him or her. But, here too, an internal differentiation is called for. As suggested by my illustration above, sadness is a spiritual feeling, albeit a comparatively superficial and passing one. Distinct from sadness is sorrow, which is less profound than grief, which in its turn is more transitory than mourning or—to put an end to the continuum—downright depression. The further a feeling is from the initial sadness, and the closer it is to the eventual depression, the more deeply the person having that feeling is immersed and caught up in it, which is to say that the person is increasingly "overwhelmed" by the feeling, coming to view not only the event(s) that gave rise to the feeling but also, ultimately, his or her whole life in light of that feeling. "For in true bliss and despair . . . all ego-states seem to be extinguished. Spiritual feelings seem to stream forth, as it were, from the very source of spiritual acts. The light or darkness of these feelings appears to bathe *everything* given in the inner world and the outer world in these acts. They 'permeate' all special contents of experience" (Fo, 343). Scheler takes this stubborn pervasiveness, the totalizing power of these feelings, to bear witness to their being "absolute" as opposed to relative. We do not mourn something or, rather, someone the way we are happy "about" or "with" something. Having, for whatever reason, arisen, the spiritual feelings "color" all subsequent experience, force the withdrawal of every other feeling or "state of mind"; being thus spontaneous and original, they "fill" the very core of our persons and gradually define—or, better, redefine—our "world." As Scheler points out, it belongs to the essence of these feelings that "either they are *not* experienced at all, *or* they take possession of the *whole* of our being" (Fo, 343). There is nothing outside the subject that "motivates" him to "achieve" a spiritual feeling. The foundation from which that feeling springs is rather to be found in the very *being* of the person himself, and "since these feelings are *not conditioned* by value-complexes exterior to the person and his possible acts, it is clear that they take root in the value-nature of the person *himself* and his being and value-being, which stand above all acts" (Fo, 344).

In summary, Scheler proposes a material ethics opposing Kant's formal moral theory, an ethics that, far from being empirical, let alone eudaimonistic, establishes strict objectivity and apriority within the domain of humanity's emotional life. The so-called emotional acts, portrayed as cases of pure intentional feeling, are to serve to establish strict objectivity and apriority in the Schelerian architectonics. Depicted as corresponding to these acts is a hierarchy of ideal values, for which strict objectivity and apriority are likewise claimed. This thesis of correspondence is but part of a larger metaphysical theory. What matters for my present purposes is that Scheler postulates a correspondence between types of feeling on the one hand and modalities of value on the other. In Scheler's model—starting from below—sensuous feelings correspond to the values of pleasure and pain; the vital feelings, to honorability and baseness; and the spiritual feelings, to values of the mind, of which the principal value is holiness. Again, it is worth emphasizing that Scheler's ethical theory postulates the same kind of objectivity, universality, and apriority on *both sides* of the correspondences, implying that the purity of an emotional act such as love is "matched" by the purity of the ideal (personality) value at which it is directed. In short, the quality of the feeling is in every case met, equaled, or mirrored in the specific quality of the value to which it correlates.

The Concept of Love in Scheler's Ethics

Scheler splits Brentano's term *vorziehende Liebe* into two parts. "Preference" is rendered purely cognitive, a receptive organ in the sense of Scheler's value-objective apriorism. "Love," on the other hand, comes to signify a peculiar way of relating to value objects, and to view this relating-to as a cognitive function is to misunderstand it—as did Brentano, according to Scheler. His thesis is that love is the foundation of all value feeling. Because love is posited as the very peak of the hierarchy of human feelings, one would expect Scheler—in order to confirm his sketched theory of correspondence—to assert that love represents a direct and unmediated grasp of the absolute and ideal value. But this is not the case. Scheler is explicit about the "objects" of love being not ideal values in themselves but rather the positively existing goods and persons. The value to which love is the correlate is therefore essentially personality value. The "what" of the original intention of love is "not a value, but rather objects which are valuable. I 'love' no value; rather I always love something which is valuable [*werthaltig*]" (Sym, 170). Yet love is not reactive; it is not a passive relating to a given value (e.g., person). To the contrary, love is truly spontaneous. Being the highest form of our intentional emotional life, it is throughout active in the sense of being a continuous *movement* from the existing person as he or she is met by our love toward the not yet, never to be exhaustively realized ideal value of that unique person. As an object of love, the person is only the point of departure for a movement toward increasingly pure ideality. Love does not create values; it discovers them *in* a person and turns its discovery into the starting point for a project of perpetual discovery of "more" value, of "higher" value. Love uncovers values in the sense of letting them come to appearance. The discovery of love stimulates an encompassing coloring of its object; "[in] so doing, love invariably sets up, as it were, an 'idealized' paradigm of value for the empirically given person" (Sym, 154). Love is the movement in the course of which its particular object is accorded the highest possible value attainable for it. Note that love does not impose an imperative-normative "ought" on its object. Though incapable, as movement, of passively letting the object be as it is, it does not intend, let alone demand, that the object change. Conditional love is not love at all, but a distortion of its essence, of what it means for it to be a movement. When imposed, that is, the movement becomes external, perhaps relative to some "pedagogical" enterprise, whereas love in Scheler signifies an internal movement, akin in form to the internal teleology of Aristotelian metaphysics. Love, then, is the intentional affirmation of the precept, Be who you are, whereby the being entailed in the "be" is neither empirical nor normative, but purely ideal. The specific quality of love's relating-to value lies in love's perpetually seeking and pursuing the *enhancement* of the value of the beloved person, thus always *transcending* the pregiven properties of its concrete object. [1]

Now, if love is the foundation of all value and itself an absolute value, is there such a thing as "absolute" love? Scheler holds that there is. Indeed, I have already pointed out that love is unconditional. However, this is restricted to the love of which only our feelings of mind (*geistige Gefühle*) are capable, to be distinguished from the "love" of our sensuous and of our vital feelings. As for the latter cases, what we often take to be love is, rather, desire, which becomes evident in the fact that the object typically loses its significance for us the moment our desire for it has been satisfied. Easily abandoned and quickly forgotten, a person we merely desire(d) is exchangeable and replaceable in a way a beloved person can never be, the former lacking the quality of uniqueness pertaining to the latter. (See the analysis of sexual love in Sym, 204ff.) But unconditionality and uniqueness are not exhaustive of love. Indeed, the inexhaustiveness in love that stems from the all too familiar embarrassment of never being quite able to explain or justify it—as my love for this person—is perhaps the very hallmark of love. All attempts to give "reasons" for our love—by making endless references to the features and deeds of the beloved one—are, notoriously, a failure. Aggregating the total "value" of the various traits found in a particular person will get us nowhere. As observed by Scheler, "There is always a surplus we cannot account for." Yet the failure to offer any sort of definitive justification for our love is by no means an intellectual one. It is rather that the *person* evades all cognitive objectification. "The element of the personal in man," writes Scheler, "can never be disclosed to us as an object" (Sym, 167). The ideal value of the person to whose enhancement an intentional act of love is directed is embodied in this very act itself and therefore inseparable from it, hence also beyond detached intellectual grasp. In this sense, to explain love means to violate its dignity; besides, it would be a kind of personal hubris.

"Love and hatred," contends Scheler, "afford an *evidence of their own*, which is not to be judged by the evidence of 'reason' " (Sym, 150). But how are we to understand this evidence? In what ways does it differ from that of intellectual cognition? Love, I have said, is a spontaneous emotional act; it is pure activity, perpetual movement; it is—and this merits emphasis—an autonomous organ of relating-to, uncovering, and enhancing (ideal) values in (real) objects. Hence, in love we gain a privileged access to the sphere of value. And this privileged status (Scheler refuses to say "function") of love, shared only by its opposite, hate, points to the *irreducibility of emotional life*. As opposed to intellectual cognition, love defies deduction as well as induction; the moment we try to decompose an act of intentional love, breaking it down into its separate parts or constituents, the act evaporates. Scheler assumes that the futility of wishing to explain love by listing features proves his point. Love is a fragile wholeness, a totality of movement "defined" by its resistance to decomposition, by its principal denial of all sorts of detachment and distancing. "Love and hatred," Scheler tells us, "necessarily fasten upon the individual core in things, the *core of value* . . . which can never be wholly resolved into values susceptible of judgment, or even of distinct apprehension in feeling" (Sym, 159).

Yet in these descriptions the more precise nature of the alleged "irreducibility" of our emotional life remains rather undetermined. In particular, we must put this straight with regard to Scheler's concept of love. In *Ordo Amoris*, Scheler criticizes all attempts to reduce love to a sensation. Conceding that we experience love as inseparable from sensations of pleasure and from a mental state of happiness, Scheler argues that the latter merely accompany or echo love, love having given rise to them, rather than the other way around. "Emotional processes," he says, "are themselves completely conditioned by the direction-, goal-, and value-determination of love and hatred, and by the worlds of objects given therein" (OA, 371; translation by the author). Again, the crucial point is that love is a spontaneous act, sensations and mental states merely reactive ones. But Scheler is not content to leave it at that. He goes on to declare the *primacy of love over cognition*, and it is in connection with this bold claim that a systematic argument for the irreducibility of man's emotional life must be sought.

Scheler's thesis of the primacy of love over cognition entails that it is only by virtue of a prior, original act of taking-an-interest-in that a particular object is given to us as an object of our (intellectual) cognition. *Feeling precedes and founds knowing*. Influenced by Goethe, Scheler maintains that "the objects that are disclosed to our senses and that reason thereupon assesses, first make their *appearance* in the processes of love."[2] So it is only through an act of intentional love or hate that an object is given to us qua object in the first place, meaning that all sensory perception as well as intellectual comprehension (e.g., analysis, assessment) of an object is conditioned by our relating to it, taking an interest in it through primordial acts of love and hate. But if this is so, then the object that is met by our senses and our comprehension must already be a carrier of value because something is loved or hated only insofar as it is a carrier of (ideal) values. In other words, the belief that our intellectual faculties (actively and originally) confer value on the objects that we have "already" sensed and—more important—felt is radically mistaken. Rather, the basic qualitative assessment of a given object is accomplished in the prior act of (intentionally) loving or hating, the work performed by our "disinterested" intellect thus being only secondary, subsequent, and, in a certain sense, "parasitic" (these terms are mine, not Scheler's). What is primarily "handed over" to the intellectual apparatus, then, is not a neutral "something" (*Sosein*) but a value-carrying object (*Wertsein*). In his late work *On the Eternal in Man*, Scheler maintains that "no truly and wholly value-free entity [can] *originally* be made the object of perception, recollection, and expectation, or, in a secondary respect, judgment, without its *value* quality or its value relation to another entity . . . having been already in some way given to us (whereby the 'already' does not necessarily have to include in itself chronological order or duration . . . .)."[3] With this, the full significance of Scheler's postulated apriority of the original emotional acts can be appreciated. There are two points to his thesis. First, the ideality and absoluteness of the sphere of value are matched by the purity and apriority of the intentional emotional acts. Second, the access to the former is obtained exclusively by way of the latter: love is matched by our loving, that is, an ideal value is matched by an intentional emotional act. But this is not all. The real thrust of Scheler's thesis is that the "matching" referred to is not a passively given one and as such not a matter of mere reception on the part of the feeling subject. Far from receiving the ideal sphere of value in anything resembling passivity, the intentional emotional act through *spontaneity* secures the very *appearance* (*Erscheinung*) of the ideal sphere of value. This, then, is my interpretation of Scheler's central claim that "all willing 'of something' presupposes the *feeling* of the (positive or negative) *value* of this something. A value can therefore never be a *consequence* of willing" (Fo, 133).

Earlier I raised the question, If love is the foundation of all value and itself an absolute value, is there then such a thing as "absolute love"? I answered that to Scheler there is. In view of the thesis just cited, I now can say not only that there is such a thing as absolute or pure love but that, for Scheler's theory to be consistent, there *must* be. If the conception of love qua ideal value is conveyed to us exclusively by virtue of acts of love, by which is meant original acts of pure loving, then it follows—mutatis mutandis—that Scheler's conception of ideal value is dependent on there being such a thing as pure love. The "pure act of love" of which Scheler speaks, tirelessly stressing its "basic character . . . [for] all forms of ethical cognition, and, indirectly, [for] willing and acting" (Fo, 581 n. 285), is thus to be looked upon as the act without which the entire conception of the sphere of ideal value would be inaccessible as well as incomprehensible to us; it takes a pure act of love to arrive at the sphere of ideal value, if my interpretation is not mistaken. Hence, our conceiving of Schelerian "love" hangs on our acts of pure loving.

So there must be pure love for Scheler's thesis to be consistent. But is there? And wherein would pure love consist? The answer that immediately springs to mind is, In love's disconnectedness from any need and inclination. To assert itself as pure and simple, love would have to free itself from the biologically determined sexual drives; it would have to be not subject to or for the sake of passion, desire, or need, but rather for its own sake or, better, *for your sake*, that is, for the sake of loving the beloved person, of affirming the genuine *otherness* of him or her, pursuing the enhancement of the value of that otherness as a value in itself. These are the terms used in Scheler's account of love. Pure love is associated with "seeing," with "coming to see"; conversely, "the 'blinding' element in an empirical infatuation is never the *love*, but the sensual *impulses* which always accompany love and by which it is actually constricted and confined" (Sym, 157–58). It is important to note here that Scheler in no way shares Kant's dismissive view of humanity's drives as constituting a "chaos"; nor does he accept the assertion, a hallmark of Kantian ethics, that impulses and the like are to be traced back to a principle of self-preservation. It is indeed a core objective of Scheler to discard the influential Kantian notion of (instinct-based) "egoism" as a primordial life-force. Far from an "original vital tendency," egoism, asserts Scheler, "is based on a *loss*, on a *removal* of the *feelings of sympathy* that belong *originally* and naturally to all life" (Fo, 278–79). Love is prior to egoism; it is prior also to sympathy, which is reactive, not spontaneous.

Yet to claim the all-encompassing primacy of love is not to have demonstrated its purity. If all sensuous pleasure, all biologically determined and sexually conditioned impulses are to be strictly abstracted from, what is the *movens* of this purified, this pure, love, through which appreciation of the sphere of ideal value is said to be exclusively facilitated? If pure love is the source of everything else, what is the source of pure love? In his book on sympathy, Scheler states, "an act of love occurs in a given biopsychic organism only where an instinctive urge is also present towards the same region of value as that to which the movement of love is directed" (Sym, 187). In his doctoral dissertation on Scheler, Alexander Altmann cites this statement in order to back up his thesis that the purity Scheler claims for the intentional act of love is nowhere actually established, and is therefore untenable. "Even given the fictitious presupposition that there exists an absolute realm of values, it follows from the psychological fact that love is never absolutely pure, in that it is always mixed with the instinctual, that the 'absolute' can never be experienced as absolute, but only as subjectively colored." In Altmann's view, there are no "pure" emotional acts, no love unconditioned by instinct, consequently no pure access to absolute values. His contention is that "the value as such is constituted first through the tendency at work primarily in instinct and secondarily in emotional acts."[4] Denying the purity of Scheler's emotional acts (of which love is the prime example) is but the other side of Altmann's central thesis that the (corresponding) notion of an absolute sphere of value is likewise unfounded.[5]

Leaving Altmann's last claim aside, I want to argue that his first one fails to stand up to closer scrutiny. Altmann's contention that the value toward which love directs itself is constituted "primarily" by instinct and "secondarily" by the emotional act is not supported by Scheler's discussion of the issue. Basically, his position is that "the instinctive system [Triebsystem] . . . determines, firstly, the actual way in which the act of love is evoked and secondly, the choice and order of preference among values, but [that] it has no bearing upon the act of loving and the content thereof (value-qualities), nor upon the superiority of the value and its position in the scale of values" (Sym, 187). I take this statement to show that Altmann's talk of value as "constituted" partly by instinct and partly by the emotional acts of a subject is unjustified. Quite to the contrary, Scheler's enterprise aims at furnishing ethics with an antisubjectivistic foundation. In accordance with this aim, the hierarchy of value he speaks about in the above quotation is posited as a priori and hence as wholly independent of instinct and emotional acts alike. By virtue of the eidetic reduction brought about by the so-called emotional epochē, the separate sphere of a priori value qualities is sought established— "separate" in the indicated sense of being a sphere independent of emotions as well as (real) objects. Herein lies Scheler's closeness to Plato: the (ideal) value of love conditions (lived, felt) love, and not the other way around, as is held by psychological and naturalistic doctrines of love. Far from constituting love qua value, an intentional act of love discovers, illuminates, and enhances the (ideal) value embodied in the beloved person. "Actual empirical organisms of any particular kind are only able to love what is at the same time appropriate to their specific instincts and of importance to them" (Sym, 188). Such, then, is the relation between instinct and love as conceived by Scheler: not a causal-genetic relation, as Altmann's critique would have it, but one where the selection of the object of love is in part performed by our instincts, whereby—significantly—the love we experience for the object chosen is in no way "exhausted" by the role played by our instincts in initially selecting it. (Strictly speaking, sexual love as understood by Scheler is not selective but wahllos, its object being not unique but exchangeable.) If our supposed love for a person vanishes once our impulses are satisfied "by" him or her, it is not the person qua person for whom we felt some affection but the person qua object of our desire; and to desire is not to love.

So in this account it appears that Scheler's doctrine of pure love is conceptually consistent and that Altmann's attempt to naturalize it fails. But, again, if love is the source of everything else, what is the source of love? My claim is that the question goes unanswered in Scheler. In the framework of Scheler's ethics, that is, love is granted the status of a metaphysical principle, an irreducible *Urphänomen*. Therefore, to seek to give a further explanation of love in philosophical terms is to misconstrue its essence, its dignity and originality. I have already noted the impossibility of (discursively) explaining our love for this or that person, an experience Scheler refers to as highly telling. But to argue that love ultimately lies beyond the reach of argument is, of course, to place Scheler's entire theory beyond that reach, insofar as it takes the metaphysical primacy of love as its systematic point of departure.

Scheler's Inverted Kantianism

The foregoing leaves Scheler's ethics susceptible to criticism of its basic premises. Such criticism would subject Scheler to the same strategy that he applies to Kant. Explicitly opposing the formality of Kant's moral philosophy, Scheler calls his own ethics "material": it is to be an "absolute, a priori *and* emotional ethics" (Fo, 254). Employing his modified version of Husserl's phenomenological method, Scheler purports to arrive at pure intentional feeling (*Fühlen*) through an emotional *epochē*. The task of Scheler's typology of the emotional life is to lay bare the separate logic, objectivity, and apriority of pure feeling, to be distinguished from that claimed for intellectual cognition in Kant's *Critique of Pure Reason*. Thus put, Scheler's enterprise is to be looked upon as a *supplement to or, more accurately, as an extension of Kant's philosophy*, rather than as a critique of it, which is of course how Scheler understood his own enterprise. In other words, what Scheler does with regard to our emotional life is but a mirroring of what Kant did with regard to our intellectual life. Scheler, that is to say, is so impressed (1) with Kant's claim that feelings are principally sensuous that he argues their pure spirituality (thus are born the concepts of *rein seelige* and *geistige Gefühle*); (2) with Kant's reduction of all emotional experience to the impulses and inclinations of a hedonistic-egoistic subject that he dissociates his notion of pure feeling not only from biological drives but from concrete subjectivity *überhaupt*; and (3) with Kant's view that emotions are but wholly subjective, contingent, and chaotic that he asserts their genuine objectivity, irreducibility, and regularity (*Gesetzmäßigkeit*), as demonstrated in his account of original emotional acts.

The philosophical framework thus erected is thoroughly Kantian, staying, as it were, unfailingly loyal to the terminology developed in Kant's first *Critique* yet argued for not along Kantian lines but from the peculiar perspective of a *Wertmetaphysik* somewhat arbitrarily equipped with the methodical devices of Husserl's phenomenology. Far from giving us the promised material ethics opposed to Kant's formal one, Scheler in fact *repeats* the Kantian outlook *within* the domain of humanity's emotional life. Scheler never actually discards this outlook and the dichotomies that go with it; what he does, rather, is claim the validity of the dichotomies—for example, a priori versus a posteriori, lawlike versus contingent—on behalf of a domain with regard to which Kant had *denied* them such validity. As I have shown, Scheler accomplishes this by *inverting* Kant's original use of the dichotomies in question, so that what was a posteriori and contingent in Kant—that is, emotional experiences viewed in toto as "heteronomous"—is turned a priori and lawlike in Scheler. Indeed it is nothing but the dichotomies inherited from Kant that allow Scheler to draw his important distinction *within* humanity's emotional life, that is to say, to maintain a division between the primitivity of sensuous and organic feelings on the one hand and the purity of spiritual ones on the other. In brief, what Scheler offers is not the announced material ethics but instead a Kantian-formal theory of the emotional life and the "laws" peculiar to it, laden with (non-Kantian) metaphysical presuppositions about the primacy of love and the subject-independent sphere of (ideal) value yet at the same time equipped with (Kantian) claims about apriority and objectivity.

Still, and in spite of the criticism just voiced, I endorse the central objective of Scheler's program: a material ethics paying systematic attention to the role of emotions and feelings in moral agency and judgment. In light of my charges against what I hold Scheler to have done, as distinguished from what it at first glance seemed he would do, the question is, Can one lend the sought-for philosophical dignity to the emotions *without* formalizing or absolutizing them? Without resorting to speculative metaphysical assumptions about the "primacy" and "purity" of love? Is it possible to break loose from the conceptual straitjacket requiring emotions to be either a priori or a posteriori, absolutely pure or wholly contingent? Why continue clinging to dichotomies allowing so little room for a conceptually unbiased inquiry into the role of emotions in ethics?

Put generally, Scheler's position is that the lower a feeling, the less suited it is to serve as a foundation for moral emotions such as compassion and sympathy. Therefore, a sensuous or a vital feeling cannot give rise to sympathy in the emphatic sense of a genuine feeling-with-another-person, whereas a spiritual feeling—for example, sadness—can. Exemplifying what he means by spiritual feelings, Scheler says that "in true bliss and despair . . . all ego-states seem to be extinguished." Feelings of this type are given to us "whenever there is no particular state of affairs or values outside or inside us that could *motivate* us feelingly to this fulfillment in bliss, and whenever the being and endurance of bliss appears phenomenally, unconditioned and unalterable by any performable acts of the will, by any deed, or by any way of life. . . . Therefore these feelings are the only ones which cannot be conceived as feelings that could be produced, or even *merited*, by our comportment" (Fo, 343–44). However, if my reading is not mistaken, this way of stating the relation between feelings on the one hand and moral emotions on the other leads to a paradox. For whereas Scheler admits to the higher "spiritual" feelings an exclusive ability to give rise to moral emotions, he also says of these feelings that they are characterized by our not having been "motivated" to experience them, by our not being "responsible" for them and in any way able to alter, let alone produce, them. Now, if spiritual feelings are the only ones rendering the phenomenon of sympathy possible, and if these feelings are defined by our inability to motivate, produce, and change them, then the conclusion seems inescapable that sympathy is reserved for feelings beyond the reach and influence of humanity, of human faculties. In short, the paradox I see consists in our having sympathy only with regard to feelings about which nothing can be done—neither by the one having them, nor by the one having sympathy with them. When Scheler later on in the same paragraph says that the spiritual feelings (e.g., bliss and despair) "only originate [*wurzeln*] in the value-nature of the person *himself* and his being and value-being, which stand above all acts" (Fo, 344), the paradox is brought to the fore once more, insofar as he elsewhere labors the point that the *Personwert* (value of the person) is principally inaccessible (see in particular Sym, 168–69). So instead of demonstrating the possibility of sympathy, Scheler appears to have shown its impossibility.

Yet there is another angle from which to approach the issue. Strictly speaking, Scheler has only argued that the person *having* a specific spiritual feeling or *being* in a specific state of mind is incapable of influencing it. This in no way a fortiori rules out one person's influencing such a feeling or state of mind in another. But though conceivable, this possibility strikes me as implausible. Indeed, Scheler holds the *Personwert* allegedly involved here to be inaccessible *in principle*. Nevertheless, according to his characterization of love, in the intentional act of pure love, what is discovered and subsequently enhanced is nothing less than the "value" of which a particular person is the carrier. The value thereby indicated is not "objectifiable," meaning that it can never be pinned down qua object of (intellectual) cognition.

To clarify the possibility of sympathy, one must first see how it differs from love. In an early formulation, Scheler says that "in contrast to love and hatred—in which values and *Unwerte* are intended, and which as *spontaneous* emotional acts must be kept distinct from the reactive ones of sympathy, but which, however, supply the foundation for the direction and centrality of sympathy—sympathy is in itself value-*blind* and already for that reason unsuited as the so-called basis for morality."[6] And in his book on sympathy, Scheler stresses that "the emotional *non*-identification of the person having sympathy with the alien feeling I [is] the phenomenal precondition of genuine sympathy" (Sym, 82). Far from threatening the possibility of sympathy, the otherness of sympathy's object is what founds it. "In sympathy we recognize that there exists such a thing as a *Fremdwert überhaupt*, which exists independently of all relatedness to one's own ego" (Sym, 72). Shown to presuppose alter's otherness from ego, the phenomenon of sympathy contains Scheler's attempt at overcoming solipsism.

So much for the clarification of the concepts. What matters here is that sympathy is a *reactive* emotion, secondary in ethical importance to the original and spontaneous act(s) of love. Founded in love, sympathy fades the moment love does; the experiences of feeling-for, feeling-into, and feeling-with have no ground on which to stand once the love preceding these emotions and making them possible in the first place is no longer present. Once again the primacy of love asserts itself at the very core of Scheler's philosophy. And whereas it is thanks to the power of sympathy that " 'other minds in general' . . . are brought home to us, in individual cases, as having a *reality equal to our own*" (Sym, 98), the specific *value* of the person qua person is not given to us in acts of sympathy but solely in acts of love, the unique discoverer of value.

Now, the paradox discussed above consisted in my coming to have sympathy only with regard to a person who experiences (spiritual) feelings which are unmotivated, unchangeable by human will, and for which the person carries no responsibility. Scheler's most-used examples are sadness and love: in both cases we are thoroughly possessed by the feeling; all endeavors to explain this pervasiveness prove futile, insofar as they are bound to leave a "plus" beyond all justification. But why exactly are we not responsible for them? Is it because we have not by any deliberate act of our will brought them into existence? Or is it because, their having arisen, we cannot "rationally" explain our having them? Or is it perhaps both? The larger question, however, is, Are we responsible for our feelings *at all*? Can we, that is, legitimately be said to be responsible for the way we feel in the same sense that we are said to be responsible for the way we act? To be more specific: Does the fact that I cannot explain why I love, or why I do not, provide "proof" that I am not responsible for the presence or absence of that feeling?

A first approach to these questions is to invoke Scheler's distinction between love and sympathy. His thesis is that "all sympathy is *based* upon love of some sort and vanishes when love is altogether absent: but the converse does not hold." It follows that "we only feel sympathy to the degree and according to the depth with which we love" (Sym, 142). So it is evident that, in Scheler's view, it is not in our power to "bring about" a feeling of genuine love for another person; love is a spontaneous act, as is the act of reciprocating or returning love. Sympathy, on the other hand, is always a reactive act; its functions are modes of social behavior. This, then, would be a first attempt to answer the questions concerning feelings and responsibility: loving and not loving are beyond the scope of human responsibility because they are spontaneous acts; feeling and not feeling sympathy are within the scope of human responsibility because they are reactive acts. Here "responsibility" means "consciously intended by a free subject." Clearly, in order to be called such, sympathy has to be intended, whereas love seems to deny intention just as it denies merit or desert; rather, it is either felt, or it is not felt.

Yet, to Scheler, sympathy is always preceded by and founded in love. So whereas sympathy is a feeling for which we can be held responsible and hence a truly *moral* emotion, this same emotion is claimed to be essentially grounded in love, which for its part is wholly spontaneous, thus denying responsibility in the sense just given. Here, then, a second paradox emerges: the paradox of grounding a feeling involving human deliberation and responsibility in one that does not. The reason this paradox arises is that Scheler's justified rejection of the various attempt to reduce love to some other particular feeling or sentiment (e.g., human benevolence in Hume, pleasure in Bentham, pity in Schopenhauer) leads him to turn the tables and postulate the reverse reductionism: namely, that all emotions, including moral ones, originate in love, being but positive or negative derivations of love. Love, that is, is not only prior to all cognitive and intellectual activity, it is also, qua metaphysical principle and *Urphänomen*, prior to *all emotions*. Indeed,

Scheler sees ethics as grounded in love, whereas Kant saw it as grounded in reason. However, as shown above, Schelerian love is just as a priori, objective, and pure as Kantian practical reason; and what is more, Scheler is just as *one-sided* in founding ethics solely in love as Kant was in founding it solely in reason. Thus, since I wish to elucidate the *interplay* between cognitive and emotional faculties in moral perception and judgment, I object to the exaggerated emphasis on emotion found in Scheler no less than to cognitivism à la Kant.

A passage from Merleau-Ponty helps close the discussion of love.

> I make the discovery that I am in love. It may be that none of those facts, which I now recognize as proof of my love, passed unnoticed by me; neither the quickened drive of my present towards my future, nor that emotion which left me speechless, nor my impatience for the arrival of the day we were to meet. Nevertheless I had not seen the thing as a whole, or, if I had, I did not realize that it was a matter of so important a feeling, for I now discover that I can no longer conceive my life without this love. Going back over the preceding days and months, I am made aware that my thoughts and actions were polarized, I pick out the course of a process of organization, a synthesis *in the making*. Yet it is impossible to pretend that I always knew what I now know, and to see as existing, during the months which have elapsed, a self-knowledge which I have only just come by.[7]

Whereas Scheler depicts love as the discoverer of value, Merleau-Ponty describes my discovery that I—undoubtedly, already, indeed for some time now—love. In the latter account, love precedes my awareness of it; the feeling is already there, unfolding, growing, bringing forward a world of its own design centered around itself (my love) and its chosen object (my beloved). Phenomenally, the feeling is inseparable from its object; the two merge and form a unit. Awareness is awareness of this already established unit, reflection is reflection on it; as acts of cognition, both *succeed* the feeling and the world as erected and as "seen" by it. By my reading, the passage quoted from Merleau-Ponty contains the following insight: my love discovers my beloved before I discover that I love. This seems at first glance to capture what Scheler had in mind when he said love was "spontaneous"; it brings about something all of itself, as it were. Yet the feeling of love must—as must *every human emotion*—be recognized as intentional, despite Scheler's claim to the contrary. We therefore have to qualify the statement according to which love, because spontaneous, was held to deny intention just as it denies merit or desert, from which we concluded that it is simply "felt or not felt." What my reading of Merleau-Ponty allows us to see is that love, precisely to the extent that it "discovers," is inescapably intentional: the discovery made by love is its particular intentional object. However, love is more. It does not merely discover the beloved, it discovers the beloved as *lovable*. Love, that is, commits an act of attribution, and it makes no sense to propose that this attribution is not intended. To say that love entails attribution is to say that love entails a *judgment* about its intentional object; it insists that the person loved is *worthy* of being loved, and it unavoidably starts fading as soon as it ceases to be committed to this (positive) assessment of its object. So, although it remains true that we cannot "make" ourselves start loving somebody just like that, as if everything turned on a simple act of the will, it is nevertheless just as true that we are in principle prepared to assume responsibility for loving the one(s) we do and for the way we do it, once we have made the discovery that the feeling is *already* there and that it is unmistakably *ours*, reflecting back on who we are by betraying what we see in another person.

But where does all this leave *sympathy* and the other moral, or altruistic, emotions? As I see it, our capacity to develop sympathy must *transcend* the narrow boundaries set up by the intimacy and physical copresence pertaining to love and hate. Sympathy, that is, must extend beyond the immediate range of the small-scale setting toward the large-scale setting and thus toward the (as yet) nonexperienced other. The scope of sympathy hence must be greater than that of love; contrary to Scheler's contention that sympathy originates in and is always derived from love, we must insist that *sympathy rests not on love but on empathy* and that our capacity for empathy can be directed to persons who are not unique to us and whom we do not love. In subsequent parts of this study, I substantiate these claims by establishing empathy as humanity's basic emotional faculty, a specific manifestation of which is sympathy; being a particular feeling, sympathy is facilitated by the basic faculty of relating to others, which I term empathy. To sum up, then, sympathy burns with a lower emotional temperature than love; and if, following Scheler, the former were really always to presuppose the latter, the phenomenon of sympathy would be unknown but in the most intimate human relations. Experience tells us that this is not so, that sympathy can have a larger audience than the narrow circle of family and friends, and that sympathy therefore does embody a truly moral potential. This potential is put to the test, however, the moment sympathy is applied to abstract and absent, as distinct from concrete and present, others. I show in later chapters that to arrest the spread of *indifference* poses the chief challenge—and the chief task—common to all other-directed moral emotions, sympathy included, and furthermore that the faculty for relating to others is a complex one *fostered* within the small-scale setting but nonetheless morally called upon to *depart* from it.

In view of the many criticisms voiced against Scheler's theory in this chapter, it may appear that I have arrived at a wholly negative conclusion with regard to its instructiveness. The overall picture is somewhat less bleak, however. I bring my discussion to a close by pointing to a difficulty as well as a lasting merit.

Given the ambitious programmatic goals Scheler set himself at the outset of his theory, what the *Formalism*, his central work on ethical theory, in fact offers must be considered a big disappointment. To be sure, Scheler does not make his task an easy one. In declaring such a monumental thinker as Kant to be his chosen adversary, Scheler in effect invites comparison with an ethical theory whose intellectual rigor his own proposal for a "material ethics" at no point succeeds in matching. Yet the same can be said about Scheler's relation to Husserl, which is basically positive. However, characteristically, Scheler's borrowings from Husserl's phenomenological method are arbitrary. To take an example—and this is the difficulty I anticipated—Scheler seeks to substantiate his claim that there is a sphere of a priori value qualities by introducing into his account the Husserl-inspired notion of an "emotional *epochē*." As far as I can see, this *epochē* is given the task of establishing a disinterested analytical access to a sphere said to exist independently of emotions as well as (real) objects. Presumably, the emotional *epochē* is held by Scheler to enable the theoretician to "bracket"—as Husserl would have implied—his or her subjectivity, including emotional being, so as to ascertain an optimally unbiased and, as it were, entirely "pure" insight into the nature of the sphere of a priori value qualities. But this conception is very unsatisfactory. It is epistemologically problematic. We may question how complete such a bracketing on the part of the inquiring subject's subjectivity can ever be. Moreover, to cast doubt on the bracketing entailed in the emotional *epochē* is not to go against but to be wholly in keeping with a key tenet of Scheler's own philosophy; his own teaching can be turned against him: Scheler, that is, time and again stresses the irreducibility (*Unhintergehbarkeit*, as Apel would have said) of humanity's emotional life and thus, by implication, of the emotional dimension of human subjectivity. I cannot but think that precisely the irreducibility thus asserted stands in flagrant contradiction to the bracketing of subjectivity required for the act of *epochē* to come about. As it stands, Scheler, in his arbitrary manner, makes use of a technical term here without bothering to give it a proper elucidation.

Now to the merit. There remain some Schelerian insights of lasting importance for the present study. They stem from his book on sympathy rather than from his *Formalism*. If we focus on his phenomenological descriptions of love, hate, and sympathy and try to liberate them from the metaphysical framework in which Scheler ultimately places them, a lot can be learned from him. When he examines love as an emotion between humans, as distinct from a metaphysical *Urphänomen* in which he wishes to ground ethics, Scheler's contribution to the philosophical study of emotions strikes me as very valuable. His notion of human love portrays it as demanding and highly selective; in this respect, it resembles Arendt's "exclusive" concept, which I endorsed in Chapter 2. Scheler tells us that in love I pursue the continual enhancement of what I perceive to be the unique value of the personality of the other, the focus of love being on the very being, the *esse*, of my beloved. Not only is this conception useful for circumscribing love in relation to the many diffuse and, in my opinion, all too comprehensive current uses of "love"; Scheler's conception of love also provides a welcome opportunity to draw some distinctions of enduring relevance to my main line of argument. As I have noted, Schelerian love must be distinguished from my notions of sympathy and empathy. Scheler has been instrumental in setting the stage for such distinctions; the demonstrated fact that I depart, in particular, from his notion of "sympathy" does nothing to diminish his role here, and I draw on his insights into human love in the subsequent discussions, notably in the section "Love, Compassion, and Empathy" in Chapter 4.

Part Two

4

The Perception of the Moral

What is the moral importance of perception, of the ability to "see" whether and to what extent the weal and woe of others is at stake in a situation? Is perception a purely cognitive matter, or does its peculiar "seeing" require the uninhibited performance of specific emotional capacities? Furthermore, if perception should require emotion, does it follow that emotions reflect morally on the person having them (or failing to have them) no less than do the actions that person performs? In short, had we better discard the influential dichotomy according to which cognition is active, something we do, and emotion passive, something we suffer, and instead postulate emotions as active *sui generis*, indeed as partly constitutive of perception and judgment alike?

In this chapter I argue for a thesis that gives a positive answer to all these questions. Emotions are active and indeed indispensable in disclosing to us that others' weal and woe is somehow at stake in a given situation. Such a situation is a moral one, in which the subject "seeing" it is a moral subject. Hence, if it is true that our access to the domain of human experience is through emotion, then our access to the domain of the moral, understood as the weal and woe of others, cannot bypass emotion but instead must be attained through it.

Overcoming the Active-Passive Dichotomy of Cognition and Emotion

"We cannot," writes Lawrence A. Blum, "help what we feel but only what we do." Not choosing to have our feelings, "we are not their initiators or authors. Thus our feelings and emotions cannot reflect on us morally" (FAM, 170). Blum takes the view portrayed here to be the typically Kantian one, where moral agency is linked with responsibility, and responsibility with follow-ing—or failing to follow—obligations and duties. The important point is that emotions are en bloc excluded from these key notions (i.e., agency, responsibility, duty), and the most crucial argument for this exclusion is given in Henry Sidgwick's contention that it cannot be a strict duty to feel an emotion, so far as it is not directly within the power of the will to produce it at any given time. Blum, though generally attacking the Kantian outlook, grants this, saying that "it is true that one cannot have a duty or obligation to have an emotion, or to act from an emotion" (FAM, 159). But the really crucial move is the next, made when the Kantian proceeds to say that that which cannot be made an object of obligation is therefore without moral relevance, from which the Kantian concludes that feelings and emotions have no moral relevance; their presence or absence, that is, cannot reflect on a person morally, since they lie outside the scope of personal agency. Opposing this view, Blum holds that "what has moral significance goes far beyond what can be made an object of duty or obligation. The good which is brought about by altruistic emotion is morally desirable, and sometimes even morally appropriate, but it is not therefore morally obligatory. It is morally good that we should respond to certain situations with care, concern, compassion, sympathy; but it is not and could not be morally obligatory to do so" (FAM, 159–60).

Blum's criticisms of the Kantian outlook terminate in a novel notion of the moral self. "The moral self," he says, "cannot be seen on a model of pure activity; . . . it cannot be identified solely with that of which we are the initiators or authors" (FAM, 177). The attitudes we possess, the values we adhere to, and the feelings we experience are not brought about "merely" through an effort of will, nor can we rid ourselves of them in such a way. Nevertheless, these attitudes, values, and feelings that we have do reflect on us morally, do form an inescapable and irreducible part of our moral self. Hence, this self "inevitably comprises a dimension of feeling and passivity" (FAM, 177). It follows that for Blum moral emotions such as sympathy and contempt reflect morally on the person having them as surely as do the actions he performs. I interpret this to mean that from the moral point of view proposed by Blum, our understanding of what is morally relevant must be altered or, better, widened so as to accord our having certain attitudes, values, and feelings the same moral significance as our performing certain acts, even though the former is "passive" in a way the latter undoubtedly is not. Note that in speaking of our feelings, "passive" does not mean "external to our true moral selves," as the Kantian would have it. What we experience, rather than choose or initiate—for example, concern, compassion, hatred, or contempt—must be acknowledged as fully a part of us. This being so, it is still conceivable that I dissociate myself from some of my attitudes and emotions. A racist, say, may change; he may cease to be one. To effect such a change, he would have to come to see his former attitudes and emotional reactions toward, say, a black person as entirely baseless and inappropriate. That is, he would increasingly view his past reactions as incompatible with his emerging understanding of himself, of the kind of person he aspires to be. A further point, made by Blum also, is that the notions of passivity, dissociation, and externality are in fact applicable to thoughts as well as to feelings. For we do not perceive ourselves as the authors of all our thoughts; many thoughts simply occur to us, and in this sense we are passive with respect to them. "Nevertheless," observes Blum, "they do reflect on us. But I can try to dissociate myself from a thought which keeps occurring to me." In the event of my successfully dissociating myself from it, the thought is "no longer part of myself"; it ceases to reflect on me morally (FAM, 182). However, in both cases of dissociation, what is required is not merely an act of one's will; to dissociate oneself from emotional reactions or thoughts that nontrivially are a part of us involves an "entire structure of one's moral being," including feelings, attitudes, behavior, desires, and so forth.

Blum's refusal to model the notion of the moral self on (Kantian) agency explodes the very distinction between activity and passivity. "On my view," writes Blum, "this distinction is to be viewed no longer as a contrast between that which, from a moral point of view, is part of us and that which is not;

rather it is a contrast between two ways in which something is part of us" (FAM, 183). Robert Solomon takes the view that we are thoroughly *active* with respect to our emotions. Instead of having them, we "make" ourselves have them. Hence, "we make ourselves angry, make ourselves depressed, make ourselves fall in love." Leading up to this statement is Solomon's thesis that "an emotion is a judgment (or a set of judgments), something we do." Echoing the existentialist pathos of the early Sartre, Solomon holds that "my [emotional] reaction is my choice"; accordingly, as for love he writes that "deciding to love is like deciding to get angry . . . ; love turns upon a *commitment* to a certain kind of seeing, a certain kind of sharing."[1] Solomon's thesis that emotions are judgments, something we entirely bring about, is implicitly rejected by Blum, since it confirms and even radicalizes the active-passive dichotomy Blum wishes to undercut. Blum, who defines "altruism" as "a regard for the good of another person for his own sake" (FAM, 9), writes:

> It is true that altruistic emotions involve judgment in some way—
> e.g., the judgment that someone is in pain, in need, suffering. In
> that sense, perhaps, one might want to say that they involve activity.
> But they are not mere reflections of such judgment, nor are they
> grounded in judgment, nor are they brought about (primarily)
> through a deliberate process of judgment. In this sense they are not
> active. Moreover, even if one wants to say that in involving judgment
> our emotions involve activity, this is not a form of activity which
> excludes passivity. For it remains true that our emotions are some-
> thing we experience or feel. (FAM, 185)

I endorse Blum's rejection of Solomon's thesis that emotions are something we bring about at will, something we "do" in the sense of deliberate decision and activity. In other words, I share Blum's view that the activity-passivity distinction is best seen as a contrast between two ways in which something is part of us, entailing that the issue—and possibility—of dissociation arises with regard to thoughts as well as attitudes and emotional reactions. Though not willed or chosen in the sense of Kantian agency, and though internal rather than external to us qua moral selves, certain attitudes and emotional reactions can be modified, changed, and gotten rid of by the people having them. So in this sense it is legitimate to say of people that they must take responsibility for attitudes and values that are genuinely a part of them "no matter what their source" (see FAM, 189).

So much for my agreement with Blum. Now, the really important issue concerns the relation between emotions and judgment. As is clear from the quotation, Blum holds altruistic emotions to be "not mere reflections of . . . judgment, nor . . . ground in judgment, nor . . . brought about (primarily) through a deliberate process of judgment." But this is to raise the issue from the wrong end. Instead of asking whether emotions are grounded in judgment, we should ask whether and to what extent *judgment is grounded in emotions*.

In explicating what is here meant by "grounded," I defend the thesis that as far as *moral* judgment is concerned, the exercise of judgment *presupposes* and is *made possible* by our "having" (or, better, having the ability to have) certain emotions. To say of moral judgment that it presupposes certain emotions on the part of the subject, however, is *not* to say—or to be committed to saying—that these emotions are "primary" and their structure "a priori" in the sense of Scheler's theory. When I hold that the exercise of moral judgment presupposes the subject's having the ability to have certain emotions, nothing whatsoever is—as yet—assumed about the primacy or apriority, or lack thereof, of the emotions referred to. In my view, Scheler was wrong in believing that the way to ensure emotions philosophical dignity is to import Kant's concepts of apriority and objectivity from the domain of pure practical reason to the (theoretically neglected and psychologically misconstrued) sphere of humanity's emotional life. To accomplish this import is not to discard Kant but to confirm him by applying his conceptual dichotomies within a field from which he had exempted them.

On the constructive side, the passing of a moral judgment is a twofold or joint accomplishment—an accomplishment, that is, possessing a cognitive as well as an emotional aspect, thereby requiring both a cognitive and an emotional faculty on the part of the judging subject. In stressing the cooperative character of the accomplishment, I imply that the passing of a moral judgment cannot come about in cases where one of the two faculties is, for whatever reason, barred from being active in the process. Thus, there is no moral judgment with only a cognitive or only an emotional component to it; neither cognition alone nor emotion alone can move us to a genuine moral judgment. Both components are needed, and to hold that one is "primary" to the other is to violate the principal *equality of importance* of the two faculties in question. In my view, then, no apriority is to be granted to either side: neither to the cognitive (Kant) nor to the emotional (Scheler).

In order to elucidate the nature of the coordination postulated by my thesis, I turn to a passage where Blum addresses the issue as he sees it. "Altruistic emotions," he states, "are intentional and take as their objects other persons in the light of their 'weal' and, especially, their 'woe.' Sympathy, compassion, or concern are directed towards others in virtue of their suffering, misery, pain, travail. And so the altruistic emotions have a cognitive dimension: the subject of the emotion must regard the object as being in a certain state (e. g., of suffering)" (FAM, 12). The question is, *How* does the subject come to regard the object thus? How does the subject come to "see" that the other person is in fact suffering? What specific type of "object" is another person's suffering? Is this seeing, *without which no object for (moral) judgment would be given in the first place*, solely a cognitive seeing, or is it rather a cognitive-emotional seeing, and a joint undertaking at that?

I hold the latter to be the case. For subjects to arrive at the phenomenon of suffering about which they are to exercise judgment, their emotional faculty (i. e., empathy) as well as their cognitive one (i. e., representative thinking) is inescapably called upon—or else the phenomenon of "suffering" would not be constituted as an object for *moral* judgment. But why, one might wonder, is the cooperation between the cognitive and the emotional faculties so seldom thematized in moral theory, indeed so often ignored? Because moral theories typically take the object of moral judgment as a *given* entity, as the more or less naïvely presupposed point of departure for inquiry. Hence, in most cases moral theories fail to inquire into the *constitution* of the object about which moral judgment is to be passed.

In recognizing a particular phenomenon as suited for *moral* judgment, a subject's cognitive and emotional faculties alike are presupposed. So, to answer the question about the original constitution of the object of moral judgment, we are referred, as it were, from the object back to the subject arriving—or failing to arrive—at it. To illuminate this point, the notion of the moral self elaborated by Blum is of great help. Blum allowed for the acknowledgment of attitudes, values, *and* feelings/emotions as internal to and fully a part of the moral self. The implication, as I see it, is that the specific emotional faculty I have spoken of is firmly installed as part of the essence of the moral self. Had we, to mention an alternative, been referred here back to the *Kantian* moral self, then we would have sought in vain for a conceptual acknowledgment of the emotional faculty shown to be required in the act of constituting the specifically moral object. This is so because of the cognitivistic one-sidedness of Kant's notion of the moral self, equating it as it does with agency and activity and hence excluding emotions en bloc.

One might object, given the example of suffering, that a distinction could be drawn between suffering qua object of moral judgment, a suffering that can be arrived at through pure cognition, and the emotional concomitants of that very same suffering, that is, the emotionally constituted sympathy or care such cognitively constituted suffering gives rise to. The distinction proposed implies a shift from our consciously perceiving a person suffering to our subsequently telling ourselves we must show that person some kind of concern. In the first case we are portrayed as disinterestedly perceiving some phenomenon; in the second, as acting on that perception in a manner involving some emotional engagement.

But the distinction is false. The implied *shift* from detached perception to emotion-based action is merely assumed, not explained. The "why" and the "how" of the shift are an enigma. In my view, the assumed shift is but a fiction. As a purported reconstruction of what is involved in my example, it is radically deficient because suffering is constituted qua object through the unimpaired interplay between our cognitive and our emotional faculties. So suffering is not a "neutral" phenomenon in the first place, and there is no "disinterested" access to the human reality of suffering. The access is pervaded by interest, by taking an interest in a piece of lived human reality. Herein lies the grain of truth in the statement I cited from Solomon. Love, or care, he said, is a certain *way of seeing*; to say of a person that he or she is suffering is already to see that person in a certain way; and to want to exempt our emotional faculty from this seeing is to undermine it, extinguish it, indeed to prevent its very emergence. Stronger still, I argue that to "see" suffering as *suffering* is already to have established an *emotional bond* between myself and the person I "see" suffering.

Again, a counterexample may be put forward. Suppose a man, Davis, happened to stumble upon a person being beaten by another. Suppose, further, that Davis proceeded with his walk, content to have given the incident a quick glance and to leave it at that. How does he feel about it? He feels nothing in particular; in fact, he couldn't care less. Is such a case a clear-cut repudiation of my claim about the phenomenon of suffering "inescapably" prompting some *emotional* reaction in us, indeed, being in part constituted by our emotional faculty? My answer is no. What we have here, rather, is a subject with impaired capacities of perception. His not perceiving suffering *as* suffering when witnessing it does not mean that we have no case of suffering here after all, no phenomenon involving emotional faculties and responses; it is, instead, a matter of *a subject failing to do justice to his object*. The described incident would refer us back to *him*, questioning his ability to *see* suffering *as* suffering, that is, to see the human reality it entails. For to have claimed that the act of constituting a phenomenon of moral judgment requires the cognitive and the emotional faculties alike is in no way to have claimed that both faculties are intact and operative in all subjects at all times.

To borrow Robert J. Lifton's term, Davis appears to be *numb*, unable to relate psychically and affectively to another person's situation; for a shorter or longer period of time, his emotional capacities toward others are inhibited, suppressed, damaged.[2] Or, to use Peter F. Strawson's term, Davis adopts an "objective attitude" to another human being, thereby precluding "the range of reactive feelings and attitudes which belong to involvement or participation with others in inter-personal human relationships." But, adds Strawson, "being human, we cannot, in the normal case, do this for long, or altogether."[3]

Strawson's observation is significant. It highlights how we take it for granted that any normal person, at any given time, is capable of "knowing" what a moral phenomenon is, of recognizing it as such whenever he or she comes across it, and of responding affectively in accordance with that knowing. Recognition and response, however, are but two aspects of the same matter. Hence, in the average case, the object, or phenomenon, is already given, already constituted; and this "already" indicates why we so seldom thematize the joint emotional-cognitive accomplishment *behind* the "given" object. Indeed, such thematization comes about only when the constitution of the object somehow fails to be soundly established; it takes a breakdown, a case where what "always" happens in fact does not, to make us ask—and see—*what* "always" happens. The upshot of Strawson's ingenious observation is that the very notion of human accountability for one's actions (or, to use Habermas's term, *Zurechnungsfähigkeit*)[4] hangs on a person's ability to "see" moral phenomena by virtue of adopting a participant reactive attitude as distinguished from an objective one; or, better still, it hangs on his *inability not to see* such phenomena.

I therefore agree with Strawson's statement: "But a thoroughgoing objectivity of attitude, excluding as it does the moral reactive attitudes, excludes at the same time essential elements in the concepts of *moral* condemnation and *moral* responsibility." Strawson distinguishes between three types of moral attitude, remarking that in general "we demand of others for others, as well as of ourselves for others, something of the regard which we demand of others for ourselves."[5] As it stands, however, Strawson forgets to mention a fourth moral attitude, no less important than the ones referred to, if not the most important one: our attitude toward ourselves. I demand, that is, something of myself for myself, just as much as I demand something of you for myself. Entertaining the idea, say, of committing murder, I say to myself, I wouldn't be able to live with having done such a thing. My attitudes toward others reflect back on my attitudes toward myself; in order to be able to view myself, for example, as a fairly decent person, I have to live up to a certain standard in my feelings, thoughts, and behavior toward others. Involved here is a normative concept of self-respect, as well as the issue of what it would take and what it would mean for me to lose it, insofar as I respect myself not with reference to other people but with reference to a standard—*my* standard.[6] In this, then, lies the standard against which the seriousness of Davis's inability to see a moral phenomenon can be put to the test. If, he, confronted with our pointing out to him his failure, should shrug his shoulders and say, "Well, so what; I don't care, it just doesn't affect me," then his conduct is explained—though of course by no means excused—insofar as we see his overall standard is such that he can live with what he did or did not do. Davis evidently does not expect of himself the reaction we on our part expect (or demand) of him, and if he can really live at peace with himself while continuing to remain indifferent to the suffering of others, then I take this to support my claim about the primacy of our attitude toward ourselves as against others' attitude toward us. It is the *former* that must change if a change in moral conduct is to be effected. (But this issue is much more complex. Thus, in Chapter 5 I show how our relations to "significant others" also help shape the standards by which we view ourselves.)

The last point was in fact anticipated in the example of the racist given above. The shift from his "being a racist" to his "having once been a racist" presupposes a shift in the nature of his attitudes toward himself. It is only by virtue of a change of these attitudes that those toward others—for example, blacks—can come about. The newly acquired self-understanding of the man renders his previous attitudes unacceptable to him; they assume the quality of contradicting rather than expressing the way he (now) sees and wishes to see himself, and thus also, in effect, the way he wishes to be seen by others. Hence, in the shift from "being" to "having once been" a racist there must be a point where the man—for whatever concrete reason—starts to subject his set of attitudes to scrutiny, with the result that he *disapproves* of what he sees—that is, of himself as "such" a person. I therefore claim that a novel self-understanding is not so much the consequence of a shift from "racist" to "former racist" as a precondition of the shift, as generating it and thereby enabling the man to regain his faltering self-respect. (To take the existentialist version, the man may see his present self as "authentic" and condemn his previous one as "inauthentic," because of the impact of prejudice, ideology, and the like.) I take this discussion to show that there is an internal connection among self-understanding, responsibility, and change. The racist's desire to change his attitudes toward others makes sense only insofar as he sees himself as responsible for the kind of attitudes he has. Put differently, he acknowledges that his attitudes—and the specific set of emotional responses that go with them—reflect on him morally, that they form an inseparable part of his moral self. So the claim I made about our demands of others being in principle dependent on and secondary to our demands of ourselves carries the implication that Blum's "being-toward-others" is not primary but rather secondary in importance to our "being-toward-ourselves."

Returning now to my central thesis, I argue not only that the moral object, or phenomenon, produces or does not produce some particular emotional reaction in the subject but, more fundamentally, that the subject actively *constitutes*—by virtue of his or her joint cognitive and emotional faculties— the moral object, or phenomenon, in the first place. Interestingly, the perspective proposed here is strikingly Kantian. What I ask is, How does a subject constitute a moral phenomenon? What faculties and accomplishments does this act of constitution require of the subject? I stress the subject's cognitive-emotional activity, whereas Blum stresses the subject's reactivity. Applied to Davis, the approach first taken fails to cut through to the fundamental question. The question initially posed was too influenced by the viewpoint of Blum, meaning that the focus was put on whether and why a specific phenomenon triggered some specific emotional reaction in the subject. But this is just one of so many ways of moving from the (pregiven) object to the subject, so as to inquire what manifest "effect" the former has on the latter. In the approach suggested by my thesis, however, the move to be made is the reverse: from the subject to the object, inquiring how the subject is *active* in disclosing the object.

But how shall we conceive of this activity? Moral perception, obviously, is a kind of activity on the part of the subject: it is recognition of the way in which a situation affects the weal and woe of the human beings involved in it. As was noted in the Introduction, moral perception does not move itself, does not arise out of itself, as it were. Rather, moral perception has its source in human *receptivity*, in the primordial capacity of human beings to be attentive to, to be alert to. It is thanks to this underlying active receptivity, this sensuous-cognitive-emotional openness to the world, that moral perception is provided with a direction, is "tuned in" to deal with specific features of specific situations.

It follows that a person's failure to display a morally appropriate reaction is to be acknowledged not as the person's original failure but as one stemming from his or her *prior* failure to be receptive to and thereupon to "see" the phenomenon at hand as a morally significant phenomenon and consequently as one that, as far as overt behavior is concerned, calls for response and possibly intervention. In a word, the failure at the manifest level of action-response originates in a failure at the primordial level of receptivity. If there is no receptivity in the sense of being attentive to and alert to, that is, of taking an interest in, the exercise of moral perception and judgment will fail to come about. Now, according to my explanatory model, an overt failure to recognize and respond to a situation involving another's suffering (recall Davis) suggests that the nonaffectedness displayed may stem from the person's diminished or even severely damaged capacity for empathy.

Perception and the Role of Emotion in Ascribing "Import"

Everything I have said here about "seeing" falls under the heading of "perception" in the explanatory scheme I launched in my discussion of Hannah Arendt:

Level: PERCEPTION $\longrightarrow$ JUDGMENT $\longrightarrow$ ACTION
Faculties involved: cognitive-emotional   cogn.-emot.   —

The application of this scheme allowed me to argue against Arendt that Eichmann's failure to judge did not stem from a failure of thinking but instead from one of perception and, further, that Eichmann's failure of perception is emotional rather than intellectual or cognitive. Having argued this twofold thesis, I conceded its lack of compelling evidence.

What was partly implicit in the discussion of Eichmann has been rendered more explicit in the present case of my Davis. Davis refrains from entering the business of passing moral judgment; throwing a quick glance at an ongoing incident, he unhesitatingly resumes his stroll. Davis epitomizes the unresponsive bystander. He makes explicit that something is wrong, conspicuously wrong, about the way he is "seeing" the incident. More directly than in the case of Eichmann, his capacity for *perception* catches our attention. Once again, that is to say, it takes a case of impaired or *failed* performance of a capacity to prompt us to examine the nature of that capacity when performed in an intact or sound manner. Breakdowns illuminate.

Above I claimed that suffering is not a "neutral" phenomenon in the first place, meaning that there is no "disinterested" access to the human reality of suffering. Rather, the access is pervaded by interest, by taking an interest in a piece of lived human reality. This taking-an-interest is what I had in mind when I introduced the category of perception; and in defining it as indispensably involving a cognitive as well as an emotional faculty, I anticipated the point I now want to develop more fully, that my taking an interest in a piece of human reality presupposes a *joint* cognitive-emotional accomplishment.

The more precise nature of this accomplishment may be approached through Lawrence Blum's reflections on the role of apprehension. Blum points out that "apprehending a situation as relating to another person's weal and woe is an essential prerequisite for acting out of regard for their weal and woe" (FAM, 132). As it stands, this is scarcely controversial. For if one holds—as I do, and as Blum does—that action, in the emphatic sense of the term contrasting it with mere "behavior,"[7] is logically preceded by perception, then it follows that there can be no altruistic action-response to a given situation without a prior apprehension of what that situation is all about. In my chapter on Arendt, I offered a tentative definition of perception in this very vein. I defined perception as the capability of recognizing and identifying the object, or phenomenon, on which judgment is subsequently to be passed; in this sense, perception "gives" judgment its object. When we want to examine *how* we identify some features in a particular situation as carrying *moral* significance, the accomplishments we focus on are those of *moral perception*. The features bearing on the weal and woe of human beings in a situation are the subject matter of moral perception, as I define it.

Consider next this statement by Blum: "My general contention is that part of what characterizes a person as caring, compassionate, sympathetic, or concerned is that he is more likely than other persons to apprehend situations in terms of the weal and woe of others" (FAM, 132). Blum then argues that the difference between the sympathetic and the unsympathetic person should be seen as having two components: the first is "apprehending the situation as involving weal and woe," and the second is "responding to that apprehension with altruistic action" (FAM, 133). Again, Blum is eager to stress how he differs from Kant. Whereas Kantian moral principles specify "what action to take in a situation of a certain kind of specification," Blum is preoccupied with "the issue of how situations do present themselves to the agent in the first place" (FAM, 137). He ends his reflections with the oft-repeated assertion that "possessing the right set of principles does not ensure correctly perceiving the situations in which they are to be applied." In the present context, this is so not because there can be no (meta-) rule by which correct rule following can be specified (cf. Wittgenstein), namely, how one is to apply the same set of rules in dissimilar situations; rather, it is so because correct perception "cannot be assumed by reason alone. Hence, what cannot be gotten from reason alone is the full-blooded moral agent, with his perception as well as his principles; all one can get . . . is the principles themselves" (FAM, 139).

I am in full agreement with this conception of the moral agent, or what I have called the moral self. Furthermore, I grant that possessing the right set of principles does not ensure correctly perceiving the situations in which they are to be applied. But what ensures correct perception? What are the general preconditions for the accomplishment of "sound" perception?

One will look in vain for a full-scale analysis of perception in Blum's book. Yet valuable observations may be found. To apprehend the features of a given situation that relates to a person's weal and woe does not require, Blum notes, "particular intelligence or sensitivity"; it only takes a person of "normal sensitivity or perceptiveness." Blum then proceeds to repeat his claim that "a sympathetic, compassionate person is more likely to act to foster the good of others" (FAM, 131). This can hardly be disputed. However, assuming that the sympathetic person is more likely than the unsympathetic to perceive others' weal and woe as at stake in situations and hence more likely to act altruistically on that perception, the question remains how great or small such likelihood is. This being so, what philosophers can do is study how perception works in so-called "paradigm scenarios."

The term "paradigm scenario" has been suggested by Ronald de Sousa. Paradigm scenarios, he explains, involve two aspects: first, "a paradigm situation providing the characteristic *objects* of the emotion (where objects can be of various sorts, sometimes more suitably labeled 'target' or 'occasion')" and, second, "a set of characteristic or 'normal' *responses* to the situation. It is in large part in virtue of the response component of the scenarios that emotions are commonly held to *motivate*; . . . for the emotion often takes its name from the response disposition and is only afterward assumed to cause it." De Sousa is committed to the view that "a child is genetically pro- grammed to respond in specific ways to the situational components of some paradigm scenarios" (ROE, 142). His account leads up to a thesis about the "rationality of emotions": "It is in terms of the relation between the evoking situation and the formal object—the quality that is tied to the paradigm situation—that the appropriateness or intrinsic rationality of an emotion is assessed." Hence, the emotion that "fits" the paradigm scenario "is by definition rational" (ROE, 149).

What bears directly on my question concerning perception is de Sousa's contention that "an emotion is appropriate in a given situation if and only if that situation is relevantly similar to, can accurately be 'gestalted' as, the situation of a suitable paradigm scenario" (ROE, 145). It follows that for de Sousa "true irrationality of emotion involves the perception of a situation in terms of a scenario which it does not *objectively* resemble" (ROE, 146).

Although de Sousa does offer a conception of what "correct" perception consists in when successfully attained, the model he has outlined contains no examination of *how* such perception is arrived at, that is, of perception as a cognitive and emotional accomplishment. Far from that, the terminology adopted by de Sousa suggests that his model is committed to some kind of stimulus-response determinism. In particular, this is the impression I get from his cited claim that "a child is genetically programmed to respond in specific ways to the situational components of some paradigm scenario" (ROE, 142). In this formulation, the vast (and undefined) category of "situational components" assumes the function of "stimuli" to which the child, in this respect somehow "genetically programmed," responds in a more or less appropriate manner. What disturbs me is de Sousa's taking the paradigm scenario as the point of departure in his model, with emotions coming to mean but "emotional responses" to the ever-preconstituted paradigm scenario. Thus, we are told that "since emotions are learned in terms of these paradigms, they cannot, at least within a given social context, be criticized for inappropriateness if they occur in response to the paradigm situation" (ROE, 143). Now, although I readily accept that emotions are learned in terms of paradigm scenarios, that is by no means the whole story about them. I find it worthwhile to ask whether the reverse in fact occurs as well, that is to say, whether paradigms are learned in terms of emotions. In other words, Is the impact of emotions confined to the "response" side, as de Sousa seems to suggest, or do emotions (also) partake in the prior and constitutive accomplishment of perceiving, or recognizing, or apprehending, the given situation as being of such and such a kind in the first place? I am committed to the latter position. Emotions such as love or care are, to invoke Solomon's expression, a certain way of seeing. Stated in general terms, emotions are active in *disclosing* a situation to us. That is, emotions are instrumental in giving us a fundamental *first access* to a situation as one where, to recall Blum, others' weal and woe is somehow at stake. Emotions are crucial in making us aware of the peculiarly *human* reality or, more broadly, the human relevance of a specific situation. Emotions make us attentive to the issue of how the *other* perceives the situation; emotions link our own perception of the situation to that of the other involved in it. This is what I had in mind when I said above that to "see" suffering as *suffering* is already to have established an *emotional bond* between myself and the person I "see" suffering.

In an earlier chapter I claimed that Eichmann was insensitive rather than thoughtless, that he failed to develop empathy with other human beings, to take an emotional interest in the human *import* of the situation in which the persons affected by his actions found themselves. This notion of import, courtesy of Charles Taylor, takes my inquiry a major step further than Blum's reflections on apprehension and de Sousa's account of paradigm scenario toward my conception of empathy.

"By import," writes Taylor (in the essay "Self-Interpreting Animals"), "I mean a way in which something can be relevant or of importance to the desires or purposes or aspirations or feelings of a subject; or otherwise put, a property of something whereby it is a matter of non-indifference to a subject" (PP, 1:48). To identify the import of a given situation means to identify what in the situation makes us feel the way we do; it entails explaining to ourselves why we are affected by, or "non-indifferent" to, the situation and, in a second step, determining the more exact nature of what we feel and assessing the justification of that feeling or, better, of feeling that way. So, concerning the ascription of the import, it is not sufficient that I feel this way, but rather "the import gives the grounds or basis for the feeling." Accordingly, "saying what an emotion is like involves making explicit the sense of the situation it incorporates, or . . . the import of the situation as we experience it" (PP, 1:49). In ascribing import to a situation I define the latter as of some particular relevance to my purposes, desires, and aspirations; hence, only beings that are taken to have purposes and the like, only subjects, can perceive a situation as carrying some import. But it is not just that my, say, being ashamed in a situation shows shame to be a subject-referring property and *eo ipso* an experience-dependent one too. For beyond the question whether I feel ashamed is the question "whether the situation is really shameful, whether I am rightly or wrongly, rationally or irrationally, ashamed" (PP, 1:55).

But when is my shame justified, and in that sense rational? How can I determine the difference between my being right and my being wrong in my identifying the import of a specific situation as the basis for the way I feel, for example, ashamed? Who is to decide? May it not be that I experience my shame as justified, as called for by the situation, whereas you, commenting on my feelings, hold it to be groundless? If import is subject referring, is it wholly relative to the one subject ascribing import and experiencing an emotion, or is import subject referring in the wider sense of referring to a plurality of subjects, a community, and a culture?

Blum asserts that the sympathetic person is more likely than the unsympathetic to perceive a situation as one where others' weal and woe is at stake, and thus more likely to act altruistically on that perception. But this, while scarcely contestable, does not provide an answer to the question just posed concerning a criterion for the appropriateness of a concrete act of perception. Now, de Sousa, to be sure, does offer a candidate for the sought-for criterion. His suggestion focuses on the way an emotional response can be said to "fit" the situation giving rise to it, the latter having been—rightly or wrongly— perceived as belonging within such and such a paradigm scenario. So emotions are justified in terms of the situation eliciting them, and the perception of the situation in its turn is justified in terms of the paradigm scenario it is assumed to belong to. Besides appearing to be very rigid, if not deterministic, de Sousa's model allows no room for emotions as being— partly but nonetheless indispensably—*constitutive* of acts of perception. Rather, his model is predominantly cognitive in the way it is framed. In particular, and as noted above, what remains insufficiently dealt with is the issue of what is required in order to take an emotional interest in how the other perceives the situation, this being what I see as the truly *moral* issue.

Taylor maintains that while emotions relating to an import, such as humiliation or shame, are subject referring, this does not entail that they are self-regarding or self-concerned; rather, the full recognition of the import involves reference to a subject, and this subject need not be the agent only, it can also comprise his or her addressee. Indeed, Taylor, using the familiar example of a person in need of help, goes on to postulate the addressee of a felt obligation as "the crucial reference to the subject. For I do not just feel desire to help this man, . . . I feel called upon to help him. And I feel called upon *qua* rational being, or moral being, or creature made by God in his image, in other words capable of responding to this like God, that is, out of agape" (PP, 1:58). So, implicit in the import is a reference to the subject, and the import the situation (e.g., seeing that somebody is wounded) bears is that it lays a specific obligation on me—"what we call a moral obligation or an obligation of charity." It therefore turns out that the import's reference to a subject is a reference to the *kind of being* on whom—and on whom alone—this obligation is laid; the fact that the situation bears this import for me reveals something about the kind of being I am; the import shows me to be the kind of being on whom a moral obligation can be laid. In the present case, "the import is that we are *called upon* to act," and this precisely by virtue of our being a certain kind of creature. The wounded person whom I feel called upon to help—insofar as I am able to perceive the call as the import of the situation, as the human reality that the situation is all about—is not merely my addressee; in responding to the obligation felt to help that person, I perceive myself as *that person's* addressee. Expanding Taylor's thesis, my point here is that I myself am the person morally addressed in the incident. In this view, to speak of subject-referring imports is not to see all motivation as narcissistic, because the class of subject-referring imports is much wider than that of *self*-referring imports; rather, subject-referring imports can have a very different structure, one that defies all attempts to prejudge whether motivation is narcissistic or altruistic.

The upshot of Taylor's account of import is that emotions are acknowledged to operate on the constitutive side of perception, as opposed to de Sousa's putting them on the side of "responses" to a somehow already constituted and recognized situation. The study of import demonstrated, first, the crucial part played by emotions in perceiving a situation as laying a moral obligation on us, or as "addressing" us, and, second, how we are the addressee of such an obligation by virtue of the kind of being we are—human subjects. As I read him, Taylor indicates, but nowhere really elaborates, a point about how the relation, or link, between the human and the moral may be conceived: The human refers to the human subject; the moral, to the moral addressee—*his* or *her* addressee. Only humans are moral; a human being is a moral being, a being on whom moral obligations can be laid and are being laid. Only human subjects are capable of initiating action in its emphatic sense, and they alone can be held responsible for the consequences that ensue from action. Only humans act morally—or fail to do so. In any case, we demand, we expect, moral conduct only from human beings; and again, only we qua human subjects can raise—to ourselves or to others—such a demand and such an expectation; we are the sole authors as well as the sole addressees of these demands and expectations. But although an animal, for example, cannot be a moral agent in the sense here defined, an animal can be, and often is, directly affected by—and on that account can be, and often is, an addressee of—an action of ours. Hence, beings that are not moral agents may still be moral addressees; the former is not required for the latter. An animal can be harmed, can be hurt, can suffer, and it can for that very reason be an object of unjust and immoral conduct. I therefore grant moral status to animals, to nonhuman beings, on account of their capacity for suffering, which I see as a sufficient condition for moral status.

Of course, the moral status of animals (to say nothing of fetuses, future generations, and the like) is the topic of a discourse in its own right, from which I must abstain in what follows.[8] I thus confine my discussion to human subjects, in the sense intended by Taylor. The proposition arrived at by

Taylor is that subject-referring feelings incorporate a sense of what it is to be human. Subject-referring imports disclose what matters to us as human subjects; they convey our sense of shame, of dignity, our feelings of admiration and contempt, of moral obligation, of remorse, of unworthiness and self-hatred. What I "know" about generosity or shame is inseparable from my knowing what it feels like to be generous or to be ashamed. I "know" that I should be generous because I am moved in some way. "Perhaps," writes Taylor, "I feel remorse when I have delivered myself of a spiteful attack . . . ; or feel morally inspired by the ideal of universal generosity. If I were quite impervious to any such feelings, these norms and ideals would carry no weight with me; I would not even be tempted to subscribe to them, and I would not describe myself as "knowing" that they were true/valid" (PP, 1:61). It is only through such a feeling as self-reproach or self-contempt or self-dissatisfaction that I develop a sense of the proper object of, for example, shame. Taylor warns against opposing knowing to feeling. Rather, his position is that "what I know is also grounded in certain feelings. It is just that I understand these feelings to incorporate a deeper, more adequate sense of our moral predicament. If feeling is an *affective awareness of situation*, I see these feelings as reflecting my moral situation as it truly is; the imports they attribute truly apply" (PP, 1:61; emphasis added).

Taylor's statement that "feeling is an affective awareness of situation" supports my thesis about the indispensable role emotions play in situation perception. But to maintain this is to be committed to a more comprehensive thesis about the cognitive dimension of feelings, that is to say, about how feelings entail judgment or belief about the way things *are*. Hence, to feel shame in a certain situation is to ascribe an import to that situation; it is to make a judgment about the way the situation is. Whether the situation is "really" shameful and thereby justifies my shame will in principle always be open to discussion, but as for the fact that I, feeling shame, judge the situation to be shameful, there can be no doubt. Yet the reverse also occurs. For there are plenty of cases where I did *not* judge a situation to be of such and such a nature, and where others may say that I *fail* to ascribe the "appropriate" import. I might be told to change my judgment, as in the often-heard appeal, You should really be ashamed of yourself! Against the double dualism of cognition-feeling and activity-passivity that I sought to explode in the section dealing with Blum, that appeal suggests that feeling can indeed become the goal (object) of the will. Yet this is not to say that the will simply "produces" feeling; rather, it is to say that the will may give rise to and may help modify feeling. As Agnes Heller aptly observes, "The person who has never been told that he should feel ashamed of himself will never feel ashamed in such cases, at least in the social average. If injunctions would not be capable to evolve feelings or to fix them, then the majority of concrete feelings would not have a chance to develop." Hence, if feelings can at all be influenced this way, the person making an appeal or injunction need not be myself but can be, and very frequently is, another person.[9]

Taylor's position is that insofar as feeling is our "mode of access to the entire domain of subject-referring imports," feelings are import attributing. Feelings incorporate a certain "understanding of our predicament, and of the import it bears." Feeling a certain way, we ipso facto judge something to be of a certain nature. In the words of Taylor, "We can feel entitled to say on the strength of certain feelings, or inferences from what we see through certain feelings, that we know that X is right, or good, or worthy, or valuable" (PP, 1:62). A feeling entails a judgment about how we hold things to be, because it incorporates a certain *articulation* of our situation. This being so, feelings also admit to *further* articulation, requiring us to penetrate more deeply into our first, or intuitive, apprehension of the situation; and this further articulation can in turn transform the feelings. As Stuart Hampshire has argued, emotions are not immediate data of consciousness, uncorrupted as it were by reflection and description. Rather, when emotion is the object of a description, the object is such that it does not exist independently of the description that we give of it; on the contrary, the emotion is partly *constituted* by the act of description. The following formulation of Hampshire's might just as well have been found in Taylor: "If my belief or assumption about the cause of the feeling is displaced by an argument that shows me that the belief or assumption about the cause is unfounded, my sentiment will change also."[10] So feelings incorporate *and* call for articulation, and then for further articulation, engaging us in a process of self-interpretation that, once started, is for all practical purposes interminable. The question whether an offered characterization is adequate can always be opened anew; characterizations of what we feel are never definitive, never complete, not least because the feelings we seek to characterize themselves alter by virtue of our continual process of characterization. Again, the perpetual activity of self-interpretation changes us: seeing ourselves differently, we become different—or at least are likely to.

But we do not merely articulate our emotions and characterize our desires, we also *evaluate* them. Evaluation involves my having a (second-order) desire about my having a (first-order) desire; that is, I evaluate my desire in terms of its desirability or lack of such. Taylor quotes Harry Frankfurt's observation that "no animal other than man . . . appears to have the capacity for reflective self-evaluation that is manifested in the formation of second-order desires" (PP, 1:16). Taylor terms "strong evaluation" the evaluation that is concerned with the qualitative *worth* of different desires. Here we make qualitative discriminations between our desires and goals; "we see some as higher and others as lower, some as good and others as discreditable, still others as evil, some as truly vital and others as trivial, and so on" (PP, 1:65). Although Frankfurt is right that the capacity for forming second-order desires and hence for engaging in strong evaluation is peculiar to humanity, not all people make use of this activity to the same extent, or at all; indeed, some seem to shun it.[11] What is more, we judge, or "evaluate," other people by their preparedness to enter strong evaluation and the radical self-reflection that goes with it; we view this preparedness as the very criterion of their being either "deep" or "shallow" individuals. What emerges from strong evaluation is a self-resolution in a strong sense, for "in this reflection the self is in question; what is at stake is the definition of those inchoate evaluations which are sensed to be essential to our identity" (PP, 1:42). A "deep" individual is one who is ready to go beyond his or her de facto desires, goals, and aspirations to question their worth, who is ready, moreover, at least to try to change those desires and thus his or her person, should those desires fail to stand up to the scrutiny of radical self-reflection. Indeed, I take *irrationality* to mean the unwillingness to engage in any such self-evaluating process. Irrationality here means a rigidity or inflexibility with regard to one's own feelings, desires, and goals. *Ceteris paribus, rationality* in this domain signifies the preparedness to question oneself and, significantly, to let others do so as well; it signifies the ability to see oneself differently and to change on account of novel insight. In general, we are justified in ascribing strong evaluation to human beings, and to human beings only, because they are such that they raise the question of what they are, who they are, and once opened, that issue can never be definitively closed. It stays with us because it defines the kind of beings that we are: self-interpreting beings, beings partly constituted by the way being that being is interpreted by that being itself.

Echoing (as I just did) Heidegger, Taylor concludes that "*Verstehen* is a *Seinsmodus*" (PP, 1:72). I will not go into the ontology expounded by Heidegger in *Being and Time* but will merely recall his thesis that "understanding always has its mood [*Verstehen ist immer gestimmtes*]"; "understanding is never free-floating, but always goes with some state of mind [*Verstehen ist immer befindliches*]."[12] Heidegger holds that the "mood is not simply a state of feeling, but rather an *Erschlossenheitsweise*,"[13] that is to say, what Taylor refers to as a "mode of disclosure." Since human emotion is interpreted emotion, my having an emotion inevitably engages me in *Verstehen*. The merit of Taylor's essays on philosophical psychology is to lay bare the basic structure of human emotion. He shows how "having" an emotion is something eminently active insofar as it involves ascribing an import in a situation, how feelings, by virtue of attributing imports, open us to the domain of what it is to be human, of what matters to us qua subjects. But what about what matters to *other* subjects? Even though Taylor emphasizes that the class of subject-referring imports is wider than that of self-referring ones, what he has to say about strong evaluation nevertheless ties it to a subject's capacity for self-reflection, for penetrating self-scrutiny. Hence, the subject of which Taylor speaks is engaged in characterization, articulation, and evaluation of his or her own feelings, desires, and goals. The interminability of such a process is brilliantly demonstrated in Taylor's essays. Yet all this appears to bear on how I perceive the way *I* feel in a certain situation. Hence my question: Does Taylor's account bear on my own feelings, desires, and so forth only, or does it also apply to *others'* feelings and desires, that is to say, to my ability to perceive how others perceive a situation?

I have already dwelt briefly on Taylor's indebtedness to Heidegger's analysis of mood (*Stimmung*), attunement (*Gestimmtsein*), and situatedness (*Befindlichkeit*) in *Being and Time*. Now, Taylor nowhere cites that work, and I shall stick to my earlier promise not to go extensively into it; but what matters in view of the question just raised is that for Heidegger, if there were no "attunement" to the world, there would be no "experience" or "perception" either. In this analysis, we could never be affected by anything if "situated being-in-the-world" had not already submitted itself to having entities in the world "matter" to it in the ways that its moods have outlined in advance; there can be no moodless apprehending of things. For Heidegger, significantly, "the affects are modes of my relating to myself [*Sichzusichverhalten*]; in them I encounter myself,"[14]—that is to say, affects signify a way of my engendering myself, of coming to terms with myself and, ultimately, of choosing myself as either authentic or as inauthentic. What concerns me, however, is the role of affect, or emotions more generally, in my relating to *others*, that is, the question of my ability to perceive how others perceive their situation and thus of the extent to which I am affected by the affectedness of others. So whereas Heidegger is concerned with the *ethical-existential* issue of how I relate to myself and conceive of the authentic (MacIntyre would say good) life for myself, my concern is with the *moral* issue of how I relate to others and perceive their weal and woe as at stake in situations.[15]

If Taylor's account of import ascription thematizes only the way I feel in a situation and the way I relate to that feeling of mine, then what is dealt with is the ethical-existential discourse that an I entertains with itself (recall Socrates' notion of an inner dialogue discussed in the chapter on Arendt). If, on the other hand, Taylor's account thematizes—or at least may be so read in order to help illuminate—the way I perceive how others perceive, experience, and feel in a situation, as well as the way I relate to all that in my judgment and action, then what is dealt with is the distinctly moral discourse that comprises two or more subjects and that in that sense opens a truly interpersonal, as opposed to intrapersonal, domain.

Taylor, at least once, does address the moral issue I just defined. He does so in the paragraph that discusses the concept of obligation. I feel called upon to help a wounded person, Taylor says, because I am a human being, that is, a being on whom such a thing as a moral obligation can be laid. Now, although Taylor nowhere makes this his central point (as it is mine), the way I read him allows me to contend that my principal mode of accessing how another person experiences, perceives, and feels in a situation is through feeling. When I "see" that another person is suffering and in need of help, I ascribe the import "suffering" to that situation, and I do so through emotion, by virtue of my ability to feel; and all this applies not only to my "own" situation but to that of others as well. Again, this is my way of putting it, rather than Taylor's; or more to the point, this way of putting the thesis shows how—to answer my question—it bears on the moral as well as on the ethical-existential issue.

My reading of Taylor's explication of obligation establishes a very strong link between the human and the moral; in an earlier section I worked out how I see the two as interrelated. The link is largely implicit in Taylor. As I have defined it, perception means the ability to "see" the human import, the human reality, of a situation. The category of perception has "cognitive" and "emotional" components, corresponding to the two basic faculties of "representative thinking" and "empathy," respectively. Taylor claims that feelings entail cognition in the sense of making a judgment about a certain situation or incident. Hence, to be ashamed is to judge a situation as shameful; it is to be committed to perceiving a situation in a particular manner. In this simple example, my distinction between a cognitive component and an emotional one is not experienced by the actor. "Shame," understood as perception of a situation, is not split into two distinct components for the ashamed person; rather, in the person's shame, feeling it (growing red, the sudden desire to hide from onlookers) is experienced as wholly inseparable and indistinguishable from judging the situation to be a shame-producing one. Terming the former the "emotion" side and the latter the "cognition" side is what theorists do, and it is what the actors themselves can do ex post facto by way of reflection. Viewed as embodying an act of perception, shame is a two-in-one, a joint accomplishment: it is a piece of emotion that is also a piece of cognition, and vice versa.

To sum up, then, an emotion as I conceive it is a feeling, a being moved and affected by something, a first, intuitive grasp of a situation, one awaiting verbal articulation, one calling for further reflection, pondering, evaluation, and—if vehement—for self-control, restraint, and carefulness, as in saying, I try not to be carried away by my emotions. Although we act on our emotions, we may also decide against doing so; emotions invariably direct our attention, but they do not dictate our course of action unless we permit them to, something for which we, however inconvenient, remain entirely responsible. Being "less" than mature and full-fledged judgments, emotions leave room for maneuver, for further, always further, reflection, pondering, evaluation.

Therefore, to "have" an emotion is not something static. It is an open-ended, dynamic mode of relating to the world, in particular to the human and thus eminently moral world. In its capacity as a first, intuitive grasp of a situation, an emotion contains a tentative interpretation of its intentional object. However, in order to evolve into a basis for action, this emotional, "gut," interpretation is in need of further reflection; it is, in a word, in need of the concentrated effort of judgment. To prepare my course of action, I subject my initial perception to further judgment. This is the sequence of moral performance as I conceive it. Through emotion, we enter into this sequence; having gained a first "take" of the situation at hand through emotion, we try to elaborate, question, modify, deepen this "gut" take of it; and in so doing, we engage in it simultaneously through the use of our cognitive powers. In this way, emotional and cognitive capacities join company and assist each other in a joint preoccupation with the situation we have tuned in to. We may, for example, want to know whether the shame we felt is after all justified, or we may wonder whether Sophie was after all humiliated by her husband Carl's remark, which we spontaneously took to be insulting, feeling the rage of indignation grow in us. Should we take action against Carl? We do not know; we need to pause, calm down, reflect. Pondering about what, if any, action to take, we employ our powers of judgment. In judging the "true" nature of Carl's conduct, we need to consult anew how we feel about his behavior toward his wife, and this brings us to a new, more mature view of the perception-through-emotion that triggered the sequence in the first place. My example illuminates the genuinely *hermeneutic*, meaning nonstatic, dynamic, character of the sequence of moral performance. There is a back-and-forth movement between the initial emotional take of, or tuning in to, the situation on the one hand and our interpretative understanding and evaluation of it on the other. And this applies to the sequence of moral performance in general; that is to say, there is a back-and-forth movement between perception, judgment, and action. I have stated above that the level of action is logically preceded by that of judgment, as is judgment by that of perception. Now, it follows from my discussion here that I acknowledge the two-way character of the movement we undertake in moral performance. Although in my view there is no action without judgment, and no judgment without perception, I acknowledge that, having moved from perception to judgment, we often move back to the former for further intake before proceeding to act. Likewise, we may interrupt our action in order to reengage in judgment or perception or both. The sequence is thoroughly dynamic.

In the work of Robert Solomon, human emotion is theorized in a particularly bold way. Solomon draws a great deal on Sartre, even more so than does Taylor on Heidegger. In Sartre's somewhat preliminary *Sketch for a Theory of the Emotions*, an emotion is depicted as a manner of apprehending the world. The manner implied is not innocent; it betrays the pursuit of a conscious strategy on the part of the feeling subject—a strategy to change the world. "Emotion," writes Sartre, "is not apprehension of an exciting subject in an unchanged world; rather since it corresponds to a global modification of consciousness and its relations to the world, emotion expresses itself by means of a radical alteration of the world."[16] Thus conceived, "in emotion it is the body which, directed by consciousness, changes its relationship with the world in order that the world may change its qualities. If emotion is play-acting, the play is one that we believe in."[17] Sartre's thesis is that a subject chooses itself as (an) emotion, for example, as sadness. "Is not," asks Sartre, "this sadness itself a *conduct*? Is it not consciousness which affects itself with sadness as a magical recourse against a situation too urgent? And in this case even, should we not say that being sad means first to make oneself sad?"[18] So instead of passively having or "suffering" an emotion, we actively choose and adopt one as a *magical* means to alter a state of affairs in the world. We are prone to do so especially in situations of failure or embarrassment or insecurity. When thus perceiving ourselves to be cornered, we aim to change the world, but if we fail this, we can at least change ourselves, which is to say that emotions frequently serve purposes of self-deception (*mauvaise foi*). To understand an emotion is to understand its meaning; the latter, asserts Sartre, is always *functional*; that is, my emotion is my answer to an awkward situation, my attempt to cope with the situation by way of seeking to transform it so as to deprive it of its "awkwardness." In Sartre's theory, to adopt an emotion is to choose to know about the world in a particular way; it is to opt for a certain kind of *cognitive* relation or, better, relating to the world. But being a primitive, "magical" means of apprehending the world, emotions are a relatively inferior strategy for coping with the entire host of situations that are viewed as somehow threatening or embarrassing or just novel. Sartre depicts emotions as having two faces, so to speak: emotions are strategies we employ in order to avoid responsibility, *as well as* something for which we are perfectly responsible; emotions are a deliberately chosen means for coping, *as well as* what we hide ourselves behind in order to plead our innocence and our complete lack of purpose.

Drawing heavily on Sartre's sketch, Solomon makes a number of bold claims about the nature of emotion, of which I present the four principal claims here. First, emotions are judgments, and so "emotions can be rational in the same sense in which judgments can be rational."[19] Second, emotions are purposive, serve the ends of a subject; they are rational responses to unusual situations. Third, and related to the second claim, the rationality of our emotions "turns on their success in maximizing self-esteem," which signifies the "common goal" that emotions have. Thus, in love, for example, "because love constitutes our equality with those whom we admire, it is consequently an emotion which *elevates* self-esteem more effectively than any other."[20] Fourth, emotions are actions, and as such aimed at changing the world; they are "our projects," concerned not only "with the way the world is but with the way the world *ought* to be." Every emotion is also "a personal ideology, a projection into the future."[21]

This admittedly superficial presentation should suffice to show the following: Solomon's theory of emotion is conducted within and restricted to what I have termed the ethical-existential discourse. As in Sartre, his philosophical hero, Solomon's focus is on a subject finding itself in a world it somehow has to relate to; it does so, "magically," but nevertheless utterly consciously, by way of emotions, that is, by invoking a certain emotion "in order" to cope with the apparently endless series of "awkward" situations with which that strange world confronts it. So emotions are something a subject relates to in the sense of having recourse to, and manipulatively at that; they are something through which a subject relates—authentically or in bad faith—

to the world so as to effect its transformation. Now, my own central concern is with the *moral* issue of how I relate to *others* through emotion, that is, with the Taylor-inspired thesis about how emotions are our principal mode of access to the experience of others, of cosubjects, in situations where I, through the import ascription furnished by emotion, perceive their weal and woe as somehow at stake. Again, the former perspective on emotion is intrapersonal, the latter interpersonal. As to the relevance of Solomon's theory, my position is that it does not succeed in illuminating the interpersonal, genuinely moral dimension and significance of emotions the way Taylor's theory does, at least in the reading I gave it.

To appreciate my claim, consider Solomon's view on love. As cited above, Solomon holds that "because love constitutes our equality with those whom we admire, it is consequently an emotion which *elevates* self-esteem more effectively than any other." But, as the analysis of Scheler revealed, what is elevated or, better, enhanced in love is not so much my self-esteem as the perceived "value" of the other qua unique person. To love is to be committed to the enhancement of the value of the beloved; it is not *essentially*—although certainly for many people it often is—to seek the enhancement of oneself. Now, however that may be in contemporary "real life," what is beyond dispute is that these are two very different perspectives on love, making visible two different theories on emotions generally: the one focuses on the self, the other on the self's cosubject. In a moral perspective, love is about the relation *between* the two, the person loving and the person being loved. So, when Solomon observes (as quoted earlier) that "love turns upon a *commitment* to a certain kind of seeing," he comes close to the moral, or interpersonal, dimension, because here "seeing" must mean seeing you, not seeing me; elevating you, or *us*, not elevating me, my self-esteem.

I contended above that there is no "disinterested" access to the human reality of suffering. Following Scheler, the access is provided by my taking an interest in the piece of lived reality qua *human* reality. Following Taylor, my emotion-grounded ascription of import is what opens me to the entire domain of what it is to be human; it is what makes me "see" the situation as involving the human reality of suffering, and this reality is, as import, something of significance to my desires or purposes or feelings as subject; it is a matter of "non-indifference" to me. The perceived human reality addresses me, calls on me, lays a *moral* obligation on me, since I am, and see myself as, a human being. This is the link I established between the human and the moral. Following Strawson, finally, there exists an alternative option to that of adopting what he would call a "participatory" attitude—namely an "objective," or detached, attitude. Adopting the latter, I would join company with Davis and share his blindness, his conspicuous not seeing the human reality of suffering; failing to perceive that reality for what it really is, for the import it carries, I would also fail to perceive myself as *addressed* by the situation, as called upon qua moral subject. Missing the human dimension of the situation, I also, and for that very reason, miss its moral dimension. This being so, emphasis must be added to the "human" in Strawson's invaluable observation, "Being *human*, we cannot, in the normal case, do this [i.e., adopt an objective attitude] for long, or altogether."

The line of argument just developed shows there to be an *emotional bond* between the cosubjects involved in the example. As anticipated, I hold the "seeing" presupposed in identifying suffering qua suffering to have established, indeed to *confirm*, an emotional bond between myself and the person I "see" suffering. *The emotional bond is not morally neutral;* on the contrary, it carries an intrinsic moral significance for the subjects affected by it—the significance, namely, that they are emotionally affected by the way the cosubjects experience their situation. It is this emotional bond that I would violate or suspend were I to adopt a so-called objective attitude. Thus, following Strawson, when I claim that we cannot—or in any case cannot for long—maintain an objective attitude, I mean that we cannot maintain for long the suspension of the emotional bond between me and my cosubjects. In other words, I cannot go on perceiving and treating cosubjects as if they were none, as if they were instead objects, as if they were not such beings that the situation in which they find themselves could call on and address me qua moral subject. Indeed, if consequently held onto, my all-around adoption of an objective attitude would disavow my very humanity.

To argue as I have done that we perceive the moral dimension of a situation by virtue of perceiving the human reality it involves is—mutatis mutandis—to argue that processes of *dehumanization* are likely to lead to *moral neutralization* and thus to immoral acts and, in the worst case, to full-scale mass murder.

The Moral Significance of Suspension of the Emotional Bond

> People never do evil so completely and gaily
> as when they do it for conscience' sake.
> —Pascal

I introduced the term "double dehumanization" in my discussion of Eichmann. My claim was that Eichmann not only failed to perceive his victims as human beings but also ceased to understand himself as one as well. Eichmann, that is, not only treated his victims as means instead of as ends in themselves (to invoke Kant) but treated himself that way too. More accurately, he allowed himself to be treated as a mere means, to be used as a mere instrument, in the destruction of the Jews. Therefore, he violated Kant's categorical imperative with respect to his own person as well as with respect to others. What takes place once this double dehumanization is accomplished is viewed as morally neutral. Since allegedly "nonhumans," the Jews are viewed as devoid of moral status and a fortiori as undeserving of the rights and justice that would accompany moral status. In theory, in ideology, and through propaganda, the way is prepared for "killing without killing," for murder with a good conscience. But what about putting such an ideology into practice? How successful is the attempt—collectively and individually— to *produce* and *maintain* a wholly objective and nonparticipant attitude toward other people?

The recent German *Historikerstreit* emphasized the "singularity" of the Nazi genocide of the Jews. However, although I agree that the Holocaust was in crucial respects an unprecedented event, it does not follow that what it disclosed about human psychology, the preconditions of immoral action, and the moral import of human proximity must be seen as strictly confined to that one event. It may not have happened before, but it did happen; and since it did, we must assume that it can happen again. Hence, we would do well to learn as much as we can about how it happened. In what follows I make use of some psychological and historical studies. The "division of labor" implicit between my overall philosophical argument and the empirical sources I draw on here is required and indeed suggests itself, since the issues just raised have been treated by psychologists, historians, and philosophers alike.

In his book *The Nazi Doctors*, Robert J. Lifton explores the psychological mechanisms involved in the individual doctor's attempt to "function" as a person in the Auschwitz environment. First of all, it must be made clear that one could not "prepare" oneself for Auschwitz: one cannot prepare for the unprecedented, for what is totally unknown. And for the average German doctor, Auschwitz was a new world. Being fundamentally unprepared for what waited, the average German doctor faced the psychological task of coping as best as one could once one got there; it was a matter of adjustment.

Adjustment, says Lifton, meant *doubling*: the division of the self into two functioning wholes, so that "a part-self acts as an entire self." The reality of the Auschwitz practice was so novel, so overwhelming in its extremity, as to call for a new self in order that the individual be capable of enduring it. This new self did not replace the old one; rather, it was developed as a counterpart to it, meaning that the resulting two selves had to exist side by side, as it were. "The individual Nazi doctor needed his Auschwitz self to function psychologically in an environment so antithetical to his previous ethical standards. At the same time, he needed his prior self in order to continue to see himself as a human physician, husband, father. The Auschwitz self had to be both autonomous and connected to the prior self that gave rise to it." Doubling follows a holistic principle: "The Auschwitz self 'succeeded' because it was inclusive and could connect with the entire Auschwitz environment." Furthermore, doubling makes for the avoidance of guilt; the second self tends to be the one performing the "dirty work." Finally, doubling involves both "an unconscious dimension—taking place . . . largely outside of awareness—and a significant change in moral consciousness."[22]

Of immediate moral relevance are the implications of doubling for feelings of responsibility and guilt. From his many in-depth interviews with former Nazi doctors, Lifton learned that doubling allowed them to avoid feelings of guilt not by the elimination of conscience but by what he calls the *transfer of conscience*. "The requirements of conscience were transferred to the Auschwitz self, which placed it within its own criteria for good (duty, loyalty to group, 'improving' Auschwitz conditions, etc.), thereby freeing the original self from responsibility for actions there."[23] What happens in doubling is that one part of the self "disavows" another part. What is repudiated is not reality itself but the meaning of that reality. The prior self would condemn the Auschwitz practice; but the individual *being there*, living there, and working there had to take a stand on his doing so that would render him capable of going on with it, one day after the other. Thus, the self that accepted the reality of Auschwitz disavowed the one that did not. So whereas the Nazi doctor knew that he selected, he did not interpret selections as murder; to the contrary, Nazi ideology assured him that by killing "life unworthy of life" (the term was coined in the book *Die Freigabe der Vernichtung lebensunwertes Leben*, coauthored in 1920 by the jurist Karl Binding and the psychiatrist Alfred Hoche, both acclaimed professors), he acted in the service of life. National Socialism picturing itself as "nothing but applied biology," to quote Rudolf Hess, the Jews were killed in order to heal the Nordic race; it was all a matter of "racial hygiene," of making sure that the blood was preserved pure, and of working toward a noble vision of organic renewal, namely, the creation of a vast "German biotic community." Lifton aptly refers to this as the "healing-killing paradox": one killed in order to heal.

Lifton, in a sweeping generalization, holds that Auschwitz "ran on doubling." Always a means of adaptation to extremity, doubling also served to motivate individuals psychologically toward engaging in atrocity. Himmler knew this very well and often played on it in his speeches. To him the killing of Jews was a "heavy task" calling for heroic cruelty. "We had," Himmler assured his SS *Gruppenführer* at Poznan in October 1943, "the moral right vis-à-vis *our* people to annihilate *this* people which wanted to annihilate us. . . . On the whole we can say that we have fulfilled this heavy task with love for our people, and we have not been damaged in the innermost of our being, our soul, our character."[24] What results is the peculiar SS morality according to which the individual's theft of a cigarette is wrong but the murder of millions right, the former being done for personal gain, as it were, the latter for the sake of the German people and the Aryan race. Hence, killing becomes a difficult but necessary form of personal ordeal. Himmler, when asked how he could bring himself to do such terrible things, is reported to have referred to the "karma" of "the Germanic world as a whole," for which "a man has to sacrifice himself even though it is often very hard for him; he oughtn't to think of himself."[25] The ethos of personal sacrifice demands that one "overcome" oneself, that one become "hard." Himmler once witnessed an open-air shooting conducted by Einsatzgruppe B under Commander Nebe in Minsk. The SS *Reichsführer* is said to have grown pale. Deeply moved by the undeniable *presence* of the atrocity taking place before his eyes, Himmler spontaneously stepped forward and addressed his men. In a short but telling speech, he told them to look at nature. Wherever they would look, they would find combat. They would find it among animals and among plants. Whoever tired of the fight went under. Raul Hilberg calls this the "jungle theory." Its essence is succinctly summed up in Oswald Spengler's grim assertion that "when the will to fight is extinguished, so is life itself."[26]

The Auschwitz self emerging from the process of doubling was a self with radically diminished capacity or inclination to feel. Lifton calls this state "psychic numbing," meaning a mental state in which one does not experience psychologically what one is in fact doing. As he points out, "*it is probably impossible to kill another human being without numbing oneself toward that victim*" (emphasis added).[27] It is by virtue of numbing that the Auschwitz self can avoid feelings of guilt when involved in killing. Doubling, numbing, and derealization are parts of the psychological process in which the self had to engage in order to become socialized into an Auschwitz self. For some people, the process was a never-ending one; for others, it would take only a few days to develop what might be called a full-fledged, autonomous Auschwitz self. Needless to say, the people belonging to the first category (significantly, the minority) would be the ones having trouble, perhaps suffering nervous breakdowns; the people in the second category would look upon the Auschwitz reality as "normal"—nothing more, nothing less. The psychological state toward which the Auschwitz socialization brought them—approximated quickly by some, hesitatingly or not at all by others— was one of *dehumanization*. In order to be able to kill, or to "kill without killing," as Lifton puts it in his healing-killing paradox, the individual had to dehumanize himself just as he had, by invoking or even internalizing Nazi race ideology, dehumanized his victims. Killing, the killer has already killed the moral person in himself. There can be no killing without a process of psychic numbing. In the end, "whether a Nazi doctor saw Jews without feeling their presence, or did not see them at all, he no longer experienced them as beings who affected him—that is, as human beings."[28]

Hannah Arendt held Auschwitz to have taught humankind that "everything is possible." There was no way in which one could prepare for what went on in the death camp. One learns about it, and then prefers not to know; one sees the evidence that it was possible, yet goes on to live as if it were not. Indeed, it is tempting to speculate that the sheer improbability of the Final Solution was a presupposition of its actually coming about; too many people for too long a time clung to the view that it could not be real—meanwhile, it became all too real. What matters is that this description goes for the participants as well as for you and me. Reflecting on his interviews with surviving Nazi doctors, Lifton confesses that they "seemed to me to be messengers from another planet. They were describing a realm of experience so extreme, so removed from the imagination of anyone who had not been there, that it was literally a separate reality. That quality—the absolute removal from ordinary experience—provided the Auschwitz self with still another dimension of numbing." Hence, "one could not believe what one was doing, even as one was doing it." Lifton cites a surviving prisoner-doctor, Marianne F., who observed that "the fact is that if you do something that is totally unbelievable, and you are incapable of believing it, you don't believe it."[29] And what one does not believe, whatever the evidence before one's eyes, one does not feel. In the extreme setting of Auschwitz reality, one derealizes what one does in the very moment of doing it. Derealization is a principal means of fending off feelings of guilt, in that it prevents them from arising in the first place.

Numbing is not only a process of adaptation to extremity, it is also a strategy for the creation and sustenance of a *situation* of extremity, that is, of an atrocity-producing situation such as Auschwitz. Numbing, that is to say, not merely helps an individual cope with a situation of extremity but also is instrumental in the very generation of such a situation. The initial production as well as the day-to-day reproduction of an atrocity-producing situation thus rests on numbing.

The Nazis achieved and secured psychic numbing in a number of ways. Consider first the role played by *ideology*. If a doctor sending Jewish children to the gas chambers sees himself as a biological soldier unselfishly engaged in purification of the blood, as taking over evolution from nature in order to prevent humanity from being "annihilated by degeneration" (in Konrad Lorenz's words), then killing turns into healing, murder into therapy, and the victim is no longer experienced as a (fellow) human being. Numbing as effected by the medico-ideological manipulation of semantics makes killing easy; the manipulation of semantics is ultimately a self-manipulation.

But numbing can also be produced by sophisticated administrative techniques. The more advanced the *technology* of killing, the greater the distance between doer and deed, perpetrator and victim, and the less the killer feels. Here numbing goes hand in hand with what I refer to as moral neutralization. Killing, once considered an inescapably moral issue, is turned into an administrative issue, a purely technical task. Albert Speer, among others, has stressed the Nazis' success in rendering their most murderous actions technical problems. Killing is industrialized. Auschwitz is an institution or, better, a *Lebenswelt* in its own right, where the victim is killed without direct interference from the perpetrator; the latter is left with the purely technical task of "making sure" that the destruction machinery is running smoothly. Industrialized killing having, so to speak, come into its own in Auschwitz, it develops the self-reproductive logic of an enormous *perpetuum mobile*. SS *Unterscharführer* Franz Suchomel practices the peculiar jargon accompanying the technification of murder when he says that "Belzec was the studio. Treblinka was an admittedly primitive, yet well-functioning assembly line of death [*Fließband des Todes*]. Auschwitz was a factory."[30] A factory indeed: when Auschwitz achieved its peak, killing more than twenty thousand Jews in one twenty-hour period, "the capacity for destruction," says a surviving doctor, "was approaching the point of being unlimited." Technology helps create a hermetic world in which ethics, according to a representative Nazi doctor, "played no part—the word does not exist."[31] It is not only that technological distancing "alters" the moral mindset, as shown by Lifton, but that the reality of killing does not come to be viewed, let alone experienced, in terms of morality at all. The numbing produced by advanced technology, removing as it does the act of killing more and more from the "embarrassment" characteristic of face-to-face interaction, apparently prevents issues of moral impact from entering the individual's field of perception. The numbed individual fails to perceive himself as a moral being; hence his actions entail no moral dilemmas to him. He is the perfect killer.

In addition to the numbing brought about by ideology and technology was that brought about by modern *bureaucracy*. "Bureaucracy," says Lifton, "makes possible the entire genocidal sequence: organization, continued function, and distancing, numbing, and doubling of perpetrators."[32] Bureaucracy helps render killing unreal. Numbing here assumes the form of impersonalization and reification; the bureaucrat views himself as a no-nonsense person eager to get on with business; in doing so, he encounters only cases (*Sachen*) and administrative difficulties awaiting their solution, never human beings. He sees nothing, hears nothing, smells nothing; he is not in a position to bear direct witness to the reality of ongoing mass murder; and therefore, he does not feel affected by that reality. He is not in a position to develop bad conscience; his concern is not with the "right or wrong" of the overall end of the process—that is, the killing of millions of human beings—but solely with his function as a means, or tool, that is to say, with the loyalty to his superiors, which the ethos of bureaucracy has taught him never to suspend. The Jew simply never appears; from the very start of the genocidal sequence, the individual Jew is subjected to a derealization making him or her invisible and nonexistent long before the actual killing itself. With mass murder thus being everywhere, but at the same time nowhere, there develops a feeling of inevitability, a sense of the inexorable, that one might as well go along because nothing can be done. As observed by Lifton, "the bureaucracy's structure and function—the murderous flow of its action—becomes itself the rationale, as clarity of cause and effect gives way to a sense not only of inevitability but of necessity."[33] The *Versachlichung* of the killing effects an extreme alienation of the perpetrators from the real "business" in which they are engaged. As described by Hilberg, ancillary bureaucracies can all too readily be enlisted to carry out the killing; transporting Jews to the death camp, the German railroad organization throughout the war held strictly to its own conventional bureaucratic routine. "By not varying their routine and not restructuring their organization, not changing a thing in their correspondence or mode of communication," writes Lifton, officials of German railroads were able to "cope with" what they were doing.[34] The sheer force of habituation and routinization within the quasi-self-sufficient environment of a gigantic bureaucratic apparatus both produces and helps sustain psychic numbing among its personnel. Thus, paradoxically, the unprecedented, some would say "unthinkable," murder of six million Jews was accomplished within an all-pervading atmosphere of business as usual, of the innocence that goes with seeming normalcy. In such a situation, "ordinary men were to perform extraordinary tasks," as Hilberg drily remarks. Prima facie, nothing was changed, because nothing had to be. The usual procedures were applied also in unusual situations; one had recourse to the familiar in the very process of producing the unprecedented. "The machinery of destruction," Hilberg notes, "was structurally no different from organized German society as a whole; the difference was only one of function."[35]

In sum, the methods and routines of the bureaucracy are totally *indifferent* to the actual nature of the "problems," or *Sachen*, to which they are applied; even in the case of killing human beings, the problems encountered can only be "technical" ones calling for improved technical solutions. The implied indifference affects the individual bureaucrat as well: performing his job, he is indifferent to the nonprofessional, nontechnical consequences of his performance. Again, the *Sache* overshadows the victims, preventing them from emerging as human beings, so that nowhere, it seems, through the whole sequence of bureaucratized and industrialized killing is the reality of that killing confronted, experienced, felt. Indifference thus seals the work done by ideology, technology, and bureaucracy to fend off feelings of guilt, in short, to produce perfect psychic numbing. And numbing is what we find to accompany mass murder. The dialectic of numbing and killing enters a vicious circle and becomes self-reinforcing: the more numb one gets, the more one kills; and the more one kills, the more numb one gets. Once set loose, this dialectic knows no internal constraints; "the ever-growing capacity for destruction," writes Hilberg, "cannot be arrested anywhere."[36] Or can it?

Lifton's claims about "doubling" and its role in the killings the Nazi doctors participated in have come under attack from a number of authors. A forceful and recent criticism can be found in Berel Lang's *Act and Idea in the Nazi Genocide.*

Lifton's starting point is that the conduct of the Nazi doctors is morally contradictory. He considers their conduct to be divided into two regular patterns of perception, judgment, and action. From this Lifton infers that the doctors were citizens of two worlds: they lived in two separate moral domains, blocking out each one in turn as the other prevailed. In this conception, the two domains are separate in the strong sense that each domain is self-sufficient and autonomous. To explain how it could be possible for a single person to live and act within two allegedly antithetical moral domains, Lifton introduces his thesis of doubling; to each of the two domains there corresponds a distinct "self": on the one hand an autonomous Auschwitz domain with a concomitant Auschwitz self and on the other hand a non-Auschwitz domain with a non-Auschwitz self. The first self is the specific by-product of the psychological task of having to adapt to and cope with the novel and extreme Auschwitz reality, whereas the second self by and large is the person's old one, that is, the self as developed before the reality of the death camp. This thesis of doubling Lifton takes to solve the problem of moral contradiction: if two autonomous selves coexist without the one interfering with the other, the fact that they are (substantively) antithetical is prevented from growing into a source of contradictions to be resolved by the person who possesses two selves.

Seeking to refute Lifton's thesis, Lang argues that

> it is not the *self* that is divided in the examples cited; [rather,] a single self has turned its attention to what it conceives as two different— morally different—objects; and this is effected within a *single* [emphasis added] moral universe of discourse. The fact that the Nazi doctors or the camp guards might act differently in different 'domains' does not mean that they are following different principles; the principles could be consistent or even identical, entailing differences in conduct because their 'objects' are judged to differ. (NG, 53)

Thus, the doctors in charge regard the medical experiments conducted on children within the camp not as experiments on children but first as experiments on Jews, a designation that overrides their identity as children. The fact that the children outside the camp, and for that matter the doctor's own, are treated otherwise, does not mean that they are subject to the rules of a different moral world. Rather, argues Lang, they are subject to the rules of the same moral world—they are treated differently "not because of differences in the categories of two domains, but because children are categorized differently within the *same* domain" (NG, 54; cf. 195).

As these quotations make clear, Lang holds Lifton's thesis of doubling to be false. In Lang's view, the conduct of the Nazi doctors can be explained without any recourse to psychological theories that assume a split into two selves—be it two selves that do not communicate with each other or that to some extent do. Far from that, the case of the Nazi doctors is one where a single self acts within a single moral universe; in doing so, the individual will act differently at different times and in relation to different contexts. But there is nothing extreme, let alone pathological, about this; it is true of much human conduct in general.

What *is* extreme in the Nazi case, however—and I proceed with this argument independently of Lang—is the significance accorded to the difference that is claimed to exist between the Aryans and the Jews, a pivotal, ineradicable difference posited between two groups or (pseudoscientifically defined) "races" within one and the same moral universe and, moreover, a difference acted on by the Nazi, remaining a single self, within that one universe. It follows that the Nazi can abuse and kill some children while adoring and loving others, without there arising any contradiction, not because the self has been split into two but because the first group of children is engendered in the moral universe as *Jewish* children and the second group is engendered there as *Aryan* ones, and this difference—internal to the one universe—is such that it justifies and calls for the displayed difference in conduct on the part of the Nazi doctors. Consequently, the new reality created by Auschwitz does not produce—and does not have to produce—as its counterpart a novel, second self. Rather, the self remains the same, and the novelty lies on the side not of the moral agent but of this agent's *objects:* within the moral universe, the Jews are singled out as a group devoid of moral status, as a group that is not entitled to specifically moral rights; hence, they are not (or no longer)—in this sense—moral addressees. What this amounts to is what I call a moral neutralization of the objects in question. It has been a central thesis of mine that, in the Nazi case, dehumanization (i.e., designating the Jews as *Untermenschen*, a process starting, judicially, with the abrogation of citizenship for the Jews of Germany in 1935 and terminating, literally, with identifying the *Nacht und Nebel* prisoners not by name but by number) has proved a sufficient condition of moral neutralization.

Having deprived the Jew of human as well as moral being—the former constituting a condition and preparation for the latter—the infliction of pain on the Jew came to be seen neither as a "human" nor as a "moral" issue; hence the asserted absence of moral dilemmas. The suffering of the nonhuman and nonmoral Jew was beyond human empathy, beyond the scope of compassion; stripped of humanity, of being a cosubject, a fellow human being, the Jew who suffered failed to elicit in the ardent Nazi—if we are to believe Höss— even the kind of emotional response the Nazi may often have shown when witnessing the suffering of an animal. The Jew, once deprived of human as well as moral being, has nothing to fall back on, not even the status granted to animals qua objects of suffering, which inspire compassion in us.

Let us assume that Lang is right and that Lifton, in effect, is wrong. The agent, then, is a single self acting within a single moral universe. I have noted how such an agent may behave differently toward different groups of children. Now, the "difference" that the Jews are considered to epitomize must be such that it makes a difference in *moral* terms—otherwise, the difference in conduct toward, for example, Aryan and Jewish children should be unwarranted. That is, what would be lacking justification is the assertion according to which the one group *merits* a treatment diametrically opposed to that reserved for the other. In short, the Jews must differ from the non-Jews in some respect that is held to be morally relevant. It might be asked here, What is the argument the Nazis offer as support for their contention that moral relevance can be attributed to the difference between the Jews and the non-Jews? *Is* there an argument—or is it just that we, engaged as we are in philosophical discourse, take it as a *petitio principii* that there must and ought to be one? Perhaps the Nazis believe in the asserted morally relevant difference without having, or wishing to have, any argument to warrant their belief? Come to think of it, do not the historians concerned with Nazism unanimously tell us that it was a deeply anti-intellectual ideology, indeed one taking pride precisely in the unsurpassed vehemence and *Konsequenz* of its struggle against everything associated with intellectual principles?

To be sure, Nazism does signify a struggle of this sort. Yet we cannot leave it at that. There is more to Nazi ideology than what follows from its notorious anti-intellectualism, and part of this "more" has to do with morality. Recall what words Himmler chose when addressing his SS *Gruppen-führer* as the Holocaust was well under way in October 1943: "We had the moral right vis-à-vis *our* people to annihilate *this* people which wanted to annihilate us." Annihilation is framed in a language appealing to, not excluding, a notion such as "the moral right." The applied rhetoric is not morally neutral; the "task" and "mission" it portrays is not morally neutral; the two peoples it depicts as meeting in struggle do not meet in a morally neutral universe, let alone in two separate domains; they clearly confront each other within a single *moral* universe.

My last observations may rightfully be taken as support for the position held by Lang. There are, however, some distinctions worth drawing here— distinctions neglected in Lang no less than in Lifton. In my opinion, it is crucial to distinguish between the level of ideology and *Weltanschauung*, on the one hand, and that of individual agency, including psychology, on the other. In view of this distinction, it is possible that Lang is right with regard to ideology, whereas Lifton is right with regard to individual agency. Hence, the two positions are not mutually exclusive. In other words, the thesis that Nazi ideology designates Jews and Aryans as confronting each other in deadly struggle within a single, morally nonneutral universe does not *eo ipso* exclude the thesis that the Nazi doctors who were engaged in the day-to-day business of carrying out the Final Solution, as demanded of them by Nazi ideology, in many cases—for psychological and wholly extraideological reasons—developed two strictly separate selves in the course of trying to cope with what they were doing. Therefore, we must be careful not to conflate the two levels. This being so, I do see a tendency on the part of Lang to collapse agency into ideology. Lang's critique of Lifton's thesis offers no clinical counterevidence, and this means that Lifton's case, based as it is on numerous lengthy interviews with Nazi as well as non-Nazi camp doctors, is the one of the two that is built on empirical material.

It is also possible to take the pragmatic (and theoretically less exciting) view that the thesis of doubling holds true for some of the cases considered, yet by no means for all or even a majority of them. To do justice to Lifton, we must bear in mind—Lang tends not to—that the concept of doubling is not applied to all cases; that is, it is not intended by Lifton to be a global or exhaustive explanation of the phenomenon he set out to examine, the mechanisms at work in psychological adaptation to extremity.

The Nazis accord moral relevance to differences related to race, on the broad collective level, and to differences related to genetic features in mentally retarded or otherwise "abnormal" individuals, as documented in the notion of *lebensunwertes Leben*, which paved the way for the Euthanasie program and the so-called T4 project. Clearly, we may have good reasons to hold that the Nazis were mistaken in according such a relevance to such differences; we may, to repeat an earlier point, question whether they, in doing this, had recourse to arguments of sufficient cogency to stand up to the test of rational inquiry. This poses an issue for those who are mainly concerned with the problematic of moral justification. My central concern, however, is with the preconditions of moral performance. Therefore, I must take as my point of departure, and take seriously, that the Nazis acted on their belief in the moral relevance of the differences referred to. They did this as a matter of historical fact, whether for good or for bad reasons. Thus, the question is, How could they do what they did?

My earlier account has stressed the importance of distancing the perpetrator from the victim, as produced by ideology, technology, and bureaucracy;

of what I have termed double dehumanization; of what I elaborate more fully below as the suspension of the emotional bond; and finally of processes of psychic numbing. To concentrate on the last (i.e., on the point relating most directly to Lifton), I have made the claim that numbing prevents issues of moral impact from entering the individual's field of perception. More boldly, I claimed that numbed individuals fail to perceive themselves as moral beings; they suppress their sensitivity to the suffering confronting them. These numbed Nazi doctors are "perfect" killers because they have suppressed the sensitivity that discloses suffering. If numbing is partly produced by a situation of extremity and partly helps produce and sustain it, then my claim is hardly too strong. Put otherwise, if there is such a thing as a perfect killer, that person can be expected to be—and to become increasingly—numb toward his or her victims, meaning, insensitive to them, emotionally unaffected by the suffering inflicted on them. A rival thesis would perhaps argue that hatred or sadism is what makes for the perfect killer, not numbing. I discuss, and repudiate, that thesis in Chapter 5. To anticipate a central argument, killers who are numb are "perfect" because, since unaffected by what happens to their victims, they are never satisfied, they have never had enough; they cannot be *sated* the way a person acting from affective engagement, that is, from an emotion such as hatred, can. By contrast, numbed individuals—in this, at one with indifferent individuals—may go on forever; if or when they stop, the reason is likely to be a nonpsychological one.

I maintain my earlier claims about the nature of psychic numbing, then, even though Lang—arguing along ideological rather than clinical and psychological lines—may have succeeded in casting Lifton's thesis of doubling into doubt. What matters for my purposes, however, is that my claims about numbing stand on their own; they are not dependent on Lifton's thesis of doubling being right. I therefore retain my account of processes of numbing while acknowledging—though not without criticism—the force of Lang's case against Lifton.

I close this section with my view on what type of moral universe the Nazi can be said to have acted within. I have observed that Himmler deems the right to annihilate the Jews a "moral" right, as does Hitler in many passages in *Mein Kampf*. I have also shown that the ideology peculiar to the "task" performed by the Nazi doctors represents killing as "healing," implying that the Nazi doctor contributes to an honorable, historical, and morally nonneutral mission. Furthermore, I have shown the SS morality to entail that while the murder of millions is right, the theft of a cigarette is wrong. The reason, I think, is that it is morally condemnable to keep for oneself something that has belonged to a Jew, not because one has any moral obligations or duties to the Jew, but because one has such to the German state, to which—and to which alone—the confiscated Jewish belongings rightfully belong. This difference reveals that one has no moral obligations to the Jew because the Jew is not a moral addressee, because the Jew is *ein Untermensch*. The Jew is devoid of moral status; at best, he is temporarily useful as *Arbeitskraft*. On the other hand, one has strictly to observe moral obligations and duties to the German state and *Volk* because the "racially superior" Germans are full-fledged moral addressees.

Apart from shedding more light on my claim that the Jews were subjected to "moral neutralization," this claim of racial superiority says something crucial about the moral universe the Nazi lives within. First, within this universe two groups confront each other, the Jews and the Germans; second, the Nazi belongs to the Germans; third, it is this group—and this group only—the Nazi owes moral obligations and duties, since of the two groups only the Germans are moral addressees and hence possess moral status. Whether the individual Nazi is able to act on these differences without developing two separate selves need not concern us now. What matters is that it is morally right and morally demanded to treat the Jews, labeled *Untermenschen*, as devoid of moral status. In short, it is morally *prescribed* to treat a group of people, engendered within the moral universe as nonmoral objects, as objects entitled to no moral standing and possessing no moral rights whatsoever. If my formulation is paradoxical, it is so because it tries to capture the highly paradoxical Nazi reality.

I have in earlier sections directed attention to the contributions to industrialized mass killings made by ideology, technology, and bureaucracy. These are extraindividual, societal forces, forces yielding an overwhelming impact on the way individuals come to see themselves and others. Nazi Germany is the historical evidence par excellence that society—or, more particularly, such societal forces as those just mentioned—by no means is always promoting, let alone in some mysterious way "guaranteeing" or "safeguarding" morality. On the contrary, what is demonstrated in the present case is the frightening effectiveness with which societal forces, when pulling uniformly in one specific direction, in fact help produce immorality rather than morality. This being so, the task for individuals qua moral agents becomes that of *resisting* what their society prescribes in the fields of moral perception, judgment, and action. It becomes their task—and their irrevocably *individual* one at that—to reject the societally upheld moral codes rather than successfully internalize and go along with them. This latter is arguably what philosophers as well as sociologists have commonly held ever since

Durkheim launched his famous view that society is a "morality-producing plant," that society by its very nature precedes, preserves, and thus always sides with morality. In this view, the individual may go wrong about what is morally right, but society may not. [37]

Whether we consider the case of Eichmann or the cases of the Nazi doctors participating in lethal medical experiments on camp prisoners, it is correct to say that "society had already appointed the objects of moral action (and disqualified others as such objects) *before* the thinking leading to moral judgment [started]." [38] Nazi society "specialized" in the ability to draw the boundaries between moral and nonmoral objects in a manner claiming unconditional, because *naturgesetzliche*, validity. It scarcely needs to be added that given such societal pressure, defiance is hard to come by.

But what is implied, as far as moral perception is concerned, in the statement that a society "specialized" in the ability to draw the boundaries between moral and nonmoral objects in a manner claiming unconditional validity?

Obviously, society—and by this I mean *any* society—presents and pre- scribes a particular way of drawing the boundaries between moral and nonmoral objects to its members. Society teaches its members that there is a distinction between morally appropriate and morally inappropriate objects. Against the background of this most general feature, a given society will encourage its members to observe that the desired and thus allegedly "correct" way of drawing such boundaries is this one particular way. It follows that individuals' inability or, worse still, outright unwillingness to observe the boundaries adhered to by their society will risk being met with some kind of sanctions from the society. Their deviation from the collectively sustained moral codes of the day will be considered a step in the wrong direction—a step, that is, away from what is recognized as sound moral performance and thus toward what is condemned as immoral.

Again, there is nothing new in this description. So far I have merely restated observations made in the discussions of MacIntyre and Arendt. MacIntyre's advocacy of a revitalized but nonetheless conventional neo- Aristotelian morality, where the prospect of ethos-transcending critique seems to me endangered, if not precluded; and Arendt's reflections on the conditions for moral conduct in a society that has turned the command, Thou shalt not kill, on its head so as to demand preparedness to endorse as morally acceptable the murder of an entire category of what has been deemed nonmoral objects—these are but two previous cases where the boundary-drawing promoted by society was set over and against the moral standards adhered to by the (more or less rebellious) individual.

I believe that there is a lesson to be learned here that is not confined to but reaches far beyond the historical experience of totalitarianism. What makes Nazi totalitarianism a special case is, first, where precisely it drew the boundaries and, second, the authoritarian fashion in which it forced the individual to comply with the suprahistorically posited quasi-natural boundaries that mark the Nazi *Weltanschauung*. But the general point I wish to stress is that in every society, whether liberal or authoritarian, the art of perceiving and observing the boundaries between moral and nonmoral objects, that is, between objects that are moral subjects and objects that are not, is something handed down to individuals by their society. Perception—*here* a boundary exists, and *this* is what it contains—is not a spontaneous making of the individual. Far from arising *de novo*, as if within a social vacuum, perception is taught to individuals, in a sense even imposed on them by society. Perception is from early on prescribed by the way significant, later also generalized, others perceive. Accordingly, society awaits and readily rewards or condemns individuals' displayed ability to adopt society's way of seeing as *their* way of seeing.

Hence, individuals are not free to pick just any moral objects they would like. Perception does not start from scratch; it is guided, channeled, given a specific horizon, direction, and target by society. Society, r.ot the single individual, selects the appropriate objects of moral concern and the like; other objects it rules out, conceals from view, demanding that the individual do so as well. Now, Habermas and other proponents of postconventional ethics will hasten to point out that the individual is an autonomous chooser among possible objects. In this domain no less than in others affected by modernity's craving for strictly rational legitimation, the individual is to have a say about where the boundaries should be drawn. This is the broad sense in which Habermas says that "actors owe their mutual understanding to *their own* interpretative performances."[39] But liberal societies' proclaimed notion of argumentative justification as the only legitimation that will do does nothing to alter the fact just observed that the boundaries exist prior to the individual. Individuals confront them as already posited and already acted on by their society. To be sure, a modern liberal society will allow individuals more room for autonomous boundary-drawing than an authoritarian one. But the point that holds for both societies is that the societal forces may predetermine—to a high degree, that is, though not completely—what is to appear as an "appropriate" object of perception in the eyes of individuals, often without their realizing that they are subject to such predetermination. This predetermining entails that individuals' *experience* of objects at hand may be blocked; instead of opening up toward the other, the other is disclosed in a pregiven, fixed manner. In short, individuals' "free choice" may be but a sham. Their perception may be preempted by the choice made by society. (I shall examine this in great detail in the section on anti-Semitism in Chapter 5.)

In this way, though only crudely indicated, the recognition of all human subjects as objects of moral perception may be barred. I have argued that moral perception presupposes empathy. However, if I am persuaded by the societal forces around me (promoting, perhaps, rigid stereotypy or abstraction of categories of others) that this and that class of objects of perception are nonmoral objects, this persuasion may prove preemptive in the sense that it may help block the activization of my faculty of empathy. "Blocking" in this case is selective, not all-encompassing; yet though "societally" rather than psychopathologically brought about, such blocking may produce effects nothing less than disastrous for the "objects" affected by the nonactivization of empathy.

If anything is established beyond doubt in the course of this discussion, it is that the faculty of empathy, so decisive in our reaching toward others as human and moral others, is a faculty that is exceedingly vulnerable to societal manipulation. The Holocaust is only the most drastic example of how relatively easily—given the momentum of the supra- or extraindividual forces of ideology, technology, and bureaucracy (properties of all modern societies)—humanity's emotional abilities can be suspended, impeded, and arrested, in ways that disallow the other to be disclosed as anything else than an abstract target, not a human face to which I can relate myself in *my* human and emotional being. This shows that empathy as required in moral perception is utterly indispensable and utterly precarious; it must be allowed to operate, to reach out toward and recognize (*anerkennen*) its specific object for moral concern to prevail, yet it is always susceptible to the larger-than-individual forces that in every society help channel the activization or nonactivization of the individual's emotional as well as cognitive-sensuous abilities. If I should pick an object that society all around me unanimously deems to be a "wrong" object, my resisting such pressure or succumbing to it is a question decided by, say, my independence as a person, my preparedness to stand up for what I—but perhaps no one else around me—believe is right.

I now return to the issue from which I broke off, that of the possibility of arresting "the ever-growing capacity for destruction."

In his book, Lifton quotes a statement by his colleagues Alexander and Margarete Mitscherlich to the effect that most Germans of the Nazi generation were incapable of confronting their guilt because its dimensions would be too overwhelming. They could not, then or now, permit themselves to feel. The argument is familiar to readers of the Mitscherlichs' *Inability to Mourn*. The absence of feelings of guilt is a main characteristic of psychic numbing. Conversely, if the individual were capable of developing feelings of guilt, there would be a possibility that the process of numbing could be arrested. Feelings of guilt, the Mitscherlichs point out, arise on the condition that the other "is experienced as 'real' [*eine wirkliche Erfahrung darstellt*]." Guilt is bound up with being affected; it depends on "the development of object-relations, that is to say, of relations with one's fellow-humans that are mutually important." This analysis is confined to interaction between humans. Here, the other will have to appear as a subject capable of feeling pain, whereas I will have to be able to experience the other as a subject having that ability. Thus, guilt essentially involves a reciprocal relation between two subjects experiencing each other as subjects in the sense just given. "Morality should prevent us from harming others."[40] The demand never to inflict pain on the other makes sense only on the presupposition that "ich ihn in all seiner Fremdheit, in dieser seiner Andersartigkeit respektieren kann." Note that the emphasis is not on my similarity, let alone identity, to the other but on the other's *difference* from me, the other's *otherness*. Indeed, "true empathy involves conscious awareness of the difference and the uniqueness of the love object."[41]

Here the Mitscherlichs suddenly speak of love: when we love, we love the other precisely in his or her otherness. Freud made the same point when he said that love is to mourning what infatuation is to melancholia. It takes the ability to love to be able to mourn. "Mourning evolves," Freud explains, "when the lost object was loved for its own sake." Hence, love is the product of difference or, to be more precise, of my conscious recognition of the otherness of the other as something that *in itself* merits my recognition. Opposed to the mourning of the other qua other in love, the depression characteristic of melancholia is a dwelling not on the loss of the other but on the loss of the self that the loss of the other is felt to bring about. "In mourning it is the world which has become poor and empty; in melancholia it is the ego itself." In melancholia, that is, the affection I felt for the other was grounded on narcissistic identification, meaning that I had picked out that particular other "because of my picture [of it] and its willingness to conform to my imagination."[42] The identification involved in melancholia thus abolishes the moment of recognized difference, or otherness, so essential in love. Having identified myself with the object (to use Freud's terminology) and made my self-esteem rest on the success of that identification, the loss of the object will throw me back on myself, which is to say, on a self that is poor, empty, impoverished. Having lost my self-esteem through the loss of the object, I develop a feeling of having been "let down" by it. What was once held to be love turns into hate; furious that the object could so radically disappoint me, furious, that is to say, finally to discover the power the object exerted because of my having in fact invested it with that power, I seek to repress the original idealization and to replace it with deprecation, telling myself that the object, after all, was not "worthy" of the dedication once felt. So whereas the immediate reaction to the loss of the "loved" object is often a cruel self-deprecation combined with bitter self-reproaches, these reproaches will later on be directed outward, toward the lost object, representing the ego's revenge on it. Psychologically, the displayed rage against the object has the function of restoring the frustrated ego's self-esteem, which was threatened with loss by the loss of the object, which was originally chosen not for its own sake (as in love) but in an act of narcissistic identification. German Nazis, the Mitscherlichs argue, can be seen to run through the sequence of melancholia just sketched; hence the competition between *Volk* and *Führer* over who had let the other down the most. The implied substitution of narcissistic identification for object-love is the essence of what the Mitscherlichs call the German inability to mourn. It arises from the inability to love.

That we abstain from inflicting pain on the ones we love may appear obvious. Equally obvious, but more problematic, is the fact that we, to be honest, do not love that many people. When love is taken to mean the full recognition of the other qua other and therefore of his or her otherness "in itself," then we have to confess that, in real life, it takes a lot to love. From this we are forced to conclude that the Mitscherlichs' demand that for there to be a morality keeping us from inflicting pain on others, we shall have to love them, seems to be without much hope of ever being satisfied. The question is, How strong a link is there between morality and love? Does the former really have to be "founded" on the latter?

Feelings of guilt, I wrote, are bound up with being affected; and to be affected by the other, the other must appear to us as a "real experience" that we have. In other words, the other must be perceived as a subject in the full sense of the term, as an autonomous person able to feel pain and to be hurt. Next, to be able to be affected by the other, we have to feel affection for him or her. This is not exactly the Mitscherlichs' way of putting it, but nonetheless it seems to capture their meaning. But does not this requisite affection equal the love necessary as a precondition of morality that was found so problematic? Love, I asserted, is my conscious recognition of the otherness of the other as something that *in itself* merits my recognition. Compare this formulation to the Kantian categorical imperative according to which we are always to treat the other not merely as a means but as an end in itself. The similarity is striking: in love, it is the otherness of the other "in itself" that I recognize; aware of my otherness from the other, I love him or her for the corresponding otherness that he or she "is" to me. The other, that is to say, represents an end in itself; I love him or her not "because of" what he or she does to me, but independently of utility and "by virtue" of the who that the other person is. To love because of what the other *does*, then—and *to me*, at that—is not to love but to confuse love with utility, with the usefulness of this or that being done by the other person. Rather, we love by virtue of what the other *is*, *in him- or herself*, the other appearing no longer as a means but as a Kantian end in itself, no longer as exchangeable but as irreplaceable.

Love in the sense here intended is not the love restricted to, say, the man-woman relationship; that is, it does not equal erotic love (though of course allowing for it). Rather, it is the love Aristotle had in mind when he described true friendship as a relationship where each wishes for the other what is perceived as best for the other. Also, in cases where our friend makes a major decision with which we disagree, we will, while signaling our disagreement with our friend, respect him or her for what he or she does, provided it be our friend's own autonomous decision. A disagreement or argument revealing the profundity of the difference between two friends ("I never realized we were *that* different") is likely to prove a challenge to our toleration and generosity, but it will not challenge the relationship per se. In love, difference is not looked upon as something to be fought and overcome but as a source of mutual enrichment. Beautiful on paper, it is hard work in real life.[43]

This tentative definition of what is here meant by love provides an approach to the problem of its connection to morality. The basic limitation from which love cannot be freed does not so much lie in the fragile nature of love itself—due to the frailty of human nature—as in the *boundaries of the setting* in which love appears. Is it not telling that the descriptions of love just offered are without exception taken from the sphere of intimacy of face-to-face interaction? And what is more, did I not in my discussion of psychic numbing repeatedly stress the connection between various types of distancing and mass murder? How can the processes of dehumanization through numbing be arrested by the humanization of love when the latter is restricted to a small-scale setting? Was not the challenge posed for an ethics of the late twentieth century that it would have to be a persuasive response to the modern scenario of killing, where, to quote Hilberg, "the perpetrator can now kill his victims without touching them, without hearing them, without seeing them"?[44]

Hilberg is right: killing is not so difficult as it used to be. Insofar as the different types of distancing produced by ideology, technology, and bureaucracy—each of which effectively separates perpetrator from victim—are permitted to develop according to their inner logic, it seems that there is indeed no way of arresting the process. The very *irreversibility* of these developments, then, seems to help make killing easier and easier. Killing, something previously possible only within a small-scale setting, has become possible—better, utterly real—within a large-scale setting and consequently has been rendered increasingly abstract.

But as Himmler knew, through the personal experience of witnessing an *Einsatzgruppe* open-air shooting, the bond pertaining to face-to-face interaction had to be systematically suspended, or else killing would produce a number of unwelcome psychological as well as moral problems. What I have in mind here is brought out in a conversation that took place between Himmler, visibly shocked by what had happened before his eyes, and Obergruppenführer von dem Bach-Zelewski:

BACH-ZELEWSKI: Reichsführer, those were only a hundred.
HIMMLER: What do you mean by that?
BACH-ZELEWSKI: Look at the eyes of the men in this Kommando, how deeply shaken they are! These men are finished (*fertig*) for the rest of their lives. What kind of followers are we training here? Either neurotics or savages![45]

Bach-Zelewski himself was to feel the effects: hospitalized with severe stomach and intestinal ailments, he experienced "psychic exhaustion" and "hallucinations concerned with the shootings of Jews."[46] As Rudolf Höss, Auschwitz camp commander, recalled in his autobiography, "Many members of the Einsatzkommandos, unable to endure wading through blood any longer, had committed suicide. Some had even gone mad. Most of the members of these Kommandos had to rely on alcohol when carrying out their horrible work." As a consequence of the obstinacy of the severe psychological obstacles involved in mass shootings, eventually only gas was seriously considered as a more "suitable" method, and this for two reasons, the first technical, the second psychological. "It would," explains Höss, "have been impossible by shooting to dispose of the large numbers of people that were expected [at the death camps in Poland], and it would have placed too heavy a burden on the SS men who had to carry it out, especially because of the women and children among the victims."[47]

Himmler's response to the unbearable horror of mass shootings was to order a "more humane" killing. Hence, face-to-face killing was replaced by the "factory" (Auschwitz), the machine gun by Zyklon-B gas, physical presence by distancing. However, significantly, one cannot say that thus one person was replaced by another. Rather, the systematic aim was the *withdrawal* of people from the process of destruction altogether; it was to kill without killers, without the interference of people. To be sure, Auschwitz, industrialized and bureaucratized mass murder, was and remains the work of people, of a vast number of individual persons—but *at the greatest distance technically possible*. In the end, there was no touching, no seeing, no hearing (except of course from the "dirty work" having to be done by the prisoner *Sonderkommandos* in removing the corpses from the gas chambers). The actual killing itself assumed a peculiar abstractness. However, such a situation had to be *created*; it was the outcome of the need, perceived perhaps first by Himmler, *to suspend the emotional tie intrinsic to face-to-face interaction*. In a word, killing had to be made abstract, and hence easy. As long as the killer could touch, see, or hear the victims, he or she remained affected by the tie, affected by the victims as *persons* and as *his* or *her* victims; hence, the killer would hesitate to kill.

Although some kind of bond or tie between perpetrator and victim may easily be granted in the case of face-to-face killing, it is far from clear wherein this tie consists. Bearing in mind the discussion of love, it would seem far-fetched indeed to claim that the perpetrator here hesitates to kill because he or she "loves" the victim physically confronting him or her. Therefore, the tie in question must be of a different, less close kind, while remaining, on the other hand, strong enough to make the perpetrator hesitate to inflict pain. Perhaps the tie is that of identification. "Identification," writes Freud, "is the earliest expression of an emotional tie with another person."[48] But insofar as Freud's main interest is in the way in which a boy identifies with his father (or, for that matter, the *Volk* with the Führer), in the sense of taking him as his ideal, his analysis throws little light on my question. A more mature form of identification is to be found in *empathy* (*Einfühlung*) in the sense given by the Mitscherlichs. Stressing the eminent moral importance of empathy, they write, "If in our situation we seek a prescription that will force us to act morally—that is, compassionately and humanely—it can be found only in a steadfast effort toward *empathetic thinking*," meaning by this "neither a sentimental feeling of unity with others nor idealistic Utopianism [*Weltverbesserungsideen*]," but rather "a willingness to put oneself in the other person's place, and critically to reflect on the 'situation' (his situation, my situation—our relationship)." Empathy establishes a *reciprocal* relation between ego and object, as opposed to the one-way relation of elementary identification. "Empathy," continue the Mitscherlichs, "calls simultaneously for detachment from oneself and for attention to others"; "understanding of the foreigner [*Fremdverständnis*] is the prerequisite for any morality based on empathy."[49] Thus, empathy differs from identification in that it rests not on infantile dependence but on mature independence, not on the introjected (assumed or wished-for) similarity of the two persons involved but on their difference. This brings out the link between empathy and love. In both, that is, what is sought for is the conscious recognition of the otherness of the other as *in itself* meriting recognition. Note also that feelings of guilt are fundamentally linked with the reciprocity achieved in empathy: a sense of guilt presupposes, as already mentioned, "the development of object-relations, that is to say, of relations with one's fellow humans that are mutually important."[50]

But what became of my question? Touching, seeing, and hearing the victim, the perpetrator hesitates. Why? What does the victim "mean" to the perpetrator? He or she does not know the victim, let alone love the victim; they are perfect strangers. Nevertheless, hesitation. Can it be that the sheer appearance of the other, the sheer concreteness of his or her copresence *as such* effects some kind of restraint and thus hesitancy? My answer is yes. We cannot, I believe, reflect on the kind of embarrassment involved here without thinking of the peculiar power of the *look* of the other, brilliantly analyzed by Sartre.[51] Part of the embarrassment must stem from the perpetrator's experiencing that his or her victim is also his or her witness, as it were. The historical evidence at hand (Himmler's reported exchange with Bach-Zelewski being a case in point) leads me to suggest that the small-scale setting, insofar as it involves proximity and face-to-face interaction, insofar as it implies the direct, meaning unmediated, physical copresence of the acting individuals, has an emotional dimension to it, one with moral impact at that.

Some peculiar force seems to emanate from the presence in person of the other, which I cannot evade—or only by effort, that is to say, only by defying this force so as to break free from it. Yet what I thus strive to oppose I cannot but confirm as being there and making an impact in the first instance. The overwhelmingness, the force, is prior; the attempt to overcome it, derivative. But whence comes this force?

Sartre turns to the look to give an answer. But I aim here to examine the eminent moral import of the book, something Sartre's account stops short of doing. When the perpetrator is looked at by his or her victim, when they each return the other's look, it is as though at that very instant the two of them are stripped bare of any presumption of indifference and anonymity: they are trapped in a suspense. However, "stripped bare" is a misleading expression; it gets the priority wrong. For—speaking of proximity—it is not as if indifference reigned first, so as to render the *Interessenehmen* (taking an interest) Scheler speaks of secondary to it. In the person-to-person encounter I examine here, the reverse is the case: not caring for the other is what is conspicuous, what calls for explanation, what catches our attention—in short, what strikes us as a breakdown to be accounted for. Under conditions of physical proximity, where the full exposure of exchanging looks is allowed for, to *matter* to one another, to be engaged in the What next? is the primordial form of relating to each other. To be sure, it is not well-nigh impossible to adopt an indifferent stance even here. But to do so is to step out. To do so presupposes an effort; it presupposes the subject's wresting himself or herself away from the condition of being engaged with the other.

What I have said suggests that the person-to-person encounter, the look meeting look, the face facing a face, amounts to a relation that is shot through with a moment of commitment. But this commitment is unlike all others; it is not a product of the subject's intentionality; it is not wanted; it simply imposes itself as a property pertaining to the very structure of this dyad in proximity. The "mattering" I speak of here is not added to proximity but resides in it. In proximity, not bothering with the other in the other's state of need lets the other down. It is as if I break a never-given promise, namely, the promise arising from the commitment inherent in the situation of engendering the other person-to-person. Here, as K. E. Løgstrup says, distrust is but a deficient mode of trust: trust is what is presupposed and acted on *as long as* it is not manifestly disappointed by one of the parties. Here trust is what we act from; its absence, what we find conspicuous.[52]

This reflection brings us closer to Levinas than to Sartre. In Sartre's analysis, the look of the other is the ultimate proof of the other's power. The look of the other transcends my transcendence, is subversive to my freedom, steals my possibilities away from me, and threatens to nullify all my projects. To be exposed to the other's direct gaze is to be exposed absolutely. In the look, the other's freedom devours mine. By contrast, in Levinas the other is not sheer force; the other's appearance is not an inescapable strength marking the boundaries of my chosen projects. My encountering the other does not spell conflict. Rather, the other is a *face*, and the other's appearing as face instead of as look means the other's coming to my attention in an ambiguous, twofold sense: as a master commanding me *and* as a being that is utterly defenseless, vulnerable, nude. Instead of stealing my freedom away from me, the other gives it meaning in presenting it with a task; the face of the other issues an appeal to me to assume responsibility for the other's fate, first and foremost, *to choose not to kill the other*. In this reversal of Sartre's portrait, it is the other as destitute, as weak, needy, and frail, that commands me. Hence, there is nonsymmetry here too; only now I am not paralyzed in my freedom through the other's transcending it from a position of strength; rather, the other as destitute, meaning incapable of resistance, meaning "an easy match" if so I wish, is what spurs me to act.

> The face is exposed, menaced, as if inviting us to an act of violence. At the same time, the face is what forbids us to kill. . . . The first word of the face is the "Thou shalt not kill." It is an order. There is a commandment in the appearance of the face, as if a master spoke to me. However, at the same time, the face of the other is destitute. . . . There is here a relation not with a very great resistance, but with something absolutely *other*: the resistance of what has no resistance— the ethical resistance. . . . [T]he face summons me to my obligations and judges me.[53]

According to Levinas, "the force of the Other is already and henceforth moral."[54] Levinas seeks to derive from the face-to-face encounter an ethic of unconditional responsibility for the other. I shall not go further into his bold doctrine. The aim of contrasting Levinas's view with Sartre's well-known analysis of the look has been to point to the possibility that it is the other— be that even the ideologically defined archenemy—who brings about the hesitancy and restraint in the perpetrator precisely insofar as the sought-out victim appears as a face, and thus as destitute and vulnerable in Levinas's sense. Vulnerability, here meaning *perceived* vulnerability, not the look qua threat, is what issues an appeal producing hesitancy instead of killing.

Love, Compassion, and Empathy

My remarks on empathy have sought to bring out its difference from simple identification and its closeness to love. What separates empathy from identification is its recognition of the otherness of two persons, of their difference and distinctness as something to be maintained rather than annulled. This statement echoes that in the chapter on Hannah Arendt, where I stated that the essence of empathy lies in one subject's *retaining* rather than abandoning his or her own standpoint and identity in the course of his or her endeavor to recognize the other as other. Empathy thus entails a *Sichmitbringen*, not a *Sichaufgeben*. Furthermore, I have just shown that the relatedness between empathy and love consists in both seeking the conscious recognition of the otherness of the other as "in itself" deserving recognition. Yet, though related, it is clear that empathy and love are not the same, that they differ.

Criticizing Scheler, I argued that the scope of sympathy must be conceived as wider than that of love. Contrary to Scheler's thesis that sympathy originates in and is derived from love, I insist that sympathy rests not on love but on empathy and that our capacity for empathy can be directed toward persons who are not unique to us and whom we do not love. The part of Scheler's conception of love that I endorsed was his claim that in loving, what I find lovable in my beloved is his or her uniqueness. In love I pursue the continual enhancement of what I perceive to be the unique value of the personality of the other, rendering him or her irreplaceable and unexchangeable. The focus of love is on the very being, the *esse*, of the beloved.

What is lacking in empathy is precisely the emphasis on uniqueness. The person with whom I empathize is perceived as different, but not as unique. In empathy, the "otherness" of the other that I view as deserving recognition does not include the strong notion of that person being irreplaceable and unexchangeable to me. Rather, empathy consists in my taking an interest in how my cosubject experiences his or her situation. Drawing on Taylor, I contended that, in general, emotions entail judgment yet are not identical with or exhausted in judgment, as held by Solomon. In my view, empathy, being humanity's basic emotional faculty, contains a cognitive dimension by virtue of which it, and it alone, *discloses* to us something about another person—namely, his or her emotional experience in a given situation. Empathy is a necessary *prerequisite* for the development of an awareness and understanding of the emotions and feelings of another person. Significantly, becoming aware of another person's emotional experience is not the same as sharing the other's feeling, that is, as experiencing it oneself. What empathy basically facilitates is my reaching out toward the other person's situation. Thanks to my faculty of empathy, I become aware that the other is in a situation of, say, distress. At this "first" stage, my empathy-based act of reaching out toward the other brings nothing more and nothing less than an initial awareness of and attentiveness to what kind of a situation the other is involved in. I tune in to, I take an interest in, the other's situation; the other's feelings are part of that situation, without, however, exhausting it. In this reaching-out, the other remains an other to me; our distinctness as individual persons is not obliterated. Likewise, no identity of feelings takes place; my awareness of the other's situation as a specific piece of lived human reality neither presupposes nor implies that I actually feel what the other feels.[55] Thus conceived, my claim is that the basic mode of ascription of import is through empathy. To sum up, then: the first access to and grasp of another person's emotional experience is through empathy, whereas the full-blown cognitive and more detached evaluation and assessment of the other's emotional experience rests on empathy's having rendered the domain of the other's experience accessible to me, an object of my awareness, in the first place. Empathy entails an intuitive and tentative judgment about the other's situation and facilitates the ensuing development of a deeper and more comprehensive judgment.

A formulation of Freud's may help cast more light on the concept of empathy that I defend. "A path," writes Freud in 1921, "leads from identification by way of imitation to empathy, that is, to the comprehension of the mechanism by means of which we are enabled to take up *any attitude at all* towards another mental life."[56] Freud's formulation helps bring out what I intend by terming empathy humanity's basic emotional faculty and by not equating empathy with one *particular* feeling. Our basic capacity for reaching out through empathy as defined here lies at the very bottom of the various "mature" emotional attitudes we may assume toward another person, such as sympathy or compassion, to name but two.

Love, I have argued, is confined to the small-scale setting; being honest with ourselves, we profess to love but a few persons. Whether it will have to remain that way for reasons that are unalterable, because apparently anthropological in nature, I cannot say. Suffice it to maintain that the love of which we know, through experience, is one pretty limited in range. This being so, the Mitscherlichs' thesis that love, and presumably love alone, can effectively keep us from inflicting pain on others seems far too demanding. Rather, less than love will have to do.

Schopenhauer suggests *compassion* (*Mitleid*). He argues thus:

> But how is it possible that a suffering that is not *mine*, that does not
> affect me, nevertheless immediately becomes my own motive, and
> one capable of moving me to act? It is possible only insofar as I *feel*
> *with* [*mitempfinde*] the suffering, that I feel it as *mine*, yet still not *in me*,
> but in *someone else*, and this even though the suffering is only given to
> me as something external, as something mediated through external
> perception. . . . This (i.e., that there is no difference between seeing
> suffering and suffering) presupposes that I, so to speak, identify
> myself with the other so that consequently the boundary between I
> and non-I is for the moment dissolved: only then . . . I no longer
> grasp him as the empirical perception discloses him, that is, as
> someone alien to me, indifferent to me, completely different from
> me; rather, I suffer with him *in him* [*in ihm* leide ich mit] despite the
> fact that his flesh does not encompass my nerves. (GM, 763)

Schopenhauer's ethics of compassion postulates *Mitleid* as "the source of
human love" (GM, 772). The capacity for suffering, not the (Kantian)
capacity for reason, establishes the criterion for a full-fledged moral status;
hence, in Schopenhauer such status is ascribed to all living creatures. "My
true inner essence," asserts Schopenhauer, "exists in all that is alive, just as
immediately as it makes itself known to me in my self-consciousness" (GM,
809). The abolition of the distinction between subject and addressee, I and
not-I, is the crucial accomplishment of compassion, and on this accomplishment rest all genuine, that is to say, *uneigennützige* (nonegoistic), virtues and
every truly good action alike. For, asks Schopenhauer, how could we
ourselves be moved to compassion, "if not so, that we place ourselves outside
of ourselves and identify ourselves with the being that suffers, that we, so to
speak, abandon our self in order to adopt his?" (GM, 784) However,
compassion, on whose basis Schopenhauer sets out to build his entire moral
theory, cannot, he says, be learned: either one has the capacity for
compassion, in which case Schopenhauer takes it to be innate (*angeboren*), or
else one is born devoid of it. "The mind is enlightened; the heart remains
unimproved" (GM, 794); learning, cultivation, and maturation are restricted
to the domain of the intellect and do not apply to human beings' emotional
capacities, to their *Herz*.

My own position differs in one crucial respect from Schopenhauer's central thesis. Compassion, in Schopenhauer's sense, requires of subjects that they abandon themselves, that they suspend their distinct selves, their very selfhood. Only to the extent that such a self-abandonment takes place, holds Schopenhauer, is the accomplishment of compassion rendered possible. Indeed, compassion *is* the proclaimed identity of two beings: the person who feels compassion is one with the being that suffers; the two melt together and can no longer be distinguished. The fundamental difference between my position and the foregoing consists in the fact that my own conception of empathy is of a *Sichmitbringen*, as opposed to a *Sichaufgeben*. Empathy is irreducibly *other*-directed; directing my capacity for feeling-with at another person—there existing no such thing as empathy with myself—I in no way abolish my awareness of being and remaining a person distinct from the person in whom I take an emotional interest. In my conception, the call for, indeed the phenomenon of, empathy arises because your pain is yours and not mine, because we are separate individual human beings; the call can be met because we are all human beings, principally sharing, through our emotional faculties, the same access to the experience of pain. A core objective in my discussion of Taylor's notion of import was to elaborate the more accurate meaning of what we are to understand by sharing an "access" to the experience of pain. I showed that our access to the entire domain of human subjects' experience of their own situation, as well as that of others, is through emotion. Deepening that thesis, I have further argued that empathy is humanity's basic emotional faculty, basic because a prerequisite for the mature development of emotional attitudes such as sympathy or care. By absolutizing the moment of identification, Schopenhauer collapses the moment of distinctness between subject and addressee, whereas I, in my definition of empathy, have incorporated the moments of sameness (principally sharing the same access to) and difference (your pain is yours and not mine) as being equally important.

To be sure, there is something very attractive about Schopenhauer's compassionate advocacy of interpersonal identification. But closer scrutiny reveals that his doctrine holds *individuality* to be but mere appearance. "Die Individuation," Schopenhauer tells us, "ist bloße Erscheinung"; in reality "ist es ein und dasselbe Wesen, welches in allem Lebenden sich darstellt" (GM, 808). In this conception, then, to draw a distinction "zwischen seinem Ich und Nicht-Ich" amounts to being committed to the (rival) doctrine of "egoism" (GM, 774). But Schopenhauer's swift inference from the one thing to the other is unjustified. To hold that individuals are different and maintain their difference is not a fortiori to be committed to seeing that difference as absolute and hence moral acts such as those of compassion as something unattainable. What disturbs me is the air of Manichaeism that comes through in the way Schopenhauer plays out the rival doctrines of compassion and so-called egoism against each other: in this purported either/or, all or nothing, the good, as it were, stands against the bad; the truly moral, against the immoral; and nothing is allowed to occupy the apparent abyss between them. As I see it, empathy does just that; its feat is to have bridged the alleged abyss. My perception of the person with whom I empathize recognizes and preserves the fact that he or she is an "alter" to me, a separate person from me; and by way of my perceiving him or her as distinctly other, I throughout maintain my own sense of self. Stated in purely logical terms, difference, or otherness, is always a *reciprocal* relation between two entities: it goes both ways. Moreover, as Scheler notes, "pity is generally recognized as a compassionate outreaching beyond the individual self [*ein mitfühlendes Hinausgreifen über das eigene Ich*],"[57] that is to say, an I's reaching out toward another I, whereby the separateness of each is not surrendered but kept intact.[58] Finally, Schopenhauer's affirmative emphasis on suffering, on suffering-with as the *sole and exclusive* source of genuinely moral acts, goes too far. Odd as it may sound, one cannot escape the impression that the phenomenon of suffering, made to constitute the very foundation of morality per se, ultimately is grossly *idealized* in Schopenhauer's ethics. But the more one succeeds in reducing the amount of suffering in the world, the more one empties morality of its sole and indispensable source. In other words, Schopenhauer's doctrine seems to contain the contradiction that the more successfully one furthers morality, the more its foundation is undermined.

It remains to subject love and compassion to a systematic comparison. On the basis of Scheler's account, love is a movement in which I enhance the other's ideal value. Love is a movement of continual discovery. Love's disclosure of the beloved is perpetual, without a fixed end point, since the qualities love renders accessible to my appreciation are taken to be inexhaustible. Love thus feeds on an everlasting source. Love is spontaneous; it discovers the other as unique and concentrates on the very being of the other, not merely on some specific traits pertaining to the other or (contingently) to his or her situation. In love, what I seek to stimulate is the full-scale repertoire of the beloved as a person, the full-blown richness of his or her personality; in wanting to stimulate the flourishing of that "unique" repertoire in the other, I make full use of the powers of my own unique person as well. The blossoming of love is that of the two persons involved. Finally, love is unconditional; it is undermined if the other is required to "prove" his or her worth through doing such and such or being such and such. If love seeks a reward, it is only that the other be him- or herself—fully.

With compassion (or pity) the picture is very different. Compassion, like love, is a way of disclosing, or "seeing," the other. Unlike love, however, compassion does not direct my attention to the other as such, to the entire personality of the other, or to the other in his or her uniqueness. The focus of compassion is narrower. Compassion is selective, but in a sense other than love is. Whereas love's selectivity stems from the exclusiveness of its human extension, that is, from its sustained focus on very few people, the selectivity of compassion concerns the light in which I see and approach the other: I here see the other as in need, as suffering, as humiliated, as threatened, and the like. Compassion thus discloses the other as being in a certain state, situation, or condition. My felt compassion is conditional upon my seeing the other in this particular kind of light; compassion calls upon me to relieve the other's suffering, yet in doing so, compassion does not involve the whole of me, or the whole of the other's personality, as love does. Compassion involves the other *as in need*, and myself as called upon to alleviate or end the other's state of need. Hence, compassion, in contrast to love, has a fixed end point and goal, namely, the end of the other's current state of need. Being situational, dependent on context, and thus reactive—my response to your lot—compassion as a feeling-for-others is temporary, is more focused on a situation-specific, passing state of affairs applying to its addressee than is love, which for its part involves a more lasting and growing involvement in the other person. This contrast between transience and permanence reflects a fundamental difference in commitment. Since compassion typically arises ad hoc and is enacted in the face of some specific state of affairs, it does not involve a very deep commitment on the part of the acting subject—or, to put it in less categorical terms, compassion need not involve the acting subject in his or her emotional depth. Again, this follows from the transience of compassion: When I have felt compassion and acted accordingly (assuming it is possible for me to intervene), the "reason" for my compassion—as experienced here and now—ceases to exist. Being deprived of its pragmatic objective, in the sense that this has now been fulfilled (i.e., the perceived suffering has been relieved), compassion is—for now—deprived of its raison d'être.

By contrast, to act on love is to strengthen it, to intensify it, to help confirm its source and thereby demonstrate love as nonconditional and noncontingent. In love, commitment and depth are profounder than in compassion; emotionally, more is involved at the giving as well as at the receiving end.

Having rejected love, on the grounds of its tie to uniqueness, and then Schopenhauer's "compassion," on the grounds of its surrender of distinctness, as viable answers to what it is that may keep us from inflicting pain on others, I argue for the candidacy of empathy. This is not to attribute to empathy the enigmatic power of a "guarantee"; I am not committed here to any bold claim about the human faculty of empathy "always" effectively preventing us from inflicting pain and "at all times" safeguarding us against evildoing. To make such a claim would be to argue a very strong thesis about the power of empathy on the (empirical) level of *action*, a full treatment of which would go far beyond the task I have set myself in this study. Far from that, what I have set out to do is to argue a thesis about the function of empathy on the level of perception, that is, about empathy as being our basic mode of access to the domain of humanity's emotional experience, and to show how the act of judgment we exercise presupposes and rests on an act of perception that logically precedes it. To sum up, the aim of my discussion has been to develop a threefold thesis about (1) the way emotions in general and the faculty of empathy in particular are crucial in making us perceive a situation as one where a cosubject's weal and woe is at stake; (2) how, in the case of, as well as because of, my missing the human dimension of a situation, I also miss—remain blind to, indifferent to, unaffected by—its moral dimension; and (3) how this failure on the level of "seeing," or perception, undermines my ability to pass sound moral judgment about the situation in question.

I have used various examples to render concrete the issues I have pursued. The examples have ranged from the (morally) extreme, as in the case of Eichmann, to the relatively innocent, as in the cases of Davis and the fictional racist. Without wanting or having to rest my case on it, I shall insert here a small passage from Rudolf Höss's autobiography, *Kommandant in Auschwitz*. It reveals the main feature of the full-fledged objective attitude to be the annihilation of one's own emotional capacities, which triggers the suspension of the emotional bond to fellow human beings and thus prepares for their (physical) annihilation. Höss writes:

> Time and again I was asked how I, how my men, over and over again, could cope with witnessing *this* process, how we could endure it. I always replied that all human inclinations and feelings had to keep silent in the face of the ice-cold consequence with which we had to

carry out the order of the Führer. Thus, I had to appear cold and heartless in front of proceedings that would cause the heart of any still humanly feeling person to turn around in his body.[59]

My Davis example focused on indifference as the prime threat to the exercise of the faculty of empathy and a fortiori to the unimpaired exercise of moral judgment. Why indifference, not hate?

I return to Scheler to give an answer. Scheler holds that love and hate, though opposites, both stem from and display a deep-seated emotional *engagement*. To love is to feel, to take an active interest in some particular person—and a positive interest at that. It is to seek the enhancement of the perceived qualities and value of that person; it entails being happy for the happiness of the other. On the other hand, to hate is also to feel, to take an active interest in some particular person—and a negative interest at that. It is to seek the deprivation of the perceived qualities and value of that person; it entails being satisfied at the misery of the other. In short, loving, I want there to be more of the other in the world; hating, to be less. Not so with indifference. To be indifferent is not to feel; it is to be unaffected. It is to take no active human interest in the situation, in the weal and woe, of another person; it is to be—and to be able to stay—uninterested in what happens to that person. Hence, there is no emotional engagement in the indifferent person; neither positively nor negatively affected by alter, by whether alter is positively or negatively affected by what is happening to him or her (even through ego), the indifferent person is simply not affected at all. As for the numb person, the type of indifference he or she shows is neither accidental nor transitory; more psychically profound, numbness signifies a *loss* of the emotional capacity to develop empathy with alter. Biographically, individuals' lack of empathy might have been caused by a lack of empathy flowing toward themselves from their primary love objects, as argued in the work of Alice Miller and Heinz Kohut. But this loss need not be definitive, and numbness is typically highly *selective*, as in the case of the Nazi doctors interviewed by Lifton, where emotional unaffectedness is confined to Jews and other so-called subhumans. Selective numbness is thus *organized* numbness, at least in this historical case; it is not original in the subject but brought about in him or her by the impact of exterior forces such as ideology, bureaucracy, and technology. In a word, it is "functional." By contrast, indiscriminate or all-around indifference toward other human be-ings—often experienced and suffered by others as "coldness"—may reveal a more generic psychopathology.

It is not my task here to do full justice to the complex causes of indifference; nor do I possess the called-for competence. My aim has simply been to show that, as far as the exercise of humanity's emotional faculty is concerned—and so *eo ipso* humanity's ability to constitute a moral phenomenon and to pass (moral) judgment on it—love and hate are linked together to form one end of a continuum at whose opposite end we find indifference. In love, our emotional engagement advances a "positive" end; in hate, a "negative" end. By contrast, indifference is characterized by obliterating or annulling *all* emotional engagement on the part of the subject—be that engagement positive or negative. What this points to is the tremendous range of indifference; it transcends all boundaries and recognizes no limits. Admittedly, we sometimes say this of love and hate as well. But we deceive ourselves in doing so. Common to love and to hate is their origin and cultivation within a small-scale and face-to-face setting. Loving or hating, it is always someone particular that we love or hate. Thus person-bound, the love or hate we feel is confined to the relative intimacy pertaining to the small-scale domain within which these feelings arise and are exchanged. Located at the opposite end of the continuum, indifference is not in principle restricted to the scope set up by personal affection and personal bonds; it is indiscriminate rather than selective. Therefore, its typical object is an anybody rather than a somebody; it is directed to the anonymous as distinguished from the unique. Indeed, indifference breeds anonymity on all sides.

From a moral perspective, the havoc indifference wreaks is, potentially, immensely greater than that brought about by felt, lived, practiced hatred. To invoke my examples: Davis is far more dangerous than the racist; his indifference is not limited to some particular cause or object, as is the hate felt by the racist. The indifferent individual is eminently mobilizable. This has to do with the peculiar insatiability of indifference, which again separates it from hate. Having sought, found, and destroyed its chosen object, hate is exhausted, its subject content. Indifference, however, is indiscriminate and hence indefatigable; as shown by Lifton's study of the Nazi doctors, the more numb the individual gets, the more he kills; and the more he kills, the more numb he gets.

If my argument is sound, there are no limits to the harm against others that can be brought about by a subject whose emotional faculty—of empathy, compassion, concern—is severely impaired. "No limits" because such a subject is beyond the very possibility of being humanly affected—affected, that is, by how his or her decisions and actions may affect other subjects.

"No limits," moreover, because a subject whose emotional capacity is damaged is *for that very reason* unable to pass moral judgment about what he or she is up to. Hence, the moral "brake" that the exercise of judgment entails is undermined. This is so because his or her failure to pass moral judgment reflects the prior and, as such, more original failure to constitute and thus "see" the phenomenon or situation in question as one calling for moral judgment, that is, as one addressing him or her qua moral subject. In other words, to be emotionally incapacitated in the sense developed here is a sufficient condition for the failure to exercise moral judgment, because there is no access to the domain of moral phenomena, of situations involving the weal and woe of others, other than the access provided by emotions in general and the faculty of empathy in particular. Empathy is our basic mode of access to the experience of another person; failing to gain access to the reality of the other's experience, we are at a loss to know how to assess and evaluate it, in short, to judge it.

Using a drastic example from recent history, I have argued that the entire logic of love and hate had to be systematically suspended by the Nazi personnel involved in the Holocaust: killing could not be permitted to stay concrete; it had to be rendered abstract, to be turned to run on indifference, not the human-emotional and hence inescapably *moral* engagement of love and hate. It was crucial that the activity of killing human beings be morally *neutralized*. This neutralization was brought about and sustained by the indicated suspension of any specifically human "interference," of any emotional affectedness on the part of the perpetrators, in short, by suspending the emotional bond between one human being and another. My "negative" examples have sought to throw light on the eminent moral significance of the emotional bond, that is to say, on what may happen in its absence. According to the thesis advanced here, to undermine the access to the weal and woe of the other through empathy is to undermine an indispensable presupposition for the exercise of moral judgment, so that—to invoke the example of Nazi Germany—having barred the emergence of empathy through processes of double dehumanization, there was no risk that the "brake" represented by judgment would come to interfere with the increasingly technologized killing. This suggests that the further one moves away from the love-hate end of the continuum and approaches the logic of indifference, the greater the danger that the subject will contribute to immoral acts, because the less likely it is that he or she will be able to "see" and subsequently pass judgment on moral phenomena.

Of course, to repeat, love is not required of us in order that we perceive a cosubject as a moral subject, judge him or her as such, and—optimally—act toward him or her as such. Linked to the felt uniqueness of the other, love is too exclusive, too selective, too narrow, for all that. Love is an entirely unsuitable criterion of moral action, and to act out of love for someone is not per se to act morally. Rather, an act performed out of love springs from an intention to do something not just for the sake of duty but for the sake of the beloved. So an act of love consists of a high degree not only of beneficence but also—indeed first and foremost—of benevolence, whereby beneficence applies to the content of action and benevolence to the motives. Being "beyond the call of duty" and thus beyond what can be morally demanded of us on the level of action, acts out of love must be classified as *supererogatory*, as advocated by David Heyd in his book on the topic.[60] In other words, although we treat those whom we love as ends in themselves, we do not love all those whom we treat as ends in themselves; and although it can never become a moral duty to love, not even an imperfect duty, it is morally obligatory to treat all human beings (indeed all beings capable of suffering, as asserted earlier) not merely as means but as ends in themselves. This is to say that the realm of morality transcends that of love; exploding the range of human love, morality cannot be based on it. As argued above, we are left with the faculty of empathy as the *emotional* foundation of morality, and the faculty of representative thinking (in the Kant-inspired sense of Arendt) as the *cognitive* foundation, the two being viewed here as *jointly* constituting the basis of morality.

In Nazi theory and practice, feeling means weakness: to display feeling is to reveal weakness. Suspecting, and fearing, their intrinsic moral significance, the Nazis endeavor to suppress humanity's emotional capacities. Self-imposed in nature, the sought-for suppression is hailed as an honorable task and taken up by the individual as an ordeal in which the strength of his or her character is put to the test. I hold the philosophical importance of the Nazi example to lie in the following. Blocking emotion in general and the capacity for other-regarding empathy in particular, these people deny themselves an access to the domain of the human and hence to the domain of the moral, understood as the weal and woe of others. The effected annihilation of feeling can be termed emotional neutralization; once established, it paves the way for, and later helps sustain, a moral neutralization of the infliction of pain, ultimately of the phenomenon of killing a human being. "Numbing" is the psychological precondition for, as well as the ensuing consequence of, the routinized killing of human beings; it signifies what one must do to oneself in order to cope with what one does to others. "Dehumanization" is the content and essential core of both types of neutralization, the emotional and the moral; the suspension of the interpersonal emotional bond is their common product. These then are the general observations allowed and even called for by the extremity of Nazi atrocities, of Auschwitz.

My argument challenges the main claims of the philosophical case against granting emotions a truly moral significance. These claims—implicit, and rarely questioned, in the tradition of Kantian cognitivistic ethics—read as follows: (1) we cannot choose what we feel; therefore (2) feelings cannot be morally required or obligatory, for it cannot be a duty to feel something, from which it follows that (3) feelings must be excluded from the domain of the moral.

 1. The claim that we cannot choose what we feel loses its intuitive plausibility when we consider that we are prepared to offer reasons for the way we feel, and we do so not only to explain the feeling but also to justify our having it—to ourselves as well as to others. If I say I feel shame, and you inquire why, I tell you the reasons for my perceiving the situation to be a shameful one. Likewise, if I love someone, I may experience the suddenness and intensity of my love as overwhelming, as taking me by surprise, and in this respect as not "wanted" or "chosen"; nonetheless, I am prepared to try to tell what inspires my love and why I find that particular person worthy of it. This shows that feelings entail judgments about the situation eliciting them, about the person inspiring them, and so on. Upon reflection we may come to see these judgments, always open to and demanding interpretation, as justified or as unjustified; and this will not be a matter of indifference to the way we feel but is likely to help sustain or help modify, change, or overcome our feeling. Although it would be too strong, and in my view misleading, to speak here of "choosing" what to feel, it does show that a feeling is tied up with a judgment (however implicit, vague, and tentative), that this judgment is open to reflection, and that reflection may produce a change in the way we feel. In feeling, therefore, there is a commitment to "rationality" in the sense that we are willing to explain and justify having a specific feeling in a specific situation or toward a specific person. What is more, we are prepared to assume responsibility for this entire process (feeling, explaining, justifying); indeed, we demand of people that they assume such responsibility, and their failure to do so is regarded as a moral issue, that is to say, as a moral failure. So feelings are not passive, something that we suffer; on the contrary, we experience our feelings as forming a part of our identity, our character;

and we view feelings as reflecting morally on the person having them, that is, as entailing specific judgments to which a person is committed and for which he or she must be prepared to assume responsibility. Related to this, finally, is the fact that we—and this is peculiar to humans—have the ability to form (second-order) desires about our (first-order) desires. The business of doing so is not morally neutral; rather, in judging, assessing, and evaluating our desires, feelings, and aspirations, we regard some as more desirable and as carrying more merit than others.

2. The inferences made at this point—namely, that which cannot be freely chosen cannot be made an object of obligation in a moral sense, and that which cannot be morally obligatory is for that very reason devoid of truly moral significance—are held to apply to feelings. According to my argument, feelings *are* required in a morally relevant sense, but it is not a (moral) duty to have this or that particular feeling. To begin with, what has moral significance goes far beyond what can be made an object of duty, or obligation, as observed by Blum. When I hold that feelings are required, I mean that they are so in a sense radically different from that in which Kant speaks of (perfect and imperfect) duties. Feelings are required, I assert, on the level of *constitution*, and thus *not* in the sense of motivation that Kant has in mind when he says that a genuinely moral act is done from (a sense of) duty instead of from inclination. Far from this, feelings are required in the sense that there can be no successful act of moral perception, or of moral judgment, without the participation of the faculty of empathy and hence of our emotional capacity, our elementary ability to feel. "Feelings are required" therefore means that the faculty of empathy is required for the accomplishment of acts of moral perception and of moral judgment alike; together with the cognitive faculty of representative thinking, empathy is constitutive of such acts. That this is true can be demonstrated by the use of negative examples: in cases where a person's basic capacity for relating to others through emotion is blocked, impaired, suppressed, or suspended, that person is unable to perceive (or "see") and pass judgment on the weal and woe of others. Why is the blocking of the emotional capacities so fatal to perception and judgment alike? It is so because a person with blocked emotional capacities is robbed of his or her mode of access to the domain of the human, that is to say, to the reality of other persons in general and to that reality's moral relevance in terms of others' weal and woe in particular. Incapable of feeling, of reaching out toward and relating to the experiences of others through emotion, such a person never gains access to, never arrives at, the domain of phenomena with respect to which perception is to be

performed and judgment to be passed. Without emotion in the elementary sense of relating to others, as intended in my definition of the faculty of empathy, a person is an outsider to the domains of the human and the moral. A lack of empathy makes for a moral blindness, as manifested in the not-seeing of the indifferent bystander.

Hence, feelings are required in the sense that the faculty of empathy is required for acts of moral perception and moral judgment to come about. On the other hand, it is not—in this thesis—a duty to have this or that particular feeling. It was Schopenhauer's mistake to believe so. What Schopenhauer does is to single out a particular feeling, that of compassion, as the (sole) foundation of morality. Taken to define morality as such, compassion is a feeling required of us in order that we judge and act "morally" in the sense of Schopenhauer. But this doctrine is vulnerable to the objection that the allegedly "natural feeling" of compassion is too narrow to serve as a motivational basis for moral acts and likewise too narrow to serve as an explanation of all moral conduct; last but not least, it is not required that someone actually suffer in order that we feel obliged to treat him or her as an addressee of moral action. These are just three ways of saying that morality transcends compassion, indeed transcends any *particular* feeling or sentiment that we may develop toward others. By contrast, what I seek to establish is the faculty of empathy as required in moral perception and moral judgment because coconstitutive of both of these. Understood as the ability to relate to others through emotion, empathy is what gives us an access to the domain of the moral. In this conception, compassion, say, or sympathy are manifestations of the faculty of empathy; as particular feelings, or sentiments, they presuppose and are facilitated by the basic emotional faculty of humanity.

3. Clearly, the falsity of the view that feelings must be precluded from the domain of the moral follows from what I have said under (1) and (2) above, insofar as excluding emotion from the moral would mean excluding us, the moral subjects, from it. Rather, our emotional faculty together with the participatory, as opposed to objective, attitude toward others that it gives rise to is what provides us with an access to the domain of the moral, making possible as it does the perception and recognition of the weal and woe of others on which the exercise of judgment is based. We experience the objects of moral judgments through emotion. Judgments do not constitute *what* is judged, nor do they define our access to the objects judged. Judgments presuppose perception—in moral life no less than in science. We pass moral judgment on things that are already given or revealed to us—

given and revealed, met and "seen", that is, through acts of perception. It is here, on this level that logically precedes that of judgment, lest judgment be empty, that we locate the emotions. Emotions anchor us to the *particular* moral circumstance, to *that* singularity, *here* and *now*, that addresses us immediately.[61] To "see" the circumstance and to "see" oneself as immediately addressed by it, and thus to be susceptible to the way a situation affects the weal and woe of others—all of this is required in order to enter the domain of the moral, and none of it would come about without the basic emotional faculty of empathy.

I have embraced Taylor's claim that "feeling is our mode of access to the entire domain of subject-referring imports," and I have expanded this claim by arguing that it follows, a fortiori, that people's capacity to feel gives them access to the domain of the moral. Thus, whereas Taylor speaks of "feeling" as the mode of access, I speak of the capacity to feel, and I specify the latter as springing from humanity's faculty of empathy. But why not, as Taylor, simply speak of "feeling"? Why this specification? Why speak here, in old-fashioned manner, of a specific emotional *faculty*? It is with the aim of showing that the term "feeling" in this connection is fundamentally mistaken, and not simply conceptually imprecise, that I turn next to a lengthy examination of these questions.

5

Emotions and Immorality

So far in this study I have been concerned with the relation between humanity's emotional capacities on the one hand and morality on the other. My argument has sought to show that the former constitute a prerequisite for the latter. However, the progression of my line of argument may have nourished a sense of dissatisfaction in the reader, and with that a growing suspicion. Can this really be the whole story about emotions and morality? Is not the argument as hitherto advanced thoroughly biased in favor of a highly selective view of human emotions? To be more precise, is not the assumed centrality of the faculty of empathy shattered as soon as we start paying attention to the other side of emotion—namely, its dark side—and, with that, to humanity's undeniable emotional capacity for destructiveness, for hatred, for cruelty? In short, is there not also a story to be told about the connection between emotions and immorality?

There certainly is. My study would be incomplete, indeed fundamentally deficient, if it were to overlook the dark side of human emotion and to neglect its inherent potential for immorality. I therefore devote the present chapter to this topic. One of my central aims is to combat the suspicion that my position is committed to the proposition that humanity's emotional capacities per se safeguard us against immorality. If this were really my position, then it would follow—or so the suspicion would have it—that the mere existence of destructiveness, of the all too human emotions of hatred and cruelty, was *eo ipso* an argument against my position.

In what follows I endeavor to show that this is not the case. I do see a link between the faculty of empathy, on the one hand, and morality, especially moral perception, on the other. This link is so strong as to allow for the thesis that empathy constitutes a prerequisite, among the faculties with which humankind is endowed, for moral performance—in perception, in judgment, and in action. Our faculty of empathy helps us gain access to the way the weal and woe of others is at stake in a situation, and thus to the domain of moral phenomena. However, I see no link between emotions as such, emotions in general, and de facto moral conduct. To assert a link here would, I take it, be to contend that as soon as some specific "emotion" is displayed in a subject, a kind of guarantee for an ensuing "moral" performance is established—a performance that contains a full recognition of the other as a cosubject in my sense, that is, as a fellow human and moral being. My position entails no such assertion. To see this more clearly, a precise and differentiated conception of human emotions is called for, one recognizing their richness and variety. It must be acknowledged that in analogy to emotions' being *an sich* neither rational nor irrational (see Chapter 4), humanity's capacity for developing emotions toward others is *an sich* neither good nor bad, neither intrinsically moral nor intrinsically immoral, for the obvious reason that there are both good and benevolent *and* bad and aggressive emotions in man. With emotions, that is, it can go both ways. What this testifies to is the mistakenness of seeking to settle the issue about the link between (general, unspecified) emotions on the one hand and morality-immorality on the other. Mistaken is the attempt to *predetermine* the connection between the two on a purely abstract level.

Hence, when we consider emotions and morality we must make sure that we know *what kind of emotions* we are talking about. In earlier sections I have at great length discussed empathy, love, sympathy, and compassion. Now the time is ripe to penetrate the nature and origin of the "other side," of human destructiveness in its various emotional and behavioral manifestations, counting hatred, masochism, and sadism among them.

The following account differs from that which dealt with emotional and psychic "numbing." My discussion of numbing illuminated the moral consequences of a neutralization and suspension of people's sensitivity to the suffering and pain of others. It showed what may happen when the development of empathy toward other people or toward a fixed category of other people is impaired and prevented. In turning now to hatred, I consider the phenomenon an *activation* of feeling—and a wholly negative one at that. Hatred seeks the destruction of the person against whom it directs itself. Whereas the killing performed in numbing is accompanied by indifference to the person being killed (who appears as exchangeable to the killer)—that is to say, by an absence of emotional engagement in the killer—the killing performed in hatred is accompanied by vehement feelings against the person being killed (who appears as inexchangeable to the killer), most typically, intense, stored-up, and "blind" rage. The manner in which the other is perceived is completely pervaded by the wish to see the other destroyed.

Although hatred is without doubt a philosophical issue (some would even venture to say it is the crux of the "problem of evil"), I want to avoid examining it merely in the abstract. Indeed, it is crucial to make the point that hatred is concrete, never abstract. And, being a specific emotion, how could it be otherwise? Hoping to do justice to this, I give hatred a face: I name for it a well-known subject and a well-known object—namely, the anti-Semite and the Jew. The justification for this particular choice is historical rather than theoretical: the havoc wreaked by anti-Semitism speaks for itself. As for Jews, theirs is a long (and disastrous) historical record as targets par excellence. One of the most influential works on this subject is the study conducted by Theodor Adorno and his colleagues, *The Authoritarian Personality*. I devote the greater part of my discussion to their theory, only later to criticize some of its claims with the conceptual means offered in the work of Erich Fromm.

In the preceding chapter it was claimed that a lack of empathy is due to a lack of empathy. I now contend that the correctness of this claim can be demonstrated by an inquiry into the ontogenetical origin of human destructiveness and hatred. In essence, what the contention holds is as follows. *First*, to say that hatred and cruelty and the like reveal a lack of empathy in the subject is scarcely controversial; some would deem it trivial. The faculty of empathy and feelings of hatred are by definition at odds with each other; if "empathy" is to possess any particular meaning at all, it must be a meaning that separates it from what we understand by hatred against others. This much, then, is beyond doubt. But now, *second*, my contention further holds that hatred and the like not only reveal a lack of empathy but that they have their origin in a lack of empathy. Hatred and the like, that is, have their source in an impairment of the development of the faculty of empathy in the subject. Thus, the presence of hatred reflects an absence or, more accurately, a deficiently established faculty of empathy. From this it follows that hatred is not a primary phenomenon; rather, it arises from and on the basis of a thwarted and impaired emotional growth in the subject (this holds for projective as opposed to reactive hatred). To understand how this impairment comes about, it is necessary to observe, *third*, that not only is the extension of empathy irreducibly intersubjective (i.e., it relates an I to a thou), but its genesis is so as well. This means that I can only develop the faculty of empathy toward others when others have displayed empathy toward me. The others referred to in the second part of this proposition are, typically, significant others, that is to say, primary self-objects. In other words, I must have experienced being the object-addressee of empathy in order to become its subject. The faculty of empathy can only evolve on the condition that it is from early on receiving stimulation from the person's human environment; it is therefore a truly intersubjective accomplishment and a very precarious one at that.

The threefold contention shows that my thesis about the link between empathy and morality is not disconfirmed by the existence of hatred and other aggressive human feelings. Undeniably, there exists a connection between hatred and (potential or actual) immorality; this is confirmed daily by empirical evidence. However, if it can be shown that hatred is not *sui generis* but instead a by-product whose origin can be located in a deficiently developed faculty of empathy, then the immorality or lack of moral perception, judgment, and conduct that hatred fosters can be overcome precisely by strengthening the capacity for empathy with others (knowing all along, of course, that this means, though necessary, may not always prove sufficient). So in this way, by advancing the argument *ex negativo*, as it were, I can demonstrate the hypothesized link between empathy and morality as the reverse side of the connection between hatred and immorality, indeed, also as the path one must choose in trying to reverse immorality into morality.

So far I have used the term "immorality" without offering any proper definition. I have merely implied that, prima facie, immorality highlights a lack of moral perception, judgment, and conduct. Few would dispute this. However, in order that the concept not remain question begging, a more precise definition is demanded.

In his book *Immorality*, Ronald Milo takes "a lack of concern (or adequate concern) for the interests or welfare of others" to "constitute the essence of immorality" (I, 81). It follows from what I have said above that I agree with this definition—at least as a point of departure for further inquiry. According to Milo, we must first distinguish between the morally concerned and the morally indifferent person. The former endeavors to judge from the moral point of view and thus to make genuinely evaluative judgments about what is morally right and wrong; in doing so, that person shows concern for the interests and welfare of others. The morally indifferent person differs from this not in moral judgment (or not necessarily), but in conative disposition. "The trouble," writes Milo, "is not that such a person lacks conviction, but that he lacks concern" (I, 182). The morally indifferent person fails to act on those moral judgments that he does make; he fails to observe them in his actual conduct toward others. From this case Milo further distinguishes what he calls preferential wickedness. Here, a person will hold that he "morally ought not to do something but nevertheless prefer (in the sense of thinking that he ought, all things considered) to do it" (I, 202). The truly wicked person is *deliberately* uninterested in avoiding moral wrongdoing; he believes that what he does is wrong, yet does it nonetheless, indeed does it willingly; in short, he prefers "promoting some desired end of his (e.g., beauty, his own welfare, or a purely Aryan society) to respecting the interests and welfare of others" (I, 54). To act on what is recognized as a morally wrong preference without having any qualms about it is the essence of what Milo terms wickedness. Finally, in moral negligence the agent fails to prevent his desires and emotions from interfering with his making the judgment that his act is wrong.

Although Milo undertakes to investigate the nature and variety of immoral behavior, thereby developing the typology just sketched, he ends his book with the claim that "there is only one ultimate source of all immoral behavior," namely, "lack of concern." If we ask why the agent of a wicked act prefers to act as he does, or if we ask why the agent of a morally negligent or a morally weak act fails to exercise certain capacities of self-control, the answer is, Because he did not care enough. In all these cases, that is, the agent "fails to be sufficiently concerned about the very feature of his act that makes it wrong" (I, 238).

In asserting that all blameworthiness reduces to a lack of moral concern, Milo attributes enormous importance to it. In his view, such a lack "not only can account for one's doing what one believes to be wrong; it can also lead to one's not believing that it is wrong." Milo infers from this that "moral concern includes more than a concern to avoid doing that which one believes to be morally wrong, since moral concern must also be able to account for *why we make moral judgments*—why we have come to believe that our act is morally wrong in the first place" (I, 239; emphasis added).

Milo's inquiry into immorality ends on this note. Hence, he does not attempt to answer his question about why we make moral judgments in the first place. To be sure, this question is so far-reaching as to merit a study of its own. In elaborating the chief categories and levels involved in the performative sequence of morality—that is, perception, judgment, and action—I hope to give an answer to the question of *how* we make moral judgments; in doing so, I defend the position that concern not only accompanies the moral judgments we make but helps facilitate them. (I have discussed the proposed link between concern and judgment in my account of "moral blindness"). But as for *why* we make moral judgments, I see no simple answer. However, what is the more conspicuous phenomenon—a person's making moral judgments or a person's failing to? I would say the latter is. This is not to say that the passing of moral judgments is something we can take for granted, just like that. Yet our actual passing of moral judgments, as well as our persistence in expecting and demanding others to do so also, is not per se experienced as problematic; we just do so, and only a philosopher would intervene and ask us why. Intrinsically problematic then, especially from a pragmatic point of view, is not the passing but the nonpassing of moral judgments; this holds true for us as agents *in medias res*, as subjects encountering other subjects within a shared lifeworld, thus sharing a life-form and the whole range of tacit assumptions that go hand in hand with such common belongingness.

If this train of thought is sound, what we take for granted is the presence of moral concern—in ourselves and in others with whom we interact. Therefore, its *absence* is conspicuous, helps cause conflicts, harm, and wrong-doing, and calls for an answer as to *its* why, as to its specific sources and origin.

To throw some light on this issue is what I seek to do in the sections that follow. In doing so, I retain Milo's very general notion of what immorality ultimately amounts to—namely, a lack of concern for the interests and welfare of others. It is my hope that the following analyses of hatred, masochism, sadism, and indifference may enrich our understanding of the factors that undermine concern for others and thereby dispose a person to immoral acts.

This chapter's inquiry into the relation between emotions and immorality starts from the assumption that among the emotions disposing a person to commit immoral action—understood as action demonstrating a lack of concern for the interests and welfare of others—*hate* seems the most prominent one. In other words, if we look to human emotions for an answer to the question What kind of motives may help explain immoral action? hate stands out as a promising candidate. But how strong is this candidacy? What forms of hatred are there? What is their—possibly common—origin? And in what ways does the behavioral importance of hatred vary with the social setting in which it emerges?

The conditions of immoral action are not of just one kind. We must distinguish between what I call small-scale and large-scale immorality. In small-scale immorality, face-to-face encounters and general conditions of proximity between subject and chosen object, or target, obtain. In large-scale immorality, different processes of distancing prevail over proximity, entailing that the human target of the action is rendered (to a varying degree) invisible, abstract, anonymous; this confers a "systemic" nature on the action sequence, as demonstrated in the Nazi extermination of the European Jews.

Projection and Hatred in Anti-Semitism

The central question explored in *The Authoritarian Personality* is, Why do certain individuals have fascist leanings, whereas others do not? The study, one part of a five-volume project entitled *Studies in Prejudice*, seeks to investigate the sociopsychological preconditions of the potential fascist, that is, of the individual particularly susceptible to antidemocratic propaganda. Using the material from more than two hundred lengthy interviews as its empirical source, the study endeavors to establish interconnections between certain character traits on the one hand and beliefs, such as racial prejudice, on the other.

Adorno and his colleagues follow Freud's psychoanalytic theory in the assumption that the proper locus in which to start their inquiry is the family. It is noteworthy that Max Horkheimer in particular holds the nineteenth-century bourgeois family to constitute the only social unit truly capable of providing the child with a stable ego identity. The transition from a feudal to a capitalist society made the (middle- and upper-class) nuclear family a relatively self-sufficient economic entity. As Horkheimer writes in his 1949 essay "Autorität und Familie in der Gegenwart" (Authority and family today), "The man, liberated from the bondage in alien quarters, became master in his own home" (AuF, 270; translated by the author). The bourgeois paterfamilias embodied strength, sovereignty, and independence; he was therefore a figure able to meet the child's (the focus is primarily on the son) need for an authority figure with which to identify. However, with the decline of the economic independence of the middle-class father brought about by the twentieth-century state capitalist society, the father increasingly ceases to symbolize an inner authority; he can no longer offer his son the kind of unquestionable autonomy that the son needs to look up to, submit to, and one day himself take over and epitomize in front of his own children. The decline of liberal capitalism entails the increasing intervention of the state in previously private realms of determination; subjected to an ever-growing pressure from the outside world, the family is progressively threatened as a place where the individual is guaranteed care and protection. The father typically becomes a mere "money earner," the woman a "domestic servant." This overall development causes a profound alteration of the nuclear family's societal position with respect to authority. Horkheimer asserts, "As the family to a considerable extent has ceased to exert its peculiar form of authority over its members, it has now turned into a place for the exercise of authority *tout court.*" "The old powers of familial subordination," Horkheimer continues, "are still operating, but they now further a pervasive spirit of accommodation and authoritarian aggression rather than the interests of the family and its members" (AuF, 276; translated by the author).

Insofar as the authority of the father rests on an economic basis, the weakening of that basis leaves the son with no adequate reason for respecting his father. The son was dependent on his father, who personified independence; the son's father no longer conveying such an image, the son, a would-be father himself, has to look elsewhere to find a figure from whom independence can be learned. Accordingly, the son directs his need outward. The more frustrated the son is in his yearning for a figure maintaining sovereignty and security *within* the family, the more susceptible he becomes to *outside* forces offering to meet such psychological needs.

In brief, this is the broad sociological background for the account of the "authoritarian personality" given by Adorno and his colleagues. In general, it can be said about the authoritarian character that he admires authority and tends to submit to it, but at the same time he wants to be an authority himself and have others submit to him. His is a Manichaeistic worldview: the good forces oppose the evil ones, the strong combat the weak; the former are worshiped, the latter are despised. Strength per se merits submission and obedience; weakness per se inspires revulsion and serves to rationalize the discharge of impulses of aggression and destructiveness.

The classic authoritarian type, Adorno argues, emerges from a sadomasochistic resolution of the Oedipus complex.[1] "Love for the mother, in its primary form, comes under a severe taboo. The resulting hatred against the father is transformed by reaction-formation into love." This transformation leads to a particular kind of superego. The transformation of hatred into love, considered "the most difficult task an individual has to perform in his early development," never succeeds completely; it is immensely fragile. Visibly influenced by Freud's "hydraulic" model, they assert that in the psychodynamics of the authoritarian character part of the stored-up aggressiveness is absorbed and turned into masochism, while another part is left over as sadism, which seeks an outlet in those with whom the subject does not identify himself, typically the out-group. Turning outward for a release of an aggressiveness denied display within the family setting from which it originally stems, the subject hits on a target long favored—the Jew. "The Jew," writes Adorno, "frequently becomes a substitute for the hated father, often assuming, on the fantasy level, the very same qualities against which the subject revolted in the father, such as being practical, cold, domineering, and even a sexual rival" (AP, 759).

Horkheimer's essay on the family shows how the father, his model function as an authority figure diminishing, comes to be substituted in this function by some collective force, for instance by the state. The more challenged, doubtful, and faltering the authority of the father, the more there is an increase in a "general preparedness to accept any prevailing authority, provided it is sufficiently powerful." With the breakdown of the father's authority image, the process of internalization in the child fails. Thus, an autonomous ego is not formed, and the resulting "ego weakness" of the subject disposes it for adherence to authoritarian ideologies. Concomitant with this development is the changed role of the mother. Upbringing becoming more and more "scientific," the modern mother does her best to conform to an ideal advocating rationality rather than emotionality. "Even love," contends Horkheimer, "is treated as a part of pedagogical hygiene"; "the spontaneity of the mother and her natural, unlimited care and warmth tend to dissolve." The upshot is that "the mother ceases to be a soothing mediator between the child and the harsh reality; she becomes the mouthpiece of the latter" (AuF, 277–78; translated by the author). No longer representing a principle different from and often at odds with the external reality, the contemporary mother instead represents the harsh reality of the outside world *at home*. This entails that the traditional distribution of roles between father and mother threatens to break down completely. The father fails to uphold the image of a self-assured authority demanding *and* deserving respect from his children. And the mother, whose task it was to make sure that the required accommodation to the outside reality as upheld by the father did not take place at the expense of the development of the individuality of the child, now fails in her traditional role too. Hence, the family is at a loss to solve its two principal tasks: the child now searches in vain for a source of unquestionable authority in the father and for a source of unfailing emotional support in the mother. An effect of this prevailing state of affairs is that the child's "hard-boiledness and reciprocal obsequiousness in the face of actual power predispose it to totalitarian ways of life" (AuF, 279; translated by the author).

It may come as a surprise that the scholars undertaking the empirical study of the authoritarian personality found the high-scorers to profess a stubborn idealization of their parents. The surprise diminishes once we appreciate that the idealization at work in these persons is of a rigid and highly uncritical kind. Closer inspection reveals their relation to their parents to be without depth; the parents are "accepted" in a conventional manner, and no emotions of profound affection and endurance seem to have evolved. Superficiality, indifference, and stereotypes prevail. As Horkheimer observes, "The abstract glorification of the family mirrors the almost total lack of a concrete relation to the parents, be it positive or negative." And he goes on to point out that the "entire affective life of the authority-bound character [demonstrates] features of superficiality and coldness," whereby he puts particular emphasis on a "general contempt for sympathy—sympathy of precisely the kind that more than anything else signifies a mother's love for her child" (AuF, 281; translated by the author). I return to the emotional origin of the *contempt for sympathy* in sections below.

Behind the lip service paid to the parents as being "wonderful" people worthy of love and respect, what emerges is not an emotional bond of real substance between child and parents but an emotional vacuum. No *binding* ties of mutual affection have been formed. I stress this once again because it connects with a point made above about the particular type of superego that is formed in these circumstances. This superego is overrigid and externalized; due to the weakness of the emotional bond with—and often also between—the parents, the child's identity remains poorly integrated and hence all the more susceptible to external pressures. To be able to cope with and if need be openly resist such pressures, the individual would have to have successfully internalized an ego-ideal of genuine authority and self-assurance; but this is what the modern father often cannot provide. Furthermore, the individual would have to be able to enter into enduring affectionate relationships with other people; but this, presupposing as it does a capacity for love and sympathy, is what the mother often fails to transmit to her child.

It goes without saying that the picture offered here is an oversimplified one. Yet I hope it delivers an adequate background for the thesis held by Adorno and his colleagues that the authoritarian syndrome is based on ego weakness. Lacking genuine inner security and having experienced a rationalized and halfhearted rather than unconditional love, the individual emerges from his or her family as a likely victim to outside forces that strive to activate and draw on the repressed urges. External authority offers to compensate for the deficient inner security; the more powerful the external authorities, the more the individual is attracted to them, trying to forget his or her own weakness by identifying and merging with the crowd, the party, or the state. Relief is gained from subordination and from the persecution of those who are picked out as "weak" and who represent traits the individual finds intolerable in his or her own self. [2]

As anticipated by Horkheimer, collective powers are attractive to the individual as a substitute for the authority that the father fails to epitomize. Accordingly, Adorno, drawing on Freud's discussion of Le Bon in his *Group Psychology and the Analysis of the Ego*, models the bond between leader and follower on that between father and son, suggesting that the former relation promises to fulfill what the latter no longer provides. The internalization of the authority of the father being unsuccessful, the fascist personality is characterized by what Freud designated the externalization of the superego. Fascist personalities typically "fail to develop an independent autonomous conscience and substitute for it an identification with collective authority which is . . . heteronomous, rigidly oppressive, largely akin to the individual's own thinking and, therefore, easily exchangeable in spite of its structural rigidity" (FT, 416). What the Führer ideology offers its adherents is precisely an omnipotent and unbridled father figure, one that appears to compensate for the frustrating experience with the powerlessness of the actual father. The narcissistic aspect of identification and idealization alike render them acts of devouring, of making the beloved object part of oneself. In this way the subject achieves a kind of "borrowed" strength and assurance that provides his or her ego with a temporal if highly vicarious satisfaction.

Yet, for all its suggestiveness, the analogy between father-son and leader-follower does not take us very far. It may succeed in demonstrating how

certain psychological mechanisms operate, but the analogy leaves us uninformed about the deeper causes of the mechanisms as such. To trace the
psychohistory of anti-Semitic prejudice, I turn to the analysis given by
Horkheimer and Adorno in their principal work, *Dialectic of Enlightenment*.

The authors of that work argue that Odysseus, as portrayed in Homer's
poem, is a prototype of the bourgeois individual.[3] A great deal of the
Odyssey, then, is an anticipation of things to come. Odysseus struggles to
become a full-fledged, self-positing autonomous subject. Horkheimer and
Adorno seek to show how this struggle for autonomy in our modern sense
has throughout Western history been linked to sacrifice, renunciation, and
repression—not only of nature, not only of others, but of the self as well.
Odysseus struggles to master nature and people. By imitating nature he
learns to adapt to it, yet in imitating nature's regularities and rigidity he
himself becomes rigid. Only through repression of instincts and continual
sacrifice—what Adorno calls a denial of nature in man for the sake of
domination over nonhuman nature and over other men—can Odysseus
survive. Autonomy is only to be attained at the price of a suppression of
man's own inner nature, a high price indeed, because "with the denial of
nature in man not merely the telos of the outward control of nature but the
telos of man's own life is distorted and befogged" (DE, 54). Autonomy
requires self-control; the subject maintains himself as autonomous over and
against nature and other men only insofar as he learns to repress instincts,
desires, and feelings. Spontaneity only betrays him. What he demands from
himself is that he restrain himself and "forget" his immediate needs and
wants. Inner no less than outer nature is mastered by rational calculation and
for the sake of self-preservation. Odysseus treats his crew as a means to his
end, but in this he makes no exception for himself: denying that he is nature
too, he treats his inner nature as an object of total domination. To Adorno,
the suppression of the nature *in* the subject *by* the subject amounts to the
annihilation of life itself. Thus, paradoxically, the very endeavor to preserve
life, in the name of "autonomy," contains a denial of life insofar as everything
living is subject to domination; predictability is to reign, not the spontaneity
of life itself. This analysis sees the history of civilization as the history of
the introversion of sacrifice; it is the history of all-encompassing renunciation. However, "everyone who practices renunciation gives away more of his
life than is given back to him, and more than the life that he vindicates" (DE,
55). Odysseus, who at all times restrains himself, renounces his life in doing
so—even though his sacrifice takes place for the sake of life itself. He saves

his life, but he dares not to live it. He is therefore himself the ultimate victim of his own sacrifice.

The total and, as it turns out, increasingly compulsive denial of everything natural and as yet untouched, of every spontaneous urge, of the desire for instant gratification, of experiences so novel as to evade the concepts already at hand—this is civilization, but it is also the price man has paid for it. Adorno's point is that as soon as man discards his awareness that he himself is nature, all the aims for which he keeps himself alive are nullified. Adorno terms this the "prehistory of subjectivity," and the irony should not escape us. For, to repeat, what he argues is that man's domination over himself, which grounds his selfhood, brings about the destruction of the subject in whose service it is undertaken. However, the transformation of sacrifice into subjectivity is not always self-sufficient, as it were. The sacrifice of the self— in the name of the preservation of the self—does not exclude the sacrifice of others. Nature that has not been transformed through the channels of conceptual order into something purposeful and predictable has a penetrating effect on the modern subject: it arouses his disgust. Uncontrolled mimesis is hence outlawed. Civilization replaces the organic adaptation to others and mimetic behavior proper by organized control of mimesis, that is to say, by purpose-rational practice, by "work." With this "rationalization" of mimesis, the indelible mimetic heritage of past experiences is consigned to oblivion. The mere recollection of this heritage poses a threat, since it dwells on what is rendered forbidden and thus must remain hidden from view. In their "Elements of Anti-Semitism" Horkheimer and Adorno write, "Those blinded by civilization experience their own tabooed mimetic features only in certain gestures and behaviour patterns which they encounter in others and which strike them as isolated remnants, as embarrassing rudimentary elements that survive in the rationalized environment." Oblivion, it now turns out, is not complete after all: "What seems repellently alien is in fact all too familiar: the infectious gestures of direct contacts suppressed by civilization, for instance, touch, soothing, snuggling up, coaxing. We are put off by the old-fashioned nature of these impulses" (DE, 181–82).

But it is not only that such impulses seem obsolete, memories from a distant past. More to the point, they pose a threat, they arouse anger, even hatred. The performers of uncontrolled mimesis must not merely be told how to behave; they must be done away with. It is not a question of pedagogy, of proper learning; it is a question of extinction. Appeals to tolerance, to the right to be different, completely miss the mark. Rather, "the mere existence of the other is a provocation" (DE, 183). But *who* is this other? The Jew. The Jew is singled out as the carrier par excellence of the mimetic features now forbidden. I pointed out that the sacrifice of the self does not exclude the craving to sacrifice others, and I have shown how remnants of unrationalized mimesis trigger feelings of revulsion. In the Jews, the two points meet: deemed the carriers of what is outlawed, *they* are the other to be sacrificed. The carrier is to be the victim. "It matters little," Horkheimer and Adorno observe, "whether the Jews as individuals really do still have those mimetic features which awaken the dread malady, or whether such features are suppressed" (DE, 185). This effect is worked by the anti-Semite's totalizing use of stereotypes. The "Jew" is a construction. He or she is never allowed to emerge as an individual. The Jews are notoriously "all alike," "the same everywhere," and so eminently recognizable. And, as Adorno points out, "there is no simple gap between experience and stereotypy"; rather, "experience itself is predetermined by stereotypy." Hence, the individual "cannot 'correct' stereotypy by experience; he has to reconstitute the capacity for *having* experiences in order to prevent the growth of ideas which are malignant in the most literal, clinical sense" (AP, 617). The stereotype keeps the world as aloof, abstract, and "nonexperienced" as it was before. Stereotypy is fundamentally inadequate to reality. It misses reality insofar as it "dodges the concrete and contents itself with preconceived, rigid, and overgeneralized ideas to which the individual attributes a kind of magical omnipotence" (AP, 665–66). And where no experience takes place, the prejudice contained in stereotypy cannot be arrested.

Thus, a link is set up between the (stereotype) Jew and the uncontrolled mimesis now under a severe taboo. The Jew is "filthy," a "vermin," a "cancer growth" within society. In Chapter 4 I mentioned that biological metaphors were exploited in the concept "life unworthy of life." To continue, the Jew is impure, and therefore dangerous, a threat that has to be dealt with without mercy, a "problem" admitting only of a "final solution" (read: physical extermination). Individual Jews are the captive of the stereotypy applied to them; precisely because they are never *experienced*, they have no chance to appear as individuals; regardless of who they are and what they have done, they cannot escape what is being made of them. "The Jews as a whole are accused of participating in forbidden magic and bloody ritual"; the Jews are trapped in a situation where "all the horror of prehistory which has been overlaid with civilization is rehabilitated as rational interest by projection onto the Jews" (DE, 186). The false projection at work in anti-Semitism, then, confuses the inner and the outer world and defines the most familiar experiences as alien, the intimate as hostile. "Impulses which the subject will not admit as his own even though they are most assuredly so, are attributed to the object—the prospective victim." The mechanism thereby exploited by fascism is as old as civilization. One must take seriously that the "person chosen as an enemy was already seen as an enemy. The disturbance"—and this is what makes the projection in question false—"lies in the failure on the part of the subject to differentiate between his own and the extraneous contribution to the projected material" (DE, 187).

The depiction of anti-Semitism as "false projection" betrays an unmistakable debt to Freud. Freud's psychoanalytic theory uncovers the transference of socially taboo impulses from the subject to the object. Under the pressure of the superego, the ego projects onto the outside world the aggressive wishes that originate from the id as evil intentions and manages to work them out as abreaction. There is nothing morbid about projective behavior per se; what makes it so in anti-Semitism, however, is a peculiar absence of reflection. Anti-Semitic subjects do not experience the object; failing this, they also fail to reflect the object as it is, for in order to do so they would have to return to it more than they receive from it. The encounter with the object therefore leaves the subjects poorer, rather than richer. They do not see that what they fear in the object is what they fear in themselves. This is so because the roots of this fear are unconscious, and they are likely to remain so in all the anti-Semite's dealings with the object. What is conscious, however, is the subject's preoccupation with the perceived otherness of the object. It is the otherness that serves as the rationale for the urge to remove from sight, to kill, to wipe out. In sociological terms, the Jews form an outgroup inescapably hostile to the in-group, and the only appropriate response to difference is to fight what is different. This mentality is part of the Manichaeistic worldview mentioned above.

The fanatical anti-Semite sees the Jews everywhere. He is therefore perpetually alerted, always on the outlook for an enemy thought to be ubiquitous. Adorno notes that the extremely prejudiced person tends toward "psychological totalitarianism," something that seems to be "almost a microcosmic image of the totalitarian state at which he aims." "As long as anything different survives, the fascist character feels threatened, no matter how weak the other being may be" (AP, 632–33). But, since the extreme anti-Semite "simply cannot stop," there emerges here a disproportion between guilt and punishment: the sought punishment of the Jews is so severe, so extreme, so total in nature, that the crimes of which they are allegedly guilty seem unimportant, indeed utterly inferior in comparison. Adorno gives the following account:

Psychologically, the idea of external Jewish guilt can be understood as a projection of the prejudiced person's own repressed guilt feelings; ideologically, it is a mere epiphenomenon, a rationalization in the strictest sense. In the extreme case, the psychological focal point is the wish to kill the object of his hatred. It is only afterwards that he looks for reasons why the Jews "must" be killed, and these reasons can never suffice fully to justify his extermination fantasies. This, however, does not "cure" the anti-Semite, once he has succeeded in expropriating his conscience. The disproportion between the guilt and the punishment induces him, rather, to pursue his hatred beyond any limits and thus to prove to himself and to others that he *must* be right. This is the ultimate function of ideas such as "the Jews brought it upon themselves" or the more generalized formula "there must be something to it." The extreme anti-Semite silences the remnants of his own conscience by the extremeness of his attitude. He seems to terrorize himself even while he terrorizes others. (AP, 633)

The thesis that anti-Semitism is based on "false projection" places great emphasis on the link that is set up between the Jew and forbidden mimetic features. The individual's fear of his or her own inner nature is projected onto the outside world, where the stereotyped "filthy" Jew is singled out as the perfect target. But a different explanation for the anti-Semite's hatred is the popular association of the Jew with the idea of freedom. Although the Jews have not been the only owners of the circulation sector, they have for many centuries been closely associated with it. In people's minds, the connection between the Jews on the one hand and circulation, money, and intellectuality on the other is a commonplace. Historically, it has stimulated myths about the "secrecy" of Jewish life, providing a fertile ground for speculations about the peculiar power of the Jews, about a Jewish world conspiracy, and so on. Operating in the sphere of circulation and hence as intermediaries rather than as clear-cut property owners or workers, being neither masters nor slaves, the Jews inhabited an "in-between" position that conferred a certain opacity and abstractness on their activities. Their societal position was one of profound ambiguity. Even though the Jews handled monetary transactions, money signifying the universal medium par excellence, as shown by Karl Marx and Georg Simmel,[4] the non-Jewish population was always struck by the seeming inaccessibility of their professional undertakings. Money travels freely; once institutionalized as the medium of exchange, money breaks down existing barriers everywhere. The eminent mobility of which money is the supreme vehicle came to be transferred onto and seen as embodied by the Jews by virtue of their key role in the circulation sector. Mobility spells freedom—freedom of movement, of course, and with that the power to transcend the limits of time and space. The Jews are accused of being parasites, of having no real home, of "belonging" nowhere; yet it is exactly for these reasons that they become the object of *envy*. Their mobility contains the promise of freedom.[5]

Hence, due to their very special position within society, the people who placed their hatred on the Jews did so out of envy as well as out of the fear of inner nature referred to above. Adorno rather downplays the role of envy as compared to that of the mimesis complex, but he does draw attention to it in a passage worth quoting:

> No matter what the Jews as such may be like, their image, as that of the defeated people, has the features to which totalitarian domination must be completely hostile: happiness without power, wages without work, a home without frontiers, religion without myth. These characteristics are hated by the rulers because the ruled secretly long to possess them. The rulers are only safe as long as the people they rule turn their longed-for goals into hated forms of evil. This they manage to do by pathological projection, since even hatred leads to unification with the object—in destruction. (DE, 199)

I close this exposition of the psychological mechanisms at work in anti-Semitism with a warning against exaggerating its scope. I want to stress that anti-Semitism is not just a question of psychology. Adorno puts the point well: "Psychological dispositions do not actually cause Fascism; rather, Fascism defines a psychological area which can be successfully exploited by the forces which promote it for entirely nonpsychological reasons of self-interest. What happens when masses are caught by Fascist propaganda is not a spontaneous primary expression of instincts and urges but a quasi-scientific revitalization of their psychology" (FT, 430). What holds for fascism in this respect holds for anti-Semitism too. In both cases—and the two often melt into one—the "regression" at work is artificial rather than spontaneous; it is brought about from above instead of arising impulsively from below. I have pointed to some of the forms this appropriation of mass psychology by the oppressors may take—for instance, the way externalization of the superego is exploited in the ideology of the fatherlike Führer, or the way the individual's conscience is expropriated by a larger apparatus the aims of which become his or her own, thus relieving the individual of feelings of responsibility and guilt. What is achieved here is the very opposite of the emancipation of humanity from the heteronomous rule of the unconscious intended in the theory of Freud: the perpetuation of dependence, not the realization of humanity's potential for freedom—this is the core of fascist and anti-Semitic "psychology."

I now turn to a criticism of specific claims in Horkheimer's and Adorno's analyses of the psychological mechanisms at work in anti-Semitism.

1. It can be said against Horkheimer that his portrait of the family suffers from a number of questionable assumptions. To start with the role of the father, Horkheimer seems to hold a very idealized view of the intrafamilial authority exercised by the middle- or upper-class father of nineteenth-century society. "In former times," asserts Horkheimer, "the loving imitation of the self-assured, wise man devoted to his duties was the source of moral autonomy for the individual" (AuF, 277; translated by the author). Obviously, and in all fairness, the family is treated by Horkheimer as an ideal type in the sense defined by Max Weber. Still, I am struck by how Horkheimer's picture of the bourgeois family verges on nostalgia. The fact that the nuclear family in former times no less than in present ones often was an arena of violence and suppression, with the father playing the lead role, is wholly neglected in Horkheimer's account. Furthermore, there is reason to question the role Horkheimer attributes to the mother. "Today," he writes, "when the child no longer experiences the unlimited love of his mother, his own capacity for love remains undeveloped" (AuF, 279; translated by the author). Again, the historical accuracy of Horkheimer's observation may be questioned—as may of course the almost reactionary way in which he reserves "authority" for the father and "love" for the mother.[6]

Despite these criticisms, some important insights can be gained from Horkheimer. First, it seems plausible that there is a connection between the frustration with a weak father figure, and the appeal of a powerful Führer: the former seems to facilitate the latter. The insecure son is a likely supporter of authoritarian ideologies that posit a rigid dichotomy between those who are "strong" and deserving of unqualified obedience and those who are "weak" and thus deserving of contempt. The fascist and anti-Semitic no-pity-for-the-poor mentality is nothing more than a brutal condemnation of anything that is deemed weak.

Next, and more important, Horkheimer's remarks about the love-giving ability of the mother suggest an idea crucial to my main argument: namely, that to give love requires a specific ability to do so, and that the individual who has not been given love, has not been the addressee of love, may fail to develop the ability to give it to others. By my interpretation, then, love is an ability that has to be learned in order to develop properly. To put it briefly, one has to have been the object of love in order to become its subject; one must have received it in order to acquire the ability to give it. Although it can be questioned whether it must be the mother who, in giving her child love, teaches it the ability to love, and whether the average mother's performance of this role today is in any way inferior to what it was in the past, the insight that I wish to keep from Horkheimer's account is that love giving requires a specific *emotional ability* and that this ability must be *learned*—by virtue of being its object—from a person who is close to the child during its primary socialization.

2. A further point of importance is the gulf between stereotypes and firsthand experience. As Adorno has stressed, stereotypes are not merely opposed to experience but highly resistant to it; thus, an established stereotype may help block the potential of the experiences de facto taken part in by the subject. The experience had is oddly impotent because the very perception of the object that is experienced is distorted. The distortion of the perception of the object is prior to the actual experience, so that the latter has no possibility of influencing or "correcting" the former. Experience is and remains the only road to a falsification of stereotype; however, this road is blocked, since the stereotype preforms the perception of the object to be experienced. The temptation to use Kantian terminology cannot be resisted: stereotypy constitutes an apriority the stamp of which shapes any object of perception.

A related point is that the beliefs contained in a specific stereotype tend to become true to reality even though initially untrue. Herein lies the supreme danger of a widely shared stereotype: an initially false belief is formed, spread, and *acted* on; after a while, it congratulates itself with being an adequate description of the brought-about reality. In a word, the belief develops into a self-fulfilling prophecy about its object. The "psychological totalitarianism" of the extreme prejudiced person is such that he or she always and everywhere strives to create a world that conforms completely to his or her fanatically held picture of how the world "is"; from this imperative no object, no event, no person is left untouched.

The Nazis were very clear practitioners of the principle of the self-fulfilling prophecy. Two important objectives coincide in their version of the principle: on the one hand, the psychological need of the extremely prejudiced person was satisfied insofar as there was no deviation from the predetermined picture of how things "are"; on the other hand, Nazi policy aims were reached insofar as the action taken produced, along the way, the rationale for its being undertaken in the first place. For example, the Nazis started out with the allegation that the Jews were notoriously filthy. They then imposed on the Jews the conditions rendering the allegation true; they forced them to gather in ghettos in circumstances of unprecedented material and spiritual deprivation. Thereupon the propaganda photographers were sent in to secure and spread the empirical evidence: the "filthy" Jews begging, lying, and dying on the streets in the Warsaw and Lodz ghettos.[7] The brought-about, "documented" filthiness could now serve its true purpose; it helped rationalize and legitimize the next, preconceived, and final step: the dissolution of the ghettos an accomplished fact, what was next in store were the death camps at Auschwitz and Treblinka. And with that, the self-fulfilling prophecy came full circle.[8]

These points are important in that they help illuminate how a *distorted perception* of the other may come about. I cannot treat here the historical, cultural, and sociological conditions of anti-Semitism. But it is not anti-Semitism as such but what we might learn from its example in terms of human psychology that is of issue. Thus, I am content if the more general underlying psychological mechanisms have been clarified. The various distortions of perception explored in the preceding paragraphs are predominantly of a *cognitive* nature. And indeed this stress on the cognitive aspects of the psychology of prejudice is very much encouraged by the approach to prejudice that is taken by Horkheimer and Adorno. With respect to my own purposes, their approach helps bring out the contribution of cognitive bias in the distortion of perception *eo ipso* of experience as well. To sum up, what distorts the perception and blocks the experience of the other qua cosubject on the "cognitive" level has been shown to include the use of stereotypes and crude generalizations; the adherence to a Manichaeistic worldview; the intolerance of deviation, nuances, and ambiguity; and the predilection for the wonders worked by self-fulfilling prophecies.

To complete the picture, however, attention must be shifted from the cognitive to the emotional level.

3. With this I come to the issue of hatred. In my reading, Horkheimer's and Adorno's reflections on anti-Semitism contain, at least implicitly, a conception of hatred. There are two main points to this conception. First, hatred emerges as part of what they refer to as "false projection." Second, hatred is studied exclusively as organized, that is to say, as "brought about" by means of fascist propaganda's clever exploitation of mass psychology.

Consequently, the nature of hate qua spontaneous sentiment, or qua deep-seated instinct, or qua sheer aggression, goes unexamined. Detlev Claussen speaks for Horkheimer and Adorno when he maintains that "organized mass murder must overcome spontaneity and emotions in order to ensure the fulfillment of its goal."[9]

When hatred surfaces in false projection, the following takes place: Feared, forbidden, and repressed aggressive impulses in the subject are projected outward onto some particular object. Once these impulses have been attributed to the object by a subject who fails to see that he or she in fact projects rather than "finds," the object—precisely because perceived as "evil," as threatening and aggressive—becomes the target of impulses whose acting out now appears appropriate and justified to the subject. Projection supports a rationalization of the aggression directed against the chosen object. The subject needs the object; the object allows the subject to turn his or her stored-up aggressive impulses outward instead of inward; the subject thus uses the object to secure his or her self-preservation and to preclude the alternative of self-destruction. "The fascist variety of anti-Semitism," assert Horkheimer and Adorno, "must first invent its own object" (DE, 207). Their statement does justice to Hitler's oft-cited remark according to which he would have had to invent the Jew had the Jew not already existed. Anti-Semitism, therefore, creates the "Jew"—or, put more generally, *hate invents its object*. However, the "creative" act of hatred is only for the sake of the act's negation: hate invents in order to destroy. (Love, let it be remembered from the chapter on Scheler, creates in order to preserve, foster, and enhance the perceived value of its chosen object.) The hate object is a creation of the subject, and the projection at work here is designated "false" because the subject is the captive of his or her own prejudice and therefore wholly unlikely to discover that the target of his or her hatred in fact stems from himself or herself and not from the object. In other words, what remains hidden is that one hates in the other what one hates—but fails to recognize—in oneself, *as* oneself. Hence, projection betrays much about the subject but discloses nothing of any reliability about the object. The characteristic exchangeability of the hate object is demonstrated by the relative ease with which the subject may shift from one object to another; the arbitrariness of object selection is one of the features Adorno had in mind when he spoke about the "ticket mentality."

Horkheimer and Adorno do not try to capture hate in its spontaneity. Their focus is on the mass psychological exploitation of hate, on its political engineering in fascism. This perspective leaves spontaneous outbursts of hatred in the individual out of the picture. Since spontaneity and individuality alike are supposed to represent threats to the "instrumental" anti-Semitism pursued by fascist ideology (an assumption also found in Hannah Arendt), these aspects of hate go largely unexamined. It seems to me to be a *petitio principii* in Horkheimer and Adorno that hate is *functional*. So, in the picture they paint of the anti-Semite, the uncovered hatred—whatever the degree of its vehemence—is interpreted so as to show the function it serves for the (biased, manipulated) individual himself or herself and for the propaganda apparatus and the socioeconomic powers that seek to exploit the prejudiced and insecure individual. Adorno expresses his preoccupation with functionality when, to pick just one example, he states that the "narcissistic gain provided by fascist propaganda is obvious," since such propaganda suggests that "the follower, simply through belonging to the in-group, is better, higher and purer than those who are excluded" (FT, 424). Although this statement does not directly address the issue of hatred, it shows very clearly the perspective from which Adorno's investigation is carried out. Put differently, when Adorno "detects" the so-called narcissistic gain in his analyses, he only finds what he is looking for. This is not to say that Adorno is wrong; it merely brings to light a key assumption he invariably (in his treatment of anti-Semitism and fascism) seems to be working from. In short, it reveals the selectivity of his perspective and thus provides some clues about its possible limitations.

The two points discussed demonstrate Horkheimer's and Adorno's debt to the psychoanalytic theory of Freud: the depiction of hatred as an instance of false projection, and the principle that hatred serves a (narcissistic) function for the subject. However, is all hatred a matter of projection? Furthermore, granted that every specific instance of overt hatred can be explained by some particular cause, does it follow that the cause in question must be understood in purely functional terms? Is not Adorno's reference to the subject's "narcissistic gain" fundamentally inadequate to explain the psychological and emotional origins of the *many faces* of hatred?

My view is that hatred is not always and not necessarily a matter of projection. This may have been the case to a large extent in fascist anti-Semitism as studied by Horkheimer and Adorno. But even if this should be correct, it does not warrant a general thesis to the effect that hatred fundamentally, according to its very nature, rests on projection. As I argue in greater detail below, projection does not exhaust the phenomenon of hate; for that, it is too narrow a model. Hate need not have its origin in the subject, or not in the subject alone; instead, the hate felt by a subject toward an object may be caused by what the object has done to the subject. Therefore, although it is probably true of anti-Semitism that the subject invents the object of his or her hatred, a conception of hatred must also be so wide as to allow for the case where the hatred felt by the subject is a response to something done by the object—by which I mean an objective case, *not* a product of the subject's projection. I term this *reactive hatred*.

To fully appreciate the view of hate I have indicated, it may prove necessary to reject Freud, or at least parts of his theory. Note, however, that I say this *may* prove necessary. For it may be that Horkheimer and Adorno have overfocused on one aspect of Freud's theory, that is, on the concept of projection, so that their (largely implicit) conception of hatred suffers from a one-sided appropriation of Freud rather than from some major flaw in his theory as such. In order to settle this question, I turn in the next section to a different reading and application of Freud, namely, the one developed by Erich Fromm. Fromm's work permits us to confront the larger issue of human destructiveness—and, as part of that, of the various kinds of aggressiveness—head-on. This being so, Fromm's theoretical framework encourages a much more differentiated conception of hatred than that considered so far. Thereupon the relation between hate and morality—or, better, hate and immorality—can be properly addressed.

A final point remains to be made. Consider the following statement from *Dialectic of Enlightenment*:

> If thought is liberated from domination and if violence is abolished, the long absent idea is liable to develop that *Jews too are human beings*. This development would represent the step out of an anti-Semitic society which drives Jews and others to madness, and into the human society. . . . Individual and social emancipation from domination is the counter-movement to false projection, and no Jew would then resemble the senseless evil visited upon him as upon all persecuted beings, be they animals or men. (DE, 199–200; emphasis added)

This passage suggests that false projection can be overcome by humanity's emancipation from domination. Such emancipation is needed in order to secure unanimous endorsement of the fact that the Jew too is a human being. According to my reading of the passage, what is called for in order to combat the hatred operating in false projection is the *abolition of the dehumanization* of hatred's chosen target. Put positively, what is required is the humanization of the hate object, in this case, the idea that the Jew too is a human being—

nothing more, nothing less. The Jew is one fellow cosubject among others. The corollary to this idea has been put forward on numerous occasions in the present study: the idea that immorality—such as it prevails, for example, in the intention to make the world *judenrein*—is linked to processes of dehumanization or, stronger still, that dehumanization is one of immoral action's key prerequisites. Conversely, this idea entails that the struggle against dehumanization in all its forms (anti-Semitic prejudice being but one) constitutes the crucial task in putting morality (as the full mutual recognition of all human subjects) where there formerly was immorality (as the acted-on nonrecognition of humans by humans). But what, it must be asked, can produce recognition of the human where there was once violent nonrecognition? To this familiar question I can offer nothing but a familiar answer: the only road leading to this goal is the road of experience. Concretely, this means to open oneself to the experience that the other is a human too. Yet the discussion of Adorno showed that anti-Semitism *blocks* this road, and very successfully at that. Still, if this is the main obstacle, then it does indicate where a solution might be found.

Fromm's Theory of Destructiveness

In his first major work, *Escape from Freedom*, Erich Fromm outlines a theory about the authoritarian personality that differs in important respects from the one defended by Horkheimer and Adorno, Fromm's onetime colleagues at the Institute for Social Research in Frankfurt.[10] But Fromm's controversy with the other Frankfurters aside, my objective in dealing with his theory is to render plausible the hypothesis that the genesis of human destructiveness is to be sought in a lack of empathy.

Fromm and the Authoritarian Character

To Fromm, authoritarianism is a mechanism of escape. It offers itself as such to individuals who seek to overcome an unbearable state of powerlessness and aloneness. In this situation, two courses are open to individuals: They may progress to "positive freedom" and trust their ability to relate themselves spontaneously to the world in love and work (Freud's *lieben und arbeiten*), thereby giving genuine expression to their emotional, sensuous, and intellectual capacities. Or they may choose to give up their freedom and try to overcome aloneness by eliminating the gap that has arisen between themselves and the world. In opting for this course, what individuals strive for is the more or less complete surrender of individuality and the integrity of the self.

This then is the general background against which Fromm attacks the problem of the authoritarian personality, whose character, he argues, is sadomasochistic. Although this is recognized by Horkheimer and Adorno (whose work on the subject was first published in 1950), Fromm places especial emphasis on sadomasochism inasmuch as it, according to his view, represents a striving for submission and domination that must be understood as a mechanism of escape. So the main difference between the two approaches is that Horkheimer and Adorno concentrate on the narcissistic gain to be had in opting for the "ticket" of fascist anti-Semitism, whereas Fromm's concern is with the wider—one could almost say metaphysical—predicament of modern humanity: its unprecedented possibility for freedom and independence, and the profound *fears* that this very possibility awakens in the twentieth-century individual. Hence the vast number of people who disavow and renounce their potential for freedom and for whom masochism and sadism appear desirable "ways out."

The masochist, according to Fromm, is riddled by feelings of inferiority, powerlessness, and insignificance. Seeking to overcome these feelings, the masochist displays a high degree of dependence on and willingness to submit to powers outside himself; he feels "alive" only through conforming to others and obeying their wishes. Having no strong sense of value, no real pride, masochistic persons tend to belittle themselves, indeed to hurt themselves and to make themselves suffer. Sadistic tendencies, though going in the opposite direction—being directed against others instead of oneself—are regularly to be found in the same kind of characters. Fromm distinguishes between three kinds of sadistic tendencies: one is to make others dependent on oneself and to exert absolute power over them; a second is to exploit others, to use them, to disembowel them, mentally as well as materially; a third is to wish to make and to see others suffer, especially mentally, by placing them in embarrassing and humiliating situations (see EF, 123–24). Fromm pays particular attention to the circumstance that the sadistic person is *dependent* on the object of his sadism. "The sadist needs the person over whom he rules, he needs him very badly, since his own feeling of strength is rooted in the fact that he is the master over someone" (EF, 125). To sum up, the masochistic as well as the sadistic individual (being often one and the same) finds himself "free" in the negative sense only, that is, alone with himself and confronting an alienated, hostile world. This makes him frightened, and he seeks to eliminate the gap, felt as an abyss, between his insecure self and the all-powerful outside world. He thus "seeks for somebody or something to tie his self to; he cannot bear to be his own individual self any longer, and he tries frantically to get rid of it and to feel security again by the elimination of this burden: the self" (EF, 130). The masochistic person seeks security by being swallowed, by dissolving himself in an outside power; the sadistic person gains security by swallowing somebody else, enlarging himself, as it were, by making another being part of himself.

Fromm's treatment of the authoritarian personality makes no explicit mention of projection, whose role in anti-Semitism Horkheimer and Adorno see as crucial, indeed as the psychological crux of the matter. By contrast, modern humanity's feeling of powerlessness is from early on the leitmotif in Fromm's dealings with the subject. Accordingly, the authoritarian character, with his or her conspicuous mixture of masochistic and sadistic tendencies, is but one among many possible ways of escape from the unbearable feeling of insecurity that Fromm takes to haunt the contemporary individual. Horkheimer and Adorno traced the hatred and destructiveness discharged in authoritarian anti-Semitism to the prehistory of a subject who pursues self-preservation and "autonomy" by waging war against his or her own inner nature and by seeking total domination over his or her outer one. Combining rather heterogeneous insights from psychoanalysis on the one hand and Marxist philosophy of history on the other, the founders of critical theory depicted anti-Semitism as the "rumor about the Jew," modeling it on a projection where what is sought annihilated in the other, in the Jew as *the* other, as otherness *tout court*, in fact stems from the anti-Semite himself or herself. Fromm differs from this approach in that he takes the assumed powerlessness of the individual as his starting point. From this perspective, the authoritarian personality emerges not as a person fighting blindly against the remnants of "outlawed mimesis," wishing to get rid of the intolerable *Natur im Subjekt* by destroying its carriers as encountered in another "race." Far from that, Fromm sees authoritarianism as an attempt to overcome an unbearable feeling of isolation, insecurity, and inferiority. Hence, strength is admired precisely because one is lacking it, and so on. To Fromm, the authoritarian personality is driven by fear rather than by hatred, and where hatred emerges, it does so as a by-product of an underlying fear that in turn develops from a sense of impotence in the midst of a forever hostile world.

For my purposes, the important difference between the two approaches is simply that Fromm's approach accommodates answers to the questions I raised by way of criticism in the section on Horkheimer and Adorno, namely: Are all acts of hatred and destructiveness cases of projection? Can it be that the model of projection permits us to grasp only one type of destructiveness but not the phenomenon itself? And moreover, is there not a class of destructive acts where the wish to destroy is objectively caused and provoked by the object, thus producing hatred as a mere reaction in the subject? If anything, these questions highlight the urgent need for a conceptual framework more sophisticated than the one found in Horkheimer and Adorno.

It is in order to gain a framework allowing me to settle the questions posed here that I turn to Fromm's assessment of the work of Freud. In doing so, my hypothesis is that the difference of opinion between Horkheimer/Adorno and Fromm, though certainly demonstrating two apparently incompatible ways of "reading" Freud, in fact reflects some basic tensions in the work of the master himself. Herbert Marcuse speaks on behalf of critical theory when he holds Fromm's "neo-Freudian revisionism" guilty of flattening out the depth dimension of the conflict between the individual and society, between the instinctual structure and the realm of consciousness: "The revisionist minimization of the biological sphere, and especially of the role of sexuality, shifts the emphasis not only from the unconscious to consciousness, from the id to the ego, but also from the presublimated to the sublimated expressions of the human existence." Against this, Marcuse insists that theory moves from the cultural to the biological, from the surface to the depth, from "finished" and conditioned persons to their sources and resources. The detection and examination of the biological, the depth, the sources and resources, Marcuse argues, requires that one be willing to maintain, first and foremost, the notion of the death instinct elaborated by Freud. [11]

Fromm's Critique of Freud's Theory of Destructiveness

In *Escape from Freedom*, Fromm draws attention to the shift in Freud's position on the issue of destructiveness. Freud's original assumption was that the sexual drive (libido) and the drive for self-preservation were the two basic motivations of human behavior. This view held sadomasochism to be a "partial drive" that, in adults, is due to a fixation of a person's psychosexual development; thus, sadomasochism is essentially a sexual phenomenon. However, Freud later came to see this early view as neglecting the fundamental importance of destructive impulses in humanity's psyche. According to his revised position, sadomasochism is the essentially nonsexual product of what he called the death instinct. Freud, that is, came to hold that there are two basic strivings to be found in humanity: a drive that is directed toward life and is more or less identical with sexual libido, and a death instinct whose aim is the very destruction of life. The death instinct refers to a biologically given tendency to destroy that can be directed either against others or against oneself. It amalgamates itself with the sexual instinct and in the amalgamation appears as masochism if directed against one's own person and as sadism if directed against others. In Freud's view this amalgamation with the sexual instinct is required if humanity is to be protected from the fatal effect the unmixed death instinct would have. Consequently, "man has only the choice of either destroying himself or destroying others, if he fails to amalgamate destructiveness with sex" (EF, 128).

Fromm welcomes Freud's late position and judges it superior to the early one. But he is critical of Freud's claim that the death instinct is "rooted in a biological quality inherent in all living organisms and therefore a necessary and unalterable part of life" (EF, 157), the claim Horkheimer, Adorno, and Marcuse wish to hold onto. In resorting to a biological explanation of this kind, Fromm feels that Freud fails to do justice to "the fact that the amount of destructiveness varies enormously among individuals and social groups"; indeed, it varies to a degree plainly disallowed by Freud's notion, Fromm continues. However, to assert the biological rootedness of an instinct does not commit one (i.e., Freud) to holding that the overt manifestations of the instinct must always and everywhere be the same. To conceive of the death instinct as part of humanity's biological constitution, as does Freud, is not *eo ipso* to see it as immune to modifications. In Freudian theory, as Marcuse rightly observes, impulses are modifiable, subject to the "vicissitudes" of history; the death instinct and its derivatives are no exception.[12] What is crucial, and what remains a matter of heated controversy, is whether the death instinct is ineradicable in humanity. Freud, for one, in choosing the term "instinct," seems to answer this question in the affirmative.

Fromm builds his answer from the principal view that what is "biological" in Freud's theory must never be treated in isolation from humanity's social environment. His position is that the given biological death (and life) instinct always enters into an interplay with nonbiological and alterable social factors. This, then, is as closely as Fromm approaches an answer to the question of destructiveness in *Escape from Freedom*: he keeps the late Freud's distinction between a life instinct and a death instinct, but wishing to speak of drives rather than instincts, he stresses the (changing and thus changeable) role played by social conditions in the "struggle" between the two major forces in humanity's existence.

The drive for life and the drive for destruction are not mutually independent factors but are in a reversed interdependence. The more the drive towards life is thwarted, the stronger is the drive towards destruction; the more life is realized, the less is the strength of destructiveness. *Destructiveness is the outcome of unlived life.* Those individual and social conditions that make for suppression of life produce the passion for destruction that forms, so to speak, the reservoir from which the particular hostile tendencies—either against others or against oneself—are nourished. (EF, 158)

Fromm's Theory of Destructiveness

In *Civilization and Its Discontents* Freud defines the meaning of the evolution of civilization as "the struggle between the instinct of life and the instinct of destruction, as it works itself out in the human species" (CD, 314). Freud says of the erotic instincts that they seek to preserve life, to "combine more and more living substance into ever greater unities," and of the death instincts that they "oppose this effort and lead what is living back to a primaeval, inorganic state" (AHD, 588; cf. 585–86). Civilization, he asserts, "has to use its utmost efforts in order to set limits to man's aggressive instincts and to hold the manifestations of them in check by psychical reaction-formations" (CD, 302–3). For this purpose, civilization seeks to stabilize the tension between the superego and the ego by the installment of the sense of guilt within each individual, "like a garrison in a conquered city" (CD, 316). Destructiveness signifies the portion of the death instinct that is diverted toward the external world, maintains Freud, adding, with the somberness marking his last works, that "any restriction of this aggressiveness directed outwards would be bound to increase the self-destruction, which is in any case proceeding" (CD, 310). The implication seems to be that self-preservation has as its sine qua non that some extraneous object be found against which the death instinct, coming to light as aggressiveness, can be directed and allowed to discharge. In a word, to prevent the destruction of the self, destruction of objects outside the self seems an absolute necessity.

It is precisely such implications Fromm wishes to avoid in his own theory of destructiveness. Perhaps this is what Marcuse was alluding to when he accused Fromm of compromising key tenets of Freud's metapsychology, in which the above stark notion of the death instinct plays a decisive role. As a proclaimed humanist, Fromm rebels against the grim conclusion that people

have only the choice between destroying themselves or destroying others—
that is, between causing suffering either to themselves or to others. Fromm
thinks that Freud was wrong in conceiving Eros and the death instinct as two
biologically given and equally strong tendencies; instead, Eros is to be
looked upon as "the biologically normal aim of development," whereas the
death instinct must be seen as "based on a failure of normal development and
in this sense as a pathological, though deeply rooted striving" (AHD, 610).

Fromm's position is worked out in his massive opus *The Anatomy of Human
Destructiveness*, completed three decades after *Escape from Freedom*. To begin
with, Fromm is disturbed by Freud's view that the basic character of the
death instinct conforms to the logic of the "hydraulic" model Freud had
originally applied to the sexual instinct, or libido. Fromm perceives in this
just one more proof that Freud's thinking throughout his entire career was
guided by the axiom that the "principle of reduction of excitation" is the
governing principle of all psychic and nervous life. Hence, to Freud, a
striving for death is constantly generated in all living substance, providing
people with the alternative of either destroying themselves or destroying
others. Fromm cites Freud's remark that "holding back aggressiveness is in
general unhealthy and leads to illness (to mortification)" (AHD, 621). In
addition to being dissatisfied with the hydraulic model and with the crude
"either-or" consequences it relentlessly leads to, Fromm finds Freud's dichotomy of the two basic instincts too crude and overlooking crucial internal
distinctions. Freud, he writes, "made the death instinct so broad that as a
result every striving which was not subsumed under Eros belonged to the
death instinct, and vice versa. In this way aggressiveness, destructiveness,
sadism, the drive for control and mastery were, in spite of their qualitative
differences, manifestations of the same force—the death instinct" (AHD,
596).

Fromm's first step in his attempt to overcome the conceptual poverty in
Freud is to introduce a distinction between two entirely different kinds of
aggression in humanity. The first kind he terms *defensive*, or benign, aggression. It is the kind that humanity shares with all animals, "a phylogenetically
programmed impulse to attack (or to flee) when vital interests are threatened." Defensive aggression is "in the service of the survival of the individual
and the species"; it is "biologically adaptive and ceases when the threat has
ceased to exist." The other kind, termed *malignant* aggression, that is, cruelty
and destructiveness, is "specific to the human species and virtually absent in
most mammals; it is not phylogenetically programmed and not biologically
adaptive; it has no purpose, and its satisfaction is lustful" (AHD, 24).

According to this distinction, defensive aggression is indeed part of human nature, even though not an "innate" instinct; Fromm argues this point against Konrad Lorenz in particular. However, and of more significance for my purposes, man differs from the animal by the fact that he is a killer: "he is the only primate that kills and tortures members of his own species without any reason, either biological or economic, and feels satisfaction in doing so." Therefore, malignant aggression constitutes the real problem and the danger to humanity's existence as a species (AHD, 26).

Fromm's distinction has it that the malignant part of human aggression is "not innate, and hence not ineradicable"; it is a human potential and, admittedly, "more than a learned pattern of behaviour that readily disappears when new patterns are introduced" (AHD, 254). He elaborates his earlier programmatic remark (cited above, EF, 158) when he writes that "I shall try to show that destructiveness is one of the possible answers to psychic needs that are rooted in the existence of man, and that its generation results . . . from the interaction of various social conditions with man's existential needs" (AHD, 294).

Obviously, a full exposition of Fromm's theory would exceed the scope of this chapter. Nevertheless, a few points may throw more light on the problem raised earlier about the nature—and different types—of hatred. First, Fromm retains his old view that sadism and masochism, both manifestations of malignant aggression, are invariably linked together and that they both spring from a sense of impotence. Both the sadist and the masochist need another being to "complete" them. "The sadist makes another being an extension of himself; the masochist makes himself the extension of another being" (AHD, 389). It is noteworthy that Fromm uses this point to criticize Horkheimer and Adorno for having treated the authoritarian character (who is described as sadomasochistic) "behaviouristically, not psychoanalytically" (AHD, 390 n. 16). To readers familiar with their study, this criticism must appear to miss the mark. Certainly Horkheimer and Adorno, in the interviews they conducted and in their application of the famous F-scale, were concerned with the study of empirical behavior or, rather, with that behavior's interplay with beliefs and values (e.g., prejudice); but to suggest that this empirically informed study of behavior was not carried out with the help of psychoanalytic theory, concepts, and assumptions is to distort the very essence of Horkheimer's and Adorno's investigations. Indeed, my own criticism of Horkheimer and Adorno addressed their, in my opinion, *exaggerated* reliance on one of Freud's chief categories, that of projection. Again, the issue at stake between the two parties is not whether to draw on psychoanaly-sis; rather, it concerns the way this is to be done and, with that, the way Freud's theory is to be interpreted.

In view of this quarrel, I find it highly interesting that Fromm, precisely on the topic of sadomasochism, applies Freudian categories in a manner doubtlessly foreign to Horkheimer and Adorno. Concentrating on the sadist, Fromm asserts that the true source of the sadistic yearning to control others is not "the powerlessness of the individual" so untiringly stressed in *Escape from Freedom* but the fact that the sadistic character is *afraid of life*. This, then, lies at the bottom of his desire to exert power over others. Life is utterly frightening to him because it is by its very nature unpredictable and uncertain. The same holds for love. Love, being equally uncertain and therefore at all times a risky undertaking, is what the sadistic character is most of all afraid of, and incapable of; the "love" he talks about is not the mutual sharing of trust and affection but the emotional satisfaction he achieves when he has gained power over the object of his so-called love. The sadist is incapable of letting go, of *living* the unpredictability and openness intrinsic to life and love; whenever he is confronted with their essence, his sole reaction is to deny it, to try to negate it by controlling what in principle defies control.

This understanding of the sadistic character, a prelude to the larger issue of hate, is interesting because it shows that although Fromm retains the Freudian categories, he uses them in a manner deviating from that of Freud himself; moreover, and mutatis mutandis, it helps highlight where Fromm departs from the other Frankfurters. Fromm's sadistic character is driven *neither* by the instinct of death *nor* by the instinct of life. Rather, what drives him is *fear of life*. Yet significantly, this fear of life does not amount to what Freud called the attraction to death as it springs from humanity's death instinct. The fear of life Fromm speaks about is not to be deduced from, is not to be seen as derivative of, the death instinct—this being the connotation carried by "fear of life" according to the antirevisionist version of Freud that Horkheimer, Adorno, and Marcuse all adhere to. To return to Fromm, the sadist does not want to kill, to destroy, to bring about the cessation of life; far from that, what he wants is to become the sovereign master of life, and this objective demands that "the quality of life should be maintained in his victim." Hence, he transforms living beings into "living, quivering, pulsating objects of control," whose "responses are forced by the one who controls them" (AHD, 388). This is what distinguishes him from the destroying person. As Fromm had observed earlier, "the destructive person wants to destroy the object, that is, to do away with it and to get rid of it. The sadist wants to dominate his object and therefore suffers a loss if his object disappears" (EF, 137; cf. 154).

Because of Fromm's conceptual superiority to Freud, he does not have to deduce all kinds of human aggression from one and the same source—the death instinct. In a first step, Fromm draws a primary distinction between defensive and malignant aggression; in a second step, he draws a number of secondary distinctions, such as that just mentioned, within malignant aggression, between the destructive and the sadistic character. As is so often the case, the conceptual differences reflect fundamental differences of opinion: whereas Freud depicts destructiveness per se, in all its various manifestations, as the product of the death instinct, Fromm—in his early as well as in his late work—sees destructiveness as the outcome of unlived life. And unlived life is not the same as death. So destructiveness is produced by frustrated life, not by a drive toward death. The thesis of the early Fromm is defended also by the later Fromm: "The more the drive towards life is thwarted, the stronger is the drive towards destruction; the more life is realized, the less is the strength of destructiveness" (EF, 158). The implication of the thesis is that sadism is fostered by "all those conditions that tend to make the child or the grownup feel empty and impotent," whereby conditions that produce fright, such as terroristic and arbitrary punishment, carry especial importance; if not stopped, early mistreatment may bear consequences that at a later stage prove fateful, if not downright fatal, not only to the would-be adult but to those close to him or her as well. A significant contributor to the generation of powerlessness is a situation of psychic scarcity, the more so the longer it endures. "If there is no stimulation, nothing that awakens the faculties of a child, if there is an atmosphere of dullness and joylessness, the child freezes up; there is nothing upon which he can make a dent, nobody who responds or even listens, and the child is left with a sense of powerlessness and impotence" (AHD, 397).

Finally, Fromm reserves the term "necrophilia" for profound attraction to death, to everything dead or dying. For the necrophilic character, what is dead rules his life—the dead rule the living; having rules being; things rule man; and attachment to lifeless objects prevails over attachment to living beings, that is, to persons (as is typically the case with autistic individuals)[13] (see AHD, 451, 469). In Fromm's scheme, necrophilia is contrasted with biophilia, that is to say, with the passionate love of life and of all that is alive. Biophilia Fromm defines as "the wish to further growth, whether in a person, a plant, an idea, or a social group." The biophilic person "loves the adventure of living more than he does certainty." He "wants to mold and to influence by love, reason, and example." To him, "good is reverence for life, all that enhances life, growth, unfolding. Evil is all that stifles life, narrows it down, cuts it into pieces" (AHD, 485–86). Fromm sees the difference between Freud's position and his own in the fact that "in Freud's concept both tendencies have equal rank, as it were, both being biologically given." By contrast, Fromm holds biophilia to refer to "a biologically normal impulse, while necrophilia is understood as a *psychopathological* phenomenon. The latter necessarily emerges as the result of stunted growth, of psychical 'crippledness.' It is the outcome of unlived life, of the failure to arrive at a certain stage beyond narcissism and indifference." To sum up: "Destructiveness is not parallel to, but the alternative to biophilia. . . . Necrophilia grows as the development of biophilia is stunted. Man is biologically endowed with the capacity for biophilia, but psychologically he has the potential for necrophilia as an alternative solution" (AHD, 486).

The Origin of Hatred

Fromm's conceptual clarifications will help me address the following questions concerning indifference, hatred, and sadism: What is their moral relevance? Can they be traced back to a common origin? If so, in what connection does this origin stand—considered ontogenetically—with humanity's faculty of empathy? To what extent may the latter help shed light on the former?

In Chapter 4, my claim was that, from a moral perspective, the havoc indifference wreaks is—potentially—immensely greater than that brought about by felt, lived, practiced hatred. In contrast to hate, indifference is not in principle restricted to the scope set up by personal encounters and personal ties. Indifference is indiscriminate, whereas hate is selective; its typical object is an anybody, rather than somebody in particular, and therefore easily exchangeable. It follows from the very essence of indifference that no bond of any depth and endurance exists between subject and object. On the other hand, having sought, found, and destroyed its chosen object, hate is exhausted, its subject content. Although the one is assumed to be even more dangerous than the other, indifference and hate both carry within them a vast potential for bringing about immoral acts. There are no limits to the harm against others that can be brought about by a subject whose emotional faculty of empathy is severely impaired. Admittedly, it may seem open to doubt whether indifference is inherently "more dangerous" than hate. Yet what matters here are the conceptual distinctions allowed for by Fromm and the way they bear on my argument about morality.

Toward the end of my discussion of Horkheimer and Adorno, I made a distinction between two kinds of hatred: one where the subject invents the object of his or her hatred and another where the hatred felt by the subject is provoked by some action on the part of the object. My claim was that Horkheimer and Adorno, in relying on the model of (false) projection, merely succeeded in capturing the former case of hatred, neglecting the latter. Equipped with the distinctions developed by Fromm, I am now able to label the former case of hatred an instance of malignant aggression and the latter case one of defensive aggression. There is nothing pathological about hatred per se; following Fromm, I hold that the hatred generated by acts threatening or even destroying one's most vital interests—such as one's own life or security, or that of the persons to whom one is most attached— is to be viewed as appropriate on psychological grounds, since defensive in nature. Whether the manner in which provoked, defensive aggression acted out against the person(s) causing it is also *justified* on *moral* grounds is a different problem altogether, one for which I think it exceedingly difficult, if not impossible, to find a definitive answer. What is certain is that the model of projection captures the perpetrator's hatred of his or her victim— for example, the anti-Semite's hatred of the Jew. Turning the tables reveals an instance of hatred qua defensive aggression, the victim's hatred of his or her perpetrator—for example, the Jew's hatred of the anti-Semite. To draw attention to the latter perspective is to complete a picture of hate that remains one-sided in the conception of Horkheimer and Adorno.

Fromm, though acknowledging that hatred may be an instance of defensive aggression, does not examine the more exact nature of this type of hatred. In fact, he confines himself to the very general definition referred to above— that such hatred is generated by acts threatening or even destroying one's most vital interests.

With regard to the question of hatred's origin, this certainly does not take us very far. Indeed, I feel that Fromm, too, fails to portray the hatred most of us are most familiar with—intuitively and intimately so—and, to be frank, not only as victims at that. To reach a more specific formulation than those considered so far, I suggest the following conception: hatred may arise as the result of an *offense to my self-esteem*. The offense afflicts the very core of my sense of personal worth and dignity. So if I take the other's action to have my self-esteem as its target, indeed *to seek to wound my self-esteem*, then I may feel so hurt as to start hating the person who wanted to do that. This I term *reactive* hatred; it is directed at persons only, since only persons can cause it.

An offense of this order, captured in the German *Kränkung*, hits me with such a profundity as to place the wound beyond mitigation and repair—and perhaps also beyond forgiveness (the latter, it must be noted, will also depend on whether the offender admits having harmed *and* wronged me, hence on whether he or she shows repentance and seeks to be forgiven). If the wound cannot heal, the person responsible for it may be beyond punishment. But beyond hate the offender is not; wounded to the very bone of my personality, I may at least start hating the offender—out of fury, out of rising, uncontrollable rage. A lust for vengeance may ensue, a desire to see the other suffer as the other has made me suffer. This, then, accounts for my hatred, yet I am forced to admit that, for all its intensity, my hatred comes *too late;* the offense, the wound, the suffering—they are all part of my world, they cannot be wished away, they will leave a scar, and they may even change the person I am, since they have affected my very personness. Even though I may convince myself that, in my case if not in others', one sin justifies another, *the other* was first. So at best my retaliation can only repeat what the other did, and I fear that my retaliation, however cruel, is but a bleak repetition, my contribution to a sequence initiated and forced on me by the other. Thus humiliated, my hatred is ignited anew.

Now, if this is a portrait of hatred par excellence, whom does it characteristically involve? Evidently, not just anyone can inflict a wound on me that cuts right through to the core of my self-esteem, to my sense of worth as a person. The offender can only be an individual with whom I entertain a personal relation. It requires knowledge of the more intimate kind to hurt with real profundity—not to want to do it, but *to know how to.* This, of course, explains why the hurt here is peculiarly inexcusable: the offender acts not in spite of his or her knowledge of weak spots but thanks to it. Still, a plea for forgiveness may be accepted, although such acceptance demands much from the offended party asked to grant it. The offense in question invariably takes place within a small-scale setting, where the subjects are significant others to each other and where the specific quality of their relationship rests on the quality of the face-to-face interaction they engage in. Only in these circumstances—normally, those in which friendships flourish—can one be hurt beyond repair, arguably also beyond the capacity for human forgiveness. That the wound should be of such depth may appear extreme, indeed a rare case. Yet the hatred I have in mind as sparked by another's deliberate—this of course being a matter of perception—blow to my self-esteem is of precisely such intensity, enormity, vehemence.

This hatred is the inversion of love. In love, to repeat Scheler's formulation, what I seek is to enhance the perceived value of the other; I want the value of the beloved qua unique person to grow; I see it as enriching the world, as making my life immensely worth living. My wish for growth in this sense is insatiable; I cannot imagine myself ever reaching a point where I would wish it to cease. As for hatred, I have said earlier that it is satiable; it rests content once its chosen object is sought, found, and destroyed. This ultimately implies a desire that the other no longer be, that the world go on without the other's being among us. But hatred need not go that far. As my portrait suggests, hatred may elicit a desire to see the other suffer, to see him or her suffer as the other has made me suffer, yes, *because* the other has made me suffer. Should the other perish, he or she would be relieved of the pain I consider owing to the other. I would ask myself whether the other had rightfully *deserved* to be thus relieved, and because I hate the other, I would probably answer in the negative. This does not show that hatred is insatiable; the earlier claim that it may reach a point of satisfaction after which it fades may still be correct. When hating, however, that point seems very distant.

But is the dividing line between the two kinds of hatred, conceptualized as instances of defensive and malignant aggression, really that clear-cut? Of course it is not. I see in this a fundamental obstacle to every attempt to settle the problem raised above concerning the moral legitimacy of acts of defensive aggression. My view is that this cannot be done; there is no "once and for all" solution to be found on a purely theoretical basis. Rather, the moral philosopher must turn around and face the cases in their empirical manifoldness. Doing so, the actor's perspective must be taken into account. How the actor draws the dividing line between the two types of aggression is, first and foremost, a matter of perception. Discussing examples of distorted perception above, I arrived at the conclusion that the distortion of the other, regardless of its particular form (to this richness there is no end), ultimately entails that the other be deprived of his or her humanity, of his or her status as a fellow human and moral being, in short, that the other be dehumanized. Apart from the psychological aspects of such a distortion, dehumanization serves a *moral* purpose, one of justification. The perceived difference of the other, whether invented or not, makes a difference to the actor also in moral terms: it throws an explanatory and justificatory light on his ensuing action against the other—"ensuing" action because he himself perceives it as a *reaction*. To be more concrete, if the Jews "brought it on themselves," if they "must have done something wrong to be so persecuted," if they are "subhu-man" and "social vermin," then the action undertaken against them is justified—*purportedly* so, the outsider would hasten to add. Now, what happens when somebody is made into a scapegoat and subsequently acted against? How does the actor perceive his action? As one of defensive or of malignant aggression? To be sure, the "scapegoat" begs the question. In other words, if we choose to take the self-understanding of the actor seriously, we find that he reverses the scheme: *he* is the victim defending himself and his vital interests against the—clever, cruel, malicious—aggressor. "Blaming the victim" here comes to mean turning him or her into the perpetrator against whom a "defensive" but nonetheless firm or even "final" response is strictly called for—and for that reason also morally legitimized.

To present the object of aggression as a dangerous perpetrator means in fact to attribute to it a significant degree of power, of strength. The object is considered equal in strength to, if not stronger than, the subject. Facing the other as posing a threat, the actor experiences him or her as an enemy causing fright. This relation contains an element of recognition: to be afraid of someone is at least to recognize him or her as sufficiently powerful to pose a threat. Brought to bear on Nazi anti-Semitism, a fear of the Jewish "race enemy" of the kind described here certainly was created in large parts of the German population. Hence, fear also belongs to the many (and often contradictory) emotional states and attitudes incited by the Nazis in their portrait of the Jews. Hatred has already been discussed, but to make the picture complete, the far from insignificant impact of contempt must be acknowledged.

Contempt differs from hatred and fear in that it feeds on the perceived weakness of the other rather than on the other's strength. And indeed, the Nazi propaganda contains all three: although the claim that the Jews pose a threat on the grounds of their (financial, political, spiritual) power is predominant, this does not exclude the contrary claim that the Jews are fit for wholesale extermination on the grounds that they are so "weak" as to be "unfit to live," as the Nazi expression has it. It is well known that according to Hitler the law of nature teaches that all that is weak must perish, and the Jews are considered the supreme case in point; indeed, they are described as subhuman. What is subhuman is, according to this race doctrine, devoid of power and strength, and therefore devoid of what it takes to command and be worthy of recognition. Only the strong merit respect and deserve to live; indeed, strength *exemplifies* a right to live. Now, whereas one fears what is deemed powerful, one despises what is deemed weak—at least when "weak" is taken to mean unfit for life.

Again, there is a lesson of general importance to be learned from the example of anti-Semitism. In examining the potential for immoral action springing from the "dark side" of human emotion, it is tempting to concentrate almost exclusively on hatred. Yet contempt contains a perhaps no less strong desire to strike out against and inflict pain on the other. In contempt, we loathe the other and see the other as worthless. To feel contempt for someone is precisely to do what I am concerned with here: it is yet another case of *disqualifying* the other as a human cosubject deserving to be treated as a moral addressee.

The dividing line between defensive and malignant aggression is vulnerable to attempts not only to blur it but also, more radically, to retain it in an inverted version, as it were. In other words, the distinction is abundantly vulnerable to manipulation. Irrespective of form and ideological content, the key aim of the manipulation is always the same: to make sure that the actor sees himself as on the right side of the line—on the side of defensive aggression. The wonders worked by projection show this. What merits emphasis, however, is the moral point of these wonders—a point omitted by Horkheimer and Adorno because it was outside the scope of their study. The terms in question—"defensive" as against "malignant"—are far from normatively neutral. "Defensive" clearly connotes "morally justified" (whether this, upon closer scrutiny, holds for all empirical cases must remain an open question); "malignant" just as clearly connotes "morally questionable," if not "downright immoral." Assuming, for the sake of the argument, that Fromm's distinction captures the alternatives between which the average actor sees himself as having to make his choice when acting "aggressively" toward others, his option—if at all articulated—is surely for the "defensive" kind of aggression. Again, this choice makes a difference to him not only on psychological grounds, thanks to the narcissistic gain it may bring, but also because the choice is eminently moral. That this is so does not escape the actor; on the contrary, it is a main preoccupation of his. Hitler's rhetoric in *Mein Kampf*, or Himmler's in the 1943 speech quoted in Chapter 2, is an exercise in the art of locating oneself on the right side of the dividing line and one's foe on the wrong side.[14] To stick to my example, the anti-Semite pictures himself as fighting against the enemy within a normatively nonneutral universe, that is to say, within a universe permeated by dividing lines that make a moral difference. In carrying out his task, in waging war and seeking a "final" solution amounting to the physical extinction of his chosen enemy, the anti-Semite is not content to have history on his side; he wants to assure himself and the world that the same goes for morality as well. What he undertakes is as old as civilization (as Adorno would put it): to present malignant aggression as defensive aggression; to reverse the roles of aggressor and victim; hence, to reap the harvest of his endeavors both psychologically and morally.

My own concept of hate, as used in Chapter 4, unambiguously links it with the destructive, as opposed to the sadistic, character conceived by Fromm. In hate, let me repeat, the subject rests content once he has sought, found, and destroyed his chosen object. Hate pursues the absolute destruction of its object. By contrast, the sadist pursues the suffering of his object. He wants to see and to make the other suffer, to cause, control, and prolong suffering—all the time being dependent on the circumstance that the other continues to live. For as long as there is life, suffering remains a possibility. The entry of death equals the cessation of suffering; accomplished destruction therefore poses a threat to the sadist in that it robs him of his suffering object and thus makes him poorer; indeed, it throws him back on the unbearable sense of powerlessness that triggered his sadistic strivings in the first place. To sum up, hatred and sadism must be separated; the sadist feels contempt for his victim but does not hate him; the person who hates wants to destroy the other, to wipe him out in the literal sense of the word. *Destruction fulfills hate but frustrates sadism.*

Analytically, it is easier to delineate the possible targets of reactive than of projective hatred, since the latter is more a product of the imagination, inasmuch as it "invents" its object. By contrast, in reactive hatred the target is the distinct person experienced to have hurt me. Common to both types is an unwillingness to recognize the person I hate as a cosubject deserving the same recognition as a human and moral being that I demand for myself from others. In this sense, hate dehumanizes: it undermines such recognition. But this is not all. Hate in the strong sense is a relation between humans. In hating you I concede the human in you; the hatred I feel for you "admits" that you are a human being, for only a creature capable of desiring to hurt me is an appropriate and, as it were, *worthy* target of hatred. Yet this does nothing to alter the fact that the objective of hate is to dehumanize. The important point is that dehumanization is a work of negation: I can only dehumanize what I originally, however reluctantly, concede as partaking in a shared humanity. Hence, the anti-Semite whose project is to deprive the Jew of all human traits, to present him as "vermin" so as to exclude him from the category of possible addressees of empathy, contradicts himself; the hatred that spurs him to dehumanize is fed by what can only be an exclusively human source. Thus, hate is from beginning to end a relation between humans and humans only.

In the preceding chapter I formulated but did not elaborate the thesis that an inability to give empathy is due (ontogenetically) to a lack of received empathy. This will become less cryptic as I proceed. In discussing "moral blindness," I traced it to a failure of perception, that is, a failure to perceive the other as a human cosubject whose weal and woe is at stake in a given situation. I then argued that the failure on the level of perception might have a specifically *emotional* failure as its source, namely, an impaired capacity for empathy with others. This provokes the question of how the hypothesized impairment of the faculty of empathy has come about. Obviously, the question, when asked in connection with a particular case, will call for a concrete, meaning empirical, answer. What theory can offer is, inevitably, only a most general answer; accordingly, it is this I now develop.

In the section on Fromm I brought attention to his observation that the psychic development of the child requires that its faculties be "awakened" and that they receive "stimulation"; short of this, growing up in a setting of psychic scarcity, the child might develop sadomasochistic and destructive tendencies. I proposed that the idea behind Fromm's observation is that a person tends to do to others what others have done to him or her. It is easily recognized that my thesis—that a lack of empathy is caused by a lack of empathy—obeys the idea or, better, principle in question.

The central idea can be spelled out like this: if a person has experienced a lack of empathy from his or her significant others during the period of his or her primary socialization, he or she will likely grow up displaying a lack of empathy toward others. I say "likely" because it is not a certainty. Yet what matters is the idea being considered. The person does what others have done to him or her or, conversely, fails to exercise what others have failed to exercise. Now, this echoes the claim I made in the discussion of Horkheimer's view of the family, namely, that one has to have been the object of love in order to become its subject; one must have received love in order to be able to give it. But though doubtless an ability, love is not a faculty. As I argued in the chapter on Max Scheler, love—like compassion, sympathy, pity, and the like—is a *manifestation*, a realization and display, of the underlying and basic emotional faculty of humanity, the faculty of empathy. To be sure, both must be fostered—the ability to love and the faculty of empathy. Yet there exists a pivotal difference between the two: the former rests on the latter in the sense that the learning of love presupposes the learning—or, more accurately, the stimulation and cultivation—of the faculty of empathy. This shows the comparative primordiality of empathy over and against love, also argued in Chapter 3. "Empathy" as I conceive of it is *inter*subjective, or interpersonal, in a twofold sense: First, it concerns others, namely, by setting up and sustaining a relation between a self and an other—thus, empathy is intersubjective as far as its *extension* is concerned. Second, empathy is a faculty whose evolution depends on its being stimulated and encouraged by others— thus, empathy is intersubjective as far as its *genesis* is concerned. Fromm delivers support for my conception of empathy when he states that necro- philia (entailing as it does a deficient sensitivity to the pain of others, to mention but the kernel common to its many forms) is a psychopathological phenomenon that "emerges as the result of stunted growth, of psychical 'crippledness' " (AHD, 486).

This no doubt needs more clarification. Alice Miller, in her study *For Your Own Good*, argues that as a matter of principle "every persecutor was once a victim" (OG, 249). At first glance it may appear highly doubtful whether this in fact obtains empirically; for my part, I prefer to take it as a sweeping theoretical generalization rather than as a proposition for which definitive empirical validity could possibly be established. Miller, like Fromm, picks Hitler as one among many famous clinical cases in which her argument receives confirmation. Applying the by now familiar principle, she writes, "If Hitler had really been loved as a child, he would also have been capable of love." However, "his whole aloof and basically cold relationships with people in general reveal that he never received love from any quarter" (OG, 181). And, to cite a further example, this time from Miller's book *The Untouched Key*, where she devotes a long chapter to the biography of Nietzsche, she contends, "As a result of having been treated brutally in childhood, fascists of whatever stamp will blindly accept their leader and treat those weaker than themselves brutally" (UK, 101). Abused children, having been subject to processes of "psychic hardening or inurement, that is to say, avoidance and suppression of all tender feelings, feelings which are despised as softness," are likely to subject their own children to the same treatment when becoming parents themselves—always according to the formula "He does unto others what others did to him."[15] Thus, Freud's concept of repetition is rendered valid for the reproduction of behavior—or, more precisely, of object relations—from one generation to the next. The implication is that the individual becomes the author of acts of which he or she was formerly the target. Miller's stark conclusion is that the psychic mistreatment or scarcity suffered as a child will cause an inability to form and maintain affectionate relations with others—an inability that may subsist throughout a person's life. The victimization of others does not free the former victim from the burden left by the wounds once inflicted on him or her. It appears exceedingly difficult to break out of the vicious circle;[16] in particular, this difficulty is shown by the pattern of cross-generational repetition revealed in cases of incest.

A more detailed inquiry into the significance of empathy in particular in the mother-child relationship is to be found in the work of Heinz Kohut. Kohut's is a theory much more sophisticated than that offered by Miller, who too often is the prisoner of her predilection for sweeping generalizations and premature conclusions. As for Kohut, two assertions stand out as especially important for my purposes. First, Kohut rejects the "equal rank" thesis of Freud's according to which Eros and the death instinct (i.e., what "produces" humanity's destructiveness) are coprimordial, biologically given instincts. In Kohut's view, the "essence of sadism and masochism . . . is not the expression of a primary destructive or self-destructive tendency, of a primary biological drive that can only secondarily be kept in check through fusion, neutralization, and other means" (RS, 128). Rather—and this is the second important assertion—Kohut in *The Restoration of the Self* argues that *destructiveness is a secondary phenomenon*, a phenomenon that is not biologically rooted or constitutionally pregiven but is instead, in all its manifestations, to be traced back to a *failure on the part of the person's primary self-object(s)*—a failure, that is, of empathy. To Kohut, then, "man's destructiveness . . . arises originally as the result of the failure of the self-object environment to meet the child's need for optimal—not maximal, it should be stressed—empathic responses. Aggression . . . as a psychological phenomenon, is not elemental" (RS, 116). The empathic failures from the side of the self-objects Kohut sees as "due to narcissistic disturbances of the self-object" (RS, 87), and these, in their turn, can be expected to be products of the *self-object's* once frustrated need for empathic responses.

Concerning the nature of Kohut's position, it is crucial to see that his explanation of destructiveness in no way diminishes its extension and centrality in human life. Kohut does not, that is, render destructiveness a mere epiphenomenon; he does not question its existence but its dynamic and genetic essence. As with Fromm, it is with respect to the latter topic that Kohut departs from Freud, and again like Fromm, Kohut elucidates his own theory with the help of a distinction between two kinds of human aggressiveness, that is, "a part of the assertiveness of the demands of the rudimentary self" that "becomes mobilized (delimiting the self from the environment) whenever optimal frustrations (nontraumatic delays of the empathic responses of the self-object) are experienced" (RS, 120–21). Under normal circumstances there is a development from primitive forms of nondestructive assertiveness to mature forms in which aggression is subordinated to the performance of tasks. Distinct from this is destructiveness (rage) and its later ideational companion, the conviction that the environment is essentially inimical (cf. Melanie Klein's "paranoid-schizoid position").[17] According to Kohut—and in this he is squarely at odds with Freud's theory of the death instinct—this second type of destructiveness does not constitute the emergence of elemental, primary psychological givens but is instead a "disintegration product," that is, a set of "reactions to failures of traumatic degree in the empathic responsiveness of the self-object vis-à-vis a self the child is beginning to experience, at least in its first, hazy outlines" (RS, 121).

Horkheimer and Adorno see "ego weakness" as the psychologically crucial precondition of fascist leanings, of hostility toward out-groups or toward otherness tout court, and of what I termed contempt for human sympathy. They hold such ego weakness to be a product (primarily) of the failure of the father to provide the child with a strong authority figure with which to identify and (secondarily) of the failure of the mother to provide the child with unconditional emotional support in the face of the harsh realities of the outside world. Kohut, tracing the origins of narcissistic personality disorders, draws a different picture, yet one throwing still more light on the sources of ego weakness (although Kohut, to my knowledge, nowhere uses this term). He aptly calls his theory a psychology of the self, implying that his chief concern is with the conditions for the establishment of a solid, as distinct from a frail and fragmented, self. In Kohut's theory the deepest level to be reached is not the drives but "the threat to the organization of the self" (RS, 123). Hence, it is only when the self is seriously damaged, or destroyed—a lack of empathic responsiveness on the part of the self-object being the prime cause of such damage—that the drives "become powerful constellations in their own right" (RS, 122). In other words, it is only when the self has not been firmly established that a phenomenon like chronic rage, that is, the desire to destroy an environment perceived as hostile, may evolve.[18]

Object-relations theory explains a person's ability to form mature and enduring relationships with others by the specific quality of that person's relationships with significant others in his or her past, especially in early childhood. Hence, W. R. D. Fairbairn defines psychology as "a study of the relationships of the individual to his objects."[19] In this view, human contact is valuable per se. The "object" is not a mere means to satisfy libidinal needs; rather, the object is sought for its intrinsic value in a relationship. The human being has a basic need for the *human* object. Drawing on ethology, John Bowlby observes that the human infant's need for human attachment is a matter of life and death.[20] Freud overlooked this need.

These theorists tend to substitute for Freud's triadic Oedipus complex the dyadic relation between a child and a primary self-object. There is little concern with the father as a symbol of authority to be respected and internalized; the almost exclusive emphasis is on the part played by the "good enough" mother (as in the work of Winnicott). Psychologically, the all-important requirement is that, at the very least, one person (it does not matter who) possess the ability and the opportunity to satisfy the child's needs to be met and "seen" by another human being.[21] In other words, it is the human other's empathic responsiveness that welcomes the infant as a comember of humankind. This approach allows the preoedipal mother-child dyad to be recognized as an independent unit in its own right, liberated from its location within the larger Freudian oedipal triad.

This shift of emphasis from the triadic to the dyadic relation helps highlight a distinction anticipated, yet not elaborated, in the critique Fromm leveled against Freud's theory of the death instinct. The distinction is that between drive needs and relational needs. Libidinal (later also aggressive) drive needs are conceptualized by Freud not only as the basic needs but also as the basic motivational source of human behavior. The drives give rise to the entire host of psychological motives, to conflict, and to the psychopathologies. Drive needs are the ultimate source of renunciation, repression, conflict, and feelings of shame and guilt in the oedipal triangle situation. By contrast, relational needs form a class of basic psychological needs in their own right whose importance in the development of an individual's sense of self Freud failed to explore. Freud failed here because his theory contains no account of affect development or of the need for a life-sustaining human object. Bjørn Killingmo, like Fromm, but in a much more accurate manner, points to the crude reductionism that Freud's instinct theory in the final analysis amounts to—the claim, that is, that the diversity of psychological motives ultimately can be traced back to two opposed yet equally original instincts in humanity. Fromm's objective has been to reveal the conceptual inadequacy of the Freudian reductionism in the face of the qualitatively different kinds of human aggression.

The relational needs coming to light once Freud's reductionism is abandoned—the dyadic relation now becoming the new point of departure—can be divided into two closely related groups. Following Killingmo, the one comprises "needs for affective attachment"; the other, "needs for confirmation of existence and value [i. e., *Selbstwertgefühl*]—usually referred to as narcissistic needs."[22] The relational needs belong to the earliest phases of human life; they are fundamental *before* the oedipal triangle situation is entered into by the child; hence, "the relational needs and their derivatives are in the experiential centre of the *pre*-oedipal child" (emphasis added). Killingmo sees the development task of this phase as twofold: "to establish both a feeling of belonging to another and the feeling of a self separated from the other,"[23] that is to say, object attachment and separation/individuation. These "post-Freudian" insights into the primary importance of the dyad and of the independent existence and evolution of relational needs allow us to draw a distinction between two separate mechanisms of pathology, that of *conflict* and that of *deficit*. Killingmo argues that although conflict and deficit are irreducible to each other and each possesses a dynamics of its own, a pathology based on conflict can arise only on the presupposition that the basic building blocks of personality structure, that is, the ability to experience the self as a strategic center of action, have been created. In other words, only when this is accomplished will the ego be in a position to "institute means of self-deception, mainly repression, to avoid finding out for *whom* he feels *what.*" In traditional psychoanalysis, pathology is ultimately based on conflict, the essence of which is invariably conceived of as "concealed meaning," that is, meaning that is established, then hidden, yet in principle detectable. The ego with a differentiated self that participates in the therapeutic undertaking is part of an alliance with the analyst whose systematic aim is the unveiling of concealed meaning. By contrast, in deficit pathology the therapeutic endeavor is to assist the ego in "experiencing *meaning* in itself"; in this case "it is not a matter of finding something else, but to feel that something has the quality of being."[24] So, instead of aiming at the unveiling of meaning, the task is to help *establish* meaning, yet this may prove exceedingly difficult because the self for whom meaning is to be attained is deficiently or at any rate only precariously established. Instances of deficit, as distinct from conflict, are therefore characterized by what Killingmo designates "intrasystemic failures such as defective self-structure, lack of object constancy, identity diffusion, splitting, and lack of capacity for emotional relating to objects."[25] Accordingly, the "person in deficit" will not "actively approach other people as *others*"; failing to build a relationship based on true reciprocity, such a person will "passively lean on others either for symbiotic comfort or to gain an enduring supply of praise and affirmation to maintain a feeling of being alive and having a self."[26] The conspicuous and, as it turns out, insatiable object-hunger displayed by these persons can be interpreted as a never-ending series of desperate attempts to compensate for the narcissistic wounds inflicted on them as a consequence of their self-object's failure to respond empathically to their basic relational needs.

The factors thus explored—the crucial importance of the preoedipal dyad, the independent existence and dynamics of relational needs, the nature of pathologies based on deficit—point toward a conception of psychopathology in terms of deprivation, empathic failure, and development arrest. This line of inquiry I consider in harmony with the direction of Fromm's attempt at overcoming Freudian reductionism on the one hand and Kohut's concern with the preconditions for the establishment of the self on the other. I find that Killingmo shares the perspective of the latter when he depicts deficit pathology as "based mainly on an emotional shortage of the objects,"[27] that is, as springing from what Kohut conceptualizes as a failure of empathic responsiveness on the part of the self-object(s). In my reading, the decisive step forward that Fromm's late work succeeds in taking consists in its making us aware, in contrast to Freud and the way his theory is appropriated in the work of Horkheimer and Adorno, of the existence of needs, affects, and object relations that qualitatively fall outside the sphere of drives and that therefore demand analysis in their own right. Having stated this, I wish to stress that it need not be a question here of choosing between the traditional theory and that expounded by the object-relations school; rather than viewing the two as incompatible, one should, as does Killingmo, endeavor to combine concepts, insights, and methods from both.

Common to Fromm, Kohut, and Killingmo, then, is a rejection of Freud's thesis of the primacy of instinctual drives. Since we observe both drive needs and relational needs, operating either separately or in some combination, there is no way of predetermining what we may encounter at the bottom of projection—whether it be an instinctual drive need, a relational need, or both. The openness of the question requires of us that we have at our disposal conceptual tools that allow for all three possibilities. Relinquishing the exclusive position of the drives, theorist and analyst alike are attentive to the basic needs of nonlibidinal and nonaggressive origin, needs, that is, for affective attachment and for the confirmation of the self that demand to be met by a self-object close to the child in a phase of development *prior to* the oedipal triad and thus also prior to the rise of the conflicts peculiar to the oedipal triad, as conceived by Freud. I emphasize that the failure of the self-object to meet the relational needs in question is predominantly an *emotional* failure. What this emotional failure helps cause is an *arrest in development*: the person who meets with a failure in this domain is arrested in the evolution of his or her own emotional capacities, that is, his or her capacity for relating to others by virtue of the basic faculty of empathy, to use my own terminology.

For my purposes in the present section, the explored emphasis on relational needs—though of course less than the whole story—suffices. It does so because it sheds additional light on the irreducibly intersubjective origin of the faculty of empathy and so helps us recognize more clearly than before the origins of the specifically emotional preconditions of perception and judgment that I have postulated in previous chapters. The emphasis suffices, that is, to give theoretical support, based on clinical case studies and thus on empirical evidence, to my thesis that a lack of empathy is due to a lack of empathy and, furthermore, that one must have been the object of empathy in order to evolve into its subject. The earlier point about the (immensely tragic) impact of intergenerational repetition in this domain serves to illuminate the overt consequences of the idea contained in the thesis.

I have argued in earlier chapters that our faculty of empathy is indispensable in moral perception, that is to say, in our gaining an access to the domain of the moral understood as a domain where the weal and woe of others is somehow at stake. I take this occasion to recapitulate the importance of speaking about the "faculty of empathy" in this connection and not, as does Charles Taylor in his otherwise invaluable work, about "emotion," or "feeling," without further demarcation. Since the latter, short of definition, comprises benevolent as well as hostile feelings, hatred as well as sympathy, it is in my opinion utterly imprecise and inadequate when it comes to assessing the true nature of the connection between emotional capacities and morality (see my introductory remarks at the beginning of this chapter). To return to my argument, we "see" the extent to which the weal and woe of others is at stake thanks to the basic capacity for relating to others, for setting up a relationship between myself and my cosubjects that is facilitated by my faculty of empathy. The claim is not, and has never been, that emotion or, more to the point, the faculty of empathy "alone" is enough; basic cognitive capacities are also required for moral perception and, subsequently, judgment to be properly achieved. To miss this would amount to the emotivistic one-sidedness I have criticized in earlier chapters, notably in that dealing with Max Scheler. So I stress that my claim holds that a lack of empathy represents a *sufficient* condition for the failure to exercise moral perception. Therefore, cases of moral blindness may have an emotional, as distinct from a cognitive, cause; they may spring from a defective capacity for empathy in the person who displays an inability to "see" that a situation involves the weal and woe of those affected by it.

What Adorno pointed out with regard to the extremely prejudiced person holds also for the sadist and the person who hates; the differences among them notwithstanding, in all these cases the *experience of the other qua cosubject is blocked.* This entails that the other (to invoke my sequence of moral performance) is not perceived, is not judged, is not treated as a fully human and moral being. Herein lies the link between prejudice, sadism, and hatred on the one hand and immorality on the other. To apply my earlier notion, the former constitute so many ways of *dehumanizing* the other, of depriving the other of status as a fellow human being. The prejudiced person projects his or her own, largely repressed fears and anxieties onto the other, who is never encountered as an individual human being but always as only a stereotyped representative of a group, race, or class that is "interesting" to the prejudiced person inasmuch as he or she promises an opportunity for the release of repressed psychic material. The other is the mirror of fears and taboos the prejudiced person refuses to perceive for what they are: his or her own. The sadist attempts to compensate for a sense of impotence by exerting power over the other, by controlling, deforming, and molding the other as "clay in his or her hands." Finally, the person who hates is also bound to the other, pursuing, however, the other's ultimate destruction, the suffering inflicted on the other being only a means to this end.

It has been the aim of this section to explore the psychological and emotional factors that are instrumental in determining whether an individual succeeds or fails to evolve the capacity for empathy with others so crucial to morality in general and moral perception in particular. The analysis has been conducted in the light of two competing hypotheses: either we regard hate— and, more generally, human destructiveness—as an elemental and ineradicable force in humanity (e.g., in the manner of Freud's death instinct), or we regard it as a secondary phenomenon, arising only on the condition that something primary to it—identified here as the faculty of empathy—fail to develop.

My line of argument has been in favor of the second hypothesis. However, before reaching a conclusion, we should consider whether the two hypotheses represent exhaustive accounts of human destructiveness in general and hatred in particular. To do so, a third possibility should be mentioned.

In speaking of "malignant aggression," Fromm had in mind an individual's wish to strike out against and inflict pain on another. In the view defended above, that of the second hypothesis, malignant aggression stands in a relation to empathy as I conceive of it, albeit a wholly negative relation: the malignant aggression surfacing in projective hatred, masochism, and sadism is a manifestation of *what may go wrong* if the faculty of empathy does not receive the stimulation required for its proper development. But note that I speak here of "projective hatred" only, leaving out "reactive hatred." I do so because ego's wish to strike out against and inflict pain on alter is not of the same kind in the two types of hatred. Projective hatred is caught well, I said, in Horkheimer and Adorno's investigations into the blend of contempt, envy, and prejudice characteristic of anti-Semitism. In this case we may speak of ego's projective hatred as inventing its object, that is, as turning the Jew into "vermin" to be gotten rid of.

Reactive hatred represents a very different case, indeed a different kind of aggression, although it does not so much represent a "third hypothesis" as it does a qualification of the second hypothesis, which I therefore wish to maintain, albeit in a more elaborate version than the one worked out in preceding sections. Employing Fromm's term, reactive hatred can be conceptualized as a form of "defensive aggression." In the example I gave in the foregoing section, I observed that reactive hatred typically arises as the result of an offense to my self-esteem. A paradigmatic case is an action I take deliberately to wound my self-esteem. Hereupon I may feel so hurt (*gekränkt*) as to start hating the person who afflicted me in such a profound way and who (I take it) *wanted* to do just that. When I start hating on this basis, namely, as a victim of what is experienced as malignant aggression, my hatred cannot be interpreted as revealing an impaired capacity for developing empathy with others. Rather, any connection with empathy in this case must be such that part of what I react against—with indignation, rage, even lust for vengeance—is precisely the lack of empathic concern *for me*, for my integrity as a person, demonstrated in alter's act. When I am deeply hurt here, I am so in my capacity as a sensitive and vulnerable human being, and what causes me tremendous pain is exactly the *lack of sensitivity* I suffer as being at the heart of alter's act against me.

I suspect that the hatred we consider here is even more easily recognized in a human relationship involving a triad as distinct from a dyad. If Martha (in my fallible interpretation, mind you) is guilty of wounding George's integrity, and (especially) if George is a person close to me, I may react against Martha with an emotional intensity best captured as reactive hatred. Hence, sensitivity and concern for others, especially dear ones, may move us to feel reactive hatred. Since this hatred arises in the form of a protest against (directly experienced or witnessed) affliction, we are prepared to view it as being, under the circumstances, an appropriate emotional response to the incident at hand; indeed, what is likely to strike us as conspicuous, as a more or less serious defect, is the case of someone apparently incapable of responding to severe afflictions with the reactive hatred that goes with strongly felt indignation. To repeat, it is not a necessary condition for the emergence of reactive hatred that I myself be the immediate target of the act against which I react; I may just as well develop such a reaction for the sake of or, vicariously, on behalf of another person. (Interestingly, some people are much better at standing up for others than for themselves; we all know some people who find affliction as suffered by others more appalling than blows directed at themselves; hence, it is not only that a person operates with different standards, it is also that the morally superior standard may be reserved for others.)

Reactive hatred as depicted here, then, represents a much-needed corrective, and in that sense a vital qualification, with respect to the second hypothesis for which I have argued above. This corrective entails that we oversimplify matters and ignore crucial internal distinctions if we view human aggression per se, in its entirety, as a by-product of an impaired capacity for empathy with others. Such a view is too crude to do justice to the qualitatively different types and different affective sources of human aggression. In fact, in describing all human aggression and all hatred in particular as a by-product of impaired empathy, we would fare no better than Freud's crude reduction of destructiveness to a death instinct inherent in humanity's biological makeup; we would, that is, substitute one kind of reductionist model for another. This being so, the corrective just outlined retains, significantly, the insight of the second hypothesis that malignant aggression, including my projective hatred, is to be looked upon as stemming from an impaired capacity for empathy; here I endorse Kohut's dyadic, interpersonal account of how such impairment and arrest in affective development is most likely to come about.

On the other hand, defensive aggression—for example, reactive hatred as triggered by another's profound injury of either my own or somebody else's integrity as a person—illustrates a type of human aggression in which the connection with the capacity for empathy is not negative, not characterized by the absence of empathy's impact on the agent's conduct. Herein lies the main reason I opt for a "corrected" and qualified version of the second hypothesis, instead of discarding it as altogether false: in defensive aggression and in reactive hatred there is also a connection with empathy, only here the connection is turned on its head, as it were, when compared with the category of malignant aggression. To be more concrete, especially in a triad of the sort portrayed above, my aggression against the aggressor to a large extent rests on my being a sensitive person, sensitive also when I am not myself the direct victim of the act of aggression.

Finally, a quite different aspect of human aggression deserves attention. If we inquire about the conditions necessary to foster the capacity to feel guilt for one's acts, an important condition is the individual's readiness to acknowledge his or her own aggression. The ability to concede the existence of aggressive urges and to relate to their manifestation—in oneself as well as in others—as representing an undeniable part of human life is vital to the development of moral-emotional capacities. Therefore, the empathic caregiver is not only a person who displays recognition of the child by giving it love and affection; the fully empathic person is also a person who readily acknowledges, rather than denies, the child's aggressive impulses as part of its (as well as one's own) emotional repertoire. (This insight is elaborated in Melanie Klein's work but downplayed in Kohut's.) The caregiver's capacity for empathy is thus required to direct itself to the child not only as someone capable of loving but also as someone capable of hating, of wishing to hurt and destroy. Now, if the existence of such aggression is disallowed, if it is invariably met with all-out disapproval and so thoroughly repressed in the child, this child is likely to grow up with a diminished ability to face and come to grips with outbursts of hatred, rage, and cruelty. Having been met with what is at best a "selective," because aggression-tabooing, empathy in its human environment, such a child will perceive him- or herself as having to suppress, hide, and censor the entire not-loving part of his or her affective experience.

The self-directed acknowledgment of aggression therefore needs to be supported by close others' recognition of it in its outward-directed form. The child who experiences being left alone by mother, and who is forced to face the painful fact that it is not the sole focus of mother's attention, is shattered by separation anxiety. Rage and jealousy, even hatred, are the child's natural reaction to being abandoned. However, if mother *meets* these negative feelings in the child, if she confirms and addresses their reality, the child is permitted to experience that it is loved and cared for even though it may feel—and act on—hatred. This is a truly precious experience. It allows the destructive impulses to appear less threatening; it helps to show that such impulses are "possible to live with," that they can be handled, even forgiven, and thus do not spell disaster. This is so because the child here experiences that the person at whom these violent feelings are directed in fact "survives" them (to use a central concept of Winnicott's).

To sum up, in defensive aggression I act in my capacity as a sensitive being—whether I or some other person may be the offended party. In acting on somebody else's behalf, in protection of his or her vulnerability and integrity as a person, I act from my empathy with that person: my empathy lets me see that his or her weal and woe is at stake in the situation. Thus, defensive aggression attests to the presence of empathy in the agent. Malignant aggression, by contrast, testifies to an absence of empathy. Such absence can be of two basic kinds: either it is selective, or it is a more general intrapersonal impairment. The first kind was studied in Chapter 4 as so many ways of producing a selective or ad hoc, as distinct from a generic and all-around, absence of empathy in the person. Extraindividual factors such as ideology, bureaucracy, and technology may supply the agent with a *Vorverständnis* (preconception) of certain others that prevents the agent's capacity for empathy from informing his or her perception of them. The present chapter has explored the second type of absence. Working mainly from the perspective of developmental psychology, I have shown how the absence of empathy in a person is a by-product of significant others' failure to stimulate its growth.

However, the presence or absence of the capacity for empathy imposes a very limited perspective on the large issue of emotions and immorality. I conclude by shifting the perspective. Using a distinction between small-scale and large-scale social settings, I raise what may appear an unexpected question: Under what conditions is hate, as far as moral performance is concerned, superfluous rather than disastrous?

The Marginality of Hate

"For three full days, we—philosophers, psychologists, novelists, and states-men—have dedicated ourselves to the problem of hate. Yet, to be frank, I must tell you this: hate still escapes us. We don't know where it comes from. The only thing we know is that, whatever the question, hate is not the answer. That is all." With these words Elie Wiesel closed the Oslo Confer-ence "The Anatomy of Hate."[28]

Wiesel's conclusion is deeply disquieting. It confers on us the status of incomprehending victims, victims of a calamity about which we know nothing at all save that its end is not in sight. If hate resists scrutiny, further inquiry seems destined to fail. What remains for us is to try and cope as best as we can with the onsets of hate the future has in store for us. If hate defies human comprehension, it also seems capable of surviving every attempt at its overthrow in real life.

Perhaps this is not what Wiesel meant to say. Perhaps I exaggerate his pessimism. However, it is also possible that we exaggerate the contribution of hate to immoral acts. Was it not one of Hannah Arendt's seminal insights that it does not take evil men to produce evil acts? So what about immorality that is not a product of hate? Let us take a fresh look at immorality by shifting the perspective from hate to indifference. This shift will provide us with a corrective to the analysis of emotions and immorality as conducted so far.

A survivor of Auschwitz, Wiesel knows from firsthand experience that the death camps ran on indifference rather than hate. "Mass destruction was accompanied not by the uproar of emotions, but the dead silence of unconcern."[29] Thus observes Zygmunt Bauman, adding weight to Wiesel's famous remark to the effect that indifference kills more efficiently than hate. This reason alone suffices to hold the connection between indifference and immorality to be pregnant with greater, incomparably greater, disasters than that between hate and immorality. Without wishing to diminish or cast doubt on the suffering wrought by hatred, the fact (hardly a disputable one after the work of historians such as Hilberg) that only minor importance can be claimed for the role played by hate in large-scale atrocities produces a certain relief as far as the statement with which I started is concerned: if hate is not at the bottom of immorality after all, then its remaining an unsolved riddle is rendered less of a scandal than initially assumed. Conversely, a solution to the riddle, should it be found, will prove less of a step forward in moral philosophy than first expected.

To appreciate the last point, a return to a former one is required. My discussion of Hannah Arendt terminated in the thesis that evil becomes banal when the motives of those involved become superfluous. To achieve this is the feat of bureaucratized murder. If pushed to the extreme, the thesis entails that the "logic" of what I term large-scale evil is in fact set in motion and sustained without its having to maintain any kind of link with or dependence on the vicissitudes of human psychology. Rather, immorality on such a scale has become independent of any specific human psychological basis. But if this is true, the entire psychology of the "authoritarian personality" as laid bare by Horkheimer and Adorno is superfluous as well. The two authors naïvely and tacitly take an assumption for granted that in fact has been turned obsolete in twentieth-century genocide: the assumption, that is, that the personality (be it "authoritarian" or not) of individuals determines their actual behavior when performing their tasks as functionaries in a bureaucratic apparatus—or, more to the point, that it makes a difference to the operations of such an apparatus just what kind of personality the individual member possesses, as if the former could be accounted for by the specific features of the latter.

Personality studies may contribute to our understanding of the grass-roots popular support for, say, fascist ideology, but they are at a loss to lay bare the nature of *cruelty and destructiveness dissociated from human motives*, that is to say, of immorality in the far too real sense here intended. An atrocity of such magnitude as the destruction of the Jews required for its accomplishment not the mobilization of feelings of hatred but the neutralization of feelings altogether.

To put the message simply, what we need to take seriously, and what I ended up observing in Chapter 2, is that it does not require an authoritarian personality (understood as one who hates and who seeks appropriate discharge) to engage in large-scale immorality, the reason being that such immorality is dissociated from personality. It is this mechanism of dissociation—that is, the distancing created between perpetrator and victim to set them mentally and, first and foremost, emotionally apart—that I wish to draw attention to when I speak about the moral consequences of the suspension of the emotional bond between people.

Distancing furthers the suspension of the emotional bond. With a change in the setting of interaction from small to large scale, the distance—physical and psychological—between those professionally performing an action, now a specialized task bearing no recognizable relation to the totality it helps produce, and those affected at the invisible and distant receiving end tends to grow to such an extent as to obliterate all bonds between them. Here, motives, save the purely professional ones, become superfluous; therefore, hate does too. Large-scale destructiveness can do without hate. The chain between destructiveness and felt, lived hatred pertaining to face-to-face encounters is broken. The obliteration of the interpersonal bond lays the foundation for immorality.

So Bauman is right when he asserts that "cruelty correlates with certain patterns of social interaction [cf. my concept of different settings] much more closely than it does with personality features or other individual idiosyncracies [sic] of the perpetrators."[30] Rather, what we find is a correlation of a very different kind, more accurately, an "inverse ratio of readiness to cruelty and proximity to its victim." The implication is familiar from the discussions of Stanley Milgram and Raul Hilberg: "It is difficult to harm a person we touch. It is somewhat easier to afflict pain upon a person we only see at a distance. It is still easier in the case of a person we only hear. It is quite easy to be cruel towards a person we neither see nor hear."[31]

These observations point in the same direction as my earlier reflections on the Eichmann case and on numbing, in Chapters 2 and 4 respectively. Bauman, whose book *Modernity and the Holocaust* has come to my attention only recently, aptly sums up what I consider the crux of the lesson to be learned: "Evidently, moral inhibitions do not act at a distance. They are inextricably tied down to human proximity. Commitment to immoral acts . . . becomes easier with every inch of social distance. . . . [M]orality looms large and thick close to the eye. With the growth of distance, responsibility for the other shrivels, moral dimensions of the object blur, till both reach the vanishing point and disappear from view."[32]

Though very suggestive, proximity is an ambiguous concept. It is useful to my discussion only if properly clarified.

On the one hand, proximity at first glance carries a strong "spatial" connotation. Broadly, this seems to be the sense of proximity illuminated in Milgram's experiments and intended by Bauman. Manipulating the space and physical barriers between subject and victim, Milgram was able to observe the difference it makes to the subject's performance whether he or she can see, hear, or touch the victim. This helps warrant the thesis of unequivocal correlation between spatial location and readiness to inflict pain.

On the other hand—and this challenges the thesis—the moral significance of proximity also derives from its nonspatial dimension. I have in mind the sense in which we declare that someone is "close" to us. Such metaphorical closeness signifies a meaning of human proximity that cannot be measured in terms of spatial presence or absence. And yet its moral impact is beyond doubt. Would it not make a difference to the subject's performance if he or she were told that the (unseen, unheard) victim was in fact someone the subject happened to know? The force yielded by this *emotionally charged* variable—knowing the absent other—would diminish the force stemming from the spatial variable; it would inspire increased reluctance in the subject to go on inflicting pain.

If we, as seems obvious, care more for a person we know than for someone who is but an unknown anybody to us, we may be expected to act in a manner showing the factor of familiarity to override the factor of physical proximity. But this implies that a person seen can matter less to us than a person out of sight. Again, conduct depends on perception; it depends on who that person "is" to us. In perception, the spatial variable is overridden by social variables such as familiarity and by extraindividual variables such as ideological stereotypes, opaque bureaucracy, and advanced technology.

My observations suffice to show that there is no *necessary* correlation between human proximity and moral conduct. As to moral concern for the other, no automatism or determinism is implied in proximity. Proximity interacts with a number of factors; it does not by itself bring about, does not by itself account for, moral conduct or lack of it. This being so, the line between morality and immorality does not coincide with that between the proximity-embedded small-scale setting and the proximity-suspending large-scale setting. "Small is not always beautiful."[33] In line with my overall argument, it is rather with respect to immorality's scope and link to human motives that a relatively clear division can be drawn between the two settings.

As for hate, the conclusion to be drawn is, in my view, as follows. Insofar as hate distorts the perception and thereby blocks the experience of the other, denying the other his or her full humanity, it constitutes a sufficient condition for immorality as performed within the small-scale setting where interaction is guided by face-to-face encounters and so by proximity. On the other hand, like every other specific personal-emotional motive, hate tends to become increasingly superfluous—hence decreasingly fatal—as a condition of immorality emerging within the large-scale setting where interaction is depersonalized, tasks routinized, and attitudes professionalized. The greater the length of the chain of intermediaries between ourselves and the consequences of our acts, the more complete will be our adoption of a detached and "objective" stance toward our activity and, a fortiori, toward those remote others affected by it. Our post-Holocaust knowledge is that such adoption, if unarrested by human intervention, breeds moral indifference and thus spells moral disaster, whose scope becomes a wholly technical and administrative matter.

Granted that hate accompanies immorality in a minority of cases, rather than as a rule, its relative absence urges us to look elsewhere for the sources on which immorality feeds. I pointed out earlier that hate is not insatiable; emotions, hate being no exception, have a natural time limit owing to their biological basis in man; lust, even blood lust, is eventually sated. Hence, when Bauman notes that "contemporary mass murder is distinguished by a virtual absence of all spontaneity,"[34] what needs to be added is "all spontaneous outbursts of *emotions*," hatred included. Hate, like love, belongs within the social microcosm, within the small-scale setting where people meet, get to know one another, and thus also get to love or hate one another—as persons at that. Hate, when produced and acted on within this domain, breeds violence; such person-to-person violence exploits and wishes to be kept a matter of privacy. A private affair—if not to the victim then at least, invariably, to the author—this violence eschews publicity.

The emotional bond of which I have spoken can obviously be of various, even opposite kinds; a person is tied emotionally to another no less by hatred than by love. This prompted me to place love and hate at the same end of a continuum and to posit indifference at the opposite end. And I further declared love too selective, exclusive, and narrow to serve as the basis for morality—pace Max Scheler. The scope of morality is immensely greater than that of love; morality transcends, explodes love. Although we treat those whom we love as ends in themselves (lest love be narcissistic, disregarding respect for the integrity of the beloved), we do not, and cannot possibly, love all those whom we are entitled to treat as ends in themselves. With this in mind, the parallelism I have proposed for love and hate can be seen to be warranted by a similarity hitherto unnoted. Hate relates to immorality the way love relates to morality: in both cases, the latter cannot be traced back to or founded on the former. It does not require love to be moral, to perceive, judge, and act morally toward another; likewise it does not take hate to be immoral, to perceive, judge, and act in a manner disrespecting or downright denying the moral status of our cosubject. Therefore, the scope of immorality is immensely greater than that of hate, in particular with respect to the large-scale setting; immorality transcends hate as morality does love.

Again, my intention is not to diminish hate but to warn against according it some kind of primacy as a source of immorality. The aim has been to put the role of hate into its proper place, which is one of marginality rather than supremacy. Yet the evaluation of hate given here does not leave immorality without an explanation altogether. I have stressed indifference: when an immoral act such as mass killing feeds on indifference as opposed to hate, exploiting the logic of routinization and depersonalization rather than the dynamics of passions and personal ties, the act in question may proceed endlessly, since the logic producing and sustaining it is insatiable. In other words, what is made independent of man, of human psychology, cannot be halted by man. If pushed to the extreme, the suspension of the interpersonal emotional bond makes for man's alienation from man, his estrangement in the face of the human.

On closer inspection, there is, paradoxically, a sense in which hate may help bring about the cessation of otherwise endless immorality. Since hate is not beyond satiation, since hate is content once destruction has reached a certain peak, since hate permits a release of accumulated aggression, the person who acts from hatred is able to say, Stop, enough, that'll do. What matters is that this is bound to occur sooner or later—"later," of course, often proving *too* late. Hatred prompts immorality, yet it possesses the capacity to intervene in it, to arrest and put an end to it. Hence, hate may eventually side with morality, more accurately, with the reemergence of morality in the wake of a temporary prevalence of immorality. By contrast, immorality that feeds on indifference or numbing, that is to say, on a suspension of humanity's emotional capacities (taking into account now that humanity's emotional capacities encompass antipathy no less than sympathy), is beyond emotions-based intervention because it is dissociated from feeling *tout court*. Such dissociation makes immorality in the sense given here truly inhuman.

My conception of a performative sequence peculiar to morality maintains that action is preceded by judgment, and judgment by perception. In Chapter 4 I defended my thesis that the faculty of empathy is a necessary, though not a sufficient, precondition for the perception of the moral. The present chapter has been devoted to the many ways in which the act of perceiving the other as a fellow human and moral being may be distorted or blocked. Special emphasis has been put on hate, since it is particularly dangerous in this respect; it deprives the cosubject of his or her humanity and turns the cosubject into an object to be destroyed and gotten rid of. In a sense, the examples invoked during the discussion so far have been so many illustrations of the more or less immoral consequences likely to ensue in cases where the perception of, judgment of, and action toward the other qua human being is undermined—be it due to cognitive or (my main focus) emotional incapacitation. Thus, the center of attention has been how humanity's emotional capacities—to speak most generally—bear on acts of perception, acts of judgment, and the action performed. So I have studied the role of emotional capacities *prior to*, preceding and facilitating, the three distinct categories the performative sequence consists of. From this perspective, a lack of empathy proves a sufficient condition of moral blindness.

But this perspective needs to be supplemented by another, one signifying a shift in the temporal point of departure. What, it must be asked, is the role of humanity's emotional capacities *subsequent* to a completed performative sequence? What is their significance ex post facto?

If we stick to the class of immoral deeds, the question invites us to reflect on the nature of such emotions as repentance and shame. In what follows, I explore only the latter, and I leave aside its—arguably intrinsic—relation to feelings of guilt. Clearly, repentance and shame are emotions with a strong cognitive component: to arise, the subject must perceive and judge the situation as calling for that particular kind of emotional response, for example, as a shameful and shame-producing situation. The subject's failure to judge it thus may therefore be of a clear-cut cognitive nature, so that, should he or she fail here, we cannot on that basis alone infer that the subject's emotional capacities are somehow impaired. As argued in earlier sections, there are in principle three ways of explaining the failure in question: it is purely cognitive, or it is purely emotional, or it is a combination of the two.

Notwithstanding the cognitive component, it is obvious that a person with deficient sensitivity to the weal and woe of others, to the suffering visited upon them, is unable to feel shame when faced with their lot. As noted above, shame is one of those feelings that arise after the act; and if we feel shame when we contemplate the idea of committing some morally dubious act in the future, the shame arises again, insofar as we think of the prospective deed as an accomplished fact. So, whether merely contemplated or actually committed, a specific, accomplished act has to be "there" for shame to arise in us.

The point is that whereas, following my analysis, an emotional incapacity such as a lack of empathy may lead to moral blindness and hence to immorality, accomplished immorality may in its turn produce, or fail to produce, a feeling of shame in the subject, the subject's response or lack of such likewise being a question of his or her emotional capacities. Moreover, the subject for whom this question arises need not be involved in the act he or she feels—or does not feel—shame about; the subject need be neither an agent nor a victim. In other words, the question of shame arises for the outsider and bystander as well as for the parties directly affected. Such shame can be of various kinds; it can reflect the shame felt and duly displayed by those involved, or—interestingly—it can arise precisely because of an *absence* of shame in one or both of the parties affected. The outsider, that is, can feel shame on behalf of subjects he feels *should* feel shame yet do not. When having such a perceived absence as its source, shame is *vicarious;* the absence it responds to is judged conspicuous; more than that, it is judged as *morally* wrong. To feel vicarious shame is to pass a moral judgment on two things at one and the same time: about the nature of the act committed by the persons involved and about the nature of the stance taken by the various parties affected by the act. Thus, to take an example, we do not feel shame only because an agent abuses a victim but also because the victim (not necessarily for reasons of masochism) appears to feel no shame about the incident. Irrespective of his or her specific role, a person's evident failure to perceive and judge the situation he or she is part of as shame-producing is what helps prompt vicarious shame.

Primo Levi, survivor, eyewitness, and chronicler of the Holocaust, captures the essence of my concept of vicarious shame in a passage relating the shock experienced by the young Russian liberators of Auschwitz. Unprepared for the unimaginable, they displayed

> that shame we knew so well, the shame that drowned us after the selections, and every time we had to watch, or submit to, some outrage: the shame the Germans did not know, that the just man experiences at another's crime; the feeling of guilt that such a crime should exist, that it should have been introduced irrevocably into the world of things that exist, and that his will for good should have proved too weak or null, and should not have availed in defence.[35]

The phenomenon of vicarious shame is particularly valuable for my purposes in that it comprises, and appears only on the condition that it bring together, what I have throughout claimed to go hand in hand: the human and the moral. In general, shame focuses on and arises in the face of a (committed or prospective) piece of action; it comes about as the upshot of an act of moral judgment on that piece of action; this act of moral judgment rests on an act of perception preceding it, in which the action to be judged is perceived and evaluated as being of this or that moral nature, that is, as carrying moral significance in the first place; finally, the act judged, thanks to its being perceived as morally relevant, is gained access to, is disclosed to the subject, thanks to the subject's capacity for relating to others by virtue of his or her faculty of empathy. In simpler terms, if the subject is lacking in his or her capacity for developing empathy with others, the entire sequence leading to a display of a feeling of shame is prevented from coming into existence. In this sense, shame presupposes empathy. The case of shame thus serves to confirm my account of the essential nature of the performative sequence peculiar to morality.

Part Three

6

Empathy and Solidarity in Habermas's Discourse Ethics

The first chapter of this study was devoted to Alasdair MacIntyre's critical assessment of contemporary moral theory, which, MacIntyre argues, has proved disastrously incapable of resolving the moral issues of the day. The longer these issues—counting Why be moral? among them—remain philosophically unresolved, the more they threaten to erode the social fabric of present-day Western culture. Since in this respect a "failure," moral theory has helped pave the way for the prevalence of emotivism, described by MacIntyre as the widely acted-upon viewpoint that morality boils down to the vicissitudes of personal preferences beyond the reach of rational justification and intersubjective agreement. To have nourished rather than prevented the current triumph of emotivism: this is MacIntyre's tough charge against contemporary ethics.

My discussion of MacIntyre's work in Chapter 1 sought to refute his critique of the moral theory he associates with the Enlightenment "tradition."

Subsequent chapters have concentrated on the case for a constructive assessment of emotions in morality. No longer explicitly concerned with Mac-
Intyre, I have developed a position that by implication shows his crude
dismissal of emotivism to do no justice to the systematic issue of the place of
emotions in moral performance. Once this issue has been rendered the main
topic, it turns out that the "emotivism" fought by MacIntyre is no real
philosophical match; for that, it is too much of a caricature. In letting
emotivism get away with its portrait of emotions as inescapably capricious,
private, and irrational, in failing to oppose the all too popular collapse of
feelings into the muddy waters of private preferences beyond argument, and
in failing to identify and examine humanity's emotional *faculty*, MacIntyre
offers a rejection of emotions in ethics that I find seriously lacking in
philosophical substance.

As I turn now to the moral theory of Jürgen Habermas, my study comes
full circle. Contrasting Habermas's position with MacIntyre's allows me to
elaborate the distinction between postconventional and conventional morality referred to in Chapter 1.

Yet my main interest in Habermas concerns his portrait of emotions in
ethics. Since this topic is an aspect of Habermas's discourse ethics, and since
his discourse ethics is a specification of his comprehensive theory of rationality and formal pragmatics, I must say something about the larger Habermasian architectonics before focusing on the place for emotions in discourse
ethics.

Characteristics of Postconventional Ethics

In *Der Sinn für Angemessenheit*, Klaus Günther distinguishes between two levels
of norm validity. The first level can be identified as conventional, the second
as postconventional. Günther stresses the following characteristics:

> 1. level: Norms are valid in concrete relations. The sum of all
> concrete relations constitutes a specific *Gemeinschaft*, or primary group.
> The other approaches me in situations in which role- and situation-
> specific expectations of conduct are actualized. Since the perspectives
> already relate to concrete others, they also apply to all situations
> where the concerned consociates encounter one another. The *concrete*
> other always and only approaches me in a concrete situation. . . .

The validity of norms [remains] linked to particular situations. Hence, validity and appropriateness (*Angemessenheit*) cannot be distinguished; both categories are mutually replaceable. . . .
2. level: Norms are valid because they can be justified by principles or in procedures in which the ideal conditions of cooperation are embodied. On this level the conditions of cooperation are separated from concrete *Gemeinschaften*. These conditions are valid for virtually all participants; they constitute conditions of possible cooperation *überhaupt*. The validity of a norm is no longer embedded in relations to concrete others, nor is it localized in specific *Gemeinschaften*; rather, it is addressed to everybody in the same way. . . . The adoption of perspectives becomes universal-reciprocal. The validity of a norm is radically separated from the situation at hand and the concrete relations in a community. The question whether a norm should be followed by everybody in every situation must be decided by all independently of the situation.[1]

I have quoted Günther so fully because the distinction between the two levels is extraordinarily rich in implications. It roughly equals the shift from "mechanical" to "organic" solidarity (in the vocabulary of Durkheim), from the relative homogeneity of traditional *Gemeinschaft* to the complexity of modern *Gesellschaft* (in the vocabulary of Tönnies), from simple role taking oriented toward the "significant" other to the more advanced form oriented toward the "generalized" other (in the vocabulary of Mead), in general terms, from small-scale to large-scale social interaction.

Günther's original contribution to discourse ethics is his proposal that a systematic distinction be made between discourses of justification and discourses of application: whereas questions concerning the validity and justification of norms call for a principal and context-free clarification, questions concerning the application of norms call for a situation-specific one. The distinction can only be drawn on the second, the postconventional, level; according to Günther's central thesis, it is a product of the historical process itself, in that "with the transition from the conventional to the postconventional level, the intertwined validity and appropriateness of norms in a particular context of shared perspectives can no longer be maintained."[2] However, both types of discourse stand under the principle of *Unparteilichkeit*, the term meaning a situation-independent, universal-reciprocal type of impartiality in the case of discourses of justification, a context-sensitive, applicative type of impartiality where all relevant aspects, including particular human needs and interests, are taken into consideration in the case of discourses of application.

What I view as the most important part of Günther's work is his systematic elaboration of discourses of application. Deontological moral theories in the Kantian tradition have tended to focus almost exclusively on issues relating to the justification, and a fortiori the generalizability, of norms; hence, the entire problem of how norms are to be "correctly" applied in shifting, novel, unprecedented situations has largely gone unthematized. In raising the complex question of how to decide which norm to apply in a particular situation, Günther promises to fill in what critics of Kantian ethics have long considered its blind or, in any case, weak spot. Against this background, what Günther's contribution may hope to achieve is to meet, on behalf of Habermasian discourse ethics, the charges of empty formalism and rigid dogmatism that Hegel leveled against Kant's ethics in general and the categorical imperative in particular. With Günther's work, moral theory professing a Kantian legacy can do so in a newly acquired confidence that it now recognizes—no less than does neo-Aristotelian ethics stressing *phronē-sis*—that a pragmatic, context-sensitive wisdom is required for the moral agent to be capable of applying abstract norms *in concreto*. (Whether Günther actually succeeds in this is a question I cannot pursue here; I will do so by implication, however, when I consider moral perception in the fourth section of the present chapter.)

The relevance of Günther's two-level scheme is this: whereas I have advocated that ethics preserve the moment of empathy derived from and fostered in small-scale, face-to-face interaction, Günther celebrates postconventional ethics' sociohistorical dissociation from any connectedness to the personal-emotional restraints of small-scale encounters. Far from finding the dissociation problematic, Günther holds it to be a major gain. In Günther's view (which he shares with Rawls, Apel, and Habermas), it is *not* desirable that any extension of the moment of interpersonally exchanged empathy be made. To urge that the morality on the postconventional level model itself on the morality of empathy peculiar to face-to-face interaction equals, these neo-Kantian philosophers would say, a regression to the concretistic and hence nonuniversalizable morality characteristic of the conventional level. What has been reached on the postconventional level, it will be pointed out, is a novel type of *reflexivity*: a fully autonomous subject, I am now able to critically assess my action not solely from the perspective of the directly affected other (be he or she a concrete or abstract, present or absent other) but also from a neutral-impartial position "above" the I-and-thou relationship, as it were, a position referred to as "the moral point of view." In other words, reciprocity is no longer person-based, particularistic, socially embedded, but universal, unrestricted by the entire problem of my knowing and experiencing the other or not. Concretistic ties of all kinds having been abstracted from and transcended, the other is, in the words of Günther, "ein *virtueller* andere." Insofar as our action extends drastically beyond the visible context in which we act here and now, reaching unknown contexts and individuals (even those not yet born), the way to secure our moral recognition of the other(s) *cannot*, it will be argued, be that of having recourse to empathy as derived from small-scale social interaction.

In the conclusion to my discussion of emotions and immorality in Chapter 5, I drew attention to the great number of empirical findings that testify to the crucial importance of *proximity* and of processes of distancing. To put it briefly, proximity—that is, the degree of closeness, of physical copresence, of visibility—makes a difference to the attitudes and behavior of a subject. Now, a proponent of deontological ethics may point out that from the moral point of view, which is neutral-impartial, the difference in question makes no difference whatsoever. It is *morally* irrelevant, the deontologist would say; the moral rights of my cosubject, the deontologist would go on to argue, are *the same* whether he or she is within or beyond the sphere of proximity; moral obligations have to be observed just as strictly toward the absent as toward the present other. I agree—on the condition, however, that this argument be acknowledged to be confined to the level of rights and duties. Rights and duties, that is, are universal in the sense that their validity is unrestricted by the contingent-particular situatedness of the moral agents. But still, and despite all this, it remains the case that there *is* a level on which proximity *does* make a difference—namely, the level of actual moral performance. The empirical research referred to in Chapters 4 and 5 shows this very clearly.

I fear that discourse ethics, in depicting the moral addressee as a "virtual other," takes a dangerous step toward abstraction. The merit of such abstraction is that it may bar false concretization such as personal bias and the like and thus secure impartiality of judgment. But the concern with impartiality overshadows the empirically persistent importance of proximity—and this is very dangerous. For in moral performance a great deal turns on whether the other is perceived as an abstract, faceless, and "formal" other or as a concrete other to which I can relate emotionally as well as intellectually. The mode in which the other is disclosed through perception makes a vital difference to the way I act. But discourse ethics, warning that concretization of the other may lead to partiality, is concerned with this danger only, not with the reverse.

Karl-Otto Apel sees the contemporary challenge epitomized in the pilot of a modern bomber: "He presses the button only on order; the effects of his release of the bomb, however, are so enormous that he no longer is able to experience them sensuously and emotionally." Therefore, a *Verantwortungsethik* (ethics of responsibility) is called for that is based not only "on a *rational foundation* but also on the mobilization of a *specifically moral imagination* that would, for example, be able to generalize the love for one's neighbor into a love for those most far off."[3] This moral imagination is to be a response to a situation where "the gap between the 'world of human effect' [*Wirkwelt*] and the organically conditioned sensuous-emotional 'world of human notice' [*Merkwelt*] has reached a new level," the implication being that "it is now scarcely possible for humans to be directly *affected* by the consequences of their actions."[4]

The processes of distancing that I have described in so many ways can now be seen to terminate in the demand that we act morally even when emotionally unaffected by the consequences of our action. The instinctual-emotional inhibitions intrinsic to face-to-face interaction within the small-scale setting having been abolished, the personal bond between a perpetrator and a victim thus suspended, it seems that a modern ethics of responsibility as advocated by Apel has no choice but to do without this dimension altogether. It is not really a question of our consciously seeking to get rid of this bond (recall Himmler), but more correctly of its having been historically lost to us. From this state of affairs, Apel concludes that the "*responsibility of reason* must now definitely take the place of a consciousness of sin based to some extent on instinct."[5] The historical developments referred to inevitably alter the meaning of the question Why should I be moral? In the eminent visibility of the small-scale setting, the instinctual-emotional inhibitions at work in the event of killing provided their own kind of answer: the immediate affectedness produced by one's witnessing the consequences of one's deeds, that is, by the physical copresence of one's victim, itself made for restraint. Today, however, the moment of emotional-personal affectedness has to be replaced by the power of reason, which is to say that now reason alone will have to do the work previously performed (at least in part) by an emotional tie. Following Apel, only the offering of reasons will produce an answer to the question Why be moral? No appeal, that is, is to be made to the individual qua an emotional being; the individual's unique capacity of *rationally justifying* his or her actions is—all by itself—to secure his or her being moral.

According to the strong thesis of Apel, the sheer asking of the question Why be moral? contains its own answer, that being discourse ethics. Apel's claim is that "given a seriously intended *question,* insofar as it is directed at all virtual addresses of an unlimited *Kommunikationsgemeinschaft,* one has already accepted the . . . normative-ethical presuppositions of a—contrafactually anticipated—ideal *Kommunikationsgemeinschaft.* In a word: there appears here the possibility of a transcendental-pragmatic ultimate justification for a discourse ethics."[6] Apel thus derives his whole ethics from the preconditions of the possibility of argumentation; to deny the *normative* implications of these preconditions, that is, of the anticipation of an *ideal* community that we cannot but make—however unwittingly—in every single act of entering discussion, means our committing a so-called performative self-contradiction. The decisive thrust of Apel's thesis is that *speech itself,* being the embodiment and carrier of humanity's rationality, transcends the here and now of our factual pragmatic context and hence the boundaries of concrete face-to-face interaction. Speech transcends, as it were, the contextuality of "conventional" morality, reaching, by virtue of its immanent ideality, toward the not-yet of the "unlimited" community to which a postconventional morality addresses itself. In speaking, that is, we are all members of an ideal community unlimited in time and space. (Apel here echoes Habermas's "formal pragmatics.")

Apel's elucidation of how the validity claims of speech are linked up with morality allows me to thematize the connectedness of language and practice in a way profoundly at odds with Viggo Rossvær's Wittgensteinian scheme. Central in Wittgenstein is the famous argument to the effect that one can never follow a rule *privatim.* "Einer Regel folgen, eine Mitteilung machen, einen Befehl geben, eine Schachpartie spielen sind *Gepflogenheiten* (Gebräuche, Institutionen)."[7] Being by definition intersubjective, language is embedded in an ongoing social practice, in a particular *Lebensform;* mediated by a specific grammar, as stressed by Rossvær, the connection between language and practice is mutual in that the one reproduces itself through the other and vice versa. Granting this, one wonders what becomes of a postconventional morality in the sense intended by Apel's discourse ethics. Apel's emphasis on the *universality* of the validity claims raised in every single speech act entails that in the speech act, the moment of contextuality, or practice-embeddedness, is being *transcended:* speaking, I not only reproduce the particular practice in which I take part, I also transcend the factual limits of that practice insofar as I—again, implicitly—address the "virtual" members of an ideal community. In other words, the reality of every act of reproduction through language produces, as it were, a moment of pure ideality peculiar to language per se.

Accepting this, we realize that the Wittgensteinian thesis of the direct reproductive mutuality of necessity restricts morality to the conventional level as defined above. Wittgenstein, that is, does not allow that the individual's following a rule or applying a norm *eo ipso* implies the rule's or norm's transcending or overshooting the ongoing practice in which it is said to be embedded; he therefore does not allow for the departure from established convention, that is, the projecting toward an ideal—the not-yet of the ideal *Kommunikationsgemeinschaft*—intended in Apel's transcendent-philosophical theory of language. In Wittgenstein's model, "the meaning of possible moral principles is determined a priori through the actual practice of habits of application that already determine the meaning of all possible rules."[8] Whereas the morality of the conventional level reproduces that which already is, the morality of the postconventional level produces something that is not yet. With regard to the problem of application of norms, the sociohistorical conditions of such application are already fulfilled in the case of conventional morality, whereas they have to be brought into existence in the case of postconventional morality, the latter addressing a contrafactually anticipated ideal community.

Discourse ethics, then, teaches that we are citizens of two worlds: qua speakers, we raise validity claims that transcend the contextuality of the practice in which we participate; qua agents, we cannot but deliberate and act within that very contextuality. Accordingly, discourse ethics is based on the awareness of "the principal difference between the ideal and the real *Kommunikationsgemeinschaft*."[9] The difference in question is one that Rossvær, following Wittgenstein, fails to take into account; moreover, it is one of which conventional morality is, happily, unaware. Derived from the juxtaposition of language and practice just made, the difference is mirrored in the abyss existing between the ideally anticipated and the de facto established conditions of communication. Apel therefore views it as part of our moral duty "to collaborate toward the approximate elimination of the reflected difference—that is, to try to see to it that in the ever necessary anticipation of the presupposed ideal conditions of communication, the word 'contrafactual' lose its ethical-practical relevance in ever more spheres of life."[10] However, the world of today, being as it is, is pervaded by the strategic rationality of agents or social systems pursuing their perceived self-interests, of the instrumentalization of humanity. In view of this state of affairs, discourse ethics demands that we be prepared "to enter into the historical situation and to reconcile the imperatives of ethical reason with those of strategic reason and of systemic rationality."[11] The task of realizing the ideal within the constraints of the real being by no means innocent, one cannot expect at all times to keep one's hands from becoming dirty: sometimes strategic reason itself is the only realistic means of bringing into existence a world in which there will be less of it and more of its counterpart, the communicative rationality on which discourse ethics is founded.

While posing a very considerable challenge to it, the abyss between reality and ideal is also that which gives discourse ethics its particular *critical* potential. Seeing no such abyss amounts to holding that (in the words of Schnädelbach) "the good already exists in the world," the crucial implication being that "no further critical standard of evaluation can then be imposed on the substantial *Sittlichkeit*, too powerful in any case, of the lifeworld."[12] When depicted as entirely embedded within and part of a given practice or mode of life, morality cannot "overshoot" and critically question but only affirm and help sustain that mode of life. Conventional morality differs from postconventional morality in that only the latter permits us to question the factual *social* validity of practice-embodied norms with regard to their *rational* validity. What we ask here is, Do these norms *deserve* the prima facie social validity granted them? Thus only a postconventional ethics enables us explicitly to make the "interests that normally underlie the conventional norms" the "subject matter of practical discourses."[13] Brought to bear on the position defended by Rossvær, this means that although it is correct to maintain an *unaufhebbare* link between rule following or norm application and practice, it must be acknowledged that a moral norm such as that laid down in Kant's categorical imperative is tied up with practice in a very special way: instead of being embedded in an existing practice in the sense of Wittgenstein's argument of rule following, the categorical imperative has its peculiar embodiment in a practice not yet empirically established, that is, in the so-called kingdom of ends—a community, to repeat, of which all of us alike are "virtual" participants as human beings regardless of location in time and space. Properly understood, the categorical imperative is not so much a concrete moral rule as a universal ethical principle; it is therefore of necessity abstract, as are all the principles—of justice, of human rights, and of the respect for the dignity of human beings as individual persons—to be identified on the level of postconventional morality. To sum up, the categorical imperative, while abstract, *is* linked with a practice—the ideal practice, that is, in which all the members of a realm of ends would take part. In his criticism of the Kantian legacy in Apel's discourse ethics, however, Rossvær, leaning on Wittgenstein, can do no justice to the practice-transcending ideal anticipated in postconventional ethical principles. Rather, Rossvær proceeds *as if* the Kantian categorical imperative were a concrete moral rule and thus belonged within—and could be criticized within—the framework of conventional morality.

Following Apel all the way up, as it were, to the postconventional level, that is to levels 5 and 6 in Lawrence Kohlberg's stage model of moral consciousness, we have reached a high level of abstraction. As I just noted, this abstraction is an important gain insofar as the potential for exercising criticism is concerned; it makes it possible to criticize what is in light of what is not (yet). In this respect, discourse ethics appears as a sounder and more convincing position than its various Wittgensteinian and neo-Aristotelian rivals. More vital to the main argument of the present chapter, however, is the fact that, with the level of abstraction attained in Apel, we certainly have been taken a very long way from the emotional tie of face-to-face interaction with which we started. I now explore the significance of that long step. Perhaps the much-celebrated gain in abstraction hides its own kind of loss.

Habermas's Discourse Ethics and Communicative Action

Habermas describes the basic intuition of discourse ethics as the intuition that an intersubjectivist interpretation of the moral point of view can be traced back to a presuppositional analysis of communicative action. To have this intuition is to hold that the presuppositions of this specific type of interaction contain the nucleus of morality; it is to hold that moral argumentation, viewed as a procedure, "inherits" the normative content of the pragmatic presuppositions of communicative action. Thus derived from the structure of interaction oriented toward mutual understanding, the moral point of view as conceived by Habermas is not the first person singular but the first person plural: it is a "we." Morality presupposes and addresses this "we." So the core phenomenon preoccupying morality is irreducibly interpersonal: the violation of norms of interaction. Discourse ethics is deontological in that it takes the primary task of moral theory to be an explanation of the normative force of interpersonal obligations and norms of conduct, and it is cognitivist in that it holds an "ought" to express a claim to objective validity, that is to say, a claim capable of finding universal consensus.

Yet what does it mean to derive the moral point of view from the pragmatic presuppositions of communicative action? And what is the normative content of these presuppositions?

Habermas has sought to clarify his position on these questions ever since his 1965 inaugural lecture in Frankfurt. In laying out the conceptual framework for his first philosophical major statement *Erkenntnis und Interesse*, Habermas argued that humanity's interest in autonomy (*Mündigkeit*) is intrinsic to the very structure of language and therefore recognizable a priori. His position was highlighted in the bold thesis that "with the very first sentence the intention of a universal and uncoerced consensus is unmistakably expressed" (TW, 163; translated by the author). Yet misunderstandings *did* arise. Subjected to scrutiny, Habermas's thesis proves to be complex and problematic: complex because every act of actual argumentation is held to rest on the presupposition of an "ideal" speech situation such as would be realized in an "ideal mode of life" only; problematic because the preconditions of an ideal speech situation clearly are far from met in real society, which means that argumentation in effect is held to have as its presupposition something that does not (as yet) exist, that is to say, an ideal that can only be counterfactually *anticipated*. The question here boils down to whether it is consistent to contend that something real, that is, argumentation, *presupposes* something purely ideal, that is, the ideal speech situation as realized in an ideal mode of life. In 1971 Habermas acknowledged that "no historical society has taken on the mode of life that we anticipate in the ideal speech situation" (VE, 126; translated by the author). Yet he maintains that it belongs to the very structure of speech that "in accomplishing speech acts, we act as if the ideal speech situation were not merely fictitious but real— precisely that is what we call an imputation [*Unterstellung*]. The normal foundation of understanding through language is therefore both: anticipated, yet as anticipated foundation also effective" (VE, 125). Habermas then summarizes his position: "For every possible communication, the anticipation of the ideal speech situation has the significance of a constitutive figuration [*Schein*] that at the same time is the prefiguration [*Vorschein*] of a mode of life" (VE, 126).

However, in 1982 Habermas withdraws this statement. He no longer wishes to uphold an internal link between raising validity claims in a speech act and anticipating—*uno actu*, as it were—an ideal mode of life (VE, 538– 39). Habermas instead seeks to reconcile his formal-pragmatic thesis about the universality of the validity claims of truth, rightness, and truthfulness with the standpoint of fallibilism. Fallibilism contends that the formal-pragmatic thesis might some day be proved wrong. The commitment to fallibilism has been a matter of perpetual controversy, however. Does it, critics have inquired, entail that the hypothesized universality of the validity claims be rejected, or does it entail that the assertion of three distinct validity claims (I omit "comprehensibility") be open to revision, so that we might tomorrow admit of more, or fewer, or altogether different, validity claims? How is a clear-cut falsification of the thesis of formal pragmatism at all conceivable?

I think that Habermas has yet to come up with a convincing reply to these questions. His current position seems to be brought out most clearly in his critique of Apel's case for a transcendental-pragmatic *Letztbegründung* (ultimate justification) of discourse ethics. The importance of this critique to my present purposes is twofold: first, it brings to light what I see as the crucial difference between Habermas's and Apel's grounding of a discourse ethics, and second, it helps elucidate the specific normative content of the presuppositions of communicative action.

In what has proved to imply an increasing opposition to Habermas's position, Apel of late insists that every speech act logically contains the anticipation of an ideal community of communication where the raised validity claims would find full approval, and that a denial of this amounts to a performative self-contradiction: the speaker who denies the presuppositions of speech *presupposes* those very same presuppositions as valid the very moment he or she seeks to deny them, insofar as the speaker—however unwittingly—demands that his or her claim be treated as valid, as true in the sense of being capable of justification. Hence fallibilism at *this* point is ruled out by Apel for the reason that an attempted refutation of the presuppositions of speech cannot but confirm what it wishes to deny. These presuppositions therefore are—and remain—a priori and universal in the sense of a "strong" transcendentalism. Significantly, Apel's version of a presuppositional analysis is not confined to moral argumentation but applies to the conditions of the possibility of speech *überhaupt*. So in Apel's view *every* subject capable of speech is always committed to the normative content of argumentation; this holds for all kinds of argumentation and from the very moment any subject opens his or her mouth and enters the argument.

Habermas's response to Apel's strong thesis is that it succeeds only in meeting the challenge of the skeptic as speaker, but not as actor. His argument against Apel is that "it is by no means self-evident that rules that are unavoidable *within* discourses can also claim to be valid for regulating action *outside* of discourses" (MC, 85–86). The commitment to the presuppositions of argumentation is a commitment every speaker cannot avoid making; but to have established this is not to have proved that every actor is bound by the same commitment; therefore, Apel's inference from the domain of discourse to that of action is unwarranted.

Habermas accordingly chooses a different path. In contradistinction to Apel's view that the normative presuppositions on which discourse ethics is based are derivable from the presuppositions of argumentation as such, Habermas holds that the nucleus of morality is to be located in a specific type of interaction, namely, communicative action, which is oriented toward mutual understanding and which, in being thus oriented, relies on language as the privileged medium of coordinating social action—"privileged" in the sense that a replacement of language as medium here is bound to have a variety of "pathologies" within the lifeworld as its upshot (TCA, 2:155). Not argumentation as such but communicative action is the locus of the normatively substantial presuppositions, these being precisely the presuppositions "*common* both to discourses and to action oriented to reaching understanding as such, e.g., presuppositions about relations of mutual recognition" (MC, 88; emphasis added). The presuppositions referred to are the following (as taken from Robert Alexy):

(1) Every subject with the competence to speak and act is allowed to take part in a discourse.

(2) a. Everyone is allowed to question any assertion whatever.
    b. Everyone is allowed to introduce any assertion whatever into the discourse.
    c. Everyone is allowed to express his attitudes, desires, and needs.

(3) No speaker may be prevented, by internal or external coercion, from exercising his rights as laid down in (1) and (2). (MC, 89)

Habermas takes these pragmatic presuppositions, which are "without alternatives" inasmuch as a speaker and actor *cannot avoid* assuming them when he or she enters discussion and interaction, to consist of the following: a *reciprocity of perspectives* is inscribed in the roles of speaker and hearer who want to come to an understanding with each other about something in the objective, social, or subjective world; a *mutuality of recognition* is presupposed in the performative attitudes that both take when they enter an interpersonal relationship; a *symmetry of expectations* is imputed from the normative context of the lifeworld they share (cf. KN, 25). Drawing on this explication of the pragmatic presuppositions of communicative action that carry a normative content, Habermas formulates the basic principle ('D') of ethical validity in terms of *rational, universal,* and *uncoerced consensus*: only those norms may claim validity that could be agreed to by all the concerned parties as participants in a practical discourse (MC, 93).

Habermas does not share Apel's problem of having to justify a *transference* of the (allegedly) universally valid presuppositions from the sphere of argumentation to that of action, because in Habermas's model the presuppositions and the normative content intrinsic to them do not merely *apply* to interaction; rather, they *determine* the very *structure* of the interaction—and thus the entire problem of a transference is gotten rid of. So whereas Apel grounds the moral point of view as depicted in discourse ethics in the presuppositions of speech (*Rede*), Habermas grounds it in the presuppositions of interaction oriented toward mutual understanding.

As indicated, the underlying difference of opinion between the two key proponents of discourse ethics concerns the issue of fallibilism. In working out his objections to Apel's transcendental-pragmatic *Letztbegründung*, Habermas draws a distinction between the rule competence of speakers and agents on the one hand and the discourse ethical reconstruction of such competence on the other. "To be sure," he writes, "the intuitive knowledge of rules that subjects capable of speech and action must use if they are to be able to participate in argumentation is in a certain sense not fallible. But this is not true of our *reconstruction* of this pretheoretical knowledge and the claim to universality that we connect with it" (MC, 97). Any attempt to infer from the pretheoretical *certainty* with which we go about applying our rule competence to the *truth* of our proposed reconstruction of this competence is illegitimate. The disagreement can be traced back to a more fundamental dispute over whether discourse ethics is a brand of reconstructive science, and thus committed to the fallibilism of such sciences, or a moral theory derived from universal pragmatics understood as a philosophical theory. Habermas opts for the former position and hence for a weak transcendentalism; Apel opts for the latter and hence for a strong transcendentalism. I take the core of the disagreement to be that Apel holds the principle of fallibilism not to apply to philosophical theories proper, such as universal pragmatics (cf. Apel in FS, esp. 19–20), whereas Habermas defends a conception of universal pragmatics and of philosophical theories in general, which commits them to the requirements of fallibilism. The quarrel over the grounding of discourse ethics is at bottom over the status—privileged or not—of philosophy.

Although far from unambiguous on the subject, it seems that in Habermas's view, validity claims, though "universal," are inescapably *provisional* insofar as they are always raised from within a specific spatiotemporal context; though transcending the here and now of this context, a raised validity claim is in principle always vulnerable to the constraints on absolute or eternally valid insight that the moment of contextuality inevitably imposes on it. In other words: "We cannot predict whether the unavoidable changes in context will one day affect a justification that is here and now accepted as sufficient. However, we must not deny this abstract possibility in order to preserve the performative meaning of the acceptance of justifications" (E, 351; translated by the author). Brought to bear on a moral discourse, this entails that the individual participant can never have access to all the relevant data or pertinent questions, simply because the correctness of moral norms—according to discourse ethics—depends on the agreement of others; and that agreement can never be fully foreseen by the one advocating a norm proposal. The point peculiar and often decisive to moral discourse is that the other, precisely as other, represents a partially hidden set not only of potential questions[14] but also of novel, because principally alterable, interpretations of needs, interests, and wants. This in its turn points to the—practically as well as theoretically—insoluble problem of possibly *distorted* interpretation of needs, interests, and wants, and, with that, to the lack of transparency of the interpersonal domain addressed in a moral discourse.

Yet Habermas's critique of Apel's strong transcendentalism is not confined to the issue of fallibilism as adhered to by all reconstructive sciences, discourse ethics being no exception. His critique extends beyond theory to the realm of practices. For Habermas, moral theory enjoys no primacy over moral practices. The assertion here is that "the *moral* intuitions of everyday life are not in need of clarification by the philosopher" (MC, 98). According to Habermas, the "idea of impartiality is rooted *in* the structures of argumentation *themselves* and does not need to be *brought in* from the outside as a supplementary normative content" (MC, 75–76). Insofar as presuppositions such as the normative one of impartiality are built into the structure of interaction oriented toward mutual understanding, and insofar as such interaction is the locus of ongoing moral practices, the task of moral theory is restricted to that of offering a reconstruction of presuppositions and intuitions that are "always already" embedded in practices. So, in addition to being theoretically untenable, because the very notion of a *prima philosophia* is so, the *Letztbegründung* stubbornly insisted on by Apel is simply superfluous: there is no *need* for a grounding of moral theory, that is, of discourse ethics, in a *prima philosophia*. This being so, the moral philosopher has no justified claim to a privileged position; he may—he even should—take part in practical discourses as "one of those concerned, perhaps even as an expert," all the while realizing that he cannot conduct such discourses "by *himself alone*" (MC, 94). So just as discourse ethics is one competitor among many in the attempt to reconstruct the pretheoretical intuitions and competencies of (lay) participants in moral practices, the moral philosopher is but one participant among others in these practices. No privileged position is to be claimed on any level—either in theory or in practice (cf. Habermas's discussion in ED, 185–99).

Although discourse ethics is a reconstructive science, in that it undertakes an explication of implicit knowledge and pretheoretical competence, it is not—as a moral theory—content to depict morality as merely mirroring some ongoing social practice. As I showed in the chapter on MacIntyre, morality portrayed as entirely embedded in a given practice or mode of life cannot overshoot and question but only affirm and help sustain that practice or mode of life. Conventional morality is reproductive in this sense. However, when the subjects attain the postconventional stage of moral reasoning, the naïve sustenance of existing practices and institutions will cease to the extent that they are now being *called into question* regarding their rational, as distinct from merely social, validity. The loss of naïveté brought about in the transition from a conventional to a postconventional level of moral reasoning signifies a gain in reflexivity; it shatters the social world as innocently "given" and brings action to a halt. The transition amounts to a moralization of the factual: "This moralization of society—that is, of the normatively integrated structure of relationships that the growing child initially had to appropriate through construction—undermines the normative power of the factual: from the isolated viewpoint of deontological validity, institutions that have lost their quasi-natural character can be turned into so many instances of problematic justice" (MC, 161). The distinction between the social and the rational validity of norms not only becomes possible at the postconventional level, it is also demanded of the individual that he or she judge and act *in view of* that distinction: "To heteronomy, that is, dependence on existing norms, is opposed the demand that the agent make the validity rather than the social currency of a norm the determining ground of his action." The emphatic conception of moral action as based on discursively redeemed, as opposed to monologically gained, knowledge of what is just, of what norms are rationally valid and for that reason alone *deserve* recognition, is unmistakably Socratic in spirit—"moral action is action guided by insight" (MC, 162).

Habermas sums up his thesis that the moral point of view is derivable from the mutual recognition built into the structure of communicative action as follows:

> The moral point of view cannot be found in a first principle, nor can it be located in an ultimate justification that would lie outside the domain of argumentation. Justificatory power resides only in the discursive procedure that redeems normative claims to validity. And this justificatory power stems in the last analysis from the fact that argumentation is rooted in communicative action. The sought-after moral point of view that precedes all controversies originates in a fundamental reciprocity that is built into action oriented toward reaching understanding. (MC, 163)

As observed above, the 'D'-principle states that only those norms are deemed valid that would find the reasonable consent of all involved and of all who are affected by its implementation. Being a "we," the moral point of view requires of every discourse participant that he or she take the perspective of all affected parties and question the validity of a norm in view of what everyone could rationally will. Hence, though recasting the basic principle of moral validity in terms of rational consensus, discourse ethics as developed by Habermas retains the formal-procedural and universalistic intentions of the typically Kantian approach. The moral point of view as defined by Habermas entails an abstraction from context under three aspects: (1) an abstraction from given motivations, (2) an abstraction from the particular situation, and (3) an abstraction from an established mode of life. All three abstractions are deeply at odds with the Aristotelian framework of MacIntyre's moral theory as outlined in *After Virtue*. Habermas's moral point of view shifts the emphasis from the question What is good for me or us? to the question What ought one to do? It imposes a differentiation between what is *good* for me or us to do and what is the *right* thing to do. Moral reasoning in the deontological sense is confined to interpersonal obligations; by contrast, all questions concerning the good life, that is, how one should live— personally and as a member of a particular community—are termed evaluative and addressed in the *ethical-existential* discourse where they are settled not in terms of their normative rightness but in terms of their authenticity. The ethical-existential discourse works from within, as it were; it takes the situatedness of the individual as its point of departure and seeks to settle the issue of what is good for him or her as concretely as possible, remaining sensitive to the context in which it arises and recognizing the uniqueness of the person posing it. Insofar as ethical questions are burdened with a person's quest for identity and self-understanding, they do not allow for an answer that can be valid for everybody; the interpretation called for here is self-related and intrapersonal in that it elucidates one's own formation processes (who I am) and a life project, or ego ideal (who I would like to be). Ethical questions are raised, discussed, and pursued in the light of an individual's or a group's notion of self-realization (see ND, 225), with regard to which there are no universally valid notions; to pretend that there were would be to violate the logic of this kind of discourse. Indeed, in political terms, it is because questions of the good life are unsuitable to universalization that there exists—and should be allowed to exist—a plurality of individual life-styles and a corresponding diversity of ideals of a good life. Now, practical reason as at work in *moral* discourses, by contrast, changes from a faculty of prudential deliberation (à la Aristotle), employed within the context of an established mode of life, to a faculty of principles of pure, context-independent reason. This context-independence is reflected in the aforementioned abstractions required of the participants in a moral discourse: they are required to adopt a hypothetical attitude toward the "givenness" of motivation, situation, and mode of life; consequently, this discourse works from without rather than from within. Having barred all evaluative questions concerning the good life, the moral discourse exclusively pursues questions of normative justification, and it does so in accordance with a procedure that demands that *everything*—that is to say, all normative validity claims built into our lifeworld and rooted in our daily practices—count as a hypothesis until it regains its validity from the authority of good reasons, and from them alone.

Having worked out the chief differences between conventional and post-conventional morality, and how the latter differentiates between social and rational validity and between ethical-existential and moral discourse, there is no need to recapitulate at this juncture the criticisms I have voiced against the moral theory of MacIntyre. I shall only repeat that if we follow MacIntyre's view that moral reasoning arises within and *must remain linked to* a living ethos (in *Whose Justice? Which Rationality?* MacIntyre prefers to speak of "tradition of inquiry"), we must be prepared to dispense with the emancipatory potential of moral universalism and to abandon the opportunity for a penetrating moral criticism of exploitative and repressive social structures. As Habermas observes, "Only the transition to a level of postconventional moral reasoning liberates our mind from distortions and constraints that grow out of our most familiar practices and discourses" (KN, 16). Only when the postconventional level has been reached does it become possible to criticize what is in light of what is not (yet); only on this level has the distinction between the legality and the legitimacy of institutions attained widespread recognition.

The distinction between legality and legitimacy is the cornerstone of Habermas's recent work on law and morality. I find it appropriate to end the discussion of the moral point of view with a brief look at the overall direction of this work. Habermas starts from the strong assumption that "legality can derive its legitimacy only from a procedural rationality with a moral impact"; the key to this is "an interlocking of two types of procedures: processes of moral argumentation get institutionalized by means of legal procedures" (L, 220). What is important here is that the procedures laid down in a moral-practical discourse provide a *normative* standard, or yardstick, for questioning the legitimacy of legal institutions: "The results of legally institutionalized practices of negotiation and argumentation count as valid or rational precisely if they come about in conformity with the prescribed procedures."[15] Echoing his critique from *The Theory of Communicative Action* (1:243ff.), Habermas charges Max Weber with falsely identifying "the procedural properties of a post-traditional level of justification with substantive values" (L, 228); failing to realize, that is, that morality in its postconventional sense is formal-procedural rather than substantive, Weber could only regard the materialization of law as its illegitimate "moralization," as the penetration of substantive justice into positive law. Habermas's argument is that the legitimacy of legality cannot be accounted for (as Weber would have it) in terms of some independent rationality that, so to speak, inhabits the form of law in a morally neutral manner; rather, it must "be traced back to an internal relationship between law and morality" (L, 228). Habermas's central thesis is that "the proceduralized law and the moral justification of principles mutually implicate one another" (L, 243). However, and significantly, Habermas warns against conflating the two. Moral argumentation penetrates the core of positive law, but it does not completely merge with it. "Morality that is not only complementary to but at the same time ingrained in law is of a procedural nature; it has rid itself of all specific normative contents and has been sublimated into a procedure for the justification of possible normative contents. Thus a procedural law and a proceduralized morality can mutually check one another" (L, 247). In the context of my study, the relevance of this thesis lies in its implicit objection to moral theories such as MacIntyre's, which tend to renounce the gulf between norm and reality, between rational and social validity, and between questions of justification and questions of application (to recall the work of Klaus Günther so warmly embraced by Habermas). In this account, neo-Aristotelian ethics oriented toward conceptions of the good or toward specific value hierarchies have not overcome Weber's belief that morality is and must remain substantial; these ethics accordingly single out particular normative contents—without, however, being able to settle the conflicting and often incompatible claims arising out of such a diversity of conceptions. Against the gloomy Weberian scenario of a permanent war between gods and demons, Habermas maintains that "only theories of morality and justice developed in the Kantian tradition hold out the promise of an *impartial* procedure for the justification and assessment of principles" (L, 241).

Why Be Moral?

Post-Kantian cognitivistic ethics in principle oppose having recourse to emotions, inclinations, and the like. The argument, made of course with particular force by Kant, has always been that the foundation of ethics must be sought in what is truly universal and exempt from empirical-historical change. Hence, a foundation is to be found in reason, and in reason alone, humanity's inclinations and emotions being too shifty and frail to warrant systematic inclusion. In short, ethics must rely on reason alone and do without the inclinations and emotions altogether. Indeed, ethics, rightly understood, addresses the task of instructing people how not to yield to their "natural" inclinations and to act, instead, wholly by virtue of their capacity for rationality. Whatever the merits of such a crude contradistinction, the argument that carries the most philosophical weight here is that reason alone guarantees objectivity in moral judgment, whereas emotions are and will always remain purely subjective and thus entirely contingent and arbitrary as guides to action. Barred from morality and philosophy proper, the emotions are handed over to psychology.[16]

　　Yet it remains to be persuasively argued that emotions can play no positive role whatsoever in the domain of morality, only a negative role as attributed to them in cognitivistic ethics since Kant. Emotions, it is held, equal subjectivity, interestedness, partiality; reason equals objectivity, disinterestedness, impartiality. Consequently, it is only on the level of postconventional morality that reason comes into its own: on this level, as was brought out by Günther, we are no longer committed to the emotional ties characteristic of face-to-face interaction or to the particular ethos of the society we belong to; rather, we make distinctions between principles having universal, prescriptive applicability and values specific to a given society, for example, our own. The higher the level of abstraction, the more the bond created by personal-emotional ties is suspended; not shame, in the form of withdrawal of love and affection, but guilt, as a reaction of conscience, sanctions our actions. All the external circumstances that were once granted normative significance—the weight of religion and tradition, the fear of punishment and of the social consequences of "being caught"—are to be stripped of their action-guiding force, giving way to the internal tribune of conscience. Because the conditions of application of postconventional morality are not yet brought into actual existence—the institutions of society only to a limited degree truly corresponding to the postconventional standards of justice—the yardstick to guide reasoning and action is not to be sought "outside" of humanity. Rather, the more mature an individual's moral consciousness, the more that yardstick is something wholly internal to that individual. Again, autonomy in the full, postconventional sense presupposes the individual's ability to stand apart from the immediate setting of his or her action, to render the validity of social values hypothetical in order that their rationality may be questioned. Autonomy, in short, presupposes impartiality, the ability to take the view, not of the other with whom I interact, but of a neutral "third" party standing above the interaction and judging it from the "moral point of view" of the ideal role taking of Kohlberg.

Postconventional morality, then, advocates withdrawal as opposed to involvement, disinterestedness as opposed to interestedness. Only thus can the impartiality of the moral point of view, which supposedly is nothing less than that of reason itself as supreme judge, be secured. What then becomes of the emotions? Are they to be entirely abstracted from in moral matters— the more so the better? Do they represent nothing but bias?

In his essay "Discourse Ethics: Notes on a Program of Philosophical Justification," Habermas reflects on the role of emotions in ethics. "The objectivating attitude of the nonparticipant observer annuls the communicative roles of I and thou, the first and the second persons, and neutralizes the realm of moral phenomena as such" (MC, 46). Recognizing that "the world of moral phenomena can be grasped only in the performative attitude of participants in interaction," Habermas proceeds to admit that feelings "have a similar function for the moral justification of action as sense perceptions have for the theoretical justification of facts" (MC, 50). To Habermas, the moral core of emotions lies in their link to universality: "Indignation and resentment are directed at a *specific* other person who has violated our integrity. Yet what makes this indignation moral is not the fact that the interaction between two concrete individuals has been disturbed but rather the violation of an underlying *normative expectation* that is valid not only for ego and alter but also for all members of a social group or even, in the case of moral norms in the strict sense, for all competent actors." Hence, the individual who has done something wrong must realize that he "has also violated something impersonal or at least suprapersonal, namely a generalized expectation that both parties hold" (MC, 48). Although the person who has been harmed will react as a particular individual having been harmed, what has been done an injustice is not the particularity of that individual but rather his or her universality. If my reading of the passage just quoted is sound, every concrete individual with whom we interact is an embodiment of universality; harming this or that individual, we "overshoot" the particularity of our cosubject; in harming that person, we *eo ipso* violate the universality of the *Verhaltenserwartung* (expectation of conduct) existing between us, which has a normative and thus impersonal import. Personal interaction triggers emotional reactions the specific moral quality of which lies in their impersonality, in the universal that is violated in the *Gestalt* of the particular.

Habermas's assertion that we gain access to the world of moral phenomena only through a performative attitude is of central importance to my own argument. I take his claim to entail that we pass moral judgments as *participants*, as engaged members of a community, not as disinterested spectators emotionally unaffected by the phenomena awaiting our judgment. Or perhaps my reading of Habermas is too strong with regard to the moral quality of emotions. Strictly speaking, that is, what Habermas says in the passages quoted is merely that our having a performative attitude in *acting* within the world of moral phenomena is what gives us "access" to it. In other words, Habermas stresses action only insofar as it discloses moral phenomena to us, whereas my thesis is that we also *pass moral judgment* in our capacity as active participants. Indeed, the mere observation that judgment is triggered by action, by agents taking a performative attitude, does not amount to much.

The case of Eichmann provides me with a suitable illustration of what is at stake here. In her analysis of the notorious Nazi, which I shall refrain from repeating, Hannah Arendt concluded that Eichmann was "merely thoughtless." In this controversial claim, I see a cognitivistic bias typical of post-Kantian ethics. My position is that Eichmann was *not* merely thoughtless, but first of all *insensitive*. While at times vaguely acknowledging this, Arendt's sole systematic interest is in the shockingly "banal" thoughtlessness she encountered in Eichmann, leading her to examine the connection between (the absence of) thinking and evildoing. At no point does she pay his undeniable insensitivity, his emotional numbness, the philosophical attention it deserves. I would argue that both features—the insensitivity as well as the thoughtlessness—contribute to the peculiar "remoteness" of Eichmann's personality. Always disinterested, never emotionally affected, Eichmann could commit the kind of crime he committed. Dehumanizing himself as well as his fellows, allowing himself and not only others to become a mere "means," and thus committing the immoral act of robbing himself of his autonomy, he remained an estranged spectator unable or unwilling to join the human lot. Failing to see his victims as human beings, as particular and unique individuals, Eichmann did not know what it means to suffer, because to know this demands an ability to *feel* what it means to suffer—an ability he seemed not to have, or to have no longer, due to the dehumanizing effect of various processes of numbing discussed above. By his *indifference* to the meaning of suffering, to the infliction of pain, Eichmann places himself outside the realm of humanity. Insofar as he adopts an objectifying attitude toward his fellows, as opposed to a participatory-emphatic one, Eichmann for all practical purposes *prevents the domain of moral phenomena from being disclosed to him*. There is no disinterested access to the phenomenon of suffering; if one bars the capacity to feel from morality, one bars humanity from it.

In my view, Eichmann epitomizes what Adorno called the "incapacity for identification with the other's suffering."[17] Arendt's thesis is that Eichmann failed to judge because he had no imagination: he failed to exercise what Kant referred to as the *erweiterte Denkungsart*, because he was incapable of representing others in his own mind. In a similar vein, Apel declares that we cannot do without "moral imagination." That is easily granted. But Apel fails to mention what place imagination is to have in discourse ethics, or how discourse ethics is thought to foster it. In the absence of this much-needed eludication, Apel tirelessly speaks of the "responsibility of reason, which must take the place of a consciousness of sin based to some extent on instinct."[18] The embarrassment here—to be traced back to Kant himself—is that Apel offers no convincing answer to the question Why should I be moral? It must be asked whether the *Vernunft* Apel appeals to is really suited to answer the question of moral motivation, being—wholly in line with the Kantian conception—purely formal and procedural. Obviously, a way out of the embarrassment—How can something purely formal inhabit empirical motivational force?—would be simply to declare the issue of motivation to lie outside the ambit of ethics proper, thereby restricting the latter to handling problems of validity, justification, and application of principles and norms. But is this not to "solve" a major problem in moral theory by way of excluding it? Or is it rather that the question Why be moral? is not a philosophical one at all, and therefore a problem purposely relinquished by deontological moral theory?

Apel sees a major shortcoming in Kant on this very issue. Kant, most evidently in his second *Critique*, was unable to offer a *reason* why we should be moral. Kant, that is, was able to offer nothing more than an appeal to the *Faktum der Vernunft*, whereby he presupposed the noumenal being peculiar to humanity. What Kant delivers is therefore—at best—a metaphysical explanation for humanity's capacity for reason, leaving, however, the question Why be moral? without a philosophical answer. Apel's view that Fichte is superior to Kant in this respect need not concern us here. [19] What matters here is twofold: first, that Apel holds the question to be a correctly posed and a truly philosophical one and, second, that Apel holds his advocated *Letztbegründung* to be able to answer it. Summing up his position, Apel writes, "By means of transcendental-pragmatic reflection upon the normative presuppositions of the possibility of thinking qua argumentation (presuppositions that cannot be set aside by any serious inquirer), it is possible to supply such a thing as a specifically philosophical ultimate justification for being logical and being moral, indeed for being rational *überhaupt.*" What this boils down to is the oft-repeated argument that "as one who seriously argues, who candidly seeks the intersubjectively valid truth . . . one is of necessity also already determined to be moral [*fürs Moralischsein entschieden*]." [20]

As far as I can see, there is a major difference between Apel and Habermas on this issue. Habermas holds the question Why be moral? to be neither correctly posed nor a truly philosophical one to be addressed by discourse ethics; it follows that he considers Apel's *Letztbegründung* a false answer to a false question.

The difference can be put as follows: Apel takes the case of the radical skeptic to confirm his thesis of a *Letztbegründung* of discourse ethics, whereas Habermas holds the skeptic to confirm his objections to Apel's thesis. Apel's argument holds only, contends Habermas, for those who already are willing to argue; and because this is exactly what the radical skeptic refuses to do,

Apel's performative self-contradiction fails to apply to him and thus, Habermas asserts, fails to provide discourse ethics with an adequate foundation. In refusing to enter the business of argumentation, the skeptic effectively places himself outside the scope of Apel's transcendental-pragmatic grounding. No *argument*, that is, can commit the skeptic to the rules of argumentation if he has—however arbitrarily at that—decided against being committed to argumentation. The implication is that "if the cognitivist persists in his analysis, he will now be talking only *about* the sceptic, not *with* him" (MC, 99). The skeptic who succeeds in maintaining his unwillingness to participate in argumentation "would be performatively right, so to speak—he would assert his position mutely and impressively" (MC, 100). He would, however, pay a price for doing so; his success would entail a failure—a failure to preserve his membership in the community into which he has been born and through whose intersubjective structures he develops and sustains his identity as individual. The skeptic who is prepared to hold onto his position at all costs, thereby also *acting* on it, puts his identity, ultimately his very existence, in jeopardy. Habermas takes the case of the die-hard skeptic to highlight the "action-theoretical bases of discourse ethics" and with that the "embeddedness of morality in ethical life [Hegel's *Sittlichkeit*]" (MC, 99). True, the skeptic can deny morality per se; he can deny observing its precepts, obligations, and duties; but he cannot deny its—and *his own*— embeddedness in a community, in a concrete ethic, or *Sittlichkeit*. The community, that is to say, the sphere of communicative action—not, as Apel has it, the practice of argumentation—is the context the skeptic cannot remain outside of without undermining his very existence qua individual. The option of leaving this context behind is but an abstraction; skepticism, when converted into a practice, has no long-term viability. Indeed, the decision for a "long-term absence [*Ausstieg*] from contexts of action oriented toward reaching an understanding . . . would mean regressing to the monadic isolation of strategic action, or schizophrenia and suicide. In the long run such absence is self-destructive" (MC, 102).

So, since individuation is for Habermas the reverse side of socialization, and since he considers argumentation to be the reflexive mode of communicative action, the issue of the identity of the individual is actually analogous to the issue of the foundation of discourse ethics. Both have their locus in the structure of communicative action: the individual receives and reproduces his or her identity through this structure, and moral argumentation as depicted in discourse ethics is derived from it in the sense of inheriting the normative content of the pragmatic presuppositions of communicative action.

Does this, one now wonders, contain an answer to the question from which I started—Why be moral? Does not the problem of bridging the deontological gap between moral judgment and action still remain? Habermas's answer is that the question is ill-conceived.

> A philosophy that no longer claims to know the telos of the good life, has to dismiss the question Why be moral?. And indeed why should a theory be capable of motivating people to act according to their insights? The disposition for responsibility depends obviously on socialization-processes and identity-formation. An identity cannot be generated by arguments. It is not a deficiency when moral theory cannot do more than rationally reconstruct the moral point of view and defend its universality. . . . To know the right answer to a moral problem means that no one has a good reason to act otherwise. This may not be a great deal, but it is more than nothing. Moral judgments possess just the degree of motivating force that the reasons possess on which they rest; and that degree varies with persons and contexts. (KN, 20)

Although Apel would oppose Habermas's contention that discourse ethics, precisely because it is a deontological ethics, must refrain from answering the question Why be moral? there is nonetheless a strong Apelian ring to the way Habermas justifies his position. This comes out in the statement that "moral judgments possess just the degree of motivating force that the reasons possess on which they rest." In the tradition of cognitivistic ethics, of course, this statement is a commonplace; as such, it is looked upon as completely unproblematic. In moral affairs, reasons—and nothing but reasons—motivate; and should something else motivate, the motivation is no longer a truly moral one. Habermas holds that a person cannot be persuaded—or, to be more accurate, persuaded by argument—to enter into moral discourse. The radical skeptic may refuse to speak, and he may even decide to act on his refusal to speak. For taking this step, however, he pays the high price of undermining his identity, ultimately his social existence. This being so, the question whether emotion, as opposed to argumentation, may be the mode of access to the domain of the moral, to what matters and makes a difference *precisely in moral terms*, that is to say, in terms of the weal and woe of our cosubjects as being at stake in some concrete situation—this question, this possibility, is not raised at all. But this is exactly the thesis I developed in the chapter on perception: that emotion provides us with an access to the domain of the moral. A way of proving this thesis is to show that a lack of emotion, that is, a blocking of the faculty of empathy, is in fact a sufficient condition for failing to enter the domain of the moral, for failing, that is, to grasp what this particular domain is all about. A lack of emotion thus amounts to a lack of moral sense, to a peculiar and often conspicuous blindness in the face of situations carrying moral significance.

The Apel-Habermas discussion about the skeptic's refusal to enter into argumentation betrays the cognitivistic framework within which both proponents of discourse ethics pose what they see as the challenge to be met with respect to the very *entry* into the moral domain. The nonspeaker, they agree, fails this entry; that I do not deny. But it should also be pointed out that the nonemphatic person, the indifferent or numb one, just as surely fails the entry. Yet this fact is wholly ignored in the debate between Apel and Habermas. What separates them indeed counts for little as compared to what they have in common. Their dispute is therefore a strictly internal one: it never puts the adequacy of the cognitivistic framework into question; it raises the issue of the failed entry in voluntaristic terms, as if it turned on the *willingness to argue*, as distinct from the possibility of an *incapacity to feel*. What is ignored, then, is that the failure to enter into the domain of the moral can be a failure of perception rather than argumentation; that the failure can be emotional, having to do with a lack (of emotional abilities) that cannot be traced back to a "decision" on the part of the subject; and, finally, that the cognitive-rendered-practical unwillingness of the radical skeptic, when compared to the case of emotional incapacity, is rarely met in real life.

As far as I can see, Habermas conceives Why be moral? as a first-person-singular question. It means, Why should *I* be moral? Habermas takes it for granted that the question asks, Why should I *act* morally, not immorally? Hence, to be moral is tacitly equated with acting morally. What is completely overlooked in such a conception is the importance of seeing, that is to say, the ability to identify and recognize a situation or phenomenon as *morally* relevant in the first place. Yet I would argue that the very notion of a subject "being" moral becomes unintelligible if the subject fails to perceive in a proper manner the distinct category of moral phenomena. Therefore, the question Why be moral? is inadequately dealt with when it is taken to address only the capacity for—presumably sound—moral action, and not just as crucially the capacity for moral perception as well. Indeed, on closer inspection the notion of action itself must refer to perception lest action be blind and as such rendered indistinguishable from mere "behavior."

But it is not only that Habermas discusses the challenge coming from the skeptic in one-sidedly cognitivistic terms or that he as a matter of course takes "being" moral to mean "acting" morally. It is exactly *because* he takes Why be moral? to be a first-person-singular question that Habermas holds it to be unanswerable by moral theory. Judging from his scattered remarks on the topic, his view is that the question Why be moral? is not a moral question but an ethical one. This admittedly is a paradoxical way of putting it, and I think it *is* a paradox. To Habermas, the question Why be moral? arises for the individual, for the subject in his or her irreducible individuality; this being so, it is for him or her—and him or her alone—to come to grips with it and to assume and "live" some particular stance toward it within the unique, narratively unfolding context of his or her life. Being or not being moral is an option, as it were, engendered within the framework of a person's biography; the question giving rise to this option is therefore an ethical-existentual one, according to Habermas's use of the term.

I, however, do not think that Habermas's position stands up to close scrutiny. Above, I have pointed out how his cognitivistic approach leads him to privilege, first, argumentation over feeling and, second, action over perception. In both cases, the primacy of the former over the latter is not established argumentatively but rather is largely taken for granted, and it is the cogency of this merely assumed order of priorities that I have wished to call into question. For all this, however, my critique aims deeper still. To see what I have in mind here, recall to begin with Habermas's remarkably crass dismissal of the question Why be moral? In the long passage I cited above, he clearly attempts to present as a virtue the unwillingness of discourse ethics to answer the question. But is not the lack of an answer that is here rendered a virtue rather the very opposite—an embarrassment? Is not discourse ethics scandalized, not vindicated, as a moral theory when it declares that it cannot answer the question Why be moral? Is not Habermas busy masking a failure as a merit?

Consider again the case Habermas makes for his position. He gives two arguments. First, a philosophy no longer knowing and committed to the telos of the good life has to dismiss the question. Second, it cannot be a task of moral theory to motivate people to act according to their insights, that is, to act morally. Both arguments can be contested; still, I limit my present discussion to the first.

The first argument holds only if it is true that the philosophy in question, namely, discourse ethics, is not committed to any specific or substantial conception of the good life, indeed to any specific good whatsoever. This demand applies to discourse ethics because it calls itself a deontological theory. Now, Habermas's maneuver here is to relegate this whole issue (Why be moral?) to ethical-existential discourse, where it is treated as a first-person-singular question answerable only by the particular individual himself or herself. But the introduced distinction between moral and ethical discourses fails to guarantee Habermas's stance its much-needed consistency.

To start with, remember Habermas's recourse to the probable, or even inevitable, loss of identity as the price paid by the die-hard skeptic. The recourse to the skeptic's identity was, so to speak, the last resort available to discourse ethics in its imagined dispute with the skeptic. But it is crucial to ask, What *is* this identity, what kind of status does it have, that is to say, what kind of status does Habermas—however implicitly—confer on it? My unhesitant answer to this question is, The status of a good. The loss of identity with which the skeptic is ultimately threatened has to be understood as the loss of a good. The issue of such a good is not a morally neutral but a full-blooded normative one. The possible loss of identity is not the loss of just any good, but of a fundamental, a constitutive one,[21] a good that must be secured lest the person perish qua person. In my view, the good of identity can be spelled out as the good of belongingness—to a society, to a community of some sort. The good of identity is inseparable from the good of belongingness because identity is unattainable without community. (I argued this in my previous discussion of MacIntyre as well.)

On a related line of thought, Habermas, in his important essay "Morality and Ethical Life," describes morality as a "compensation for man's extreme vulnerability." He writes, "In anthropological terms, morality is a safety device compensating for a vulnerability built into the sociocultural forms of life. Creatures that are individuated only through socialization are vulnerable and morally in need of considerateness [*schonungsbedürftig*]" (MC, 199). In this view, morality is a social institution whose chief purpose is to safeguard us against our vulnerability as human persons. But is not morality when portrayed as an institutionalized compensation along these lines, *eo ipso* looked upon as a good? Stronger still, is not the gist of Habermas's account that morality is *for the sake of* this good of belongingness?

If my analysis is not mistaken, these are two instances in Habermas's work on moral theory where he, in seeking to clarify and defend his version of discourse ethics, has recourse to arguments that rest on a notion of a constitutive good—in both cases the good of belonging to a community. Now, the fact that his theory, being a moral theory, is committed to some such good may appear to have but minor significance. But it is not so. On the contrary, it is highly significant, since Habermas, in wanting to develop

discourse ethics as a deontological ethic, has forbidden himself any commitment to some notion of a good. So it is because his moral theory takes pride
in its purported "liberation" from any commitment whatsoever to specific
goods that the analysis I have given can be seen as radically challenging the
consistency of the program for a discourse ethics. Strictly speaking, Habermas's strong affirmative reference to our vulnerability, to our susceptibility to
suffering and pain, seems to be ruled out a priori, as it were, by the principles
of deontology to which Habermas so expressly wants to adhere. (This point
I elaborate at greater length in a separate discussion below.)

In view of the assertion mentioned above that morality is a social
institution the raison d'être of which lies in its securing its members a
protection against their peculiar vulnerability as persons, it seems obvious
that morality is an institution in whose sustenance all people must take an
interest. This, it appears, is the answer to the "unanswerable" question Why
be moral? In other words, people's interest in morality qua protection-
providing institution contains a plausible answer to, gives them a good reason
for, "being" moral themselves and *thereby*—for how could it otherwise be
done?—supporting this institution. Needless to say, morality—precisely
when depicted as a precarious institution—breaks down as soon as people
stop being moral, that is, to use my own terms, as soon as they cease to
perceive, judge, and act with a concern for the weal and woe of fellow
humans as at stake in some situation. With this, we are at the very core, we
address the very locus, of morality as *inter*- as opposed to intrapersonal. In
saying what I say here, I address the irreducibly and unmistakably *moral*, and
not—as the "official" Habermasian stance toward Why be moral? has it—the
ethical-existential. Hence, Why be moral? starts off as and remains a moral
question, despite deontology's claims to the contrary.

Yet, and perhaps far from uncharacteristically, this is another case where
the answer that seems to offer itself, indeed to grow out of the very arguments
with which Habermas on some occasions operates, is one squarely disallowed
by the overt or proclaimed aims of the kind of moral theory he wishes to
advocate. What I have demonstrated in the preceding discussion is how, on
the one hand, the issue of a commitment to some notion of good and, on
the other, the issue of moral motivation are linked together, indeed *come*
together to produce, in effect, one and the same response to both issues.
The response intended is the one just given. The conception of "identity" as
well as "vulnerability" has been shown to invoke, and very crucially so, a
recourse to belongingness—to a community, to morality as a social institution. What matters is that the recourse to belongingness amounts to a

recourse to a (constitutive) good, even though this latter is never openly acknowledged by Habermas. He believes himself to be true to deontology and hence to be prudently silent on the good ultimately involved in both issues; in reality, however, he—as any close reading reveals—conducts his defense of discourse ethics in a manner secretly, as it were, invoking the selfsame forbidden good. What I have detected here is a pragmatic contradiction the full implications of which I cannot analyze here, although I briefly return to them below.

Hence, according to my use of the terms, Why be moral? is not an ethical-existential question but a moral one, because it involves what I throughout have defined as the moral issue—that is, the issue of how I relate to others and perceive their weal and woe as at stake in concrete situations. Even though we may say that it is always an *individual* who is *addressed* by the question Why be moral? the question does not remain, as it were, within the single individual's domain, does not merely bear on his or her biography; far from being thus restricted, the question—and the way an individual responds to it—affects the interpersonal, the social, domain. The individual's response here will be a matter not only of his or her "being with him- or herself" but of his or her "being with others" as well.

It has been necessary to labor this point because Habermas's use of the concepts differs from mine. In his terminology, an individual who engages in a so-called ethical-existential discourse ultimately faces the "ethical" question par excellence, What should I do? in the light of the "existential" question par excellence, Who am I, and who do I want to be? By denying Why be moral? the status of a moral question and by declaring it an ethical one, Habermas in effect sees it as belonging to the class of questions headed by What should I do? Within this class, Why be moral? assumes the form Should I be moral? and if yes, then why? To Habermas, "ethical questions do not in any way require a full-blown breach of the egocentric perspective, for all these questions are related to the telos of *my* life" (ED, 105; translated by the author). Habermas furthermore understands the "moral" question as the "question whether a norm or an action is right" (ED, 47). Criticizing the position of Bernard Williams, Habermas states that "morality does not concern the telos of a successful life under the aspect of the question addressing who I am (or we are) and wish to be; rather, it deals with the categorically different question of which norms we wish to live by and how action disputes can be resolved in the interest of all" (ED, 124).

I hope that these references help clarify the different terminologies involved here. Habermas subscribes to a Kantian definition of a moral question; accordingly, the question requires "an assessment of interpersonal conflicts with a view to what *everyone* may agree to desire" (ED, 124; translated by the author). In my conception, on the other hand, the moral question is the very broad one of how an individual relates to others and perceives their weal and woe as at stake in a concrete situation; accordingly, I recognize a moral dimension in the issue of being with others per se. That is to say, my being with others is not a morally neutral matter: it is not morally neutral in the cases where I recognize that the others with whom I am are moral beings, and it is not morally neutral in the cases where I fail to be the author of such recognition of others.

However, although Habermas's Kantian view of the moral question prima facie may appear much more specific and "focused" than mine, what he says is in fact very general too. In the passage quoted above, he speaks of the moral question as touching on "the norms we wish to live by." Now, the way the individual members of a society respond to the question Why be moral? even when translated into What should I do—be moral or not? (see above), will inescapably have an effect on the norms we live by, and wish to live by. In a similar vein, when Habermas speaks about the moral question as addressing the impartial judgment of "interpersonal conflicts," this is also something that cannot be strictly divorced from how the question Why be moral? is understood and responded to. Indeed, it is not far-fetched to imagine cases where interpersonal conflicts arise precisely because individuals have failed to respond to the question in a manner their cosubjects feel is legitimate to expect—from others no less than from themselves.

> What moral and, especially, immoral action means is something we experience and learn *prior to* all philosophy; it confronts us no less compellingly in compassion for the hurt integrity of others than in suffering over one's own afflicted identity or in anxiety at its being endangered. The inexplicit socialization experiences of forbearance, solidaristic help, and fairness inform our intuitions and teach us more about this than all arguments are capable of. (ED, 185; translated by the author; cf. TK, 144)

I agree. Like Habermas, I see the limitations to attempts to argue a person into "being moral." But if a person's being moral and having the intuitions Habermas refers to turns on something else than what can be achieved by argumentation, the nature of this "else" demands scrutiny. This Habermas's moral theory abstains from offering. Again, is that a virtue or a failure? What

I can say, regardless of the answer, is that my own attempt to account for the preconditions of moral performance aims to shed light on the prephilo-sophical "socialization experiences" Habermas speaks of as informing our moral intuitions. To explore these experiences and intuitions, I have been forced to explode Habermas's cognitivism.

Empathy and Solidarity in Discourse Ethics

In a passage seldom paid attention to, Habermas writes that "where sociocul-tural distance is a factor, concern for the fate of one's neighbor [Nächsten]—who more often than not is anything but close by—is a necessary emotional prerequisite for the cognitive operations expected of participants in dis-course." Does this indicate that Habermas is ready to accommodate his theory to the previously discussed difference that proximity makes to humanity's moral performance? Moreover, what does it take, in terms of specific faculties, to turn the distant other into the Nächsten? Habermas acknowledges a "connection between cognition, empathy, and agape," and he observes that "this integration of cognitive operations and emotional dispositions and attitudes in justifying and applying norms characterizes the mature capacity for moral judgment" (MC, 182).

Now, these are scattered remarks in Habermas's Moral Consciousness and Communicative Action, which is to say that he there indicates rather than elucidates the importance granted emotions in discourse ethics. However, the topic is taken up at greater length in an essay entitled "Justice and Solidarity," which is Habermas's response to the conception of level 6 in Kohlberg's model of moral consciousness. Kohlberg argues that benevolence (Wohlwollen) is as primary a moral principle as justice. On level 6, that is, the two principles mutually support each other: "Benevolence checks the alleged interest in justice so that it remains compatible with the demand for the contentment of all, and considerations of justice restrict benevolence so that it can be combined with a respect for the rights of others as autonomous subjects."[22] The coordination of the two principles ensures that I advance the well-being of others while still respecting their inviolable rights, and vice versa. Accordingly, the moral point of view is concerned with the good for everyone to the same extent. The principle of justice demands that I have equal respect for the integrity and worth of every individual person, and to have the same respect for every person as autonomous subject means to treat all persons equally. In treating all persons equally, the attitude I adopt is one of impartiality. The principle of benevolence, on the other hand, demands that I advance the well-being of other persons and that I protect them against being harmed, against suffering. In seeking to advance another person's well-being, the attitude I adopt is one of identification or empathy; I identify with the other person insofar as he or she is a member of the human race, "bears a human countenance," as Max Scheler puts it. Kohlberg's central thesis, to repeat, is that the two principles are equally fundamental. However, a certain primacy is nonetheless admitted to benevolence: "As a mode of interaction between self and others, which expresses a considerateness for the respect for others that characterizes 'level 6,' benevolence precedes—logically as well as psychologically—that which we term justice."[23] The benevolence postulated for the postconventional level is no longer that guided by empathy—that is to say, the more or less vague relation between two persons—but that of *sympathy*, meaning the understanding of the other person in terms of his or her understanding of him- or herself. The sympathy characteristic of level 6 implies that I recognize the worth and the integrity of other persons in their very uniqueness as individual persons. Recognizing that uniqueness, I cannot claim to have a true understanding of a person's interests; the knowledge of the actual nature of such interests remains a privilege of each person. Persons are understood as "self-determining actors pursuing the actions in which they have an interest."[24]

Habermas welcomes the intention behind Kohlberg's suggestion that the principle of justice be supplemented by one of benevolence, without, however, being prepared to follow Kohlberg all the way. Kohlberg's construction implies an "emotivistic one-sidedness" Habermas finds unacceptable. For Habermas, emotions have a role to play only up to a certain point, beyond which the accomplishments of moral reasoning are exclusively cognitive, or intellectual. Kohlberg's model starts with the simple interaction between at least two communicatively acting individuals. First, it is demanded of ego that he have a sympathetic understanding of alter's situation in the sense of sympathy given above. That is, he must identify with alter in order to understand the perspective from which he would view his hopes, interests, and values in the event of a moral conflict. Second, ego must presuppose that his taking over alter's perspective is reciprocated by alter, that alter takes over the perspective of ego. Finally, ego must transcend the concrete context of his dyadic relation to alter; he must ask whether his proposed course of action, viewed as a universal practice, would find consent among all persons affected by it. This last step demands the universal exchangeability of the perspectives of all persons affected; ego has to imagine himself in the place of every other person. These then are the three basic mental operations demanded of the individual in ideal role taking.

I take Habermas's central claim to be that the move from concrete interaction to the adoption of an abstract-universal perspective that encompasses all particular ones implies a move from an emotional-cognitive accomplishment to a purely cognitive one. He writes, "What was sympathetic empathy and identification under the concrete initial conditions is sublimated at this level [6] to accomplishments that are purely cognitive." To imagine oneself in the place of everyone else, so the argument goes, is a purely cognitive task; as such it involves the "*understanding* for the claims of others that result in each case from particular interest positions" as well as "*consciousness* of a prior solidarity of all concerned that is objectively grounded through socialization." This means that the emotional tie characteristic of face-to-face interaction is suspended or, better, left behind when role taking turns ideal in the sense of becoming abstract-universal as opposed to particular and concrete. As Habermas puts it, "At this level of abstraction, sensitivity to individual claims must be detached from contingent personal ties (and identities), just as the feeling of solidarity must be detached from contingent social ties (and collectivities)" (JS, 234). Emotions—or, more accurately, our faculty of empathy (*Einfühlungsvermögen*)—thus cease to be part of the mental accomplishments demanded of the individual as soon as his or her role taking becomes universal in the sense of level 6.

If this is what Habermas is claiming, he in fact implies that the *act* of transcending, given contextuality toward universality, is exclusively intellectual, neither prompted nor accompanied by our faculty of empathy. To appreciate the full significance of this—which provides the real setup for my discussion—it must be recalled that Habermasian discourse ethics conceives role taking as a discourse model, as a "rational will formation" in the course of which "attitudes are changed through arguments." Now, if emotions are taken to be exhausted in "attitudes," and if the latter are to be subjected to the scrutiny and modification of arguments, the shared primacy and the equality in the division of labor between the principles of justice and benevolence are both shattered in favor of an unequivocal priority of the cognitive faculty over the emphatic one. Viewing role taking as entirely discursive is what prompts Habermas to charge Kohlberg with emotivistic one-sidedness. In Habermas's reading, "the presentation by Kohlberg . . . demonstrates a tendency . . . to view 'dialogue' not as a form of argumentation but as a method from group dynamics for sharpening the capacity for empathy and strengthening social ties." So Habermas's complaint with Kohlberg's equalization of justice and benevolence is that the centrality therein granted our faculty of empathy is maintained *throughout* in the Kohlbergian model of role taking. Hence, the upshot of the so-called emotivism in Kohlberg is that it overshadows what Habermas sees as the "purely cognitive meaning of ideal role-taking as a procedure for the impartial judgment of moral states of affairs" (JS, 234).

Kohlberg and Habermas thus offer two different pictures of what goes on in ideal role taking: whereas Kohlberg depicts the ascendance from context-specific to universal role taking as having throughout the form of a joint undertaking of our cognitive and emotional faculties (in which we cognitively reach an increasingly higher level of reflexivity and abstraction, and in which we emotionally move from simple identification through diffuse empathy toward sympathy as recognition of the integrity *and* uniqueness of alter), Habermas admits our emotional faculty a role only at the start of this movement and not at its final stage, level 6. In Habermas's view, that is, emotions are crucial in the *disclosing* of the world of moral phenomena. However, in the practical discourse itself, on which role taking is now modeled, no place is allowed for the *continued* impact of emotions. The role of emotions is restricted to the initial "opening up" of the moral phenomena to be discussed from a hypothetical point of view, discussion here meaning the purely cognitive redeeming of the validity claim of normative rightness. Such, then, is the difference in overall outlook. But Habermas also pursues a more internal critique in his rejoinder to Kohlberg. The first claim here is that Kohlberg is unsuccessful in establishing "respect" as inherent to his proposed concept of sympathy. Habermas points out that I can have respect for the integrity of another person without caring for his or her well-being, charging that Kohlberg has failed to demonstrate a necessary link between that respect and that caring. The second, related claim is that the principle of equal respect relates to individuals, and to individuals only, thereby precluding my caring for the *common* well-being, or *Allgemeinwohl*. The third, more important claim is that the postulated equality between justice and benevolence remains "associative" rather than convincingly argued for in Kohlberg's model. Here Habermas's stand is the by now familiar one that "with the transition to universalized, completely reversible perspective-taking, not much more is left of a sympathy that is initially directed to concrete reference persons than a purely cognitive feat of understanding" (JS, 243). One may wonder whether this last statement is at all compatible with the tenor of the passage cited above where Habermas contends that the "integration of cognitive operations and emotional dispositions and attitudes in justifying and applying norms characterizes the *mature* capacity for moral judgment" (MC, 182).

Habermas's response to Kohlberg has constructive elements as well. Habermas shares Kohlberg's endorsement of G. H. Mead's thesis that persons are individuated only through a process of socialization, or *Vergesellschaftung*. The development of the individual's identity takes place within a community in which he or she is looked upon as a competent and responsible speaker and actor. Hence, the integrity of individual persons is dependent on the integrity of the interpersonal relations of reciprocal recognition of which they are part. So if the identity of the group they belong to should be threatened, their identity as individuals would be endangered too. While professing commitment to this scheme, Kohlberg fails to do it full justice, insofar as he transposes the concept of equal respect for the worth of everyone into his own, novel concept of the benevolence for the concrete other (*den Nächsten*). Habermas claims that Kohlberg's "benevolence" is unable to ensure the interest for the common good that is supposed to go hand in hand with the care for the well-being of the concrete other; as it stands, benevolence remains tied up with and thus limited to the care for the single individual. Now, the simple preoccupation with the single individual is precisely what care must be capable of transcending, according to Habermas, hereby taking himself to be more loyal to Mead's scheme than Kohlberg. This leads Habermas to replace Kohlberg's individual-centered benevolence with a concept of *solidarity*. The principle of solidarity "is rooted in the realization that each person must take responsibility for the other because as consociates all must have an interest in the integrity of their shared life context in the same way. Justice conceived deontologically requires solidarity as its reverse side." So justice and solidarity are principles of equal status and import, just as justice and benevolence were in Kohlberg. For Habermas, justice refers to the "equal freedoms of unique and self-determining individuals," whereas solidarity refers to the "welfare of consociates who are intimately linked to an intersubjectively shared form of life" (JS, 244). In recognizing the one, moral norms cannot but preserve the other; acknowledging the equal rights and liberties of every individual entails pursuing the well-being of concrete others as well as the community to which they belong. Postulating justice and solidarity as two aspects of the same issue, Habermas purports conformity with Mead's dictum that we are what we are only through our relations with others.

I am not satisfied with Habermas's criticisms of Kohlberg. First, it is not clear to me what is gained by Habermas's exchanging Kohlberg's benevolence for a concept of solidarity. The alleged gain is that solidarity secures the concern for the common good, or the good of the community, whereas benevolence does not. Benevolence, Habermas holds, remains bound up with a care for the concrete other. Benevolence, as understood by Kohlberg, that is, fails to embrace the collective *unity* that a plurality of persons makes up. Habermas's critique of Kohlberg at this point would be an internally valid one only if he succeeded in showing that Kohlberg's "sympathy," being the form benevolence assumes on level 6, fails to comprise the social dimension Habermas has in mind when he, by way of criticism, introduces the alternative concept of solidarity. But as Habermas's argument stands, it contains no discussion of the Kohlbergian sympathy. Habermas keeps referring simply to the "benevolence for the other," only to proceed to make his case for his notion of solidarity in its place, as it were. But the term "benevolence for the other," receiving no further explication, in no way captures the meaning of sympathy as defined on level 6. As far as I can see, Habermas's complaint about social inadequacy might be valid with reference to Kohlberg's notion of empathy, but not with reference to sympathy, the latter having been introduced in Kohlberg's model as a more mature and sophisticated version of the former. "Sympathy," writes Kohlberg, "contains an understanding of the empathic ties existing within at least two connected social dimensions: (a) an understanding of what a 'person' is and (b) an understanding of the *condition humaine*, in which persons exist and interact."[25] So the *condition humaine* is the social dimension implied in sympathy, which is to say that sympathy is *not* restricted to a care for the concrete other only. Far from that, the term *condition humaine* must be interpreted as embracing *all* social settings, all collective unities, insofar as they are made up of human beings. The conclusion to be drawn from this is that benevolence understood as (Kohlbergian) empathy is indeed socially restricted and thus less comprehensive than solidarity; whereas benevolence understood as sympathy—this, significantly, being how Kohlberg defines it on level 6—is just as socially extensive as its purported "improvement," solidarity. Provided my interpretation is correct, Habermas's objection to Kohlberg's concept of benevolence is untenable.

The second, far more important reason for my dissatisfaction with Habermas's critique concerns the role granted to emotions. I take it that one of the main objectives of Kohlberg's admitting the principle of benevolence a shared primacy with that of justice was to develop an argument to the effect that the emotional faculty is principally just as indispensable in moral reasoning—all the way up to level 6—as is the cognitive one. I am sympathetic with such an objective, but I am unhappy about the way Kohlberg actually argues for it. At this point, however, my primary concern is with Habermas.

If the concept of solidarity is to replace that of benevolence, one wonders what becomes of the part played by emotions—be it in the form of simply empathy, be it in the form of comprehensive sympathy—in Kohlberg's coining of benevolence. Put differently, the question is, Does Habermas's solidarity admit emotions the same role as Kohlberg's benevolence? That is to say, Does Habermas allow emotions any systematic impact on the moral deliberation taking place on level 6, where such deliberation is supposed to recognize solidarity to the same degree as justice? Now, I have already given an initial answer to this question. Earlier on, I wrote that for Habermas the move from simple to universal role taking is a move from an emotional-cognitive accomplishment to a purely cognitive one. There can be no doubt that Habermas's overall position is that what we exercise as participants in a practical discourse is but "rein kognitiven Leistungen," that is, a purely cognitive accomplishment. Habermas, therefore, in exchanging benevolence for solidarity, seems to disavow the emotional component of the Kohlbergian conception. Indeed, it would seem that emotions do not survive the concep-tual change, which is to say that the concept of solidarity is robbed of the emotional ballast with which Kohlberg's benevolence is so strongly—and rightly—equipped. Hence, for Habermas to remain faithful to his overall view, he has to make sure that the deliberation on level 6 bars the impact of emotions and remains purely cognitive; were he, on the contrary, to remain faithful to Kohlberg's premises, he would be forced to allow equal importance to the emotional and cognitive faculties alike.

Contrary to expectation, in the essays "Morality and Ethical Life" and "Justice and Solidarity," Habermas asserts the equal importance of both principles, observing that "without unrestricted individual freedom to assess validity claims, the agreement that is actually reached could not be truly universal; but without the empathy of each person in the situation for everyone else, which is derived from solidarity, no resolution capable of consensus could be found" (JS, 247; cf. MC, 202–3). In other words, *solidarische Einfühlung* (a solidaristic feeling-into) is called for in the delibera-tions taking place in a practical discourse. Emotions, then, are not altogether left behind the moment discourse is entered into; it now appears that the role of emotions is not restricted to that of giving us an access to the world of moral phenomena *überhaupt*, that is, to that of disclosure. So far so good.

But what precisely does the empathy of the *solidarische Einfühlung* referred to mean? How does it compare with Kohlberg's sympathy? This, I claim, is a question that goes unanswered in Habermas's account. The notion of *Einfühlung* in Habermas remains unexplicated; it is paid lip-service to rather than elaborated on.

But how could it be otherwise? Given Habermas's expressed intention to correct the alleged "emotivistic one-sidedness" of Kohlberg by way of interpreting the "role-taking model from the outset as a discourse model," the answer to the question I have raised is clearly predetermined in favor of a cognitivistic outlook—an outlook, I claim, *more* one-sided than the Kohlbergian one, where emotions, far from overshadowing cognition, are granted *equal* importance. As far as I can see, once the model of role taking is held to be wholly translatable to the model of discourse, the question of the systematic place for emotions is decided, and decided *negatively*, meaning that emotions are left out: being from *vornherein* (the very outset) discourse, role taking is turned into an exclusively cognitive process. Viewing role taking as discourse means submitting it to a cognitive purification emotions have no prospect of surviving; it means focusing exclusively on the vindication of the validity claim of normative rightness. Discourse, we read, is the "reflective form of communicative action"; it is "in fact . . . argumentation" (JS, 235).

Yet in introducing the concept of solidarity, Habermas has given himself an opportunity to confront his discourse ethics squarely with the issue of emotions, for the simple reason that "solidarity" evokes in us the recollection of experiences that are not so much cognitive-intellectual as emotional. When we say that we "have" solidarity with somebody, this having is determined as well as accompanied by some kind of feeling, of *engagement* (in French), for the particular somebody concerned. A person incapable of feeling affection for others, that is, of empathy in the sense of a feeling-into, would be unsuccessful in convincing us that he or she had solidarity with another person. Perhaps this is overemphasizing the emotional component of solidarity; it is not intended to present solidarity as merely emotional, but rather as fundamentally resting on ego's ability to become affected (*betroffen*) by alter's situation or, put negatively, by ego's inability to remain emotionally indifferent with regard to the situation in which alter finds himself. These are just so many words to make the point that *solidarity presupposes empathy*. Although Habermas retains the Kohlbergian connotation of benevolence as care for the well-being of the concrete other, he shifts the basic reference of solidarity from the person-intimate to the larger social domain. The principle of solidarity, he writes, "is rooted in the realization that each person must take responsibility for the other because as consociates all must have an interest in the integrity of their shared life context the same way" (JS, 244). Thus, to care for another person is never a private matter; care in the sense here intended always transcends the particular person to whom it is directed; it comprises the community of which both persons are members, so that in caring for you, I care for us, and in caring for us, I care for our community, and in caring for our community I contribute to its sustenance as an identity-producing social unit.

So Habermas explains his notion of solidarity by appealing to the "experience that the one [ego] must stand up to the other." What sort of experience is this? Evidently it cannot be a purely cognitive or intellectual matter; it must involve feelings of some kind or another. But what sort of feelings do we have for the community to which Habermas's concept of solidarity ultimately refers? Are not feelings, so to speak, by definition directed to concrete persons rather than abstract collective entities? Indeed, it must be admitted that feelings always arise within some socially narrow context, that they are shared and cultivated by and between individuals who see each other as in some way personally related, and that feelings therefore are prompted by my experiencing another person in a specific way, that is, by my taking an interest in that person. Hence, when we react emotionally, we do so as concrete persons moved to act or react by other concrete persons. Conversely, the more abstract persons are rendered to us, the smaller is the probability that we become emotionally involved in their well-being or lack of such. So a correlation obtains between concreteness and affectedness, and likewise between abstractness and indifference. The moral significance of this is that the more abstract alter appears to ego, the more emotionally and morally indifferent ego will be toward alter.

Habermas seems to hold that in his discourse ethics, the indicated problem of having to bridge the apparent abyss between the concrete and the abstract, between the individual and the community at large, does not arise. His view is the Hegelian one that the individual person is a carrier (*Träger*) of the society to which he or she belongs, so that what we encounter in the concrete person is not merely particular but also universal. Brought to bear on the concept of solidarity, this entails that my having solidarity with you is *eo ipso* my having solidarity with the social unity or lifeworld of which both of us are members. So the whole is met in each of its parts. Thus, the individual who has done somebody wrong must realize that "in offending the particular person, he has also violated something impersonal or at least suprapersonal, namely a generalized expectation that both parties hold"

(MC, 48). Personal interaction generates emotional reactions the specific moral quality of which lies in their impersonality, in the universality of the normative *Verhaltenserwartung* that is violated in the *Gestalt* of my particular cosubject. I take it that this model is inspired by the young Hegel's analysis of the criminal—approvingly dealt with in Habermas's *Theory and Practice*—where he shows how the criminal, in failing to respect the shared morality and ethos of his or her society, profoundly undermines his or her own identity and self-respect.[26]

The interaction from which Habermas's reconstructive account of solidarity starts involves a "we," implying that I violate an established norm in my behavior toward you, thereby *eo ipso* violating the "we" that is the community we both belong to. Accordingly, solidarity as defined by Habermas is an "experience" where recourse is had to the circumstance that "as consociates all must have an interest in the integrity of their shared life context in the same way" (JS, 244). Hence, the interaction that generates solidarity is conceived of as one in which I myself take part, and the social unity that is violated through the relevant piece of interaction is one I already belong to; it is a "we." But can this really be all there is to solidarity? Does it capture its essence? I think not. Rather, I take solidarity to concern others, abstract and absent, rather than concrete and present, others at that, so that our ability to have solidarity is put to the test not so much when we are participants in interaction as when we are not, which is to say that solidarity addresses a "they" rather than a "we." Solidarity in my sense is expected primarily of the spectator, secondarily of the participant. *A* might be expected by *B* to have solidarity with *B*'s being harmed by *C*, keeping in mind that *B* and *C* might belong to different societies than *A*. Hence, solidarity more often than not assumes the form of my being called upon to take a step toward interaction, as opposed to Habermas's conception where I am already engaged in some ongoing interaction. The call for solidarity is contained in the question (actually a moral demand) How can you remain passive? How can you be content to go on as if this did not happen to us here?

My proposal, then, is that the subject exercising solidarity is initially passive rather than active, a spectator rather than a participant, emotionally indifferent rather than affected. The demand of solidarity, its moral challenge, is that I *turn* active and affected, that I negate the passivity in which I find myself toward the persons who are being harmed and who therefore are the addressees of my act of solidarity. What is involved in this demand is, first, that we are *appealed* to—appealed to as individuals who might live somewhere else and be preoccupied with other worries but who, significantly, are first of all human beings. That is, the appeal sets up an identity that purports to bridge the given gap—be it political or social, religious or geographical. Second, the appeal demands that we are moved to engage in actions that appropriately express our solidarity. For us to actually make such a move, it would seem that something more real, more concrete, is needed than the sheer appeal to our "being humans too," this seeming very abstract and elusive. In short, the bridging of the gap referred to cannot take the highly abstract form of a shared identity as men or women, as embodiments of "humankind"; some moment of particularity is required to trigger the act of genuine concern for a distant "they." We must, that is, be somehow personally affected by being informed that B is affected by the harm done by C. Now, being thus affected cannot be a purely intellectual matter; it must also—rather, it must in the first place—involve our emotional faculty. A Mr. Harris, in a letter to the *Guardian* (London) on the students' revolt in China, succinctly expresses this idea when he writes that "I wept as I read of what happened in Beijing. Despair turns to anger, and then to shame. I consider how I, as a citizen of the 'free West,' am implicated in the killing" (7 June 1989, 2). Being a spectator, this writer directs the demand for solidarity to himself, and a fortiori to the entire public of spectators. The peculiar moral content of his appeal to himself lies in the feeling that he cannot go on viewing himself as a human being in the full sense of the term, that is, as the kind of person he wishes to be, were he to remain passive. Note that his appeal for action invokes the notion of shame; in professing that he would be ashamed not to negate his passivity, he implies that others too would be ashamed of themselves if they remained passive onlookers. The moral thrust of this "would be" lies in its characteristically being a "should be": others *should* perceive the killings in China as the same kind of challenge to their view of themselves, to their self-respect, as does Mr. Harris. What his letter helps illuminate, then, is the internal link between shame and self-respect. As Gabriele Taylor correctly points out, "if someone has self-respect then under certain specifiable conditions he will be feeling shame. A person has no self-respect if he regards no circumstances as shame-producing. Loss of self-respect and loss of the capacity for feeling shame go hand in hand."[27]

What Mr. Harris captured in so few words is precisely what Charles Taylor—to recall Chapter 4—has in mind when he speaks about "import." In identifying the import of a given situation, Mr. Harris picked out "what in the situation gives the grounds or basis of our feelings, or what could give such grounds, or perhaps should give such grounds, if we feel nothing or have inappropriate feelings."[28] In this sense, the import of the current events in China for Mr. Harris was that he felt himself called upon to act; the demand that he show solidarity was prompted by external events but, significantly, was nonetheless self-imposed, in that it, by invoking shame, referred him to his self-respect. Such an act of solidarity presupposes that the event in question represents a violation against some specific rights of another being, insofar as these rights are viewed as constitutive of the very being of that being, and that the event carries an import for us in the sense of demanding a response from us by virtue of our being the kind of beings we are, that is, moral beings. Hence, solidarity sets up a correspondence; it contains a recognition of the inviolable humanity of the threatened other that I feel called upon to exercise in order that I continue to recognize myself in my full humanity; in respecting the inviolability of the other, I preserve my self-respect. I cannot, in a word, go on recognizing myself without recognizing the other. Now, as Mr. Harris's unmistakable display of indignation helped show, our direct, intuitive experience of import is through feeling; and feeling, asserts Charles Taylor, "is our mode of access to the entire domain of subject-referring imports [e.g., shame], of what matters to us qua subjects, or of what it is to be human."[29]

The notion of solidarity I advance here represents a supplement to Habermas's in that I stress the relation with the "foreign" other, whereas his focus is on the "near" one. But what is philosophically important is the precise nature of the interplay between the faculties of empathy and imagination in solidarity, and this interplay is best appreciated in acts of solidarity with foreign and distant others because here the faculty of empathy is in need of the assistance yielded by the faculty of abstraction (i.e., imagination) to be led to its object. It is on this formal level of constitution (viz., how we arrive at the specific object of solidarity), rather than on the sociological one of concrete extension ("near" versus "distant" addressee), that I see the more vital philosophical issue.

It might be objected here that my discussion has rendered solidarity so wholly dependent on empathy as to be virtually inseparable from it. In short, I am charged with reducing solidarity to empathy. My response is that this is not the case. Yet I realize the need for making a more systematic distinction.

Empathy is our basic emotional faculty; it is captured in the German *Einfühlungsvermögen*, that is, the capacity of "feeling into." Empathy originates and is fostered within a small-scale setting, where communication takes place on a face-to-face basis and where the participants are physically copresent. The genuinely *moral* significance of empathy lies in its other-directedness. It is not only that ego's empathy relates to alter, sets up a relation, and establishes some emotional tie and personal bond between the two; it is also that the very origin and initial cultivation of ego's capacity for empathy can be traced back to an interpersonal relation (typically that between mother and child) as the setting that is the *conditio sine qua non* for the emergence of empathy. Simply put, the implication here is that a lack of empathy is due to a lack of empathy, meaning that individuals whose primary love objects or self-objects have failed to display empathy toward them may thus themselves fail to develop empathy toward others. Because of the relative narrowness of empathy's original social range, it takes an act of imagination, of mental abstraction, to extend one's empathy to unknown and nonexperienced others (or, to be more precise, to secondary, as opposed to primary, experienced others). *This extension is exactly what takes place in solidarity.* Solidarity is directed toward persons with whom we, at least initially, entertain no ongoing business; its social context therefore is that of a large-scale setting. Thus, solidarity initially presupposes some social distance between subject and addressee, whereas the act of developing and demonstrating solidarity is likely to bring about a—temporary more often than permanent—*suspension* of that very distance. Every act of solidarity renders this pregiven distance less psychically real—for both parties. The suspension of the distance between the subject and his or her addressee(s) is the work of empathy in solidarity, without which it would not come about. This, then, is my conception of the relation between empathy and solidarity.

Returning again to the discussion of Habermas, the question is, What follows for discourse ethics from my thesis that solidarity presupposes empathy? The concept of solidarity introduced by Habermas is too narrow to capture its full meaning; solidarity, that is, involves our relation to otherness, to them, and not primarily our relations with one another; it is eminently *inter*communal in addressing a "they" as opposed to a preestablished "we"; indeed, it concerns the very relation *between* us and them. Solidarity challenges us to respond in a morally appropriate manner to what happens to abstract and absent others with whom we have never interacted. We sustain our self-respect qua moral beings through acts displaying our respect for others; what is demanded from us in solidarity with others is only what we demand from ourselves qua moral beings; though triggered by external events, the peculiar moral obligation in solidarity is fundamentally a self-imposed one. According to the argument I have offered, to develop and foster solidarity is not one-sidedly or even predominantly a cognitive accomplishment; rather, it is a complex process involving the interplay of cognitive and emotional faculties. More specifically, the function of our empathy peculiar to promoting solidarity is *to render the abstract concrete*, to turn the situation of those remote and unknown others into something to which we can relate qua human beings *schlechthin*. Note that the movement thereby indicated goes in a direction opposite to the movement demanded in the domain in Kant's "pure practical reason": whereas empathy as presupposed in solidarity requires of us that we turn the situation of the abstract, absent, alien other into something concrete, present, familiar, to which we can always relate qua subjects already "knowing" what it would mean to find ourselves in "such a situation," Kant's practical reason as employed in moral judgment demands of us that we transcend the narrow particularity of our interaction context in order to make sure that *everybody* likely to be affected by our proposed course of action would approve of it. So whereas empathy as presupposed in solidarity is a movement from the abstract to the concrete, the practical reason of Kant is a movement from the concrete to the abstract, concerned with the universalizability of our maxim of action and thereby thematizing its implicitly raised normative validity claim. Let me repeat here that the accomplishment involved in solidarity is by no means solely "emotional." Emotions alone would never move us to genuine solidarity. For us to arrive at the absent other, the principal addressee of solidarity, in the first place, an act of *imagination* is called for wherein empathy is led to its object, as it were, and without which our capacity for empathy would remain restricted to a socially pregiven "we," as distinct from the "they" on which solidarity focuses. The *interplay of faculties* at work in solidarity can be described as follows: whereas our faculty of imagination, in the sense of a transcendence of given spatiotemporal contextuality, provides us with a mental access to what is absent and unknown, our faculty of empathy, in the sense of a feeling-into, brings the initially absent and unknown—to which it is led by an act of imagination—"back" to us, this bringing-back implying the psychical suspension of the distance between subject and addressee from which the process started out. Thus, whereas Habermas's conception takes a preestablished intracommunal "we" as its focus, my account shows the act of solidarity, pictured as intercommunal, to *produce* an encompassing "we" where at first there were a "we" and a "they."

The interplay of faculties by virtue of which solidarity gains its object, its specific addressee, is neglected in the account given by Habermas. Its neglect can be explained, I believe, by the fact that Habermas's treatment of solidarity assumes the addressee to be already *given* to the subjects expected to display solidarity. This givenness of the addressee is not accounted for; it is merely presupposed, and as such *prior to* the entire analysis. Consequently, Habermas is silent on the question how the *access* to the addressee of solidarity is gained. To raise this question means to raise the issue of perception, and this is exactly what Habermas fails to do. In speaking of "concern for the fate of one's neighbour—*who more often than not is anything but close by*" (MC, 182; emphasis added), Habermas in my view captures the kernel of what solidarity is all about. But he leaves us ignorant of how his "concern" comes about as long as he overlooks the interplay between imagination and empathy just sketched. As I see it, this interplay explains the *possibility* of *der Fernste* becoming *der Nächste*; that is to say, his or her becoming so is the accomplishment not of judgment (and be it that judgment peculiar to level 6 in Kohlberg) but of perception, whereby perception "gives" judgment its distinct object. My analysis of perception aims at going beyond the naïvely presupposed "givenness" of the object and subjecting its occurrence to a separate inquiry. Note again (to recall the above section on Apel and Habermas) that the question dealt with in my analysis of perception— that is, how a subject gains access to the object on which judgment is passed—is to be strictly separated from the question of motivation. Put differently, the aim of the above analysis is to show how empathy is an indispensable precondition for an act of solidarity to come about; the aim is not to investigate what kind of motives people have for showing solidarity with others. Indeed, I consider such a topic to lie outside the scope of moral theory.

This discussion bears on the issue of the extension of empathy raised in the chapter on perception. My treatment of empathy in the preceding section applies to the issue of its extension as directed to *absent others*. It is precisely the nonpresence of the addressee that necessitates the assistance yielded to empathy by the faculty of imagination. Hence, in the many cases where the other is absent and unknown, there can be no question of my "feeling" how the other feels; what happens here is rather that my empathy capacity is guided by imagination to the place of the other, to the particular context in which his or her weal is at stake. Admittedly, these are very general observations. To hold that they must be so is, however, part of the position I wish to defend. At this point in the argument, it is easily recognized that a number of philosophers have been struggling to find the appropriate formulation for a powerful idea that has long been one and the same: to perceive *der Fernste* as if he or she were *der Nächste*. Kant captured the idea in his concept of *die erweiterte Denkungsart*; Hannah Arendt, drawing on Kant's third *Critique*, termed "representative thinking" the process of "being and thinking in my own identity where actually I am not"; and Habermas, most recently, has started from the same idea in his attempt to accommodate Mead's ideal role taking and Kohlberg's principle of reversibility within the model of a practical discourse. Yet for all their insight and merit, these three formulations suffer from the same weakness: they all commit themselves to a *monistic* view of the accomplishment required of the moral subject; they all, that is, seek to trace the accomplishment back to *one* specific faculty of humanity; and they all identify this faculty as being wholly cognitive-intellectual. Arendt, in particular, typically plays empathy and imagination against each other—as if they represented profound opposites—only to discard the former and absolutize the latter; she thus never entertained the hypothesis that the two might *support* each other and inhabit equal performative importance. In this latter view, which of course is my own, "imagination" is the most promising answer to the problem of the extension of empathy precisely because monistic and reductionistic theories are misguided; empathy, that is to say, cannot by itself, of its own inherent force, reach out toward and embrace the addressee in cases where he or she is situated outside of the context in which the faculty of empathy is ontogenetically fostered and socially exchanged. Here, the assistance yielded by our capacity for imagination, for rendering the absent present and thus for "being and thinking where actually I am not," is downright indispensable. To sum up, then, solidarity as conceived of in my account presupposes imagination no less than empathy; the point is to leave room for both.

Recent history bears witness to the eminent moral force of the "we"-identity produced by empathy's suspension of distance, for example, of the psychic distance between a perpetrator and his or her victim(s). Hence, it was a systematic aim of leading Nazis to *prevent* the distance-suspending and "we"-identity–producing force of empathy from coming about. In short, one had to make sure that killing was rendered and subsequently *kept* abstract and, so, "beyond" emotional involvement and the moral concerns that go hand in hand with it. As long as the killers, that is, could touch, see, and hear the victims, they remained affected by the emotional tie intrinsic to face-to-face interaction, affected by the victims as *persons* and as *their* victims. To apply the terms just elucidated, the Nazis sought to prevent the perception of a larger "we" that is the accomplishment of empathy and to set up—by way of dehumanization—a supposedly unbridgeable gap between a constructed "us" and a constructed "them," between humans and so-called subhumans. [30]

Habermas's theoretical preoccupation with solidarity is foremost sociological, as demonstrated in his use of the term in *The Theory of Communicative Action* (esp. 2:139ff.). "Solidarity" in that work refers to the ongoing social integration of a group of individuals; it is distinctly intracommunal in that it partakes in the symbolic reproduction of a lifeworld. So whereas solidarity as understood by Habermas helps reproduce an already established shared social identity, solidarity as depicted in my model above helps produce a novel, enlarged "we"-identity where previously there were a "we" and a "they," that is to say, two separate and unrelated we's. Thus, my intercommunal solidarity *sets up* a social relation and a novel identity, where Habermas's intracommunal solidarity presupposes one and addresses the question of its future sustenance.

What follows from the position outlined here is that Habermas has—as yet—failed to pay adequate attention to the specific function of empathy in his discourse model of ideal role taking. My account has sought to bring out the internal link between empathy and solidarity. I have wanted to show that the intracommunal aspect of solidarity—which I of course do not deny—cannot be all there is to solidarity when viewed from a moral, as opposed to a sociological, perspective. Solidarity, that is, is not morally exhausted in the intracommunal setting but rather comes to its fore in the intercommunal one, namely, as an act prompted by the moral obligation to recognize *others*. The *Einfühlungsvermögen* invoked in *solidarische Einfühlung* remains a blind spot in discourse ethics, albeit less so in Habermas than in Apel; it is occasionally referred to but never systematically accounted for within the larger theoretical framework. The irreducible emotional features in Kohlberg's discarded notion of sympathy were thrown overboard the moment Habermas exchanged the principle of benevolence with that of solidarity. Introduced in its stead was a concept of solidarity whose emotional features went practically unthematized and whose social setting was the implausibly limited one of a given "we" in which both the subject and the addressee of solidarity were already participating. Thus, the more important moral problem of the solidarity of the spectator-subject was neglected, and with that the crucial function of empathy. However, the very narrowness of this "solidarity" provided me with the possibility of advancing an immanent critique; the concept simply failed to do justice to even a commonsense understanding of what we in fact do when we exercise or, conversely, call for solidarity. In the course of exploding Habermas's notion of solidarity from within, the function of empathy could finally receive its due attention. My larger claim is that the exercise of solidarity may help highlight what goes on in moral reasoning *überhaupt*. Both versions of one-sidedness are to be avoided: qua moral act, solidarity is neither a purely cognitive nor a purely emotional process; it inevitably presupposes both faculties alike, granting primacy to neither of them. Solidarity, then, involves the cognitive faculty of universalization, or rendering the particular abstract, as well as the emotional faculty of being affected, or rendering the abstract concrete, the alien human. The practical reason at work in Kant's *erweiterte Denkungsart* and in Hannah Arendt's "representative thinking" helps me relate intellectually to the all-embracing community of "all affected parties"; the empathy at work in our ability to be affected by the affectedness of the other helps me relate emotionally to the particular situation of an often unknown and nonexperienced other. It is our capacity to employ both faculties in seeking to come to grips with moral issues that makes us the beings we are; it is the systematic attention to the role of both faculties alike that makes for a sound moral theory.

Habermas and the Place of Emotion in Moral Judgment

I have tried to show that Habermas's case against an alleged emotivistic one-sidedness in Kohlberg fails to recognize the consistency with which Kohlberg's model of role taking maintains a *balance* between the accomplishment of humanity's cognitive and emotional abilities. Seeking to substantiate my critique in a constructive manner, I put forward a conception of solidarity that does justice to the interplay between our cognitive and our emotional faculties, that is to say, between imagination and empathy, respectively.

However, my critical discussion of Habermas is in need of an addendum. Based on his publications up to 1986, the above account fails to capture the complexity of Habermas's position as it emerges in the light of his most recent writings on discourse ethics. Since Habermas has asserted that the "role-taking model from the outset [is to be interpreted] as a discourse model—in fact, [as] argumentation" (JS, 235), I maintained that his portrait of what goes on in ideal role taking appears to render it *wholly cognitive*; and this, to be sure, is the prominent tendency, or "pull," in Habermas's theorizing about morality that I have focused on above. However, in other contexts of discussion, Habermas articulates a view of ideal role taking that in fact, as far as I can see, is more differentiated than the conclusion reached in his critique of Kohlberg.

Consider this passage in Habermas's 1990 interview with Hviid Nielsen: "At least empathy, that is, the capacity for feeling into [*einfühlen*] and overcoming the cultural distances to foreign and prima facie incomprehensible life conditions, reactions, and interpretations, is an emotional prerequisite for an ideal role taking in which the adoption of the perspective of all the others is demanded of everyone" (NR, 143; translated by the author). This statement invites comparison with the cited criticisms of Kohlberg. Whereas Habermas, in taking Kohlberg to task for his so-called emotivistic one-sidedness, had argued that emotions (i.e., Kohlberg's "sympathy") have no legitimate role to perform once we engage in "universalized, completely reversible perspective-taking" (JS, 243), Habermas now argues that precisely this accomplishment is made possible for the subject with the help of a "generalized sympathy." Habermas says about this sympathy that it "sublimates itself into the capacity for empathy and goes beyond the affective ties to those others who are close to us; it opens our eyes to the 'difference,' that is, to the separateness and uniqueness of the other stubbornly claiming his otherness" (NR, 143).

Habermas here goes so far in according empathy an indispensable moral significance that he, in effect, challenges or at least downplays his cited cognitivist objections to Kohlberg's model. His position on the matter thus comes to resemble my own. The statements cited from the interview with Hviid Nielsen grant empathy a continued impact on the moral subject's performance even at the level of universal reversibility of perspectives. The claim could be put like this (in my own terminology): the faculty of empathy sensitizes us to the vulnerability we as humans are endowed with; empathy also, guided to its addressee by imagination, helps us recognize the vulnerability of others when they are distant and unknown to us, rather than encountered in conditions of proximity. In this view, there is no point or level of ideal role taking at which the sensitizing function of empathy would cease to fulfill a legitimate function. Empathy possesses a potential for transcending the narrow confines of proximity-based face-to-face interaction, as Habermas now also acknowledges; yet to accomplish this act of transcendence so as to reach the distant and unknown other(s), the faculty of empathy needs to be accompanied by the faculty of imagination.

Moral emotions, Habermas implies in a recent essay, are not to be dismissed as arbitrary and capricious. "Moral emotions, in which a sense of justice inheres, are not merely spontaneous affects; they are intuitions rather than impulses; what is articulated in moral emotions is, in an emphatic sense, a correct insight" (TK, 112; translated by the author). But this is not to say that what our feelings tell us will always be right when seen from the moral point of view. As I pointed out in Chapter 5, there is no link between emotions in general and a sound moral performance. Habermas, albeit from a different perspective, makes what I take to be a similar point when he observes that "moral emotions, however, despite their indispensable cognitive function, have no monopoly of truth. In the final instance, it is up to moral judgments to bridge a gap unbridgeable by emotions. In the end we must have recourse to moral *insights*, when everything carrying a human countenance is to have a claim to moral considerateness" (NR, 143; translated by the author). So, although Habermas sees a place for feelings—"in questions of justification of norms and their application, feelings have an invaluable heuristic function"—he is quick to mark the limits to the moral importance of feelings: "for the assessment of the phenomena they disclose, [feelings] cannot be the final instance" (NR, 144).

I have no difficulty endorsing these statements. As I read them, they are wholly compatible with my own views as developed in preceding chapters. Our emotional abilities sensitize us to and thus help us see that a phenomenon or situation carries moral relevance, that is, that it involves the weal and woe of others. This is the crucial sense in which our capacity to feel opens up the world of moral phenomena to us. The faculty of empathy is recognized as constitutive in the exercise of moral perception (Habermas first argued to this effect when he, speaking of feelings rather than empathy, discussed Strawson in 1983 [see MC, 45–50]). However, although feelings thus conceived help us see the moral phenomenon, they are not to be taken as being the yardstick by which the normative *rightness* and *justice* of a norm, or a proposed course of action, are determined. The yardstick for the justification of the act must be localized elsewhere than in the feelings. In discourse ethics, this yardstick is Kantian. As Habermas says, "The prototype is Kant's categorical imperative, understood not as a maxim of action but as a principle of justification." This means that the "point of view of impartial judgment is assured through a universalization principle that designates as valid precisely those norms that *everyone* could *will*" (JS, 228, 229).

So Habermas allows a place for feelings in perception but excludes them from the procedure of justification. The latter is a matter of practical reason, conceived dialogically, not monologically. Actions and norms are justified by way of argument; the central criterion for their justification is whether the norm under consideration can be assented to by all affected parties. Consent is given or withheld on the exclusive basis of the rational force (*Überzeugungskraft*) of the arguments. We undertake the justification of norms from "the moral point of view." We adopt the moral point of view, Habermas implies, solely in our capacity as rational beings, as Kantian *Vernunftwesen*, and not in our joint cognitive-emotional capacities. To repeat, Habermas's main criticism of Kohlberg's model was that it failed to acknowledge the "purely cognitive accomplishment" we perform on the level of a "universal inter-changeability of the perspectives of all concerned" (JS, 233–34).

As far as I can see, if feelings are crucial to the disclosure of the domain of moral phenomena (as Habermas has argued since 1983), this must mean that our emotional capacities are instrumental in guiding us to and thus in helping us gain a moral point of view, that is, to the point of view from which moral conflicts can be, first, recognized *as such* and, second, judged in terms of the interests of all affected parties. In other words, our emotional capacities—by which I of course here intend the faculty of empathy—in helping us see "the moral," help us adopt the point of view from which we can argue about and judge affairs deemed "moral." (To be sure, a deeper question is buried here. For is it not more convincing to say, as I have implied on numerous occasions, that to exercise our faculty of empathy toward others *is already* to be committed to a "moral point of view," than it is to say that our emotional capacities "guide us" to the—not yet adopted, as it were—moral point of view? Indeed, in my thesis, to perceive, encounter, and approach the other in my capacity as *(mit)fühlendes Wesen* is to perceive him or her in a moral light. Again, this helps explain why insensitivity entails moral blindness.)

But if the line of thinking before the parentheses is a correct exposition of Habermas's view, it makes no sense to bar, as does Habermas in his critique of Kohlberg, our emotional capacities from the performance required by the subject at the level of a universalization of perspectives. Rather, the moral subject *throughout*, that is to say, on all levels of ideal role taking, exercises his or her cognitive-emotional capacities. It is qua emotional as well as rational being that the subject gains and retains a moral point of view. So the exercise of moral capacities and the adoption of a moral point of view presuppose an emotional as well as a cognitive faculty.

However, the yardstick by which the validity claim of normative rightness is vindicated is of a different nature. As indicated above, feelings neither establish nor embody this yardstick. It is easy to see why this is so. If actual feelings were to be the locus of the yardstick, no common-meaning intersub-jective yardstick would be found; most likely the yardstick would not only differ from person to person but also change in the same person from one situation to the other. Justification, if thus subject to the arbitrariness of (in the last instance) personal sympathies and antipathies, would be but a sham. I therefore agree that *actual feelings* are unsuited as a yardstick for the resolution of conflicting normative validity claims. Obviously, such a yardstick must be the same, and equally binding, for all moral subjects. Like Habermas, I see no candidate here that would be superior to the criterion of universalization worked out by Kant.

Even though the Kantian criterion of universalization—that is, considering whether a proposed course of action would be consented to by all affected parties—is in my opinion superior to other yardsticks to guide moral judgment, a number of factors may call its adequacy into question. On the concrete level, to judge how best to act so as to be in keeping with the Kantian yardstick is something that will often run into serious difficulties. In the many cases where the conditions of perception and judgment are far from ideal, much less transparent, what we, from the standpoint of theory, demand of the actor is that he or she—always *in medias res*—be able to judge soundly in the face of unprecedented events while being affected by cognitive fragmentation and while having only exploded categories at his or her disposal (cf. the discussion of Hannah Arendt in Chapter 2). This, of course, is to push the less-than-ideal circumstances of moral perception, judgment, and action to an extreme. But it serves as a useful reminder that, however convincing and consistent in theory, any candidate for an overriding yardstick in moral affairs is likely to prove exceedingly hard to live up to in actual practice.

Another field of problems, on the level of theory, is the critique of the Kantian-Habermasian universalization criterion to the effect that there is no single criterion to decide what is the morally right thing to do, just as there is no single principle to decide about all goods, so as to rank them in a manner valid for all arising conflicts. Charles Taylor, in a particularly forceful critique, combats the penchant of the mainstream form of moral philosophy "for a unitary conception of the 'moral,' based on a single criterion." In Taylor's view, there exists a "diversity of goods for which a valid claim can be made"; "the goods may be in conflict, but for all that they don't refute each other."[31] I will not go into the contestation over the primacy of the right over the good that lies behind Taylor's argument. I only wish to make the point that we as moderns are committed to a plurality of rights and goods in view of whose often rivaling claims a *single* criterion to resolve the rivalry is perhaps simply not to be had. Indeed, it may limit our moral perception and judgment and so shrink "our" moral universe if we in all arising situations wish to subsume their features to a unitary, overriding principle. This may lead to selectivity, dogmatism, and blindness; it may thus undermine moral performance instead of guiding it. A preparedness to "consider all affected parties" may be grossly inadequate to guide the actor's judgment; in any case, much situation-specific interpretation is called for. [32]

In subjecting moral phenomena to normative evaluation, that is, in judging a moral issue with a view toward acting rightly concerning it, the agent cannot allow his or her feelings to prevail as the yardstick of evaluation. If the agent simply acts on what he or she feels, unmediated by judgment, his or her action may turn out to be, well, moral *or* immoral, there being no way to decide which a priori, as it were. To observe this is only to recall my argument in Chapter 5. This may appear unproblematic. But it does not mean that my position here is at one with Habermas's. If I am not mistaken, there is in Habermas an inference typical of the tradition of moral philosophy within which he writes. The inference is as follows: (1) since the yardstick by which we distinguish between morally right and wrong is upheld by practical reason and hence of a cognitive nature, thereby securing the impartiality of the "moral point of view," it follows that (2) the powers we exercise in passing moral judgment are of an exclusively cognitive nature. In other words, one infers from the yardstick that we relate to *a fronte*, to the resources in the moral agent that he draws on *a tergo*. Since the yardstick is cognitive, the powers required in the judging subject are taken to be so as well.

The inference is false: (2) does not follow from (1). To hold that it does is to misconstrue what goes on in moral performance. In the sequence triggered by perception, passing through judgment, and issuing in action, the relevance and impact of the agent's emotional abilities are not restricted to the level of perception. Rather, the emotional abilities—by which I mean the faculty of empathy—also participate on the level of judgment. Habermas disagrees; he limits the impact of emotional abilities to the level of perception. As far as the exercise of moral judgment is concerned, I take Habermas to remain a spokesman for the (common) view that to grant emotional abilities an impact here would mean to jeopardize the impartiality of judgment.

I will not repeat my case for the thesis that the exercise of moral judgment requires emotional as well as cognitive capacities in the subject. The reader will recall my argument in Chapter 2, where I discussed the case of Eichmann. To show why the inference referred to is false, I invoke an illustration introduced in Chapter 4.

The example runs like this: I take Carl to make an insulting remark to his wife Sophie. I take him, that is, to humiliate her in front of me, and I deliberate about whether to intervene, to act against Carl. Before deciding what, if any, action to take, I face a number of questions. Did he humiliate her? My instant indignation no doubt suggests he did, but I could be wrong. If he did humiliate her, why does Sophie let him get away with it? Didn't she notice? Can it be that she doesn't care? Or is it, rather, that she wants, and expects me to intervene—on her behalf, as it were? If so, do I have any right to interfere in the situation, and does Sophie have any right to expect me to? Should I rather leave an argument to the two of them? But if I do take Carl to have humiliated her, would it not be cowardly of me to pretend I don't notice, or to pretend I don't care? And what about the prehistory? Is Carl retaliating?

To be sure, my illustration fails entirely when it comes to raising moral issues of the most profound and principal order. Yet the illustration has the merit of realism; it is intended to capture the kind of everyday-life moral dilemmas we struggle to come to terms with on the run-of-the-mill microlevel of moral performance. Prima facie, it appears as if only cognitive capacities are required of me in the scene I have portrayed. I want to reach a sound judgment about how to act. If I am to act, I must do so pretty soon. Now, as in the discussion of the example in Chapter 4, my endeavor to reach an appropriate judgment directs me back to a renewed engagement with my first intuitive perception of the scene at hand. The original perception reads, He humiliates her. It is instantly accompanied by a mounting feeling of indignation in me. The perception is, phenomenally, inseparable from the feeling that accompanies it. Humiliation is the "import" that my perception (through emotion) of the situation attributes to the latter as being its content, as being what the situation is about. What allows me to take Sophie to be humiliated? I take an interest in her situation, and an emotionally charged one at that. Through my emotional abilities, I engage in her position, in her possible or most likely response; by virtue of taking up her position, of "being there," at the receiving end of Carl's remark, I can—in a second move, as it were, one made possible by my *return* to my original act of perception—proceed to reflect about, evaluate, and question the nature of Sophie's reaction. Since the scene involves a triad, I have to go on to assess the nature of my part in it, in order finally to reach a decision about what would be the morally appropriate and justifiable thing to do.

My immediate access to the nature of Sophie's situation is through my faculty of empathy. Empathy allows me to enter into, to engage with, Sophie's situation. I explained this process in Chapter 4. But, to invoke the example again, there is more. Perception needs to be supplemented by judgment if deliberate action is to ensue. As became clear from the example, judgment takes the form of a return to and concentrated reengagement with the original act of perception through empathy. This is the point of disagreement between Habermas's position and mine. For the judgment I exercise here cannot close itself off from what I learn about the scene at hand by virtue of my emotional capacities. Rather, my exercise of judgment grows more mature, balanced, well founded, the more it succeeds in entering into a dialogue with the intake of the scene facilitated by my emotional capacities. My emotions bring me in touch with the situation about which judgment is to be passed; my emotions—here, the rage of indignation mounting in me—let me notice the situation at hand; they alert me to the human reality of the scene before me. Emotions, as I have noted earlier, anchor us to the *particular* moral circumstance, to the singularity, *here and now*, that addresses us immediately. Yet emotions do not tell us, of themselves, as it were, what is morally right. But they provide us with the perceptual material we need to engage in order to judge what is morally right. Judgment does not let emotions have the final say in settling matters of right and wrong; in this I agree with Habermas. However (and in this my emphasis differs from Habermas's), judgment must remain *sensitive* to the original insight into the situation—that is, into the other's weal and woe—that my emotional capacities make possible. Hence, the exercise of judgment is characterized by an interplay between emotion, "gut" feelings, original intake, on the one hand, and cognition, evaluation, reflection, on the other. So, to conclude, whereas the yardstick to which we relate in order to judge right and wrong is cognitive (i.e., demanding of us that we consider the rights and interests of all affected parties), the resources we draw on and the abilities we exercise in passing moral judgment with a view to this yardstick are of a joint emotional and cognitive nature.

7

Morality, Emotions, and Gender

The dichotomy of reason and emotion continues to be at the center of contemporary moral theory, as just witnessed in the case of Habermas. Though today less crudely framed than in its Kantian fashion, this dichotomy continues to lead many philosophers to regard emotions as suspicious, as a dark and possibly uncontrollable force in the midst of the otherwise rational moral agent.

Despite its stubborn impact, however, there exist dichotomies other than the reason-emotion one that also involve emotion in a manner relevant to my argument about the place of emotion in moral performance. Anthropologist Catherine Lutz draws attention to another influential dichotomy involving emotion when she observes that "one important aspect of [the category of emotion] is its association with the female, so that qualities that define the emotional also define women." And she adds, "For this reason, any discourse on emotion is also, at least implicitly, a discourse on gender."[1]

Lutz's observation is a vital one. To be sure, gender has not been brought into play as a distinct category in the account given of emotion in the preceding chapters. But, to echo Lutz, this does not mean that theorizing about emotion is, or can be, neutral with respect to gender. I said at the outset of the study that what we know about emotion we know from experience. Now, the way in which an individual experiences the world or others or him- or herself is conditioned by a number of factors, counting the issue whether this individual is a he or she among them.

So I agree with Lutz's observation about the impossibility of a gender-neutral discourse on emotion, and I grant that my own is no exception. Still, the fact remains that I have developed my account without any explicit, let alone systematic, reference to gender. Is this mere coincidence or (scarcely better) a case of ignorance or forgetfulness?

It is none of these. While admitting the validity of Lutz's statement, I have nevertheless proceeded as if gender makes no, or at least no systematically important, difference to what I have had to say about morality and emotion. In what follows, I will try to explain why that is—why, to be more accurate, the proposed theory of moral performance has been put forward without reference to gender.

The "Different Voice" of Carol Gilligan

In the piece from which I quoted, Lutz goes on to claim, "As both an analytic and an everyday concept in the West, emotion, like the female, has typically been viewed as something natural rather than cultural, irrational rather than rational, chaotic rather than ordered, subjective rather than universal, physical rather than mental or intellectual, unintended and uncontrollable, and hence often dangerous."[2] Lutz's point is that these dichotomies are not innocent and neutral with respect to gender; rather, these are gendered dichotomies, albeit in ways of which we—as theorists no less than as lay agents—for the most part fail to be aware. The celebrated categories of the cultural, the rational, the ordered, and the universal (all of which are widely cherished values in the West) are associated with the male; the natural, the irrational, the chaotic, and the subjective, in contrast, are associated with the female. Most significantly, and explaining the largely unconscious reproduction of the associations in our everyday life, "everyday cultural models [link] women and emotionality."[3] One may think about how the culture industry—films, pop music, youth magazines, life-style advertising, and the like—spread stereotypes about the "masculinity" of being cool and detached, set over and against the "femininity" of being emotional and impulsive. To Lutz's list can be added another key dichotomy, that between the public and the private, or the polity and the household, whereby the former is associated with the male and the latter with the female.[4] It goes without saying that this outlook helps prepare and sustain men's oppression of women. As Simone de Beauvoir has pointed out in her classic work *The Second Sex*, the male is endowed with the power of transcendence; his is a freedom from the constraints and dark powers of nature, a freedom required for cultural and artistic activity. In stark and, as it were, irrevocable contrast, the female merely reproduces the course of nature in giving birth, providing nurturance, and preparing food. Moreover, since the "feminine" is linked with emotionality, impulsiveness, desire, body, and sensuousness, the male, in order to assert himself and claim his identity as "masculine," must suppress these allegedly feminine traits in himself. This being so, we may say that the female is also the otherness within the male that the man must deny.[5] A situation is created between the sexes that is well captured in Jessica Benjamin's remark that "gender polarity deprives women of their subjectivity and men of an other to recognize them."[6]

Feminist theorists have set out to explode these outworn dichotomies and to expose the male and so utterly gender-biased perspective that has produced them and continues to do so today. At most, the dichotomies convey what men think of themselves and, by way of negation and thus characteristic dismissal, of women. Yet it is precisely this nonadmittedly gendered "view from nowhere" that has, for thousands of years, been permitted to present itself as the whole and impartial truth about the sexes. This means that the largely implicit assumptions about gender differences and about their "natural," "biological," and, as it were, "precultural"[7] origins have perpetuated, also in the common self-understanding of women, a perspective where the male is the norm.

What, then, is the role of gender in the discourse on emotions and morality?

I turn to Carol Gilligan to confront this question head-on. This choice suggests itself immediately, since Gilligan's book *In a Different Voice* has unleashed a remarkably broad and enduring interdisciplinary debate.

A main thesis of Gilligan's is that Kohlberg's six-stage model of the development of moral judgment from childhood to adulthood (dealt with in some detail in Chapter 6) is in fact gender biased in that it throughout takes the male as the norm. Gilligan points out that Kohlberg's model is based empirically on a study of eighty-four boys whose development Kohlberg has followed over a period of more than twenty years. Yet this gender selectivity in his empirical sample has not prompted Kohlberg to take up the problem this may entail for the generalizability of his findings; that is, the selectivity has not prevented Kohlberg from conceiving his stage theory as neutral with respect to gender, and so as equally valid for men and women.

However, the lack of validity of Kohlberg's theory for both sexes can only be scientifically proved when an equally comprehensive longitudinal empirical study is carried out among a sample of female individuals, adolescents and adults at that. Only this will allow for a comparison where systematic attention is paid to the gender of the participants. Having at our disposal the material required for such comparison, we will be able to ascertain whether the sexes approach and judge in the same way or in different ways with regard to moral issues and dilemmas.

This is the sort of empirical research undertaken by Gilligan. Her sample consists of female college students from age fifteen upward, to whom she returned for new interviews after a five-year interval, thus tracing into maturity the growth of their moral reasoning. Strictly speaking, the existence of gender difference in dealing with moral issues is not a "thesis" of Gilligan's or what she set out to prove; rather, it is a central finding of hers, resting soundly on the basis of her empirical research. As Gilligan states in the introduction to her work, "the different voice I describe is characterized not by gender but theme. Its association with women is an empirical observation" (DV, 2).

Gilligan found a "voice" distinctly different from the speaking in the studies of Kohlberg and his collaborators, and it is the pervasiveness of this hitherto uncovered difference that moves Gilligan to charge Kohlberg's stage model with gender bias: it is a bias painting what is really, or merely, the male point of view as "the" moral point of view, just as Piaget (a chief influence on Kohlberg) made the mistake of equating male development with child development (see DV, 10).

The different voice engendered in Gilligan's interviews with adolescent and adult women in one where the main focus is placed on human bonds, relationships, and interdependence, and where the concrete context of the situation demanding a moral resolution is given top priority, as are the feelings and the individuality of the persons involved. To synthesize and give her (far from completely homogeneous) findings a label, Gilligan identifies the kind of moral reasoning she typically finds among her subjects as an "ethic of care and responsibility." She distinguishes this ethic from the "ethic of justice and rights" she holds to be typically found among the male subjects in Kohlberg's research.

To get an idea of the main characteristics of the two ethics in question, consider the following excerpts from Gilligan's book:

> Considering the moral dilemma to be "sort of like a math problem with humans," [eleven-year-old Jake] sets it up as an equation and proceeds to work out the solution. Since his solution is rationally derived, he assumes that anyone following reason would arrive at the same conclusion. (DV, 26–27)

> Amy [sees] in the dilemma not a math problem with humans but a narrative of relationships that extends over time. (DV, 28)

> [For Ned] morality is a prescription, a thing to follow . . . [it is] a kind of balance, a kind of equilibrium. . . . If you want other people not to interfere with your pursuit of whatever you are into, you have to play the game. (DV, 98)

> [For Sharon, morality is about trying] to be as awake as possible, to try to know the range of what you feel, to try to consider all that's involved, to be as aware as you can be of what's going on. . . . The [general] principle would have something to do with responsibility, responsibility and caring about yourself and others. (DV, 99)

Gilligan sums up her findings as follows:

> The moral imperative that emerges repeatedly in interviews with women is an injunction to care, a responsibility to discern and alleviate the "real and recognizable trouble" of this world. For men, the moral imperative appears rather as an injunction to respect the rights of others and thus to protect from interference the rights to life and self-fulfillment. (DV, 100)

Hence we have to distinguish

> between a morality of rights that dissolves "natural bonds" in support of individual claims and a morality of responsibility that knits such

> claims into a fabric of relationship, blurring the distinction between self and other through the representation of their interdependence. (DV, 132)

> While women thus try to change the rules in order to preserve relationship, men, in abiding by these rules, depict relationships as easily replaced. (DV, 44)

Gilligan's findings suggest that men wish to see themselves—and wish to be seen by others—as self-sufficient agents, as having no need for the other. Autonomy is taken to equal independence; concomitantly, there often surfaces in the voice of the male an all-out rejection of dependence on others. As shown by Barry Richards, this mentality is at work not only in the private domain of relationship (Gilligan's main focus) but also in the public domain of politics, in particular in pro-marketeers' celebration of the omnipotently free individual, of the *homo oeconomicus* unfettered by binding forms of relatedness to others.[8] And despite Margaret Thatcher, we *do* think of the jungle of the market as a "man's world."

Several other psychological observations are worth making, too. C. Fred Alford discerns vital similarities between the justice-and-rights orientation and what he, drawing on the Frankfurt school, calls instrumental reason. The depiction of human relationships and bonds as "easily replaced" counts for Alford as an example of "how instrumental reason regards its objects, even people, as interchangeable, fungible units."[9] The universalist ethic of justice and rights, contends Alford, subjects moral judgment to rigid symbolic equation; it is inflexible in the face of new experiences, geared toward subordinating reality to a particular equation. As against this, "reparative reason" (a term inspired by Melanie Klein's analysis of our capacity for reparation, for making good the harm our aggression may cause others) employs loose symbolic equation; it "lets experience take the lead in formulating the categories by which we apprehend experience."[10] Guided by care for the object, for the concrete suffering of real individuals, reparative reason, when forced to choose, "loves the person more than the idea, the individual more than the principle."[11]

Alford advances the argument that instrumental reason comes to the fore in "paranoid-schizoid morality." Here, "every act of love and concern is purchased by hatred and aggression directed elsewhere; that is, by splitting and idealization."[12] At work in this morality is a rigid tendency to force reality into prefabricated categories, coupled with an inability to come to terms with ambivalence, with one's love and hate for one and the same person. As a result, the object of our good and bad feelings is split in two, into what Klein metaphorically described as the "good" and the "bad" breast. The mechanisms of idealization and splitting deny the complexity of the object; "shades of grey disappear as the all-good aspects of the other are idealized and its all-bad aspects are split off and parceled out."[13] Paranoid-schizoid morality is characteristic, I may add, of the construction of the other I examined in the discussion of anti-Semitism in Chapter 5. In the paranoid-schizoid position, the intrapsychic origins of aggression are denied. Seeking to escape the guilt caused by aggression and the fear of persecution it gives rise to, the subject projects impulses of destructiveness, hatred, and envy onto (allegedly hostile) others. In violent anti-Semitism, the annihilation of the loathed, all-bad Jew illustrates the potential for (group as well as individual) immorality pertaining to the paranoid-schizoid position as theorized by Klein.

By contrast, the reparative reason Alford discerns in Gilligan's interviews with women is taken to express what Klein termed the depressive position. In this position, the common task faced by every human being, to integrate his or her love and hate for the same object, is successfully met. In Richards's formulation, Klein sees the experience of depression to "rest on the capacity for guilt and concern about the consequences of one's destructiveness. With this concern comes the wish for reparation, the impulse to make good the damage, the unconscious basis of many of our constructive dealings with the world."[14] Alford considers women's primary preoccupation with preserving bonds and relationships—if necessary, at the cost of giving the exception primacy over the rule, the individual case primacy over universalistic principles—to testify to their attainment of a depressive, as distinct from a paranoid-schizoid, position.

Though in my view somewhat crude and speculative, Alford's use of key Kleinian concepts provides an illuminating psychological underpinning for Gilligan's findings.

In Gilligan's work, a number of questions are prompted by her implication of two distinct ethics. She states that the "different" voice is "characterized not by gender but theme" and that "its association with women is an empirical observation" (DV, 2). How exactly are we to conceive the link between distinct ethic and gender? That is, of what kind is the link claimed to obtain between an ethic of care and responsibility on the one hand and the female sex on the other? Why is it that "women"—and Gilligan increasingly employs the plural as her argument proceeds—come to constitute a different voice than men in matters of morality? Does the difference between the sexes highlighted in her book derive from biology, or from different patterns of socialization? Or is the gender difference, rather, a cultural construct, unwittingly supported by women but suited to the purpose of securing the continuing reign of patriarchy?

Owen Flanagan and Kathryn Jackson are among the many commentators to raise questions about the status of Gilligan's findings. They point out that Gilligan "shifts between the ideas that the two ethics are incompatible alternatives to each other but are both adequate from a normative point of view; that they are complements of one another involved in some sort of tense interplay; and that each is deficient without the other and thus ought to be integrated."[15] In my reading, too, Gilligan provokes such questions where one would expect her work to go a long way toward answering them. The exact nature of the link between ethic and sex remains open. There are passages where Gilligan acknowledges this. She emphasizes that "these findings were gathered at a particular moment in history, the sample was small, and the women were not selected to represent a large population." Consequently, "these constraints preclude the possibility of generalization and leave to further research the task of sorting out the different variables of culture, time, occasion, and gender" (DV, 126).

Despite the many unanswered questions, there is one variable that is invoked more systematically than others in Gilligan's study, and that is the different patterns of socialization of boys and girls. "The elusive mystery of women's development," we are told, "lies in its recognition of the continuing importance of attachment in the human life cyclus" (DV, 23). The biological fact that women are the sex giving birth gives rise to an especially deep-seated consciousness of human attachment and interdependence on the part of any woman becoming mother of an infant who is entirely dependent on her for nurturance, physical closeness, and emotional assurance. (I touched on this point from a different angle when I observed in Chapter 5 how the preoedipal mother-child dyad, and thus the emotional aspects of mother-hood, has stood at the center of modern object-relations theory.) The sexes achieve their respective gender identity by following very separate paths into adulthood. Whereas boys grow into men by way of separating themselves from the early primary tie with the mother, shifting their identification to the father, girls need not go through such a reorientation but instead intensify and deepen the one that already exists, that is, the identification with the mother. Therefore, the task of separation is more clear-cut and, in a sense, more pressing for boys than for girls. On the other hand, the continuation into adulthood of mutual feelings of identification between daughter and mother will supply girls with a richer and more enduring experience than boys have with attachment and connectedness. (Yet this achievement of identity through continued identification, as against separation, is a deeply precarious task, one ripe with conflict not least in the period of adolescence.)[16]

In the words of Nancy Chodorow, "Girls emerge from [the experience of identification with mother] with a basis for 'empathy' built into their primary definition of self in a way that boys do not."[17] For women, then, the basis for empathy is developed in the course of two phases of their (typical) life history: in the first phase, a basis for empathy derives from the factor of enduring identification with their primary caretaker; in the second phase, a basis for empathy derives from becoming mothers themselves, thus experiencing dependence and attachment from the perspective of the adult caregiver. Particularly in her interviews with women who have had to decide about abortion, Gilligan discerns the articulated emergence of a distinctly female moral language. "This is the language of selfishness and responsibility, which defines the moral problem as one of obligation to exercise care and avoid hurt. The inflicting of hurt is considered selfish and immoral in its reflection of unconcern, while the expression of care is seen as the fulfillment of moral responsibility" (DV, 73).

Implications for Moral Theory

The introduction of the issue of empathy marks an obvious point of similarity between my theoretical concerns and Gilligan's, at least prima facie. Recording the reflections of Claire, a twenty-seven-year-old married woman about to enter medical school, Gilligan writes, "[Claire now] ties morality to the understanding that arises from the experience of relationship, since she considers the capacity to 'understand what someone else is experiencing' as the prerequisite for moral response" (DV, 57). Statements such as this clearly overlap with my account of the preconditions of moral performance. More specifically, we recognize in Claire's outlook the emphasis on morality as having fundamentally to do with interpersonal relations, hence with what the other is experiencing. Indeed, the capacity required for understanding what the other is experiencing is considered indispensable for moral response to come about.

So there are obvious points of commonality between my focus on the emotional capacities presupposed in gaining access to the domain of the moral (understood most generally as the domain where the weal and woe of others is at stake) and Gilligan's focus on care and the prerequisites of caring for others. However, whereas my study has been about what I take to be the preconditions of arriving at *the* moral point of view, always depicting that point of view in the singular and analyzing its necessary preconditions on the level of specific cognitive and emotional faculties in "the" human agent, Gilligan pursues her notion of an "ethic of care and responsibility" by way of *contrasting* it with *another* (rival? or complementary?) ethic, that of "justice and rights"; she views the one ethic as involving, for example, emotional abilities more decisively and prominently than the other. That is, she regards women as typically more on the "emotional" side and men as typically more on the "cognitive" side. This contrast is brought out in the way "female" care for relationship is contraposed to "male" preoccupation with principles and rule following.

But what consequences should be drawn from the fact that mine is throughout a one-morality account and Gilligan's a two-ethics one?

A possibility suggesting itself is that since there exists such an overlap between my interest in emotional abilities (i.e., the faculty of empathy) and Gilligan's focus on care, it follows that my analysis of moral performance captures the ethic of care much better than it captures the ethic of justice, meaning that my analysis expresses a female, as distinct from a male, perspective on what we are up to when we deal with matters of morality. If this is found to be the case, it would entail an irony of no small magnitude, the author of the present study being a male.

However, I do not hold the possibility sketched here to capture the truth. To realize why this is so, we must distinguish between the different levels of inquiry involved in my analysis and in Gilligan's. The central claims in my analysis of moral performance are that moral action is logically preceded by moral judgment, that moral judgment is logically preceded by moral perception, and, further, that the cognitive faculty of representative thinking (and imagination; cf. Chapter 6) and the emotional faculty of empathy are equally indispensable for the exercise of moral perception and moral judgment. Accordingly, my analysis has concentrated on the *constitution* of the specifically *moral* phenomenon, or situation, or issue, as the subject matter for the performance of (moral) perception and judgment. I have explored what this type of phenomenon is and what is required in the human agent to arrive at it in acts of perception and judgment.

In contradistinction to this, Gilligan's inquiry is not carried out at the level of logical connection between the categories making up the sequence of moral performance. Rather, it is an attempt to give, on the basis of empirical research, a descriptive account of how women "typically" approach, judge, and resolve what they regard as matters of moral importance. Gilligan undertakes her study without investigating the *philosophical* question of what it takes—indispensably and in terms of logical necessity—to constitute and arrive at a "moral" phenomenon in the first place. True, part of what Gilligan wishes to show is that crucial differences obtain between the sexes concerning *what* is to count as a "moral" issue in the first place and, moreover, *how* one is to go about judging and resolving the topics deemed moral.

Since the levels of investigation are categorically different, I see no possibility for a direct one-to-one comparison between the two inquiries. This conclusion may appear disappointing, but nonetheless, to explain it may serve to clarify points that would otherwise remain unnoticed.

My conclusion implies that there is no way in which claims or findings in the one inquiry can be treated as verification or falsification of those in the other. Now, prima facie, it appears that an "overlap" obtains between my thesis about the importance of empathy in moral performance and Gilligan's finding concerning the centrality of empathy in an ethic of care. One might wish to interpret this overlap to the effect that each inquiry is confirmed, or at least supported, by the other.

But I maintain that there is no case of valid confirmation here, or the opposite, for that matter. It is true that my emphasis on empathy is reflected in Gilligan's ethic of care. Yet the validity of my claims about the logical function of empathy at the level of the constitution of the object addressed in moral perception and judgment is neither strengthened nor weakened by the circumstance of "empathy" (conceived by Gilligan not as a faculty but as a manifest feeling, among others) surfacing in Gilligan's portrait of the self-understanding characteristic of the proponents of an ethic of care.

Gilligan speaks of empathy in terms of relative degree, not in terms of function in moral performance. She operates with "more" or "less" as indications of the degree to which empathy qua manifest feeling prevails in the two ethics; she thus speaks of empathy in the context of (gender-oriented) comparison. Again, this differs from my inquiry, where attention is focused on the indispensability of cognitive and emotional faculties, not their respective "priority" in the self-understanding of agents, as this lends itself to empirical study with specific regard to gender.

There is much in Gilligan's work to suggest that women are relatively more concerned with (context-sensitive, particularized) *perception*, whereas men are relatively more concerned with (principle-oriented, universalizable) *judgment*. Assuming that this is empirically the case in a Western society like the United States, this difference between the sexes does nothing to alter my conception of the general and logical preconditions of moral perception and moral judgment *per se*. In other words, because I have set out to explore the necessary preconditions involved at the distinct levels of moral performance, there can in my conception be no question of some preconditions being more vital for women than for men: if the joint contributions of the faculties of empathy and representative thinking are required for moral performance to come about, the faculties are required for both sexes, not only for one of them.

Gilligan's interpretation of the ethic of care and the ethic of justice as rivals constitutes another difference. I began this study by questioning the way moral philosophy has tended to view the principles of respect and of concern for others as opposed, thus claiming the primacy of the one over the other. Against such claims, I have tried to demonstrate that the one moral principle is in fact included, not precluded, in the other. Similarly, on the level of abilities required in the subject's exercise of moral perception and judgment, my thesis has been that there is an *interplay* between cognitive and emotional faculties. Here, too, I oppose the philosopher's predilection for hierarchy and suggest that the capacities in question need to collaborate and be in balance for sound moral performance to be attained. In my account, the sequence of moral performance is undermined once one of the two basic faculties in the subject (sex making no difference) is for some reason impaired or impeded, or otherwise overshadowed by its counterpart. My notion of interplay is one of equilibrium, if you like; there is no either/or here.

The same line of reasoning can be applied to the contraposition of care and justice. I would argue that just as concern for others implies respect (and vice versa), and just as the one basic faculty needs the contribution of the other, so the justice and the care approaches to morality need to be in dialogue with each other if a balanced and mature grasp of moral affairs is to evolve in the agent—whether the agent is a he or a she. As Flanagan and Jackson remark with regard to the empirical level, "most individuals use both orientations some of the time."[18]

A rejoinder to this deserves to be made on behalf of Gilligan. What motivated her research was her deep dissatisfaction with Kohlberg's (vastly influential) model of moral development. Gilligan set out to correct what she regarded as a one-dimensional and restricted conception of how moral reasoning proceeds and of what its subject matter consists of. Part of the narrowness of Kohlberg's theory has to do with the priority given to cognitive skills of problem solving, with the result that sensitivity and emotional capacities are underplayed. If Gilligan is guilty of overemphasizing this narrowness, such overemphasis is an easily understandable effect of her attempt to bring into the open what she found neglected in Kohlberg.

Viewed in this light, there *is* a significant overlap between Gilligan's objectives and mine. On the level of moral theory, the intellectualism and cognitivism of Kohlberg's stage model of moral development (notwithstanding the vital nuances noted in Chapter 6) need to be overcome if we are to give a valid account of the abilities required in moral judgment. On the level of moral practice, it is crucial that the emotional capacities indispensable for moral performance be fostered and given opportunity to evolve and flourish in the individual human agent, allowing care, concern, and sensitivity for others to guide their conduct no less than a well-developed awareness of the principles suited to resolve conflicts of claims or rights.

The empirical side to the preclusion of emotional abilities from much of moral theory is the suppression of these abilities in the individual. The suppression of emotion in oneself as well as in others is widespread; it is encouraged and sustained not only by theory but—much more penetratingly—by values and assumptions deeply embedded in contemporary Western culture. To say this is to indicate a much bigger canvas than I can paint here. (But recall the discussion of emotivism in Chapter 1. In passing, it should be noted that modern Western culture in many areas appeals to, manipulates, and exploits people's hunger for authentic emotional experience. Current trends in advertising, personnel management, and "human interest" mass media precipitate a commercialization of feelings, that is, an explicitly voiced concern with how *you* are feeling, what *your* special needs are. It is as if the "tyranny of intimacy" offered a psychological compensation for the anonymity experienced and suffered by many people in present-day capitalist society. Alienated by the incomprehensibility of modern politics, people turn their attention to the personal life and style of the politicians, whose sex life and handshake become no less vital than their actual views.) In earlier parts of this study, I have thematized the repression of emotion and sensitivity that takes place in numbing and somewhat differently in indifference. Moreover, much has been said about the moral—or, rather, immoral—consequences likely to ensue from a deficiently developed capacity for empathy with others, viewed as a developmental product of early affective ties with significant others. However, these discussions have either been of a general, largely theoretical nature (drawing in particular on object-relations theory), or they have been linked to particular historical illustrations and ideological outlooks—such as, for example, the cognitive and effective components of the *Feindbild* (enemy portrait) in anti-Semitism. So, although there have been certain references to culture, politics, and ideology, there has been no attempt to link the suppression of emotion to gender. This, of course, is the point where Gilligan's research can serve as a supplement to my own account.

Let me, finally, make a point about emotions, gender, and culture. I have noted that patterns of socialization are a source for the commonplace link between women and "emotionality." However, the particular ways in which a biological difference—here, between the sexes with respect to childbearing and caretaking—comes to make a difference in the lives and identities of the persons involved are not decided by biology. Rather, biological differences are rendered meaningful, become carriers of meaning, by the significance attributed to them in a cultural system: the culture, that is, works upon the meaning of biological differences in highly contingent ways, in ways conditioned by time, place, tradition, religion, power relations, and so on. To give a familiar example, a given cultural system may assert that women's (biologically conditioned) gender-specific function in childbearing renders them closer to "nature" than are men and that *therefore* the status of women is inferior to that of men. My point here is merely that no such "inference" follows from biology pure and simple. Biological features do not "of themselves" dictate implications, for example, for social organization or power relations; if they did, we would be at a loss to explain the existence of numerous and essentially different social and political relations between the sexes, known to us to obtain in the world today. Ideologies of all sorts seldom leave a biological difference between the sexes alone and permit it to remain "merely" biological and thus devoid of cultural and social meaning. [19]

To be sure, to observe this is only to remind the reader of a major concern in modern feminism, politically no less than intellectually. This is the context in which we must understand the attack by feminists on the mainstream moral theorizing that—however naïvely—presents itself as neutral with respect to gender, or at least as uncommitted to any "ideologically" infected (and thus possibly controversial) views about it. However, as far as I can see, it is the selfsame—and indeed inevitable—culture-specific aspect of the gender issue that in fact returns with a vengeance once a theorist wishes to advance the case for its full inclusion in moral theory. If the status, content, and meaning of the (biologically conditioned) gender difference are so contingent, that is to say, so dependent on eminently changeable cultural, political, and historical factors, then this may be seen as making it exceedingly difficult to find a systematic place for gender in moral theory. Or, at any rate, it goes a long way toward explaining why such a place has for so long not been found. Put otherwise, if there is no *essentialist* and, so, enduring connection between moral reasoning and gender—and the claim that there is not is a common one among feminist theorists eager to judge as invalid any "naturalization" of gender difference[20]—then the gender variable must perhaps remain at the margins of systematic moral philosophy.

I see two points of lasting importance in Gilligan's work. First, there is her answer to a question raised at the outset of my inquiry: Why is it that emotions are a largely neglected topic in philosophic theorizing about morality? The answer Gilligan offers is that this neglect in a crucial sense is due to a powerful, albeit often unacknowledged, propensity of moral philosophers of various persuasions to paint a "male" picture of what moral reasoning consists of. This is a picture where the agent's development toward maturity is conceptualized and "measured" in terms of intellectual and cognitive skills. Moreover, the view of emotions, widely held in Western society, as being sharply opposed, even harmful, to the attainment and performance of mature moral judgment and as having for biological or "natural" reasons a closer link to "feminine" ways of dealing with moral affairs has contributed to keeping emotions at arm's length from moral discourse proper. It is the merit of Gilligan's work to have enhanced our awareness of the contestable nature of both assumptions, and not least to have shown that neglect of emotion is (also) due to neglect of women.

Second, Gilligan questions the way mainstream (i.e., Kohlbergian, Rawlsian, Habermasian) theory defines the moral domain and what is to count as a moral issue. Consider Kohlberg's widely shared position on the nature of morality. Kohlberg contends that all moral judgments possess certain formal features such as prescriptivity (i.e., they entail obligations) and universalizability. He also maintains that "*moral* judgments or principles have the central function of resolving interpersonal or social conflicts, that is, conflicts of claims or rights." Kohlberg further asserts that his notion of "morality as justice best renders our view of morality as universal. It restricts morality to a central minimal core, striving for universal agreement in the face of more relativist conceptions of the good."[21] As will be recalled from Chapter 6, this echoes Habermas's reduction of morality to questions that it is possible to resolve by means of consensus in a practical discourse.

Gilligan and a host of other critics have called into question the adequacy of such a conception of morality. For example, Flanagan and Jackson urge us to imagine "a complex judgment about how one can best help a friend who is depressed." To arrive at this judgment, the personality of the friend, his or her life experience, and patterns of interaction and depth of commitment between the two friends will need to be taken into consideration; these are the factors that constitute the context for the passing of judgment. Now, as Flanagan and Jackson observe, "it is implausible to think that there is anything interestingly universalizable about such a judgment or that there is necessarily any judgment of obligation involved."[22] The task for judgment in this example is not the resolution of "conflicts of claims or rights" in the light of universal principles. Kohlberg, who must agree that this is so, will perhaps defend his conception of morality by saying that the example, falling short of the formal features listed above, is therefore not a case belonging within the moral domain, and so not a case of moral judgment.

But this is too high a price to pay. It means that the moral domain is given an implausibly restricted meaning. In the words of Flanagan and Jackson, "There is too much moral energy expended on self-improvement and the refinement of character, on respectful interactions with loved ones, friends, and strangers," for cases such as the one given to be considered devoid of moral importance.[23]

A consequence of the Kohlbergian restriction of morality to matters of justice and conflicts of claims or rights is that a boundary is set up between issues of genuine moral import and "personal" issues. Thus, in his rejoinder to Gilligan's critique, Kohlberg, intent on preserving his formal-universalist restriction of morality to a "central minimal core," contends that "the spheres of kinship, love, friendship, and sex that elicit considerations of care are usually understood to be spheres of personal decision-making, as are, for instance, the problems of marriage and divorce."[24] But, as Seyla Benhabib is quick to point out, these issues are "obviously both personal and highly moral." Kohlberg shrinks the moral universe in a way that simply will not do. It is exceedingly hard to see that issues facing us in the "spheres of personal decision-making" are not and cannot hope to qualify as genuinely moral issues. In Benhabib's formulation, "the moral issues which preoccupy us most and which touch us most deeply derive not from problems of justice in the economy and the polity, but precisely from the quality of our relations with others in the 'spheres of kinship, love, friendship, and sex.'"[25] In Gilligan's interviews with women struggling with the eminently moral issue of reaching a decision about abortion, many regarded this as the most crucial moral decision in their lives, and the one involving most personal pain. Again, "the morally relevant situation is not a situation of justice."[26] The examples of friendship, marriage, and abortion suffice to demonstrate the implausibility of conceiving morality in a way categorically *opposing* pressing personal (or, rather, interpersonal, i.e., involving a you as well as an I) issues to the truly moral ones. The assertion that justice defines the core of morality and that justice is trump applies first and foremost to the arrangement of social and political institutions (to allude to Rawls);[27] it does not capture the boundaries of morality per se.

Let me conclude. In Kohlberg no less than in Habermas there is an exaggerated preoccupation with the demand for impartiality in moral reasoning. The result is that features such as impersonality, justice, formal rationality, and the criterion of universalizability constitute the acid test that issues and dilemmas must pass in order to qualify as being of truly "moral" import. Both philosophers pay a price for their preservation of the Kantian legacy. In Kohlberg, much of what we as lay actors view and try our best to come to terms with as moral issues is said to be nothing of the sort; in Habermas, issues not touching on justice and rights are said to be evaluative matters of the good life and individual self-realization. Concomitant to the narrowing of the moral universe is the advocacy of what in the end is an implausibly ascetic ethical theory. It is no wonder that from the standpoint of such a theory, the emotional abilities in "man" at the center of my study are largely overshadowed by cognitive and intellectual ones. It is the merit of feminist theorists such as Gilligan and Benhabib to have thrown more light on why this is so.

Notes

INTRODUCTION

1. VanDeVeer, *Paternalistic Intervention*, 446. See the distinction between "reasons of respect" and "reasons of concern" in Benn, *A Theory of Freedom*, esp. 7ff., 105ff.

2. MacIntyre, *Whose Justice? Which Rationality?* 260ff.; Taylor, *Sources of the Self*, 248ff.

3. Kohut, *The Analysis of the Self*, 300ff.; idem, *The Restoration of the Self*, 304ff. The work of the object-relations school is discussed in Chapter 5. A useful overview can be found in Alford, *Narcissism: Socrates, the Frankfurt School, and Psychoanalytic Theory*, esp. 29–72.

4. A. O. Rorty, ed., *Explaining Emotions*; Blum, "Compassion," in ibid., 507ff.; idem, *Friendship, Altruism, and Morality*; Solomon, *The Passions*; idem, *About Love*; Solomon and Calhoun, eds., *What Is an Emotion?*

5. The claim that empathy not only fundamentally but also exclusively—that is to say, by its very nature—is other-directed is not original. Edith Stein, assistant to Husserl in Freiburg, writes, "The experience [*Erfahrung*] to which the knowledge of others' experience [*fremdes Erleben*—the distinction between *Erfahrung* and *Erlebnis* cannot be captured in English] refers back is called empathy" (*Zum Problem der Einfühlung*, 20; translated by the author). In a similar vein, psychologist Martin L. Hoffman observes that "empathic distress has certain dimensions that clearly mark it as a moral motive. The arousal condition (another's misfortune), the aim of the ensuing action (to help another), and the basis of gratification in the actor (alleviating the other's distress) are all contingent on someone else's welfare" ("Empathy, Its Limitations, and Its Role in a Comprehensive Moral Theory," 294).

6. Gadamer, *Wahrheit und Methode*.

7. *Concern For Others*, 100. I find Kitwood's notion of "moral space" very suggestive and therefore regret that he does not give it a comprehensive elucidation. Kitwood states that moral space is created by "free attention plus free attention"; it signifies the "very antithesis of distance, for it is something shared, into which both (or all) persons involved may enter freely" (98). He goes on to say that "the heartland of morality is a complete particularism; a person is taken and accepted as nearly as possible exactly as he or she is, and not made an instance of anything else, be it a social category, a moral principle, or whatever. Also, moral space involves no prescription at all; no one

'ought' to do anything, for it is a place of being, relating, and discovery" (99). Notwithstanding the epistemological difficulties that arise with respect to such a purportedly unbiased and "free" approach to others, what Kitwood's remarks convey is that in his conception moral space is a vision and an ideal rather than a well-defined analytical category; hence, its heuristic potential is fairly limited. But Kitwood's emphasis on the dangers pertaining to "distance" and "prescription" is well taken. In the section "The Moral Significance of Suspension of the Emotional Bond" in Chapter 4 and in the section on anti-Semitism in Chapter 5 I probe more deeply into the ideological and psychological factors that promote a distorted perception of the other, thereby preventing the emergence of moral space between individuals. In the worst case, the suppression of moral space understood as the arena on which individuals meet in mutual recognition may prove a crucial step toward the implementation of orchestrated immoral action on the part of one (political, religious, ethnic—witness Yugoslavia) group toward another. Here individuals will perceive each other not as individuals but as instances of preconceived categories; thus Kitwood's formula—"free attention plus free attention"—will be extinguished.

8. For Heidegger's critique of cognitivism in epistemology, see *Sein und Zeit*, §§12ff., 29ff., 44. A good overview can be found in Hubert L. Dreyfus, *Being-in-the-World*, esp. 45ff., 173ff., 195ff., 265ff.

9. The term "receptivity" is mine, not Heidegger's. In *Sein und Zeit* Heidegger uses a number of terms to describe the phenomenon I very broadly denote "receptivity." For example, he states that "the discoveredness [*Entdecktheit*] of intraworldly entities is grounded in the world's disclosedness [*Erschlossenheit*]. But disclosedness is that basic character of Dasein according to which it is its 'there'. Disclosedness is constituted by affectedness [*Befindlichkeit*], understanding [*Verstehen*] and telling [*Rede*] and pertains equiprimordially to the world, to being-in, and to the self" (*Being and Time*, 263; cf. *Sein und Zeit*, 220). It would complicate matters unnecessarily to explain Heidegger's almost untranslatable technical terms here. For my purposes, the above quote suffices to demonstrate what is Heidegger-inspired about my notion of receptivity.

CHAPTER 1

1. *Being and Nothingness*, esp. 559ff. on "freedom."

2. *Philosophical Profiles*, 124–25.

3. *A Treatise of Human Nature*, III, i, i, (p. 521); see also the discussion of the naturalistic fallacy in Williams, *Ethics and the Limits of Philosophy*, 122ff.

4. Rawls, *A Theory of Justice*, 255.

5. Vetlesen, "Heideggers Auseinandersetzung mit Nietzsche," 24ff. (Norwegian version in *Agora* 3 (1992): 36–68.

6. Koselleck, *Vergangene Zukunft*, 300ff.

7. C. Taylor, *Philosophical Papers* 2:231–32.

8. C. Taylor, *Hegel*, 297ff., 414ff.

9. C. Taylor, "Die Motive einer Verfahrensethik," 120; translated by the author.

10. Schnädelbach, "Was ist Neoaristotelismus?" 50; translated by the author.

11. Apel, "Kann der postkantische Standpunkt der Moralität noch einmal in substantielle Sittlichkeit 'aufgehoben' werden?" in *Diskurs und Verantwortung*, 131; translated by the author.

12. Ibid., 133; translated by the author. See my discussion of Habermas's critique of Gadamer's "conservative" conception of tradition in "Habermas' kritikk av Gadamers tese om hermeneutikkens universalitet."

13. Habermas, *Moralbewußtsein und kommunikatives Handeln*, 71ff.

14. *Liberalism and the Limits of Justice*, 180.

15. Rawls, *A Theory of Justice*, 554, 560.

16. Ibid., 563.
17. I return to these issues in Chapters 2, 4, and 6.
18. *Philosophical Papers* 2:197–98; emphasis added.
19. Ibid.
20. Hegel, *Grundlinien der Philosophie des Rechts*, §153 (p. 303).
21. Sartre, *Being and Nothingness*, 302.
22. Blum, *Friendship, Altruism, and Morality*, 4.
23. Blum, "Compassion," 514.
24. *Morality and the Emotions*, esp. ch. 3, "Kantian Arguments Against Emotions as Moral Motives," 86–122.
25. *Aristotle on Emotion*, 18.
26. Ibid., 75.
27. Sherman, *The Fabric of Character: Aristotle's Theory of Virtue*, 49.
28. Ibid., 169.
29. Ibid., 47. See Chapter 6, note 32, on Martha Nussbaum.

CHAPTER 2

1. Husserl, *Die Krisis der europäischen Wissenschaften und die transzendentale Phänomenologie*. Schütz's analyses of the natural attitude, routinization, and idealization help illuminate the consciousness-raising effect of "breakdowns"; when something that "always" works all of a sudden no longer does so, we start asking *what* exactly it is that always works. See Schütz, *The Phenomenology of the Social World*; idem, *The Structures of the Lifeworld*, esp. 47ff., 238ff.
2. Adorno, *Negative Dialektik*, 355; cf. idem, *Minima Moralia*, 313.
3. *Grenzen der Aufklärung*, 43.
4. Lanzmann, *Shoah*, 88; translated by the author.
5. *The Destruction of the European Jews*, 1187.
6. Milgram, *Obedience to Authority*, 188.
7. Adorno et al., eds., *The Authoritarian Personality*, 127ff., 198–99; idem, "Freudian Theory and the Pattern of Fascist Propaganda," 416, 430; cf. Arendt, *On Revolution*, 130–31, on "conscience."
8. *Vergangene Zukunft*, esp. 349ff.; Vetlesen, "Erkjennelse og historisk endring," 104ff., 177ff.
9. See Brumlik, "Über die Ansprüche Ungeborener und Unmündiger: Wie advokatorisch ist die Diskursethik?" 265ff., esp. 298 n. 4.
10. Forst, "Hannah Arendt and the Postmodern Moment," 13.
11. Sartre, "Existentialism Is a Humanism," in Robert C. Solomon, ed., *Existentialism*, trans. P. Mairet (New York: Random House, 1974), 199; cf. idem, *Critique of Dialectical Reason* 2:263ff.
12. *Philosophical Profiles*, 298.
13. Beiner, *Political Judgment*, 156–57.
14. Habermas, *The Theory of Communicative Action* 2:353ff.; Vetlesen, "Towards a Theory of Fragmentation: A Critique of Critical Theory"; idem, "Erkjennelse og historisk endring," 173ff.
15. Hilberg, *The Destruction of the European Jews*, 1009.
16. Broszat, introduction to *Kommandant in Auschwitz*, by Rudolf Höss, 17–18; translated by the author.
17. Jean-Paul Sartre, *Anti-Semite and Jew*, trans. George J. Becker (New York: Grove Press, 1962), 54.
18. Horkheimer and Adorno, *Dialectic of Enlightenment*, 168–208.
19. Sartre, *Being and Nothingness*, 532ff., esp. 534.
20. *Stichworte*, 187; translated by the author.
21. Habermas, *Moral Consciousness and Communicative Action*, 46–47, 50.

22. *Phänomenologie des Geistes*, 431ff.
23. See Beiner, *Political Judgment*, 61ff.
24. Dilthey, *Der Aufbau der geschichtlichen Welt*, 252ff.; Gadamer, *Wahrheit und Methode*, 205ff.; Habermas, *Knowledge and Human Interests*, 181ff.; idem, *Zur Logik der Sozialwissenschaften*, 550; Vetlesen, "Erkjennelse og historisk endring," 29–30.
25. *The Nature of Sympathy*, 65.
26. "Hannah Arendt: On the Concept of Power," in *Philosophical-Political Profiles*, 184; cf. Vollrath, "Hannah Arendt über Meinung und Urteilskraft," 85ff.; Benhabib, "Hannah Arendt und die erlösende Kraft des Erzählens," 150ff.

CHAPTER 3

1. See the discussion of love as my conscious recognition that the otherness of the other is something that in itself merits my recognition, in Chapter 4.
2. Scheler quoted in Leonardy, *Liebe und Person*, 95; translated by the author.
3. Scheler quoted in ibid., 101; translated by the author.
4. Altmann, *Die Grundlagen der Wertethik*, 72, 73; translated by the author.
5. Ibid., 69.
6. Scheler quoted in Leonardy, *Die Grundlagen der Wertethik*, 87.
7. Merleau-Ponty, *Phenomenology of Perception*, 380.

CHAPTER 4

1. Solomon, *The Passions*, 191, 185, 379, 418.
2. See the definition of "numbing" in Lifton, *The Nazi Doctors*, 442ff.
3. *Freedom and Resentment*, 9, 10.
4. See the discussion of the notion of "normality" in Habermas, "Überlegungen zur Kommunikationspathologie," in *Vorstudien und Ergänzungen zur Theorie des kommunikativen Handelns*, 226–70, esp. 245ff.
5. *Freedom and Resentment*, 21, 15–16.
6. Cf. the distinction drawn between self-respect and self-esteem in Walzer, *Spheres of Justice*, 274.
7. The intended understanding of "action," which sees it as strongly linked with intentionality, i.e., as an agent's *deliberate* way of acting, and thus as distinct from mere "behavior," is elaborated in C. Taylor, *The Explanation of Behaviour*, esp. 196ff.
8. See Wolf, "Haben wir moralische Verpflichtungen gegen Tiere?" and Habermas, *Erläuterungen zur Diskursethik*, 219ff.
9. Heller, *A Theory of Feelings*, 32.
10. Hampshire, *Freedom of Mind*, 241.
11. Martin Löw-Beer has taken up the question of Taylor's meaning in the assertion that it is "necessary" for human persons to engage in strong evaluation. See Löw-Beer, "Living a Life and the Problem of Existential Impossibility," esp. 225ff.; see also C. Taylor, "Comments and Replies," esp. 249ff.
12. Heidegger, *Being and Time*, 142H, 339H.
13. Tugendhat, *Selbstbewußtsein und Selbstbestimmung*, 200; translated by the author.
14. Ibid., 204; translated by the author.
15. The distinction between an ethical-existential and a moral discourse is suggested by Habermas

in "Vom pragmatischen, ethischen und moralischen Gebrauch der praktischen Vernunft," in *Erläuterungen zur Diskursethik*, 100ff. I return to it in Chapter 6.

16. *Being and Nothingness*, 509.
17. Sartre, *Sketch for a Theory of the Emotions*, 65.
18. *Being and Nothingness*, 104.
19. Solomon, "Emotions and Choice," in *What Is an Emotion?* ed. Solomon and Calhoun, 317.
20. Solomon, *The Passions*, 242, 243, 264.
21. Ibid., 212.
22. Lifton, *The Nazi Doctors*, 419.
23. Ibid., 421.
24. Himmler quoted in Hilberg, *The Destruction of the European Jews*, 1009.
25. Himmler quoted in Lifton, *The Nazi Doctors*, 435.
26. Spengler quoted in Hilberg, *The Destruction of the European Jews*, 137, 293.
27. Lifton, *The Nazi Doctors*, 442.
28. Ibid., 444.
29. Ibid., 447.
30. Suchomel quoted in Lanzmann, *Shoah*, 88; translated by the author.
31. Lifton, *The Nazi Doctors*, 493, 178.
32. Ibid., 495.
33. Ibid., 496.
34. Ibid., 446. See also Hilberg, *Sonderzüge nach Auschwitz*.
35. Hilberg, *The Destruction of the European Jews*, 264.
36. Ibid., 1187.
37. A critique of Durkheim's immensely influential view that "all morality comes from society," that "there is no moral life outside society," that "society is best understood as a morality-producing plant," and that "society promotes morally regulated behaviour and marginalizes, suppresses or prevents immorality" is to be found in Bauman's *Modernity and the Holocaust*, esp. 169ff.; the quotations are from page 173. I discuss Bauman's book in the last part of Chapter 5.
38. Bauman in personal correspondence, 14 July 1991.
39. *The Theory of Communicative Action*, 2:133.
40. Mitscherlich and Mitscherlich, *The Inability to Mourn*, 290, 166.
41. Ibid., 158; cf. 39.
42. Freud, "Mourning and Melancholia," in *On Metapsychology*, 254. Cf. Bowlby, *Attachment and Loss*, vol. 3, *Loss*, 245–62.
43. See Aristotle's famous account of friendship (*philia*) in *Nicomachean Ethics*, e.g., 1156a3–5. My short paragraph on friendship mixed the Aristotelian and the Kantian conceptions, without being systematically committed to either. Whereas for Aristotle the friend is perceived not merely as useful and pleasant to me but also as a supreme addressee of my goodness, i.e., as a subject possessing intrinsic value, for Kant the friend is perceived as a person for whose inherent dignity and right to autonomous decision making qua person I show respect, or *Achtung*. I am indebted to Seyla Benhabib and Jon Wetlesen for pointing this distinction out to me. An excellent analysis of friendship is given by David Norton in his *Personal Destinies*, 303ff.
44. Hilberg, *The Destruction of the European Jews*, 1187.
45. Ibid., 332.
46. Lifton, *The Nazi Doctors*, 159.
47. Höss quoted in ibid.
48. *Group Psychology and the Analysis of the Ego*, 134.
49. Mitscherlich and Mitscherlich, *The Inability to Mourn*, 187.
50. Ibid., 290.
51. See the chapter on the look in Sartre, *Being and Nothingness*, 340ff.

52. Løgstrup, *Den etiske fordring*, 28.
53. Levinas, *Ethics and Infinity*, 86, 89; idem, *Totality and Infinity*, 215.
54. *Totality and Infinity*, 225. Levinas's discussion of responsibility, subjection, and substitution, in his book *Otherwise than Being or Beyond Essence*, contains numerous implicit references to Sartre's account of freedom and choice in *Being and Nothingness*. For example, Levinas writes: "Responsibility for another is not an accident that happens to a subject, but precedes essence in it, has not awaited freedom, in which a commitment to another would have been made. I have not done anything and I have always been under accusation—persecuted" (114). "We discern in obsession a responsibility that rests on no free commitment, a responsibility whose entry into being could be effected only without any choice. To be without a choice can seem to be violence only to an abusive or hasty and imprudent reflection, for it precedes the freedom non-freedom couple, but thereby sets up a vocation that goes beyond the limited and egoist fate of him who is only for-himself, and washes his hands of the faults and misfortunes that do not begin in his own freedom or in his present. It is the setting up of a being that is not for itself, but is for all, is both being and disinterestedness. The for itself signifies self-consciousness; the for all, responsibility for the others, support of the universe. Responsibility for the other, this way of answering without a prior commitment, is human fraternity itself, and it is prior to freedom" (116). For a critical discussion of Levinas's account of responsibility for the other as absolute and unconditional, see my "Why Does Proximity Make a Moral Difference?"
55. Since the completion of this chapter, I have become aware of a passage in Paul L. Harris's *Children and Emotion*, 52, which seems to contain the same point. Harris writes, "Our everyday understanding of emotion scarcely requires such emotional contagion or congruence. [We] can also understand another person's emotion without feeling the same emotion. . . . Even when we comfort someone in distress, we are likely to do so out of a feeling of concern for the person, rather than because some equivalent distress has been aroused in us." Harris, however, shows the latter condition to prevail frequently in young children. On behalf of my own conception, I only wish to add that the "feeling of concern for the other person" Harris refers to presupposes and hence arises from the faculty of empathy and that although a person "need not" feel what the other feels, it is necessary, in order for "a feeling of concern" to arise, that the person showing such concern has developed a *capacity* for doing so. This may seem a trivial addition to make, but it is not, since research in developmental psychology has brought us to recognize that many people are rigidly selective in what kind of feelings they allow themselves—and by implication, allow in others—to feel. To pick an example, a man may have experienced being rebuffed rather than cared for when experiencing grief as a child. Seeking to adjust to this, the child will be afraid to display feelings of grief; he tries to hide them from others and perhaps later to deny their existence to himself as well. As an adult, such a person may be expected to demonstrate a conspicuously low tolerance for others' open display of grief and need for comfort and reassurance. The person closes this part of the human emotional repertoire off from his field of perception; his selectivity rules this part out; he cannot comfort in others what he has come to extinguish in himself. I am indebted to Siri Gullestad for explaining the nature of this process to me. See also Daniel Stern, *The Interpersonal World of the Infant*, 207ff., on "selective attunements."
56. Freud quoted in Kohut, *The Restoration of the Self*, 306.
57. *The Nature of Sympathy*, 52.
58. Cf. Blum, "Compassion," 512.
59. *Kommandant in Auschwitz*, 132–33; translated by the author. In this characteristic manner, Höss at the beginning of his autobiography relates the following about his upbringing: "My parents brought me up to approach all adults and especially elders with respect and reverence, regardless of their particular background. It was made my supreme duty to be of service whenever it was necessary. I was told with particular insistence that I always had to carry out and follow the desires and regulations of my parents, of my teachers, the clergy, and so on, indeed of all adults, including the domestic servants. Nothing should keep me from complying instantly with their wants. What

they said was always right. These principles of my upbringing have penetrated my very blood and body. I can still remember how my father . . . always assured his friends that, in spite of all opposition, the laws and arrangements of the state had to be obeyed unconditionally" (25; translated by the author). (One would, let me add, be hard put to come up with a more adequate testimony to what "conventional morality" in early twentieth-century Germany boiled down to; see Chapters 1 and 6.) Some may find that I have placed too little emphasis on obedience and the notorious *Pflichtbewußtsein* of the Nazis. But these factors are well documented in the general literature. Besides, my discussion of Eichmann in Chapter 2 pointed out how he renounced moral responsibility for his actions as he became engaged in the carrying out of the Final Solution. I have also referred to Stanley Milgram's classic study *Obedience to Authority*, whose analysis of the "agentic state" (132ff.) gives a well-founded explanation of the "I was merely following orders from my superiors" syndrome, of which Eichmann and Höss were part. For my purposes in this chapter, however, the suppression of sensitivity is a more important factor than the ones just referred to.

60. *Supererogation*, 102; cf. Rawls's remarks on supererogation in *A Theory of Justice*, 192, 438ff.

61. My position on the relation between emotions and judgment has been influenced by discussions with Chris Latiolais.

CHAPTER 5

1. Cf. the useful discussion in Held, *Introduction to Critical Theory*, 144ff.

2. See Canetti, *Crowds and Power*.

3. Cf. the appendix in Held, *Introduction to Critical Theory*, 401ff.

4. See Simmel, *The Philosophy of Money*, esp. 272ff., 349ff., 476ff.

5. See Claussen, *Grenzen der Aufklärung: Zur gesellschaftlichen Geschichte des modernen Antisemitismus*, 34.

6. By implication, Jessica Benjamin in her book *The Bonds of Love* criticizes the portrait of the mother given by Horkheimer—and by a host of other authors writing within the orthodox psychoanalytic tradition under the enduring impact of Freud's account of the Oedipus complex. Benjamin states, in my opinion correctly, that "the father's ascendancy in the Oedipus complex spells the denial of the mother's subjectivity, and thus the breakdown of mutual recognition. At the heart of psychoanalytic theory lies an unacknowledged paradox: the creation of difference *distorts*, rather than fosters, the recognition of the other." Furthermore, in the model upheld in the Oedipus complex—as that complex is commonly interpreted, that is—"the boy does not merely disidentify with the mother, he repudiates her and all feminine attributes" (135). I take this observation of Benjamin's to help cast light on the emergence in male subjects of what I elsewhere in this chapter talk about as "contempt for sympathy." In other words, the boy strives to confirm—in his own eyes as well as in others'—his "masculine identity" and "ego strength" precisely by way of disavowing his own femininity; he sets affection, sensitivity, and receptivity over and against the willpower and independence attributed to the father. Subjected to the influence of this powerful dichotomy, the boy seeks to disavow traits considered "feminine" and to model his own identity on traits considered "masculine." But, as Benjamin remarks in her critique of Christopher Lasch's analysis of narcissism, "Why, indeed, should the ego ideal or the superego be assigned a gender?" (158). Her question retains its thrust when put to Horkheimer as well.

7. On the history of the ghettos, see Dawidowicz, *The War Against the Jews, 1933–45*, esp. 247ff., 357ff.; Loewy et al., *"Unser einziger Weg ist Arbeit": Das Getto in Lodz, 1940–1944*.

8. See Lasch, *Haven in a Heartless World*, esp. 96ff.

9. Claussen, *Grenzen der Aufklärung*, 37; translated by the author.

10. On the controversy between Fromm and the other Frankfurters, see Jay, *The Dialectical Imagination*, 100ff.

11. *Eros and Civilization*, 247–48, 264–65, 273.

12. Ibid., 272.

13. See the excellent discussion of the emotional aspects of autism in Harris, *Children and Emotion*, 193ff. I thank Martin Löw-Beer for this reference.

14. In a speech to the German people on 30 September 1942, to pick an example, Hitler said, "In my Reichstag speech of September 1, 1939, I have spoken of two things: first, that now that the war has been forced upon us, no array of weapons and no passage of time will bring us to defeat, and second, that if Jewry should plot another world war in order to exterminate the Aryan peoples of Europe, it would not be the Aryan peoples which would be exterminated, but Jewry." Quoted in Hilberg, *The Destruction of the European Jews*, 407. For analyses of Hitler's rhetoric, see J. P. Stern, *Hitler: The Führer and the People*; Fest, *Hitler: En biografi*, esp. 105ff.; Ofstad, *Vår forakt for svakhet*; Vetlesen, "Romantikken, Nietzsche og nazismen," 27ff.

15. Anita Eckstaedt, *Nationalsozialismus in der "zweiten Generation": Psychoanalyse von Hörigkeitsverhältnissen*, 211; see also 112, 253ff, 379. In his collection of papers *The Making and Breaking of Affectional Bonds*, John Bowlby puts forward an accurate description of the process of doing unto others what was formerly done to oneself. Bowlby writes, "Whatever representational models of attachment figures and of self an individual builds during his childhood and adolescence, tend to persist relatively unchanged into and throughout adult life. As a result he tends to assimilate any new person with whom he may form a bond, such as spouse or child, or employer or therapist, to an existing model (either of one or other parent or of self), and often to continue to do so despite repeated evidence that the model is inappropriate" (141–42).

16. See Winnicott, *The Maturational Processes and the Facilitating Environment*; idem, *Playing and Reality*; Storr, *Solitude*, 69–70.

17. Klein, *Envy and Gratitude and Other Works, 1943–1963*.

18. Kohut's focus on how crucial it is that a child's need for empathic responsiveness be met by at least one person in the immediate human environment has been criticized by Jessica Benjamin for failing to take into account that the person offering such response must from early on be recognized as a person *in his or her own right* by the child needing response. That is, the child must meet and be able to acknowledge and welcome resistance as opposed to unfailing and unconditional support; it must encounter difference, the otherness of the other, as opposed to the undynamic affirmation of sheer mirroring. This is the message of Donald Winnicott's seminal paper "The Use of an Object and Relating Through Identifications" (in *Playing and Reality*). "To use an object," observes Winnicott, "the subject must have developed a *capacity* to use objects." He describes the origin of such a capacity as follows: "In the sequence one can say that first there is object-relating, then in the end there is object-use; in between, however, is the most difficult thing, perhaps, in human development; or the most irksome of all the early failures that come for mending. This thing that there is between relating and use is the subject's placing of the object outside the area of the subject's omnipotent control; that is, the subject's perception of the object as an external phenomenon, not as a projective entity, in fact recognition of it as an entity in its own right. This change (from relating to using) means that the subject destroys the object. . . . [A]fter 'subject relates to object' comes 'subject destroys object' (as it becomes external); and then may come *object survives* destruction by the subject" (105). Here Winnicott, though employing a different terminology, echoes my own insistence on the subject's ability to recognize and allow for, not distort or refuse, the fact that the other encountered in what I term moral perception is different, is an *other* in the strong sense of the word. A lack of this ability may lead to so-called projective hatred. See Winnicott, *Playing and Reality*; idem, "The Theory of the Parent-Infant Relationship," 233ff.; cf. the section "Intersubjective Relatedness," in D. Stern, *The Interpersonal World of the Infant*, 203ff.

19. *Psychoanalytic Studies of the Personality*, 60. Fairbairn criticizes Freud's view that libido is primarily pleasure seeking; he argues that "libido is primarily object-seeking," and that "libidinal aims are inherently bound up with object-relationships" (126, 138).

20. "The Nature of the Child's Tie to His Mother." Bowlby's central thesis in this early paper,

which he would come to revise in later works (see 153n), is that "unless there are powerful built-in responses which ensure that the infant evokes maternal care and remains in close proximity to his mother throughout the years of childhood he will die" (192).

21. See Miller, *The Untouched Key*, 50–51, 168–69, on the vital importance of a child's experiencing that "at least once in their life," a particular person, a "witness," "helps the child experience his feelings to some degree."

22. Killingmo, "Characters on the Stage: Ibsen's 'Life-Lie' Revisited," 11; cf. idem, "Problems in Contemporary Psychoanalytic Theory, I: Controversial Issues," 55.

23. Killingmo, "Characters on the Stage," 11.

24. Killingmo, "Conflict and Deficit: Implications for Technique," 67.

25. Ibid., 65.

26. Killingmo, "Characters on the Stage," 12.

27. Ibid.; cf. Killingmo, "Problems in Contemporary Psychoanalytic Theory, II: Lines of Advance," esp. 64, 67.

28. Elie Wiesel, concluding oral statement at the Oslo Conference "The Anatomy of Hate," Oslo, 30 August 1990.

29. Bauman, *Modernity and the Holocaust*, 74.

30. Ibid., 166.

31. Ibid., 155.

32. Ibid., 192.

33. Bauman, personal correspondence, 19 June 1991.

34. *Modernity and the Holocaust*, 90. See the interesting chapter "Political Opinion and the Extermination of the Jews" in Ian Kershaw's study *Popular Opinion and Political Dissent in the Third Reich*, 358ff. Kershaw, a historian, writes, "The abstraction of the Jew had taken over more and more from the 'real' Jew who, whatever animosity he had caused, had been a flesh-and-blood person. The depersonalization of the Jew had been the real area of success of Nazi policy and propaganda on the Jewish Question" (360). However, and highly significantly, "compared with the simmering unrest and discontent on economic matters and the depth of feeling which gave rise on occasion to explosive and . . . often effective outbursts of opposition on Church issues, the detachment and general lack of active interest and involvement when it came to anti-Jewish policies and measures is depressingly striking" (377). "Ultimately . . . dynamic hatred of the masses was unnecessary [for carrying out the Final Solution]" (372).

If Kershaw is right that "dynamic hatred of the masses [ultimately] was unnecessary," this leaves open the possibility that, at some earlier point, such hatred was in fact necessary—namely, as popular backing of the official Nazi policy on the "Jewish Question." To dwell on this point means to elaborate also on Bauman's assertion, cited earlier, that "mass destruction was accompanied not by the uproar of emotions, but the dead silence of unconcern."

My knowledge of German Nazism suggests that we can distinguish between two phases of Nazi anti-Semitism. The first phase is part of the so-called years of struggle when leading Nazis, most notably Hitler and Goebbels, tried to whip up anti-Semitist feelings in the population. This was the phase of mobilization: Nazi propaganda urged the German *Volk* to let loose their presumably deep-seated hostility to the Jews. For this purpose, outworn anti-Jewish stereotypes and ideas of "conspiracy," of links to "world communism," of the Jews as "social vermin," a "cancer growth," as "unfit to live," were thoroughly exploited. However, this phase came to an end as the war approached. From 1938 to 1939, Nazi anti-Semitism took on a different form and entered a second phase. Spontaneity gave way to purposiveness, mobilization to secrecy; public pogroms gave way to deportations to the "East" and, with that, to an *Endlösung* entrusted to the smallest possible circle of professional functionaries, the guiding idea becoming that the less one talked and knew about the (post-1939) fate of the Jews, the better. Whereas the first phase had been marked by a sought-for involvement of the German people, in which the party leadership hoped to exploit the masses' hatred, the second phase was marked by measures of concealment, with the German population at large becoming increasingly indifferent to the now rarely seen and heard-of Jews.

If an exact date should be proposed for what may in retrospect be held to mark the end of the first phase and to prepare for a shift to the second, 9 November 1938 seems a plausible candidate. This, of course, is what is known as the Crystal Night, the *Reichskristallnacht*. Significantly, the pogroms carried out all across Germany this night were intended by Goebbels and his associates in the *Propagandaministerium* to provide an opportunity for the "people's" hatred of the Jews to come out in the open and so spark grassroots support for the aggressive Nazi stance on the Jewish Question. However, what was meant to be an orgy of stored-up mass hatred of the Jews turned out to be nothing—or, rather, almost nothing—of the sort. Not that the *Aktion* was not an experience of terror for its victims, but its participants were relatively few in number, and the response of the average citizen seems to have been one of disgust rather than delight. In his chapter "Reactions to the Persecution of the Jews," Kershaw gives a detailed account of the event. I present some excerpts: "So far as Goebbels had reckoned with spontaneous popular support for the pogrom, however, he was disappointed. The disapproval of large sections of the population was abundantly clear, even if open protest was in the circumstances hardly conceivable" (260). "It was perfectly obvious that the whole affair had been directed and orchestrated by the Party—all the more so where the demolition had been carried out by SA squads brought in from outside" (263). "Jewish eye-witness accounts abound with references to the kindness of 'Aryan' and 'Christian' neighbours and are anxious to point out the overwhelming rejection of the pogrom by the vast majority of the population" (269). "There were few occasions, if any, in the Third Reich which produced such a widespread wave of revulsion— much of it on moral grounds—as the 'Crystal Night' pogrom" (270–71). This may come as a surprise. It may appear that Kershaw is giving a one-sided account. But this is not so. The conclusion he reaches is a balanced one, and it merits being quoted *in extenso*: "The unceasing barrage of anti-Jewish propaganda had not been without effect. People's minds were increasingly poisoned against the Jews in at least an abstract way; the conviction was spreading that there *was* a Jewish Question. In November 1938, as earlier, it was therefore *the method rather than the aim* [emphasis added] of Nazi policy which most people were condemning. Just as the Nuremberg Laws of 1935 had been widely acclaimed in contrast to the condemnation of the primitive brutality of the 'individual actions,' so now approval for the 'legal measures' was juxtaposed with wide condemnation of the brutality and destruction of the pogrom itself. 'Anti-Semitism—o.k., but not like that' seems to sum up much of the mainstream response to 'Crystal Night,' and to the chequered course of Nazi radical attempts to solve the Jewish Question before 1938" (272–73). Thus, the biggest pogrom was also the last one, a mistake not to be risked another time. What hatred there was gave way to noninvolvement at the grassroots level; as more "humane methods" (in the vocabulary of Himmler) and "rational" means were developed, emotionally and morally charged proximity was replaced by processes of abstraction.

35. Levi, *If This Is a Man* and *The Truce*, 188; cf. 398. In his essay "Useless Violence" in *The Drowned and the Saved*, Levi reflects on the various Nazi techniques of humiliation. In particular, he calls attention to "excremental coercion" and "the coercion of nudity." From my perspective, both can be understood as stages in robbing the Jews of their status as human beings. Indeed, as many camp survivors have pointed out, it seems that the ultimate goal of the Nazi humiliation of the Jews was to persuade the Jews themselves to adopt and accept the Nazi view of them as nonhuman, as unworthy of human existence. In other words, the actual physical extinction was to be preceded by a spiritual extinction on the part of the victim himself or herself; physical death would add nothing, as it were, to the already accomplished spiritual death. "Excremental coercion" serves to render men and women indistinguishable from animals. As Levi observes about the ride in packed freight cars to the death camps in Poland, "The doors were opened another time, but during a stop in an Austrian railroad station. The SS escort did not hide their amusement at the sight of men and women squatting wherever they could, on the platforms and in the middle of the tracks, and the German passengers

openly expressed their disgust: people like this deserve their fate, just look how they behave. These are not *Menschen*, human beings, but animals, it's clear as the light of day" (88–89). The "coercion of nudity" is only a logical follow-up. "One entered the Lager naked: indeed more than naked, deprived not only of clothing and shoes . . . but of the hair of one's head and all other hairs. . . . Now a naked and barefoot man feels that all his nerves and tendons are severed: he is a helpless prey. Clothes, even the foul clothes which were distributed, even the crude clogs with their wooden soles, are a tenuous but indispensable defence. Anyone who does not have them no longer perceives himself as a human being, but rather as a worm: naked, slow, ignoble, prone on the ground. He knows that he can be crushed at any moment" (90). Having been thus degraded before dying, the victim is perceived in a manner allowing the murderer to be less burdened by guilt. As Levi comments, this is "an explanation not devoid of logic but which shouts to heaven: it is the sole usefulness of useless violence" (101; cf. the chapter on torture in Amery, *Jenseits von Schuld und Sühne: Bewältigungsversuche eines Überwältigten*, 37ff.; Nyiszli, *Auschwitz*). I have found it vital to include these observations, because they help to bring out what has been somewhat neglected in my earlier account—namely, the existence of meticulous techniques of humiliation, of inflicting psychical as well as physical pain on the victims, under conditions where the method of killing had become technified and industrialized. Beyond that, the observations highlight how the perpetrators' dehumanization of their victims was rendered easier and more "plausible" to the former once it came to be (to a varying extent) adopted by the latter.

CHAPTER 6

1. Günther, *Der Sinn für Angemessenheit*, 157–58; translated by the author.

2. Ibid., 257.

3. Apel, *Diskurs und Verantwortung*, 17–18; translated by the author.

4. Ibid., 44.

5. Ibid.

6. Ibid., 448.

7. Wittgenstein, *Philosophische Untersuchungen*, §199. The references to Rossvær are to his essay "Transzendentalpragmatik, transzendentale Hermeneutik, und die Möglichkeit, Auschwitz zu verstehen," 187ff.

8. Apel, *Diskurs und Verantwortung*, 460; translated by the author.

9. Ibid., 141.

10. Ibid., 144–45.

11. Ibid., 215.

12. Ibid., 131.

13. Ibid., 133.

14. Rehg, "Discourse and the Moral Point of View: Deriving a Dialogical Principle of Universalization," 27ff.

15. Habermas, "Towards a Communication-Concept of Rational Collective Will Formation: A Thought Experiment," 150.

16. As it stands, the characterization of Kant's position on the role of emotions in ethics given here fails to do him justice. I may have been too uncritical in my endorsement of Lawrence Blum's important book *Friendship, Altruism, and Morality*.

I think that Blum's book, which I drew on in Chapter 4, is often too undifferentiated in its portrait of the "Kantian view." To cite a representative passage, Blum states that "Kant does not see idle wishes, emotions, desires, or even intentions as having in their own right any moral significance; what counts are our motives for endeavouring to bring about certain states of affairs (even though the success of those endeavours is not regarded as significant)" (141). And further: "The Kantian view [is that] while emotions or sentiments may have value beyond the motivating of beneficence, the kind of value they have is not moral value" (152). Although I agree with Blum's overall position—that " 'emotion for the sake of emotion' is alien to my view"; "it is because altruistic emotions are forms of (appropriate) responsiveness to others' weal and woe that they are claimed to be morally desirable" (153)—the formulations I have cited are too simplistic. They put excessive emphasis on Kant's distinction between actions performed *aus Neigung* and those performed *aus Pflicht*, on the one hand, and on the distinction between actions done *pflichtmäßig* and those done *aus Pflicht*, on the other, that is, between their *Legalität* and their *Moralität*. Now, in the section in *Critique of Practical Reason* where Kant discusses these concepts, he writes that "it is of the utmost importance in all moral judgments to pay strictest attention to the subjective principle of every maxim, so that all the morality of actions may be placed in their necessity from duty and from respect for the law, and not from love for or leaning toward that which the action is to produce" (A145, p. 84). Kant sums up: "Such is the nature of the genuine incentive of pure practical reason. It is nothing else than the pure moral law itself, so far as it lets us perceive the sublimity of our own supersensuous existence and subjectively effects respect for their higher vocation in men who are conscious of their sensuous existence and of the accompanying dependence of their pathologically affected nature" (A158, p. 91). Kant certainly demands a careful interpretation, meaning a more complex one than those given, at least on occasion, by myself as well as Blum. What complicates matters is that Kant also speaks of the *Gefühl* of *Achtung* for the moral law laid down in us qua self-legislating rational beings. But what type of a feeling is the *Gefühl* Kant has in mind here? The German philosopher Harald Köhl has put Kant's view like this: "Kant wished to stress that there exists no feeling that precedes the moral law and that forms the moral law's psychological and justificatory basis. Rather, the moral feeling is elicited of the condition that one adopts a moral point of view and—independently of feelings—judges actions from it. That the moral law is itself the moral motive [*Triebfeder*; cf. the Kant quotations above] is only Kant's shorthand expression of the more complex fact that the law appeals to our powers of sensitivity and thereby elicits a feeling of respect [*Achtungsgefühl*] that in its turn should constitute the basis for the performance of moral acts. . . . Kant's feeling of respect is not only *caused* by the moral law—that is, by the consciousness of the law—but it is, as respect *for* the law, also directed intentionally at the moral law" ("Kant und Schopenhauer in der Ethik: Die Theorie der moralischen Motivation," 13–14; translated by the author). With this I hope to have done some justice to Kant—on his own terms, as it were.

17. Adorno, *Stichworte*, 187; translated by the author.

18. Apel, *Diskurs und Verantwortung*, 17–18; translated by the author.

19. Ibid.

20. Ibid.

21. Charles Taylor discusses "constitutive goods" in his *Sources of the Self*. Taylor's use of the term is complicated and cannot be elucidated without entering into the main argument of his massive book. I must confine myself to the following. "Constitutive goods," writes Taylor, "are empowering"; "they empower as 'moral sources' " (338). "The constitutive good is a moral source"; "it is a something the love of which empowers us to do and be good" (93). A central thesis in Taylor's book is that contemporary deontological moral theories are "grounded on an unadmitted adherence to certain life goods, such as freedom, altruism, universal justice" (93). Taylor thus makes his contribution to the liberalism-communitarianism controversy over the (contested) primacy of the right over the good. In my discussion, "belongingness" is a constitutive good Habermas has "forbidden" recourse to, in the sense that without the individual's belongingness to a community, all life goods or life aims the individual may have will be threatened, since deprived of belongingness the individual's very identity is undermined—as Habermas himself acknowledges (see note 26 below).

22. Kohlberg, Boyd, and Levine, "Gerechtigkeit, Wohlwollen, und der Standpunkt der Moral," 213; translated by the author.

23. Ibid., 212.

24. Ibid., 222.

25. Ibid.

26. In his younger days, particularly in the early sixties when he wrote the collection of essays entitled *Theory and Practice*, Habermas took considerable interest in the writings of the young Hegel. Central to the latter is the analysis of "the struggle for recognition," the origins of which date back to Hegel's fragment *Der Geist des Christentums*. Hegel here shows how the "criminal" destroys the dialogic relation of "recognizing oneself in the other." Habermas gives the following account: "The 'criminal' who revokes [*aufhebt*] the moral basis, namely the complementary interchange of noncompulsory communication and the mutual satisfaction of interests, by putting himself as individual in the place of the totality, sets in motion the process of a destiny which strikes back at him. The struggle which is ignited between the contending parties and the hostility toward the injured and oppressed other makes the lost complementary interchange and the bygone friendliness palpable. The criminal is confronted by the power of deficient life. Thus he experiences his guilt. The guilty one must suffer under the power of the repressed and departed life, which he himself has provoked, until he has experienced the deficiency of his own life in the repression of others' lives, and, in his turning away from the lives of others, his own alienation from himself" (*Theory and Practice*, 148). Since the late sixties, Habermas has departed from the Hegelian path and, inspired by the linguistic turn in modern philosophy, embarked instead upon that of a formal pragmatics concerned with the universal presuppositions of speech acts. Despite this shift, I find that the sketched Hegelian *Gedankenfigur* continues to exert influence on Habermas's way of thinking about the consequences of challenging the dialogic preconditions of communication. An obvious case in point is Habermas's claim—discussed in the second section of this chapter—about the skeptic's project being "existentially" self-destructive, if not ultimately lethal. Hegel agrees.

27. *Pride, Shame, and Guilt*, 80.

28. *Philosophical Papers*, 1:49.

29. Ibid., 62; cf. my discussion in the first section of Chapter 4.

30. I have discussed the Nazis' notion of *lebensunwertes Leben* at length earlier in this study, especially in Chapter 4. Here I only wish for a moment to view the notion from the viewpoint of a survivor and to ponder survival as experienced by someone who narrowly escaped the death intended for him, by someone declared unfit to live, unworthy of life, by, say, the only person out of four hundred thousand to survive—in short, by someone like Simon Srebnik, the sole known survivor of Chelmno. "1 : 400,000. Simply ridiculous. But every life is for every individual completely hundred per cent, so perhaps there is some sense to it after all" (translated by the author). Thus Hannah Krall reminds us in her book *Schneller als der liebe Gott*, 146–47. I am grateful to Daniela Hirsekorn for this reference.

31. Taylor, *Sources of the Self*, 102, 502.

32. Martha Nussbaum's book *Love's Knowledge*, has come to my attention since the completion of my text. Nussbaum's excellent account of Aristotle's theory of moral perception and judgment, and of practical deliberation in general, seems to overlap with my own ideas in all essential aspects. Nussbaum reminds us that in Aristotle's view, "priority in practical choice should be accorded not to principle, but to perception, a faculty of discrimination that is concerned with apprehending concrete particulars" (68). With respect to practical matters, says Aristotle, "the discernment lies in the particulars and in perception" (*Nicomachean Ethics*, 1126b2–4; cf. the discussion of judgment in Chapter 2 above). Aristotle sees practical matters as "mutable, or lacking in fixity. A system of rules set up in advance can encompass only what has been seen before"; "people of practical wisdom must meet the new with responsiveness and imagination"; through experience they must learn to "improvise what is required" (71), knowing full well that practical wisdom or *phronēsis* is not and cannot be *epistēmē*, that is, systematic scientific understanding. The latter is ruled out, furthermore, because practical matters are "indeterminate or indefinable"; we must observe the "variety of practical contexts and the situation-relativity of appropriate choice" (71); finally, "the concrete ethical case may simply contain some ultimately particular and non-repeatable elements" (72).

CHAPTER 7

1. "Engendered Emotion: Gender, Power, and the Rhetoric of Emotional Control in American Discourse," in Lutz and Abu-Lughod, eds., *Language and the Politics of Emotion*, 69.

2. Ibid.

3. Ibid., 78.

4. See Pateman, "Feminist Critiques of the Public/Private Dichotomy," 281ff.; Young, "Impartiality and the Civic Public: Some Implications of Feminist Critiques of Moral and Political Theory," 382.

5. See Simone de Beauvoir, *The Second Sex*.

6. *The Bonds of Love*, 218.

7. In her interesting book *Unnatural Emotions: Everyday Sentiments on a Micronesian Atoll and Their Challenge to Western Theory*, Lutz offers a comprehensive critique of the "Western" view in which "emotions are primarily conceived of as precultural facts, as features of our biological heritage that can be identified independently of our cultural heritage" (70).

8. See Richards, *Images of Freud*, 154.

9. Alford, *Melanie Klein and Critical Social Theory*, 166.

10. Ibid., 167.

11. Ibid, 165. Note Alford's attack on Habermas: "Habermas allows needs to emerge, to reveal themselves, only to the degree that they are detached from the hopes, sufferings, and dreams of real people and are rendered utterly transparent in discourse, as though all spoke the same language of needs, words and needs being virtually interchangeable. However, in treating needs in this fashion, Habermas has already gone a long way down the road toward instrumental reason" (163). This is not fair criticism; it is in fact the type of charge that makes Habermas furious. Whatever the shortcomings of Habermas's position (cf. my discussion in Chapter 6), to see it as an instance of "instrumental reason" is to misconstrue it beyond recognition. Alford overlooks the perspective from which Habermas argues for the inclusion of needs, wants, and interests in discourse—his perspective is that of *Ideologiekritik*. The aim of the critique (with which Alford is certainly familiar) is to go beneath the positive givenness of (social and individual) needs and reveal the power structures that sustain and reproduce them. Wishing to address needs in discourse does not amount to seeing them as entirely transparent, let alone wishing to force them to become so. Alford would do well to take a (second?) look at Habermas's 1982 "Reply to My Critics." Here Habermas states, "If the actors do not bring with them, and into their discourse, *their* needs and wants, *their* traditions, memberships, and so forth, practical discourse would at once be robbed of all content" (255). In my view, excessive abstraction *is* a problem in Habermas's theory, but not in the fashion of "instrumental reason," as Alford contends.

12. Alford, *Melanie Klein and Critical Social Theory*, 148.

13. Ibid., 89; see also Melanie Klein, *Envy and Gratitude*, esp. 14ff., 34ff.

14. Richards, *Images of Freud*, 44.

15. "Justice, Care, and Gender: The Kohlberg-Gilligan Debate Revisited," 43.

16. See Nancy Friday, *My Mother, My Self*.

17. Nancy Chodorow quoted in Flanagan and Jackson, "Justice, Care, and Gender," 44.

18. Ibid., 50.

19. See the brilliant book *Culture and Practical Reason*, by Marshall Sahlins.

20. A case in point is Catherine Lutz, who takes John Bowlby to task for "naturalizing" "feelings of love for the child on the part of the mother"; in this respect, Bowlby merely "follows the prevailing cultural emphasis on women's emotional qualities when he focuses on the emotions of women and their children" (Lutz and Abu-Lughod, *Language and the Politics of Emotion*, 81–82). It seems to me that (some) feminists sometimes want to have it both ways: while they assert that the oppression of women and the suppression of emotions are two sides of the same coin, they vehemently reject as

"ideological" and "naturalizing" the view that women are the more emotional of the two sexes. This strikes me as inconsistent.

21. *Essays on Moral Development*, vol 2, *The Psychology of Moral Development*, 293ff., 306.
22. "Justice, Care, and Gender," 47.
23. Ibid.
24. *Essays on Moral Development*, 2:229–30.
25. *Situating the Self*, 184.
26. Ibid., 186.
27. Cf. Flanagan and Jackson, "Justice, Care, and Gender," 48.

Bibliography

Adorno, Theodor W. *Minima Moralia*. Frankfurt: Suhrkamp, 1951.
———. *Eingriffe*. Frankfurt: Suhrkamp, 1963.
———. *Negative Dialektik*. Frankfurt: Suhrkamp, 1966.
———. *Stichworte*. Frankfurt: Suhrkamp, 1969.
———. *Zur Metakritik der Erkenntnistheorie*. Frankfurt: Suhrkamp, 1970.
———. *Erziehung zur Mündigkeit*. Frankfurt: Suhrkamp, 1971.
———. "Freudian Theory and the Pattern of Fascist Propaganda." In *Soziologische Schriften*, vol 1. Frankfurt: Suhrkamp, 1972.
Adorno, Theodor. W., et al., eds. *The Authoritarian Personality*. New York: Harper & Row, 1950.
Alford, C. Fred. *Narcissism: Socrates, the Frankfurt School, and Psychoanalytic Theory*. New Haven: Yale University Press, 1988.
———. *Melanie Klein and Critical Social Theory*. New Haven: Yale University Press, 1989.
Altmann, Alexander. *Die Grundlagen der Wertethik*. Berlin: Reuter & Reichard Verlag, 1931.
Amery, Jean. *Jenseits von Schuld und Sühne: Bewältigungsversuche eines Überwältigten*. Munich: Deutsche Taschenbuch Verlag, 1988.
Apel, Karl-Otto. *Diskurs und Verantwortung*. Frankfurt: Suhrkamp, 1988.
———. "Normative Begrundung der 'Kritischen Theorie' durch Rekurs auf lebensweltliche Sittlichkeit." In *Zwischenbetrachtungen: Im Prozeß der Aufklärung, Festschrift für Jürgen Habermas*, ed. Axel Honneth et al., 15–66. Frankfurt: Suhrkamp, 1989.
———, ed. *Hermeneutik und Ideologiekritik*. Frankfurt: Suhrkamp, 1971.
Arendt, Hannah. *The Origins of Totalitarianism*. New York: Harcourt Brace Jovanovich, 1951.
———. "Understanding and Politics." *Partisan Review* 20, no. 4 (1953): 377–92.
———. *The Human Condition*. Chicago: University of Chicago Press, 1958.
———. *Between Past and Future*. New York: Viking, 1963.
———. *Eichmann in Jerusalem*. New York: Viking, 1963.
———. *On Revolution*. New York: Viking, 1963.
———. "Thinking and Moral Considerations." *Social Research* 38 (1971): 417–46.

————. *The Life of the Mind.* 2 vols. London: Secker & Warburg, 1978.
————. *Lectures on Kant's Political Philosophy.* Chicago: University of Chicago Press, 1982.
————. *Nach Auschwitz.* Berlin: Tiamat, 1989.
Aristotle. *The Politics.* Translated by T. A. Sinclair. Harmondsworth, Middlesex: Penguin, 1962.
————. *Nicomachean Ethics.* Translated by Terence Irwin. Indianapolis, Ind.: Hackett Publishing, 1985.
Augstein, Rudolf, et al. *Historikerstreit.* Munich: Piper, 1987.
Bauman, Zygmunt. *Modernity and the Holocaust.* Cambridge: Polity, 1989.
Beauvoir, Simone de. *The Second Sex.* New York: Harper & Row, 1952.
Beiner, Ronald. *Political Judgment.* London: Methuen, 1983.
Benhabib, Seyla. "Hannah Arendt und die erlösende Kraft des Erzählens." In *Zivilisationsbruch: Denken nach Auschwitz,* ed. Dan Diner, 150–75. Frankfurt: Fischer, 1988.
————. "Judgment and the Moral Foundations of Politics in Arendt's Thought." *Political Theory* 16, no. 1 (1988).
————. *Situating the Self.* Cambridge: Polity, 1992.
Benjamin, Jessica. *The Bonds of Love.* New York: Pantheon, 1988.
Benn, Stanley. *A Theory of Freedom.* Cambridge: Cambridge University Press, 1988.
Benn, Stanley, and G. F. Gaus, eds. *Public and Private in Social Life.* London, 1983.
Berlin, Isaiah. "Two Concepts of Liberty." In *Liberalism and Its Critics,* ed. Michael Sandel. Oxford: Basil Blackwell, 1984.
Bernstein, Richard J. *Praxis and Action.* Philadelphia: University of Pennsylvania Press, 1971.
————. *Beyond Objectivism and Relativism.* Oxford: Basil Blackwell, 1983.
————. *Habermas and Modernity.* Cambridge: Polity, 1985.
————. *Philosophical Profiles.* Cambridge: Polity, 1986.
Bettelheim, Bruno. *The Informed Heart.* New York: Avon, 1971.
Blum, Lawrence. "Compassion." In *Explaining Emotions,* ed. Amelie O. Rorty. Berkeley and Los Angeles: University of California Press, 1980.
————. *Friendship, Altruism, and Morality.* London: Routledge & Kegan Paul, 1980.
Böhler, Dietrich, et al., eds. *Die pragmatische Wende.* Frankfurt: Suhrkamp, 1986.
Bowlby, John. *Attachment and Loss.* Vol. 1, *Attachment.* London: Pelican, 1984.
————. *Attachment and Loss.* Vol. 3, *Loss.* London, Pelican, 1985.
————. "The Nature of the Child's Tie to His Mother." In *Essential Papers on Object Relations,* ed. Peter Buckley, 153–200. New York: New York University Press, 1986.
————. *The Making and Breaking of Affectional Bonds.* London: Routledge & Kegan Paul, 1989.
Brumlik, Micha. "Über die Ansprüche Ungeborener und Unmündiger: Wie advokatorisch ist die Diskursethik?" In *Moralität und Sittlichkeit,* ed. Wolfgang Kuhlmann. Frankfurt: Suhrkamp, 1986.
Buckley, Peter, ed. *Essential Papers on Object Relations.* New York: New York University Press, 1986.
Canetti, Elias. *Crowds and Power.* London: Penguin, 1980.
Claussen, Detlev. *Grenzen der Aufklärung: Zur gesellschaftlichen Geschichte des modernen Antisemitismus.* Frankfurt: Fischer, 1987.
Dawidowicz, Lucy. *The War Against the Jews, 1933–45.* Harmondsworth, Middlesex: Penguin, 1975.
de Sousa, Ronald. "The Reality of Emotion." In *Explaining Emotions,* ed. Amelie O. Rorty. Berkeley and Los Angeles: University of California Press, 1980.
Dilthey, Wilhelm. *Der Aufbau der geschichtlichen Welt.* Frankfurt: Suhrkamp, 1981.

Diner, Dan, ed. *Ist der Nationalsozialismus Geschichte? Zur Historisierung und Historikerstreit.* Frankfurt: Fischer, 1987.

———, ed. *Zivilisationsbruch: Denken nach Auschwitz.* Frankfurt: Fischer, 1988.

Dreyfus, Hubert L. *Being-in-the-World.* Cambridge: MIT Press, 1991.

Eckstaedt, Anita. *Nationalsozialismus in der "zweiten Generation": Psychoanalyse von Hörigkeitsverhältnissen.* Frankfurt: Suhrkamp, 1989.

Edelstein, Wolfgang, ed. *Zur Bestimmung der Moral.* Frankfurt: Suhrkamp, 1986.

Fairbairn, W. R. D. *Psychoanalytic Studies of the Personality.* London: Routledge & Kegan Paul, 1952.

Fest, Joachim C. *The Face of the Third Reich.* Harmondsworth, Middlesex: Penguin, 1979.

———. *Hitler: En biografi.* Oslo: Gyldendal, 1979.

Flanagan, Owen, and Kathryn Jackson. "Justice, Care, and Gender: The Kohlberg-Gilligan Debate Revisited." In *Feminism and Political Theory,* ed. Cass Sunstein, 37–53. Chicago: University of Chicago Press, 1990.

Forst, Rainer. "Hannah Arendt and the Postmodern Moment." Frankfurt, 1988. Manuscript.

Fortenbaugh, W. W. *Aristotle on Emotion.* London: Duckworth, 1975.

Forum für Philosophie, Bad Homburg, ed. *Zerstörung des moralischen Selbstbewußtseins: Chance oder Gefährdung.* Frankfurt: Suhrkamp, 1988.

Freud, Sigmund. *On Metapsychology.* Pelican Freud Library, vol. 2. Harmondsworth, Middlesex: Pelican, 1984.

———. *Civilization and Its Discontents.* In vol. 12 of the Pelican Freud Library. Harmondsworth, Middlesex: Pelican, 1985.

———. *Group Psychology and the Analysis of the Ego.* In vol. 12 of the Pelican Freud Library. Harmondsworth, Middlesex: Pelican, 1985.

Friday, Nancy. *My Mother, My Self.* London: Fontana, 1979.

Fromm, Erich. *Escape from Freedom.* London: Routledge & Kegan Paul, 1960.

———. *The Anatomy of Human Destructiveness.* London: Penguin, 1977.

Gadamer, Hans-Georg. *Wahrheit und Methode.* Tübingen: Mohr, 1960.

Giddens, Anthony. *The Constitution of Society: Outline of the Theory of Structuration.* Cambridge: Polity, 1984.

Gilligan, Carol. *In a Different Voice.* Cambridge: Harvard University Press, 1982.

Günther, Klaus. *Der Sinn für Angemessenheit: Anwendungsdiskurse in Moral und Recht.* Frankfurt: Suhrkamp, 1988.

Habermas, Jürgen. *Technik und Wissenschaft als "Ideologie."* Frankfurt: Suhrkamp, 1968.

———. *Knowledge and Human Interests.* Translated by Jeremy J. Shapiro. London: Heinemann, 1972.

———. *Theory and Practice.* Translated by John Viertel. London: Heinemann, 1976.

———. *Communication and the Evolution of Society.* Translated by Thomas McCarthy. London: Heinemann, 1979.

———. "A Reply to My Critics." In *Habermas: Critical Debates,* ed. John Thompson and David Held. London: Macmillan, 1982.

———. *Zur Logik der Sozialwissenschaften.* Frankfurt: Suhrkamp, 1982.

———. *Moralbewußtsein und kommunikatives Handeln.* Frankfurt: Suhrkamp, 1983.

———. *Philosophical-Political Profiles.* Translated by Frederick G. Lawrence. London: Heinemann, 1983.

———. *The Theory of Communicative Action.* Vol. 1. Translated by Thomas McCarthy. Cambridge: Polity, 1984.

———. *Vorstudien und Ergänzungen zur Theorie des kommunikativen Handelns.* Frankfurt: Suhrkamp, 1984.

——. "Entgegnung." In *Kommunikatives Handeln*, ed. Axel Honneth. Frankfurt: Suhrkamp, 1986.

——. *The Philosophical Discourse of Modernity*. Translated by Frederick G. Lawrence. Cambridge: MIT Press, 1987.

——. *The Theory of Communicative Action*. Vol. 2. Translated by Thomas McCarthy. Cambridge: Polity, 1987.

——. "Kohlberg and Neo-Aristotelianism." Frankfurt, 1988. Manuscript.

——. "Law and Morality." Translated by Kenneth Baynes. In *The Tanner Lectures on Human Values*, ed. Steve McMurrin. Salt Lake City: Salt Lake City University Press, 1988.

——. *Nachmetaphysisches Denken*. Frankfurt: Suhrkamp, 1988.

——. "Die drei Gebrauchen von der praktischen Vernunft." Frankfurt, 1989. Manuscript.

——. "Justice and Solidarity." Translated by Shierry Weber Nicholsen. In *The Moral Domain*, ed. Thomas Wren. Cambridge: Harvard University Press, 1989.

——. *The New Conservatism*. Translated by Shierry Weber Nicholsen. Cambridge: MIT Press, 1989.

——. "Towards a Communication-Concept of Rational Collective Will Formation: A Thought Experiment." *Ratio Juris* 2 (1989).

——. *Moral Consciousness and Communicative Action*. Translated by Christian Lenhardt and Shierry Weber Nicholsen. Cambridge: MIT Press, 1990.

——. *Die nachholende Revolution*. Frankfurt: Suhrkamp, 1990.

——. *Erläuterungen zur Diskursethik*. Frankfurt: Suhrkamp, 1991.

——. *Texte und Kontexte*. Frankfurt: Suhrkamp, 1991.

Hampshire, Stuart. *Freedom of Mind*. Princeton: Princeton University Press, 1971.

Hare, R. M. *Freedom and Reason*. Oxford: Oxford University Press, 1963.

——. *Moral Thinking*. Oxford: Clarendon Press, 1981.

Harris, Paul L. *Children and Emotion*. Oxford: Basil Blackwell, 1989.

Hegel, G.W.F. *Grundlinien der Philosophie des Rechts*. Frankfurt: Suhrkamp, 1970.

——. *Phänomenologie des Geistes*. Frankfurt: Suhrkamp, 1970.

Heidegger, Martin. *Nietzsche*. 2 vols. Pfullingen: Neske, 1961.

——. *Being and Time*. Translated by John Macquarrie and Edward Robinson. New York: Harper & Row, 1962.

——. *Sein und Zeit*. Tübingen: Max Niemeyer Verlag, 1979.

Held, David. *Introduction to Critical Theory*. Berkeley and Los Angeles: University of California Press, 1980.

Heller, Agnes. *A Theory of Feelings*. Assen: Van Gorcum, 1979.

Heyd, David. *Supererogation*. Cambridge: Cambridge University Press, 1982.

Hilberg, Raul. *The Destruction of the European Jews*. New York: Holmes & Meier, 1985.

——. *Sonderzüge nach Auschwitz*. Frankfurt: Ullstein, 1987.

Hoffman, Martin L. "Empathy, Its Limitations, and Its Role in a Comprehensive Moral Theory." In *Morality, Moral Behaviour, and Moral Development*, ed. William M. Kurtines and Jacob L. Gewirtz. New York: John Wiley, 1984.

Honneth, Axel, ed. *Kommunikatives Handeln*. Frankfurt: Suhrkamp, 1986.

Honneth, Axel, et al., eds. *Zwischenbetrachtungen: Im Prozeß der Aufklärung, Festschrift für Jürgen Habermas*. Frankfurt: Suhrkamp, 1989.

Horkheimer, Max. "Autorität und Familie in der Gegenwart." In *Zur Kritik der instrumentallen Vernunft*. Frankfurt: Fischer, 1985.

Horkheimer, Max, and Theodor W. Adorno. *Dialectic of Enlightenment*. Translated by John Cumming. London: Verso, 1979.

Höss, Rudolf. *Kommandant in Auschwitz*. Munich: Deutsche Taschenbuch Verlag, 1963.

Hume, David. *A Treatise of Human Nature*. Harmondsworth, Middlesex: Penguin, 1969.
Husserl, Edmund. *Die Krisis der europäischen Wissenschaften und die transzendentale Phänomenologie*. The Hague: Martinus Nijhoff, 1954.
Jay, Martin. *The Dialectical Imagination*. Boston: Little, Brown, 1973.
Kant, Immanuel. *Critique of Judgment*. Translated by J. H. Bernard. New York: Hafner Press, 1951.
———. *Critique of Practical Reason*. Translated by Lewis White Beck. New York: Macmillan, 1956.
———. *Grundlegung zur Metaphysik der Sitten*. Frankfurt: Suhrkamp, 1974.
Kershaw, Ian. *Popular Opinion and Political Dissent in the Third Reich*. Oxford University Press, 1983.
Killingmo, Bjørn, "Problems in Contemporary Psychoanalytic Theory, I and II." *Scandinavian Journal of Psychology* 26 (1985): 53–73.
———. "Characters on the Stage: Ibsen's 'Life-Lie' Revisited." Oslo, 1989. Manuscript.
———. "Conflict and Deficit: Implications for Technique." *International Journal of Psycho-Analysis* 70 (1989): 65–79.
Kitwood, Tom. *Concern for Others*. London: Routledge & Kegan Paul, 1990.
Klein, Melanie. *Envy and Gratitude and Other Works, 1946–1963*. London: Virago, 1988.
———. *Love, Guilt, and Reparation*. London: Virago, 1988.
Kogon, Eugen. *SS-staten*. Oslo: Gyldendal, 1981.
Köhl, Harald. "Kant und Schopenhauer in der Ethik: Die Theorie der moralischen Motivation." Göttingen, 1989. Manuscript.
Kohlberg, Lawrence. *Essays on Moral Development*. 2 vols. San Francisco: Harper & Row, 1981.
Kohlberg, Lawrence, Dwight Boyd, and Charles Levine. "Die Wiederkehr der sechsten Stufe" and "Gerechtigkeit, Wohlwollen, und der Standpunkt der Moral." In *Zur Bestimmung der Moral*, ed. Wolfgang Edelstein, 205–41. Frankfurt: Suhrkamp, 1986.
Kohlberg, Lawrence, and D. Candee. "The Relationship of Moral Judgment to Moral Action." In *Morality, Moral Behaviour, and Moral Development*, ed. William M. Kurtines and Jacob L. Gewirtz. New York: John Wiley, 1984.
Kohut, Heinz. *The Analysis of the Self*. New York: International University Press, 1971.
———. *Introspektion, Empathie, und Psychoanalyse*. Frankfurt: Suhrkamp, 1977.
———. *The Restoration of the Self*. New York: International University Press, 1977.
Koselleck, Reinhart. *Vergangene Zukunft*. Frankfurt: Suhrkamp, 1979.
Krall, Hannah. *Schneller als der liebe Gott*. Frankfurt: Suhrkamp, 1980.
Kuhlmann, Wolfgang, ed. *Moralität und Sittlichkeit*. Frankfurt: Suhrkamp, 1986.
Kurtines, William M., and Jacob L. Gewirtz, eds. *Morality, Moral Behaviour, and Moral Development*. New York: John Wiley, 1984.
Lang, Berel. *Act and Idea in the Nazi Genocide*. Chicago: University of Chicago Press, 1990.
Lanzmann, Claude. *Shoah*. Düsseldorf: Claassen, 1986.
Lasch, Christopher. *Haven in a Heartless World*. New York: Basic Books, 1977.
———. *The Minimal Self*. London: Picador, 1985.
Leonardy, Heinz. *Liebe und Person*. The Hague: Martinus Nijhoff, 1976.
Levi, Primo. *If This Is a Man* and *The Truce*. Translated by Stuart Woolf. London: Abacus, 1987.
———. *The Drowned and the Saved*. Translated by Raymond Rosenthal. London: Abacus, 1988.
Levinas, Emmanuel. *Ethics and Infinity*. Pittsburgh, Pa.: Duquesne University Press, 1985.
———. *Otherwise than Being or Beyond Essence*. Translated by Alphonso Lingis. Dordrecht: Kluwer, 1991.

————. *Totality and Infinity*. Translated by Alphonso Lingis. Dordrecht: Kluwer, 1991.

Lifton, Robert J. *The Nazi Doctors*. London: Macmillan, 1986.

Lifton, Robert J., and Eric Markusen. *The Genocidal Mentality*. New York: Basic Books, 1990.

Loewy, Hanno, et al. *"Unser einziger Weg ist Arbeit": Das Getto in Lodz, 1940–1944*. Frankfurt: Löcher Verlag, 1990.

Løgstrup, K. E. *Den etiske fordring*. Copenhagen: Gyldendal, 1991.

Löw-Beer, Martin. "Living a Life and the Problem of Existential Impossibility." *Inquiry* 34 (1991): 217–36.

Lutz, Catherine A. *Unnatural Emotions: Everyday Sentiments on a Micronesian Atoll and Their Challenge to Western Theory*. Chicago: University of Chicago Press, 1988.

Lutz, Catherine A., and Lila Abu-Lughod. *Language and the Politics of Emotion*. Cambridge: Cambridge University Press, 1990.

MacIntyre, Alasdair. *After Virtue*. London: Duckworth, 1985.

————. *Whose Justice? Which Rationality?* London: Duckworth, 1988.

McMurrin, Sterling M., ed. *The Tanner Lectures on Human Values*. Salt Lake City: Salt Lake City University Press, 1988.

Marcuse, Herbert. *Eros and Civilization*. London: Ark, 1987.

Mead, George Herbert. *Mind, Self, and Society*. Chicago: University of Chicago Press, 1973.

Merleau-Ponty, Maurice. *Phenomenology of Perception*. Translated by Colin Smith. London: Routledge & Kegan Paul, 1962.

Milgram, Stanley. *Obedience to Authority*. New York: Harper Torchbooks, 1974.

Miller, Alice. *For Your Own Good*. London: Virago, 1987.

————. *The Untouched Key*. London: Virago, 1990.

Milo, Ronald D. *Immorality*. Princeton: Princeton University Press, 1984.

Mitscherlich, Alexander, and Margarete Mitscherlich. *Die Unfähigkeit zu Trauern*. Munich: Piper, 1967.

————. *The Inability to Mourn*. Translated by Beverly R. Placzak. New York: Grove Press, 1975.

Mosse, George. *The Crisis of German Ideology: The Intellectual Roots of the Third Reich*. London: Allen & Unwin, 1964.

Nietzsche, Friedrich. *Werke in drei Bänden*. Munich: Hanser, 1969.

Norton, David. *Personal Destinies*. Princeton: Princeton University Press, 1979.

Nussbaum, Martha. *Love's Knowledge*. Oxford: Oxford University Press, 1990.

Nyiszli, Miklos. *Auschwitz*. Translated by Tebere Kremer and Richard Seaver. London: Granada, 1973.

Oakley, Justin. *Morality and the Emotions*. London: Routledge & Kegan Paul, 1992.

Ofstad, Harald. *Vår forakt for svakhet*. Oslo: Pax, 1971.

Pateman, Carole. "Feminist Critiques of the Public/Private Dichotomy." In *Public and Private in Social Life*, ed. Stanley Benn and G. F. Gaus. London, 1983.

Piaget, Jean. *The Moral Judgment of the Child*. Harmondsworth, Middlesex: Penguin, 1977.

Plato. *The Works of Plato*. New York: Modern Library, 1956.

Plessner, Helmuth. *Die verspätete Nation*. Frankfurt: Suhrkamp, 1974.

Rawls, John. *A Theory of Justice*. Oxford: Oxford University Press, 1973.

Rehg, William. "Discourse and the Moral Point of View: Deriving a Dialogical Principle of Universalization." *Inquiry* 34 (1991): 27–48.

Reif, Adalbert, ed. *Hannah Arendt: Materialien zu ihrem Werk*. Vienna: Europaverlag, 1979.

Richards, Barry. *Images of Freud*. London: J. M. Dent & Sons, 1989.

Ritter, Joachim. *Moralität und Sittlichkeit: Studien zu Aristoteles und Hegel*. Frankfurt: Suhrkamp, 1969.

Rorty, Amelie O., ed. *Explaining Emotions*. Berkeley and Los Angeles: University of California Press, 1980.

Rorty, Richard. *Contingency, Irony, and Solidarity.* Cambridge: Cambridge University Press, 1989.

Rossvær, Viggo. "Transzendentalpragmatik, transzendentale Hermeneutik, und die Möglichkeit, Auschwitz zu verstehen." In *Die pragmatische Wende,* ed. Dietrich Böhler, et al., 187–202. Frankfurt: Suhrkamp, 1986.

Sahlins, Marshall. *Culture and Practical Reason.* Chicago: University of Chicago Press, 1976.

Sandel, Michael. *Liberalism and the Limits of Justice.* Cambridge: Cambridge University Press, 1982.

———, ed. *Liberalism and Its Critics.* Oxford: Basil Blackwell, 1984.

Sartre, Jean-Paul. *Being and Nothingness.* Translated by Hazel E. Barnes. New York: Washington Square Press, 1956.

———. *Anti-Semite and Jew,* trans. George J. Becker. New York: Grove Press, 1962.

———. *Sketch for a Theory of the Emotions.* London: Methuen, 1971.

———. "Existentialism Is a Humanism." In *Existentialism,* ed. Robert C. Solomon, and trans. P. Mairet. New York: Random House, 1974.

———. *Critique of Dialectical Reason.* Translated by Quintin Hoare. Vol 2. London: Verso, 1991.

Scheler, Max. *The Nature of Sympathy.* Translated by Peter Heath. London: Routledge & Kegan Paul, 1954.

———. *Schriften aus dem Nachlass.* Bern: Francke, 1957.

———. *Ordo Amoris.* Bern: Francke, 1967.

———. *Vom Ewigen im Menschen.* Bern: Francke, 1967.

———. *Formalism in Ethics and Non-formal Ethics of Values.* Translated by Manfred S. Frings and Roger L. Funk. Evanston, Ill.: Northwestern University Press, 1973.

Schnädelbach, Herbert. "Was ist Neoaristotelismus?" In *Moralität und Sittlichkeit,* ed. Wolfgang Kuhlmann, 38–64. Frankfurt: Suhrkamp, 1986.

Schopenhauer, Arthur. "Über die Grundlage der Moral." In *Sämtliche Werke,* vol. 3. Frankfurt: Suhrkamp, 1986.

Schütz, Albert. *The Phenomenology of the Social World.* London: Heinemann, 1967.

———. *The Structures of the Lifeworld.* Ed. Thomas Luckmann. Evanston, Ill.: Northwestern University Press, 1973.

Sherman, Nancy. *The Fabric of Character: Aristotle's Theory of Virtue.* Oxford: Clarendon Press, 1989.

Simmel, Georg. *The Philosophy of Money.* London: Routledge & Kegan Paul, 1978.

Solomon, Robert. *The Passions.* New York: Anchor, 1976.

———. *About Love.* New York: Touchstone, 1988.

Solomon, Robert, and Cheshire Calhoun, eds. *What Is an Emotion?* Oxford: Oxford University Press, 1983.

Stein, Edith. *Zum Problem der Einfühlung.* Halle: Buchdruckerei des Waisenhauses, 1917.

Stern, Daniel. *The Interpersonal World of the Infant.* New York: Basic Books, 1985.

Stern, Joseph P. *Hitler: The Führer and the People.* Berkeley and Los Angeles: University of California Press, 1975.

Storr, Anthony. *Solitude.* London: Flamingo, 1989.

Strawson, Peter F. *Freedom and Resentment.* London: Methuen, 1974.

Sunstein, Cass, ed. *Feminism and Political Theory.* Chicago: University of Chicago Press, 1990.

Taylor, Charles. *The Explanation of Behaviour.* London: Routledge & Kegan Paul, 1964.

———. *Hegel.* Cambridge: Cambridge University Press, 1975.

———. *Philosophical Papers.* 2 vols. Cambridge: Cambridge University Press, 1985.

———. "Die Motive einer Verfahrensethik." In *Moralität und Sittlichkeit,* ed. Wolfgang Kuhlmann, 101–36. Frankfurt: Suhrkamp, 1986.

————. *Sources of the Self*. Cambridge: Cambridge University Press, 1989.
————. "Comments and Replies." *Inquiry* 34 (1991): 237–54.
Taylor, Gabriele. *Pride, Shame, and Guilt*. Oxford: Clarendon, 1985.
Thompson, John, and David Held. *Habermas: Critical Debates*. London: Macmillan, 1982.
Toulmin, Stephen E. *An Examination of the Place of Reason in Ethics*. Cambridge: Cambridge University Press, 1950.
Tugendhat, Ernst. *Selbstbewußtsein und Selbstbestimmung*. Frankfurt: Suhrkamp, 1979.
Turner, Henry A., ed. *Nazism and the Third Reich*. New York: Quadrangle Books, 1972.
VanDeVeer, Donald. *Paternalistic Intervention*. Princeton: Princeton University Press, 1986.
Vetlesen, Arne Johan. "Romantikken, Nietzsche og nazismen." Oslo, 1982. Manuscript.
————. "Teknologi og menneskelig erkjennelse." Oslo, 1984. Manuscript.
————. "Towards a Theory of Fragmentation: A Critique of Critical Theory." Frankfurt, 1985. Manuscript.
————. "Erkjennelse og historisk endring." Master's thesis, Department of Philosophy, University of Oslo, 1987.
————. "Habermas' kritikk av Gadamers tese om hermeneutikkens universalitet." *Norsk Filosofisk Tidsskrift* 23 (1988): 27–38.
————. "Utkast til en kritikk av Habermas' samfunnsteori." *Norsk Filosofisk Tidsskrift* 26 (1991): 1–29.
————. "Heideggers Auseinandersetzung mit Nietzsche." Norwegian version in *Agora* 3 (1992): 36–68.
————. "Why Does Proximity Make a Moral Difference?" *Praxis International* 12 (1993): 371–87.
Vollrath, Ernst. "Hannah Arendt über Meinung und Urteilskraft." In *Hannah Arendt: Materialien zu ihrem Werk*, ed. Adalbert Reif, 85–109. Vienna: Europa-Verlag, 1979.
Walzer, Michael. *Spheres of Justice*. Oxford: Basil Blackwell, 1983.
Williams, Bernard. *Ethics and the Limits of Philosophy*. London: Fontana, 1985.
Winnicott, Donald W. *The Maturational Processes and the Facilitating Environment*. London: Hogarth Press, 1965.
————. *Playing and Reality*. Harmondsworth, Middlesex: Penguin, 1980.
————. "The Theory of the Parent-Infant Relationship." In *Essential Papers on Object Relations*, ed. Peter Buckley, 233–54. New York: New York University Press, 1986.
Wittgenstein, Ludwig. *Philosophische Untersuchungen*. Frankfurt: Suhrkamp, 1960.
Wolf, Ursula. "Haben wir moralische Verpflichtungen gegen Tiere?" Frankfurt, 1988. Manuscript.
Wren, Thomas, ed. *The Moral Domain*. Cambridge: Harvard University Press, 1989.
Young, Iris Marion. "Impartiality and the Civic Public: Some Implications of Feminist Critiques of Moral and Political Theory." *Praxis International* 5 (1986).
Young-Bruehl, Elisabeth. *Hannah Arendt: For Love of the World*. New Haven: Yale University Press, 1982.

Index

absolute love, 136–37

Act and Idea in the Nazi Genocide (Berel Lang), 186, 187

action
moral, 5
morality and, 309–10
thinking and, according to Arendt, 101–4

actuality, Aristotelian concept of, 29

Adorno, Theodor, 89, 112, 221, 225–27, 229–46, 249–50, 253, 257, 262, 265, 267, 268, 272

After Virtue (Alasdair MacIntyre), 24–29, 31–34, 36–44, 58, 60–61, 73, 74, 77, 93, 299

aggression
defensive, 248–49, 257, 268–70
malignant, 248–49, 257, 267–70

Alexy, Robert, 295

Alford, C. Fred, 346–47, 372n. 11

Altmann, Alexander, 140–42

altruism, 79, 156–58

The Anatomy of Human Destructiveness (Erich Fromm), 247–52

anger, 131

animals, 169

anti-Semitism, 221, 347, 354, 367–69nn. 34–35
authoritarian personality and, 244
and defensive vs. malignant aggression, 257–58

dehumanization and, 180, 185, 188–92
fear in, 256
hatred and, 253
"legal" basis for, 88–89, 111
projection and hatred in, 232–42
Sartre's definition of, 112

Apel, Karl-Otto, 9, 64, 68, 97, 149, 286, 288–92, 294–98, 305–9, 331

apprehension, 164–65

Arendt, Hannah, 12, 70–71, 74, 85–125, 183, 193, 240, 272, 304–5, 329–30, 332

argumentation, 295–97, 307–10, 314

Aristotle and Aristotelian tradition, 23, 24, 26, 28–41, 45, 57, 60, 63–67, 70, 74–76, 81–82, 93, 198, 300

Aristotle on Emotion (W. W. Fortenbaugh), 81–82

attentiveness, 8–9, 162

attitudes, moral, 160–62

Auschwitz, 180–84, 187, 200, 210, 215, 272, 278

authoritarian personality
Fromm's view of, 242–45
origin of, in family, 236–37
sociological background for, 226–29

The Authoritarian Personality (Adorno et al.), 221, 225–27, 232–34

"Autorität und Familie in der Gegenwart" (Max Horkheimer), 225–28, 236

Köhl, Harald, 370n.16
Kohlberg, Lawrence, 292, 303, 315–22, 329,
    330, 333, 335, 343, 352–53, 355–57
"Kohlberg and Neo-Aristotelianism" (Jürgen Ha-
    bermas), 296, 301, 308
Kohut, Heinz, 7–8, 211, 261–62, 265, 269,
    270
Kommandant in Auschwitz (Rudolf Höss), 210,
    364–65n.59
Koselleck, Reinhart, 93
Krall, Hannah, 371n.30
Krisis der europäischen Wissenschaften (Edmund Hus-
    serl), 86

Lang, Berel, 186–91
language, 289–90, 293
Lanzmann, Claude, 90
large-scale immorality, 225
law/legality
    legitimacy vs., 301–2
    under totalitarianism, 88–90
    totalitarianism and, 92
Lebenswelt, 86
Lectures on Kant's Political Philosophy (Hannah
    Arendt), 93, 95, 96, 107–8, 120
legitimacy, legality vs., 301–2
Levi, Primo, 279, 368–69n.35
Levinas, Emmanuel, 202–3, 364n.54
liberalism, 26, 47, 55–72, 75
Liberalism and the Limits of Justice (Michael Sandel),
    67
libido (sexual instinct), 248
The Life of the Mind (Hannah Arendt), 87, 94, 95,
    98, 100–103, 120
Lifton, Robert J., 180–87, 189–91, 211, 212
Locke, John, 67
Logstrup, K. E., 202
Lorenz, Konrad, 184, 249
love, 213–14, 259
    Arendt on, 117
    compassion vs., 208–10
    empathy and, 201
    engaged nature of, 211–12
    as learned ability, 236–37
    limited range of, 205
    morality, as precondition for, 197–98
    mourning and, 196
    sadist's fear of, 250
    in Scheler's material ethics, 135–42, 150

Solomon's view of, 178
    sympathy vs., 145–47, 204
Lutz, Catherine, 341–42, 372n.20

Machiavelli, Niccolò, 67
MacIntyre, Alasdair, 7, 12–14, 23–83, 93, 173,
    193, 283, 300, 302
    on Enlightenment's justification of morality,
        38–46
    on liberalism, 55–72
    on loss of Aristotelian tradition, 29–38
    on problem of emotivism, 24–29
    on rationality of tradition-constituted in-
        quiry, 46–55
malignant aggression, 248–49, 251, 257, 267–
    70
Marcuse, Herbert, 245–47
Marx, Karl, 234
masochism, 243–44, 249
material ethics, Scheler's program for, 128–35,
    142–43
Mead, G. H., 285, 319, 330
Mein Kampf (Adolf Hitler), 191, 257
melancholia, 196–97
Merleau-Ponty, Maurice, 147–48
Milgram, Stanley, 90, 112, 274
Miller, Alice, 211, 260–61
Milo, Ronald, 222–24
Mitscherlich, Alexander M., 196–98, 201
Mitscherlich, Margarete, 196–98, 201
Modernity and the Holocaust (Zygmunt Bauman),
    273, 363n.37
money, anti-Semitism and, 234–35
mood, 172–73
moral action, 5
moral attitudes, 160–62
moral blindness, 259, 278
moral concern, 223–24
morality
    love as precondition for, 197–98
    reason for, 302–15
    role of gender in emotions and, 341–57
Morality and the Emotions (Justin Oakley), 5
moral judgment. See judgment(s)
moral law, Kantian concept of, 41–42
moral neutralization, 10, 179, 213, 215
moral perception. See perception
moral performance, 2–3, 85
    epistemology and notion of, 16–18
    human-centered focus on, 3

Lightning Source UK Ltd.
Milton Keynes UK
07 June 2010

155237UK00001B/310/P